CIRCUIT LISTENING

# Circuit Listening

CHINESE POPULAR MUSIC IN THE GLOBAL 1960s

Andrew F. Jones

*University of Minnesota Press*
*Minneapolis*
*London*

The University of Minnesota Press gratefully acknowledges the financial assistance provided for the publication of this book by the University of California, Berkeley.

Portions of chapter 1 were published in "Circuit Listening: Grace Chang and the Dawn of the Chinese 1960s," in *Audible Empire: Music, Global Politics, Critique*, ed. Ronald Radano and Tejumola Olaniyan (Durham, N.C.: Duke University Press, 2016). A portion of chapter 2 was published in an earlier version as "Quotation Songs: Portable Media and the Maoist Pop Song," in *Mao's Little Red Book: A Global History*, ed. Alexander C. Cook (Cambridge: Cambridge University Press, 2014).

Copyright 2020 by the Regents of the University of Minnesota

All rights reserved. No part of this publication may be reproduced, stored in a retrieval system, or transmitted, in any form or by any means, electronic, mechanical, photocopying, recording, or otherwise, without the prior written permission of the publisher.

Published by the University of Minnesota Press
111 Third Avenue South, Suite 290
Minneapolis, MN 55401-2520
http://www.upress.umn.edu

Printed in the United States of America on acid-free paper

The University of Minnesota is an equal-opportunity educator and employer.

27 26 25 24 23 22 21 20          10 9 8 7 6 5 4 3 2 1

Library of Congress Cataloging-in-Publication Data
Names: Jones, Andrew F. author.
Title: Circuit listening : Chinese popular music in the global 1960s / Andrew F. Jones.
Description: Minneapolis : University of Minnesota Press, [2020]
Identifiers: LCCN 2019033216 (print) | ISBN 978-1-5179-0206-3 (hc) | ISBN 978-1-5179-0207-0 (pb)
Subjects: LCSH: Popular music—China—1961–1970—History and criticism. | Popular music—Social aspects—China—History—20th century. | Music and state—China.
Classification: LCC ML3502.C5 J58 2020 (print) | DDC 781.630951—dc23
LC record available at https://lccn.loc.gov/2019033216

CONTENTS

| | | |
|---|---|---|
| | Acknowledgments | vii |
| | Introduction. The East Is Red: Toward a Sonic History of the 1960s | 1 |
| 1 | Circuit Listening at the Dawn of the Chinese 1960s | 29 |
| 2 | Quotation Songs: Media Infrastructure and Pop Song Form in Mao's China | 53 |
| 3 | Fugitive Sounds of the Taiwanese Musical Cinema | 79 |
| 4 | Pirates of the China Seas: Vinyl Records and the Military Circuit | 109 |
| 5 | Folk Circuits: Rediscovering Chen Da | 133 |
| 6 | Teresa Teng and the Network Trace | 169 |
| | Appendix: "Listening to Songs in the Streets of Taipei" *Hsu Tsang-Houei* | 197 |
| | Notes | 203 |
| | Index | 255 |

ACKNOWLEDGMENTS

This book is itself the product of a complex and far-flung circuit of friends and colleagues and collaborators, spanning two oceans and more than a few islands. I am deeply grateful for all those who have powered the project, whether through their support, provision of archival materials, intellectual inspiration, or conversation. While I cannot hope to enumerate all of those debts here, their traces resonate throughout the chapters that follow.

Without the help of a number of institutions across three continents, I would have had neither the wherewithal to conduct research nor the time to write. I am grateful for the generous fellowship support of the John Simon Guggenheim Foundation, the Chiang Ching-kuo Foundation for Scholarly Exchange, and the University of California President's Faculty Research Fellowship in the Humanities. I was able to present the initial framework of the book as a Rayson Huang Fellow in the Department of Music at the University of Hong Kong, and the final chapters crystallized during a residency at the École des Hautes-Études en Sciences Sociale (EHESS) in Paris. In between, the Graduate Institute of Musicology at the National Taiwan University (NTU) served as a kind of second academic home. I am also grateful to St. John's College, University of Oxford, as well as to the Center for Research in the Arts, Social Sciences, and Humanities (CRASSH) in Cambridge, for hosting me during a formative period in the gestation of the book.

A book is only as strong as its sources. Here in Berkeley, the C. V. Starr East Asian Library has been essential to my work, and I am grateful as ever for the initiative of its director, Peter Zhou, and the boundless enthusiasm and energy of our librarians, Jianye He and Susan Xue. In addition, I relied heavily on the resources of the East Asia Library at Stanford

University; the National Central Library and National Taiwan Libraries in Taipei; the National Library of China in Beijing; and the Shanghai Library, among many others.

I am grateful to Ronald Radano and Teju Olaniyan for organizing the "Music–Race–Empire" conference in Madison, Wisconsin, in 2011, which brought together a diverse group of scholars to listen to popular music, across borders and with fresh ears. I have also benefited immensely from presenting and discussing my work with colleagues in ethnomusicology, film studies, and Chinese studies at the University of Hawai'i, UCLA, the University of Toronto, the University of Chicago, Rice University, Duke University, the School of Oriental and African Studies, Aarhus University, the National Chengchi University in Taipei, and Shanghai University's Institute of Film.

The middle chapters of the book revolve around Taiwan. For more than a decade, the poet and environmental activist Yung-feng Chung has been my dear friend and closest comrade-in-arms in exploring the island's music, history, and culture. This book would be inconceivable without his tutelage. I came to understand the sonic wonders and historical weight of Taiwanese folk music through the work of Lin Sheng-xiang. It was also Sheng-xiang who first played for me one of Chen Da's records on the stereo in his upstairs room at home in Meinung and later patiently explained his *yueqin* techniques. I am honored and humbled to be able to relay some of the stories Yung-feng and Sheng-xiang have shared with me here.

My colleagues at the Graduate Institute of Musicology at NTU—Fumitaka Yamauchi, Chien-chang Yang, Tung Shen, Ying-fen Wang, and Szu-wei Chen—have been staggeringly generous, nurturing this project in numerous ways. C. S. Stone Shih was an invaluable and empathic guide to the musical geography of Taipei and made possible a series of meetings with the inimitable icon of Taiwanese music Wen Shia and his lovely family. Professor Wu Rung-shun shared his work on the preservation of Taiwanese vernacular music and his memories of his mentor, Hsu Tsang-Houei, while Charles Hsu graciously spoke with me about the legacy of his father, Hsu Shih. The photographer and pioneering music critic Chang Chao-Tang helped me map out the artistic and musical milieu of the 1960s and 1970s, of which he was such a pivotal part. Shihlun Chang and Tunghung Ho were unstintingly openhanded in sharing archival materials, advice, and perspectives. Tom Davenport provided not only his riveting stories of encountering Chen Da as a young documentarian in 1967 but also his massive and invaluable photographic archive of the vanished world of the Taiwanese 1960s. More than seven thousand of his images now reside in the East Asian Library at Berkeley as the Tom Davenport Collection; a selection of those pictures graces this book as well, providing readers with a sense of the visual texture of those years.

The conceptual compass of the book has widened enormously as a result of stimulating conversations with colleagues in ethnomusicology, including Michael Denning, Steven Feld, and Martin Stokes, and fellow travelers in Chinese cultural and sound studies, among them Guo-Juin Hong, Nicole Huang, Jean Ma, William Schaefer, and Andreas Steen. John Pilgrim helped me familiarize myself with vacuum tubes, transistor electronics, and circuit topologies.

My departmental colleagues Robert Ashmore, Weihong Bao, and Alan Tansman have been constant companions and teachers, making Berkeley a happy model of what an intellectual community can and should be. Our students, of course, have made that community whole and have inspired me to do the best work I could do. They have contributed to this project in ways great and small. I am particularly thankful for ongoing exchanges about Taiwanese literature and film with Evelyn Shih and about sonic culture and the Chinese 1960s with Laurence Coderre; for Lawrence Zi-qiao Yang's fresh perspectives and detective work in local archives on my behalf; and for Xiaoyu Xia's insightful readings of my work-in-progress. Hua Yao accompanied me to archives in Beijing and Shanghai and elegantly translated my prose into Chinese. Chenyu Qu assisted me with my research on Teresa Teng. Jon Pitt generously helped me locate records in Japan. Julia Keblinska, finally, worked tirelessly and imaginatively to ensure that the book came together in its final form.

The book is dedicated to Lanchih, who brought me into the orbit of her island, and to my father, who connects me to our island home in Jamaica and continues to ground the circuit of my life.

INTRODUCTION

# The East Is Red

## Toward a Sonic History of the 1960s

How might we listen to the 1960s otherwise—not from the metropolitan center but from its rural margins? How can we hear our way into a fresh understanding of the musical and media history of this era of decolonization and the Cold War? More broadly, how do recorded musical artifacts speak of the historical moments that produced them, and how can we attune ourselves to what they have to say and decode their messages? This is a book about music in the Chinese-speaking world in those years, but perhaps the global questions with which it grapples might be best approached from the vantage point of outer space. In December 1968, at the conclusion of a fractious and frantic year of youthful utopian longing, political uprisings, and fierce reaction across the world, the Apollo 8 mission beamed back a serene image of the earth rising over the moon—a now iconic reminder of our common destiny as denizens of an embattled planet.[1] A little more than one year later, on the evening of April 24, 1970, China launched its first manmade satellite. Thirteen minutes into flight, as the satellite cleared the atmosphere and took up its orbital path around the globe, an ultra-shortwave radio transmitter began to broadcast a melody back to earth: "The East Is Red." The song, a paean to Chairman Mao Zedong 毛澤東 and the Chinese Revolution, programmed to play twice per minute on an infinite loop, "rang out across the universe," as one jubilant report in the *People's Daily* 人民日報 put it, for as long as the eponymous "The East Is Red 1" 東方紅一號 remained operational.[2] The broadcast was in many ways a fitting swan song for the 1960s, signaling China's triumphant if belated entry into the space race, which had been initiated by the Cold War contest between the West and the Soviet bloc. And to the extent that the space race had been, at least since the 1962 advent of Telstar, the first communications satellite capable of beaming televisual signals across Europe and North America, a contest for broadcasting dominance, the satellite was a manifestation of the determination to break out of circumscribed media circuits and project Mao's revolutionary fervor across the world and into the furthest reaches of space.

"The East Is Red" was an appropriate musical vessel for this project, not only by virtue of its infectiously catchy pentatonic melody but also because it was arguably the most widely known and frequently broadcast song of the decade, saturating the quotidian life of nearly a quarter of humanity to an extent undreamed of by any entrant to the Western hit parade, including the Beatles. The song had begun its ascension to the status of de facto national anthem in 1964 with nationwide screenings of an eponymous "song and dance epic" mythologizing the history and achievements of the Chinese Revolution. The initial performance of "The East Is Red" in the Great Hall of the People in Beijing featured a choir of more than one thousand singers and a symphony orchestra, accompanying hundreds of dancers as they performed magnificent Busby Berkeley–like musical numbers in precisely synchronized formations, flowing across the vast landscapes projected by a coordinated battery of lantern slides across the stage.[3] In the title song, which was also the overture for the film, the Chairman and his Party are deified as the Daystar of the people, radiating light, warmth, and liberation across the land:

> The east is red, and the sun has risen
> China has produced a Mao Zedong
> He works for the happiness of the people
> Hu'er hai'yo, he is the saving star of the people!
> Chairman Mao loves the people
> He is our guide on the road
> to build a new China
> Hu'er hai'yo, leading us forward!
> The Communist Party, like the sun
> Wherever it shines is bright
> Wherever the Party is,
> Hu'er hai'yo, the people are liberated![4]

By the mid-1960s, the song and the film had come to constitute a kind of self-perpetuating media loop, propelled by and propelling the personality cult surrounding Mao Zedong. Its solar imagery—visualized in the opening sequence of the film by a massive phalanx of chorines, arrayed in the shape of a sunflower, swaying heliotropically toward an image of the Chairman—saturated Chinese media culture. In cinema, color posters, printed materials, and myriad objects of everyday use, Chairman Mao is imagined as a radiant medium, emitting the effulgent rays of his thought and suffusing the spaces beneath his Delphic gaze with beams of light (see Plate 1).

In the summer of 1966, with the Chairman's support, a massive new revolutionary campaign erupted against his own Party apparatus, led by high school and college students fired by utopian promises and disaffected by the bureaucratic structures and stultifying educational institutions of the actually existing socialist order. "The East Is Red" emerged as the soundtrack to this "Great Proletarian Cultural Revolution" 無產階級文化大革命, displacing the official national anthem, "The March of the Volunteers" 義勇軍進行曲, and crackling nearly incessantly for nearly a decade over a wired broadcast system, consisting of a network of nearly 100 million loudspeakers, that the Party had constructed across the country beginning in the late 1950s. By the late 1960s, the Central People's Broadcasting Station's daily broadcasts began before dawn and ended deep into the night with a rendition of the melody played on a set of ancient stone chimes. Schoolchildren began their day by singing the anthem, and public meetings were called to order with its recitation. In a nationally publicized act of revolutionary fervor during the summer of 1966, a consortium of student activists, Red Guards, and skilled factory workers in Shanghai labored day and night to design and install a new mechanism to allow the clock tower of the British-built Customs building on the Bund to sound the hours not with the colonial cadence of the Westminster chimes but with the melody of "The East Is Red."[5] Public buildings throughout the country, including the Beijing Railway Station, followed suit. The song, like church bells in medieval Europe, drew the boundaries of collective space and limned the very movement of time.[6]

The satellite was thus an almost perfectly self-reflexive realization of the song's lyrics and of the logic of the one-to-many media network of which it was part. Rising into earth's orbit like a little sun, "The East Is Red 1" would broadcast its Maoist message across the globe, shedding light across the dark reaches of space, a singular beacon of liberation for the wretched of the earth below.

The dream of opening new and unprecedentedly global media circuits, however, was by no means unique to China in those years. In fact, "The East Is Red 1" had long since been beaten to the punch and was doubtless intended to rival similar communications efforts in the Soviet Union and the West. The first simultaneous, worldwide live satellite broadcast, "Our World," had taken place on June 25, 1967, executed by a consortium formed by the British Broadcasting Corporation, Canada's CBC, Japan's NHK, NET (National Education Television) in the United States, and ten other agencies. Conceived as a global event that would unite television viewers across the Cold War divide, "Our World" reached an estimated 400 million viewers distributed across twenty-four countries, even after the Soviet Union and other Eastern bloc nations withdrew their participation at the last moment in protest of the Six-Day War in the Middle East. Appropriately enough, the two-and-a-half-hour program began in Canada with an interview of media theorist and apostle of the electronic "global village," Marshall McLuhan, and culminated with a live studio performance by the Beatles of a new song they had written expressly for the occasion, the title of which would come to stand in for the utopian spirit, countercultural sensibility, and collective aspirations of the late 1960s moment: "All You Need Is Love."[7]

"The East Is Red" and "All You Need Is Love," of course, could hardly be more different. The former is unabashed propaganda, an ideological broadside predicated on a folk melody, slowed to a stately tempo and amplified a thousandfold by orchestral bombast so as to proclaim Chairman Mao as savior and solution; the latter is a pop song that playfully undermines its own premises ("no one you can save that can't be saved") and gleefully punctuates its disarmingly simple refrain ("love, love, love") with the melodic shards of earlier musical monuments. From the opening fanfare citing the French revolutionary anthem "La Marseillaise," to closing allusions to Bach, "Greensleeves," Glenn Miller, and the Beatles' own breakthrough hit "She Loves You," "All You Need Is Love" takes pleasure not only in its own historical self-consciousness but also in the dissolution of all fixed or fast-frozen conceptions of musical genre.[8] And yet, somehow, both songs are unmistakably and emblematically products of the 1960s and emerge from a shared historical moment. That "somehow" is both the starting point of this book and also its most pressing historiographical question. What connects the worlds of these songs, and in what sense can we say that they are of the same historical moment? Is it possible to write a sonic history of the global 1960s from the perspective of a place that is usually dismissed as marginal to the musical revolutions of those years? Can we bring China back into the narrative of how we hear the explosion of popular music for which these years are famous and, by the same token, reinsert the global into our sometimes hermetic sense of Chinese cultural history at midcentury? To what extent does it make sense to speak of a common 1960s sound across the geopolitical fractures of the Cold War and the struggle for decolonization? Is any historical era, for that matter, coherent unto itself? Or is our sense of period style invariably an ex post facto imposition of a false historical unity that never really existed at the time?

## INTRODUCTION

The juxtaposition of "The East Is Red" with "All You Need Is Love" suggests one approach to these questions. As ideologically and aesthetically distinct as these songs are, they were united by reliance upon—and were in a very real sense *about*—the unprecedented reach of the communications networks by which they were disseminated. Not the ubiquity nor the political power nor the particular aesthetic qualities of "The East Is Red" can be understood in isolation from the socialist media network by which it was borne. The ecumenical cheer and open-ended universalism of "All You Need Is Love" was, from its very inception, inseparable from its mode of transmission. Nor could its subsequent success be separated from the radio sets and record players that sent the single to the top of the charts after its televised debut. The ubiquity of medium, to once again invoke Marshall McLuhan, was precisely the message.[9] Even John Lennon's enigmatic lyrics for the song seem to echo something of the recursive logic of McLuhan's pronouncement: "There's nothing you can do that can't be done / Nothing that you can sing that can't be sung. . . . Nothing that you can know that isn't known / Nothing that you can see that isn't shown."

By the late 1960s, what could be sung, known, and shown increasingly reached audiences by way of transistorized electronics. Indeed, it is precisely the transistor that distinguishes the 1960s from all earlier musical and medial epochs. Invented in 1947 at Bell Labs by a trio of American scientists, the transistor was a deceptively simple device that, in sending electricity across a semiconductor material such as germanium or silicon, amplified its signal or "gain." The technological gain thus generated constituted nothing short of what Ernest Braun and Stuart Macdonald have termed a "revolution in miniature." By the 1960s, mass-produced transistors had begun to replace older, far more cumbersome, and less energy-efficient vacuum tube electronics, spurring the explosive growth of a new consumer electronics industry worldwide. Vacuum tubes require the application of enough voltage to heat a filament: only when the cathode has been excited to a red glow will electrons begin to flow. Solid-state transistor circuits, by contrast, run cool and, because they did not require an evacuated glass enclosure, were smaller from the start and only became tinier over time. It is exactly their rapid and exponential diminution in size, famously posited by Moore's Law, which has yielded the complex integrated circuits and microelectronics that have irrevocably transformed every aspect of our world and media environment. Writing one of the first histories of the semiconductor industry in the late 1970s, Braun and Macdonald averred that the transistor had made "other technological innovations pale into insignificance," for with its advent:

Whole new industries arose, new professions, new ways of production and new organisations. Without solid state electronics, we would have no powerful computers, no large-scale automation, no communications satellites or space exploration. There would be no electronic calculators or digital watches, no transistor radios, portable tape recorders or bugging devices . . . the list could be extended almost indefinitely and is growing daily.[10]

By the late 1960s, transistorized electronics had made new ways of producing, disseminating, and listening to music not only possible but also increasingly common. This is in no small part because they were inexpensive to produce and to own and energy efficient enough to be driven by batteries, even in remote rural regions far from metropolitan centers or electrical mains. They were not only the common denominator between the Beatles' worldwide popularity and the Maoist propaganda network but the very condition of possibility for both. The giddy rise of rock and roll—and the advent of its distinctly punchy and compressed sonic aesthetic—has long been attributed to the new popularity as well as to the technical limitations, of portable, monophonic transistor radios beginning from the late 1950s.[11] Transistor technology was equally as decisive for defining and diffusing the sound of the Chinese Revolution. Disassemble one of the tens of millions of public-address speakers that were strung across Chinese city streets and village squares beginning in the late 1950s and you will find cheap transistors. Scratch the surface of a satellite, whether "The East Is Red 1" or the series of Intelsat stations that beamed the Beatles to the world, and you will find an array of transistor circuits, turning solar radiation into usable energy and routing ultra-shortwave signals back to earth. Transistors, in rendering recorded music ever more portable and accessible, whether deep in the hinterlands or in outer space, allowed mass-mediated musical networks to scale up, to aspire to new and more expansive territories, and to bring together national, cross-regional, or even global communities of listeners.

**Circuit and Ground**

A satellite like "East Is Red 1" was short-lived and exceptional—a kind of signal flare sounding out the developmental aspirations of the socialist nation-state. On the ground and in everyday practice, the "revolution in miniature" wrought by the transistor was always uneven, subject not only to the gravitational pull of geopolitics but also to the contingencies of local histories, conditions, and practices. This book relates how transistors left their imprint on musical practices and aesthetics in the People's Republic of China between the 1950s and the 1970s, affording the state the means to construct an unprecedentedly pervasive socialist media network. The transistor also served as the agent of that same system's dissolution, as an influx of portable consumer electronics playing popular music imported from Taiwan via Hong Kong transformed the Chinese soundscape in the post-Mao era. Much of the book is devoted to chronicling the emergence of those newly electrified forms of popular music on the littoral fringes of the mainland, in the British crown colony and port city on China's southernmost edge, and on the island-nation, former Japanese colony, and American Cold War proxy, some one hundred miles distant from China's southeast coast, often referred to in those years as "Free China." Taiwan is a particularly rich site for the study of the technological mediation of music in the 1960s, not only because of its precarious position along the geopolitical rifts of the Cold War but also because of its rapid industrial development as one of the world's most prolific exporters of consumer electronics and of pirated music: ground zero of a musical "revolution in miniature." Throughout the book, I chart the ways in which transistor circuits served as a material conduit for the production and electronic dissemination of new sounds, be it the revolutionary anthems of the socialist era in China, mambo in Hong Kong, or pop balladry from Taiwan.

Transistor circuits allowed these sounds to circulate across time and space, as popular genres radiated out from London, New York, and Los Angeles to the rest of the world, formerly remote areas were brought into the musical orbit of rapidly industrializing cities, and rural sounds migrated into and left their mark on urban soundscapes. Contrary to the technological triumphalism of which critics have sometimes accused Marshall McLuhan, the transistor did not and could not effect an Aquarian age of open borders, across which nomadic "information-gatherers" were free to range.[12] There would be no phonographic "music hall without walls," in which a newly tactile "electronic man" levitates free of print culture and its train of ancient linguistic prejudices.[13] Instead, and perhaps predictably, electronic circuits operated across, within, and in complex and often complicit relationships with existing social topologies. In this book, then, I listen for the new musical possibilities opened up by the transistor and how media technology has left audible traces on the music of the period. Yet I am also concerned throughout with another kind of circuit—the particular linguistic, ideological, and economic pathways, cut by the passage of historical time, along which particular genres of music could (or could not) travel. Their topologies have been indelibly traced by colonial histories and etched by the sharp declivities of social inequity, both within and across different societies. Circuits function not only to enable but also to *delimit* or prevent the flow of musical current. All but the simplest circuits employ both capacitors (to pool potential energy) and resistors (to reduce the flow of current, divide a voltage, and reroute or terminate the transmission of a signal). Different circuits run on different power sources and are designed for divergent purposes. From the putatively "open circuits" that patched the commerce and culture of Hong Kong, Taiwan, and Chinese diasporic communities throughout Southeast Asia to the metropolitan West and Japan, to the seemingly "closed circuit" of a revolutionary media system on the Chinese mainland, I listen in the following pages to the fractured topography of the global 1960s and attempt to diagram its contours.

That topography was often rural and at a remove from the major metropolitan centers in which the political uprisings, student movements, and cultural upheavals of the era took shape. Our accounts of the 1960s revolve around places like Paris in May 1968, Swinging London, and the Summer of Love in San Francisco. Any itinerary of the decade's upheavals should surely also include Eastern bloc cities like Prague, where protestors fought and lost a battle for "socialism with a human face," as well as Beijing, where what was arguably the largest and fiercest antibureaucratic youth movement of those years, that of the Red Guards, erupted in 1966. Other major cities in East Asia were also caught up in this global wave. Tokyo became the site of massive demonstrations against the United States' imperial presence in East Asia, beginning with a blockade of the Legislative Diet in protest of the Treaty of Mutual Cooperation and Security (ANPO) in 1960 and culminating in student occupations of Tokyo University in the late 1960s in protest of the Vietnam War. In Seoul, at the very dawn of the decade, striking students toppled the U.S.-backed Syngman Rhee regime in the April Revolution of 1960. Nor were the rapidly expanding capital cities of the global South exempt, from Mexico City (site of a vibrant counterculture as well as the deadly massacre of student strikers at the Universidad Nacional Autonóma de México [UNAM] in 1968) to São Paulo (where student protest, popular music, and the artistic avant-garde for a brief moment came together under the banner of Tropicália despite brutal martial law).

How can we explain the global simultaneity of this outburst of political and cultural energy? Fredric Jameson, in his 1984 essay "Periodizing the 1960s," asks us to look to the countryside for an answer.[14] In Jameson's macrohistorical account, the First World 1960s with which many of us are familiar were first set into motion by the "great movement" of Third World decolonization, from Ghana's independence in 1957, to the victories of the Algerian war of liberation and the Cuban Revolution in 1959, and on to the "wrenching" liberation struggles led by Patrice Lumumba in the Congo in 1961.[15] Jameson's list here is necessarily partial, for the period between the 1950s and the mid-1970s witnessed the birth of dozens of new postcolonial states across Africa, Asia, Latin America, and the Caribbean as the British, French, German, and Portuguese empires relinquished their hold on former colonial possessions. Vietnam's decolonization struggle and the ensuing U.S.-led war to contain communism in Southeast Asia became a particularly potent geopolitical and ideological flashpoint as the decade wore on. As "natives became human beings," Jameson asserts, their struggles became the inspiration and the strategic blueprint for social movements and insurrections in the First World as well.[16]

Jameson's point is not solely to celebrate the creative energies unleashed by decolonization. In dialectical fashion, he shows instead how those forces had themselves been set into motion by the penetration of metropolitan capital into its agrarian hinterlands:

> in a process generally described in the neutral but obviously ideological language of a technological revolution in agriculture: the Green Revolution, with its new applications of chemical procedures to fertilization, its intensified strategies of mechanization, and its predictable celebration of progress and wonder-working technology, destined to free the world from hunger.... The older village structures are now systematically destroyed, to be replaced by an industrial agriculture whose effects are fully as disastrous as, and analogous to, the moment of enclosure in the emergence of capital in what was to become the first world. The "organic" social relations of village societies are now shattered, an enormous landless preproletariat "produced," which migrates to the urban areas (as the tremendous growth of Mexico City can testify), while new, more proletarian, wage-working forms of agricultural labor replace the older collective or traditional kinds.[17]

Crucially, the Green Revolution's incorporation into global markets of heretofore resistant pockets of countryside coincided with an ever more thorough colonization of everyday life by the consumer society and its mass media in the city. Migrants were freed from the drudgery of the land, only to be brought into a new electronic fold. Urbanites were fired by the pastoral promise of a global village, just as actual villages were being plowed under by the pitiless logic of commodity markets. Borrowing his metaphor from Mao Zedong, Jameson likens this "dialectical process in which 'liberation' and domination are inextricably combined" to the smashing of an atom, producing, for a brief time, "a prodigious release of untheorized new forces" in the political and cultural realm.[18]

While Jameson's "unified field theory of the 60s" is sketched out in admittedly broad strokes, it does provide a useful heuristic with which to listen to the worldwide efflorescence of popular music of the period. This is not merely a matter of the ways in which the momentous topical issues of those years began to seep into Anglo-American mass-mediated music, informing the zeitgeist and shaping entire genres, as in the indelible associations between the American folk revival and the civil rights movement, soul music and Black Power and between rock music and student protest and Vietnam.[19] Nor is it limited to the no less important, if less often remarked, ways in which the sounds of the colonies, both internal and more far-flung, turned the harmonic forms of metropolitan musical inside out, while at the same time introducing a host of new timbral possibilities into the pop music palette. Much has been written about the ways in which the British Invasion appropriated the idiom of black American blues. Nor is it a secret that English folk-rock and psychedelia mined techniques and timbres appropriated from Britain's former colonial possessions on the Indian subcontinent.[20] Something similar could also be said about the ways in which innovators like Miles Davis and John Coltrane drew on the modalities of West African, North African, and South Asian music to transform the harmonic language of jazz.[21]

Yet these stories about 1960s music, as important as they are, remain provincial and one-sided. The real virtue of Jameson's "unified field theory" is that it allows us to see a bigger picture and to ask different kinds of questions. Is there a sense in which the various vernacular musics of the 1960s, across a vast variety of locales, share some sort of historical determination or period style? How might listening to the rural peripheries, as opposed to the metropoles, change our sense of the dynamics of this period? In a manner strikingly analogous to the global upsurge of new urban idioms that Michael Denning has charted for the late 1920s in his brilliant history of the decolonizing impact of electrical recording, *Noise Uprising* (of which more later), we hear an unprecedented wave of new vernacular styles emerge across the world beginning in the late 1950s and on into the mid-1970s, just as transistor radios, record players, and tape recorders begin to percolate across the developing world.[22] Many of these new genres emerged as country people, rendered redundant by changes in the agrarian economy, migrated to the makeshift slums surrounding the industrial centers of the Global South. Examples abound, from the hard-driving accordion-driven forró music of rural migrants to São Paulo, to the bass-heavy reggae music, fusing American soul with Afro-Caribbean revivalist rhythms, which bubbled up from the shantytowns of Kingston, Jamaica, in the late 1960s.[23] By the mid-1970s, myriad hybrid styles, riffing on rural sounds with electric guitars and keyboards and drum kits, recorded with modern studio equipment and pressed on vinyl, began to circulate within urban media circuits from Johannesburg, Lagos, Lusaka, and Nairobi to Bangkok, Jakarta, and Phnom Penh.[24]

Around the same time, and almost simultaneously around the globe, there arose a vogue among youthful urban audiences for various forms of folk revivalism. The American folk revival, initially driven by trade unionism and left-wing mobilization by figures like Woody Guthrie and the Weavers, began to enter mass-mediated circuits with a vengeance in the late 1950s with the sudden popularity of records by the Kingston Trio and Peter, Paul, and Mary and reached its apogee with Bob Dylan's ascent to stardom and his apostasy with regard to folk orthodoxy in 1965, when he dispensed with the traditionalist acoustic repertoire and plugged in an electric guitar at the Newport Folk Festival.[25] Developments in the United Kingdom closely tracked those across the Atlantic, as a generation of folkies such as Donovan, the Pentangle, and Fairport Convention began to experiment with the possibilities of an electric folk-rock sound by the late 1960s. In Brazil, the defining moment of the decade came in 1967 with a televised clash at the Festival de Música Popular Brasileira between the earnestly political, strummed acoustic guitars of folk revivalism and the self-consciously indigenized "tropicalist" rock music—buzzing with fuzz guitar, batería, and berimbau—championed by Caetano Veloso and Gilberto Gil.[26] Analogous developments unfolded across the Eastern Bloc as well, where the massive underground popularity of guitar-toting folk "bards" like Russia's singer-songwriter Vladimir Vysotsky had helped to spawn electrified folk-rock and folk-pop hybrids such as Pojuschie Gitary and Pesnyary by the 1970s.[27] For a brief moment, folk troubadours commanded enormous cultural prestige and even political power across the world: the abortive insurgency of Salvador Allende in Chile is almost unimaginable in the absence of the music of Víctor Jara and the *nueva cancion*, and a radio broadcast of the folk *fadista* José Afonso's "Grândola Vila Morena" served as the trigger for Portugal's Carnation Revolution in 1974, bringing down the authoritarian Salazar regime.[28] In Vietnam, the noted poet and antiwar folksinger Trịnh Công Sơn ran afoul of both the South Vietnamese and the communist regimes.[29] In Japan, Okabayashi Nobuyasu 岡林信康 gave voice to the left wing and antiwar concerns of student protesters, while innovative countercultural folk-rockers like Happy End, recording for the Underground Record Club (URC), pioneered a lyrically localized folk-rock idiom.[30] In South Korea, a genre of Dylanesque folk known as *t'onggit'a umak* vied for urban listeners with rock tinged by *minyo* folk revivalism.³¹ There are many more examples of this global wave from locales around the world. What is interesting is that each of these local scenes traced a dialectic arc between the acoustic and the electric and between the valorization of pastoral sounds and their circulation within urban commercial circuits.

The remarkable simultaneity of these phenomena can doubtless be attributed in part to the global reach of American and British media networks. That many of the guitar-strumming singer-songwriters of those years were referred to as the "Bob Dylan" or "Joan Baez" of their respective nations speaks volumes about the hegemonic power of the stylistic norms and musical forms of British and American counterculture in those years. The omnipresence of the guitar, whether acoustic or electrically amplified, as the nearly inevitable medium for this panoply of local idioms also suggests something of this dominance.³² In places like Taiwan and Hong Kong, plugged more or less directly into English-language media circuits by dint of their position on the front lines of the Cold War, the influence of guitar-driven folk and rock music was palpable and nearly immediate.

Rather than speaking in terms of unidirectional influence or of stable musical categories, however, it may be more helpful to understand these genres as effects of the circuits in which they moved. In chapter 1, "Circuit Listening at the Dawn of the Chinese 1960s," I trace the advent of the transistor era back to the glamorous and globe-trotting diva of the Mandarin musical cinema in Hong Kong Grace Chang (known as Ge Lan 葛蘭 in Chinese). Tellingly, Chang's musical idiom is difficult to categorize or to position. Displaced from "Red China" by the revolution, Chang had little truck with her adoptive city and its prevailing Cantonese idiom. She harked back instead to the interwar tradition of jazz-inflected "modern song" from the colonial entrepôt of Shanghai and employed standard Mandarin as a lingua franca connecting her to a pan-Chinese pop circuit.³³ What does it mean, then, that Grace Chang's music trafficked freely in fashionable Afro-Caribbean genres like mambo and calypso or that this "Mambo Girl" 曼波女郎 (as she was known to her fans across the Chinese diaspora) was marketed back to North American audiences as an archetypically "Chinese" singer? In this chapter, I listen to Grace Chang as a kind of sonic flare, one who enables us to trace the contours of a circuitous media network, extending from Havana and Mexico City to Manhattan and Hollywood and linking Hong Kong to Taiwan and its diasporic Chinese hinterlands in Southeast Asia. While much of the chapter focuses on the high-flying world of Mandarin musical cinema, I also show what happens when mambo crosses over into a profoundly different and far more down-market entertainment circuit, one catering to the linguistically marginalized Taiwanese migrant workers crowding the industrial districts of Taipei. Just as Grace Chang's records bear what we might call the "network trace" of the transnational media matrix in which they were produced, the mambo music of Hong Yifeng 洪一峰 registers the imprint of a Taiwanese media circuit situated between the lingering legacy of Japanese empire and the ascendency of the Pax Americana and shuttling uneasily between rural roots and urban accommodations.

That dialectic organizes the history of postwar Taiwanese popular music and cinema that I provide over the course of three chapters at the heart of the book. Inextricably intertwined with the particularities of the military and economic presence of the United States on the island, Taiwan's media history also emerges out of the global confluence of the Green Revolution and transistorization that I have touched upon earlier. In fact, Taiwan is a uniquely compelling historical case in this regard, for the island was firmly situated at the forefront of both processes. Soon after the Chinese Nationalist Party's (KMT) defeat by the Communist Party (CCP) and its retreat to the island in 1949, Chiang Kai-Shek's 蔣介石 government-in-exile embarked on an ambitious program of rural land reform, designed to counteract the structural legacy of fifty years of Japanese colonialism and facilitate the island's industrial modernization and incorporation into the U.S.-backed economic order then taking shape. With the intellectual and strategic cooperation of the Sino-American Joint Commission on Rural Reconstruction (JCRR) and with economic assistance from the United States Agency for International Development (USAID), large-scale projects introducing new and higher-yielding rice cultivars, mechanizing agricultural processes, and encouraging the use of industrial fertilizers and pesticides resulted in stratospheric economic growth.[34] These agricultural gains were expropriated to aid the expansion of the manufacturing sector. By 1953, the Taiwanese firm Tatung 大同 had begun, with the financial assistance of USAID, to transfer electronics manufacturing expertise from a resurgent Japan.[35] Japan's success in the early 1950s, sparked by licenses of proprietary transistor radio technology from American firms, had been fueled by a steady supply of rural and predominately female laborers, who propelled its electronics assembly lines to profitability and helped establish the country as a world-beating force in the television manufacturing industry.[36] That model was replicated in Taiwan. In 1962, the Japanese electronics conglomerate Matsushita 松下, later known as Panasonic, set up shop in an industrial suburb of Taipei, manufacturing a variety of consumer electronics and home appliances for local and global markets. Six other joint ventures were to follow by 1963.³⁷ By 1964, an exports-processing area had been established in the southern port city of Kaohsiung, anchored by General Instrument, an up-and-coming U.S. manufacturer of semiconductor circuits. Between 1966 and 1971, the electronics sector grew at an annual rate of 58 percent.³⁸ By 1968, electronic goods had become Taiwan's second largest export, after textiles.³⁹

As the economy took off, rural populations increasingly left their villages behind, pouring into urban Taipei and Kaohsiung along Japanese colonial-era railways in search of new mobility and opportunity. As a militarized outpost of the United States' strategy of Cold War containment, however, where the often brutally repressive martial law of the KMT still held sway, the 1960s of emancipatory possibility, decolonization, and dissent largely bypassed the island. Yet Taiwan's position at the margins of the Pax Americana meant that the sounds of a globally circulating counterculture still arrived on its shores, taking on new and sometimes nearly unrecognizable forms. Chapter 3, "Fugitive Sounds of the Taiwanese Musical Cinema," presents a close reading of a 1969 Taiwanese-language or *Taiyu* 台語 musical called *Goodbye, Taipei* 再見台北 featuring one of the most celebrated singers of the era, Wen Shia 文夏.⁴⁰ Made for precisely the sorts of rural migrants whose native idiom had been marginalized by official government policies favoring standard Mandarin Chinese and whose lives had been upended by rapid modernization, this black-and-white film features an oddly anachronistic cinematic aesthetic, reminiscent of Charlie Chaplin–style slapstick comedy, the Keystone Cops, and Buster Keaton chase films. The old-fashioned flair of the film is belied by its soundtrack, which teems with cover versions of the very latest sounds from the Anglophone and Japanese hit parade, from soul to psychedelia. This reliance on the cover song was part and parcel of the larger cultural logic of a multiply colonized milieu, surviving in the interstices between a vanquished empire and a newly dominant global power. Like many other Taiwanese-language films of this era, *Goodbye, Taipei* cheerfully turns our ready distinctions between original and cover, anterior and posterior, the pursued and pursuer, upside down. Its frenetic narrative pace, moreover, registers both the excitement and the wrenching displacement of the island's developmental steeplechase. Ironically, Wen Shia's work thrived throughout the decade in the context of an itinerant media circuit in which live performance and cinema reinforced each other in surprising and counter-intuitive ways. That particular circuit, however, was not to survive the 1960s and the unrelenting onrush of mass-mediated modernization. *Goodbye, Taipei* was Wen Shia's last film before a new Mandarin-only media system, underwritten by the authoritarian state and by the rise of television, rendered his work obsolete. Wen Shia's fugitive sound, in its apparent backwardness vis-à-vis the global 1960s, allows us a visceral look back at the uneven social topography of this fleeting temporal moment.

In chapter 4, "Pirates of the China Seas: Vinyl Records and the Military Circuit," I explore the antinomies of Taiwan's marginal position at the military frontiers of the Cold War. In the wake of the Chinese Revolution and the Korean War, Taiwan was pressed into service as an "unsinkable aircraft carrier" in the containment of Communist insurgencies and by the late 1960s had become a major staging point for the transfer of men and materiél to the war in Vietnam. Up and down what Bruce Cumings has called the archipelago of empire running from South Korea, Japan, Okinawa, and Taiwan to the Philippines, military bases served as the single most important conduit for the dissemination of Anglophone pop music into East Asia. Military installations and their broadcasting stations served as a kind of semiconductor, amplifying musical signals from abroad and powering the coming together of new and quite unforeseen local circuits of cultural production and consumption. One important material substrate for this circuit was vinyl. Just as Wen Shia and other musicians created locally inflected cover versions of Japanese and Western hits, Taiwanese record pirates were quick to press foreign sounds to local profit. Taiwan was notorious in these years as a source of cheap copies of U.S. long-playing records, pressed on colored vinyl with mimeographed covers and marketed to U.S. servicemen in cities such as Taipei and Kaohsiung as well as to local enthusiasts. As pirate records thrived in the interstices between the KMT censorship regime and international copyright conventions, they also enabled new ways of feeling and being, embodied by a flowering of a late 1960s youth culture revolving around the consumption of Anglophone "hit music." The history of one of the most intrepid of these pirate firms, First Records 第一唱片, also discloses a revealing paradox—it was precisely the business of piracy that subsidized the rise of an altogether different structure of feeling: the rediscovery of local folk music and its entry into mass-mediated circuits in service of an anticolonial agenda. By 1979, when the United States formally broke off diplomatic relations with the Republic of China and withdrew from its military bases, a "campus folk" revival was in full flower across the island. Inspired by the folk singer Li Shuangze's 李雙澤 anticolonial call to "sing our own songs" but modeled in large measure on globally portable norms and musical forms, campus folk was poised not only to transform Mandarin popular music in Taiwan but also to remake the soundscape of mainland China as well.

Chapter 5, "Folk Circuits: Discovering Chen Da," the final chapter of this trilogy on Taiwanese music, turns to an examination of the internal contradictions of the Taiwanese folk revival. Why did a movement dedicated to the recovery of an indigenous voice remain so stubbornly in the shadow of a globally circulating folk aesthetic? The story begins with an epochal encounter in 1967 at the southernmost extremity of the island between the eminent modernist composer and musicologist Hsu Tsang-Houei 許常惠 and a blind, impoverished *yueqin* 月琴 (moon lute) player named Chen Da 陳達.[41] Reminiscent in many ways of the "rediscovery" of African American blues pioneers like Mississippi John Hurt and Furry Lewis, which helped define the music of the American 1960s, Hsu Tsang-Houei's advocacy of Chen Da's folk balladry made him into a legend. For Hsu and his collaborator Shih Wei-liang 史惟亮, Chen Da represented the missing link: a living revenant on whose body was inscribed the essence of a Chinese folk music in imminent danger of extinction. The agent of that destruction was the inundation of the Taiwanese soundscape by mass-mediated music, much of it from abroad. But having been discovered, Chen Da was recorded, his performances televised, his image rendered iconic, and his art remade into a neatly packaged and annotated artifact, despite its distinctly improvisatory quality. The migration of Chen Da and his music into urban media circuits allows us to see the way in which the culture of the transistor rendered not only distant sounds but also even rural places portable and open to new kinds of modernist appropriation and imagination. In a close reading of Shih Wei-liang's long-playing document of Chen Da from 1971, *Musician of Our Nation* 民族樂手陳達和他的歌, we can also hear the way in which that transistorized media network left its traces on his music. Tellingly, the earthy sound of these field recordings could not be replicated in campus folk and its pop-rock offshoots. The legacy of Chen Da and his signature song, "Remember When" 思想起, was secured, in a final irony, not by being discovered but because it had long since been covered—by the same pop musicians Hsu and Shih had blamed for its demise.

The fate of folk music was profoundly different in the People's Republic of China—so different, in fact, that one might wonder in what sense these stories belong in the same book, or speak to the same historical era. I am not interested in imputing to these two cases an underlying commonality based on some vague or unsubstantiated notion of linguistic or cultural affinity.[42] What interests me instead are the actual and abiding historical intersections between these very different musical circuits and their mutual imbrication in the geopolitical dynamics of the global 1960s. Those intersections speak, of course, to history in the long and the short *durée*, from the early migration of Hokkien and Hakka settlers to Taiwan in the seventeenth century to the massive influx of two million mainlander refugees to the island in the wake of the Chinese Civil War, Shih Wei-liang and several other of the dramatis personae in this story among them. Indeed, a daughter of that exodus named Teresa Teng 鄧麗君, as I recount in the final chapter of the book, went on to become the most estimable and effective weapon in the Cold War sound clash between the rival states across the straits, leaving an indelible mark on Chinese music in the process. Until the late 1970s, when cassette tape recorders began to trickle into the mainland and, along with them, pirated cassettes of Teresa Teng's music, its media ecology, with some significant exceptions, had been sealed off from the outside world.[43] Just as Taiwanese record pirates smuggled a new sensibility to the island in the 1960s and 1970s, the opening up of this alternative musical circuit signaled the advent of a new structure of feeling in the 1980s and tolled the knell of the high socialist era.

Teng's story is instructive in that it shows the extent to which the Cold War divide was a matter of media infrastructure. In chapter 2, "Quotation Songs: Media Infrastructure and Pop Song Form in Mao's China," I provide an account of how the socialist state marshaled the same technology available elsewhere to design and construct a very different kind of media system, one premised on fixed state-run installations at odds with the portability and domestic use we usually associate with the transistor as a technology. The wired broadcasting network of the Maoist years resonated across urban streets, schools, and workplaces, but its most salient feature was its reach. Radiating out from the center, broadcasts traveled deep into the countryside via an array of provincial and county-level relay stations and rediffusion lines, rewiring the affective life of the peasantry.

The countryside in question was far larger, more populous, and much poorer than a place like Taiwan. Throughout the 1960s, rural electrification was the exception, rather than the rule. Unlike in most other agrarian nations in the postwar period, the peasantry was also something of a captive audience. The People's Republic began to implement strict controls on rural–urban migration in 1954. A regime of "Household Registration Regulation," referred to in Chinese as the "*hukou*" 戶口 system, was signed into law in January 1958, effectively consigning more than 80 percent of the population to de facto exclusion from urban residency and amenities.[44] These rules not only helped facilitate the top-down implementation of state directives in a command economy. They were also designed to prevent precisely the sorts of uncontrolled mass migration and urban growth that had been occasioned by the Green Revolution elsewhere across the Third World.[45]

This is not to say, as the historian Sigrid Schmalzer has shown, that the global tide of the Green Revolution passed China by. Chinese socialists were understandably wary of American-led efforts to modernize rural economies (with Taiwan serving as a notable test case). After all, those efforts—and even the term "Green Revolution" itself—had been championed by the director of USAID, William Gaud, as a bulwark and guarantor against "Red Revolution."[46] Nonetheless, Chinese officials "embraced the causes of science and modernization, and so in some important ways, the green revolution in red China looked strikingly similar to the green revolution as Gaud imagined it."[47] Chinese scientists and activists, using a "patchwork" of methods, moved assiduously to introduce modern machinery and chemical fertilizers, implement large-scale irrigation and land-terracing projects, and encourage the use of higher-yielding seeds.[48] The extension of wired media into the countryside was, in this sense, a vital part of the infrastructure for this program of modernization, serving as a mouthpiece for Party directives as well as a means of mobilizing the peasantry.

As Brian Larkin reminds us in his study of northern Nigerian media history, however, media systems do not always work as efficiently as advertised; infrastructural connections are "frequently messy, discontinuous, and poor," especially in rural regions far from the urban centers of advanced industrial economies.[49] A media theory extrapolated from abstract models of unimpeded technical advances risks mistaking the ideal for the actual. Larkin advises us to listen as much for noise generated by "technical interference and breakdown" as for the official signal the network is supposed to relay.[50] Following Larkin, I explore here how the local exigencies of the revolution in the Chinese countryside necessarily complicate technical histories of the "revolution in miniature" that take the advanced industrial economies of the West as their fulcrum. The implementation of transistor technology in rural China was distinctly nonlinear. Mandated by the central authorities, broadcasting networks were often jerrybuilt by local authorities in the absence of state funding or even electrical mains. Engineers were forced to improvise, and the technical choices they made were governed by thrift and expediency rather than by engineering efficiency or audio quality, let alone high fidelity. Transistorized public address systems and portable film projectors were often driven by makeshift generators, hand-cranked by peasants, or even propelled by teams of oxen. Relays traveled down telephone lines, and interference was common. Speakers were rudimentary at best and always shrill. The network was *noisy*.

That noise is distinctly audible in the musical aesthetics of the era. I listen for its traces in one of the more curious cultural products of the Cultural Revolution—quotation songs. Adapted from what was surely one of the most iconic and widely distributed books of the global 1960s, the

"Little Red Book" 紅寶書 of *Quotations of Mao Zedong* 毛主席語錄, "quotation songs" were short, fast, loud, repetitive, and astonishingly catchy.[51] Engineered to cut through the noise of public spaces, their narrow frequency range exploited the limitations of the horn reflex speakers through which they resounded. Their brevity, in turn, encouraged memorization and collective recitation. The quotation song, not unlike the contemporaneous hits of the Beatles or the Rolling Stones, was built around an insistent melodic or rhythmic hook and as such was not only instantly recognizable but also easily replicable across disparate media and contexts. In this regard, quotation songs reflected the relentlessly cross-platform interactivity of the socialist media system, in which print, posters, cinema, radio broadcasts, and records mimicked one another's formal logic and responded to the same political imperatives. This culture was so catchy, in fact, that it crossed over, resonating among youthful radicals worldwide, like the Parisian Maoist insurgents portrayed in Jean-Luc Godard's 1967 film *La Chinoise* who tune in and are turned on by the sound of Radio Peking. In Godard's cinema, we see not only the presence in Paris at the apogee of the 1960s of a distinctly Maoist cultural formation but also its formal affinity and even convergence with the countercultural pop of the Atlantic world.

Godard's stylish radicals, listening in to Radio Peking on a shortwave transistor radio, would surely have reveled in the nowness of "The East Is Red" and its declaration of the dawning of a new era. I have already suggested in this introduction and pursue in more instantiated detail in the chapters that follow the notion that with close listening to recorded artifacts, we can discern something like a "network trace," a sonic signature that bears the indexical imprint of its historical moment. We can hear, in Larkin's terms, not only the signal but the noise; not just the song but also the sound of the particular linguistic, social, and technological circuits in which it moved. Circuits can be local and restricted to a particular audience or milieu, but, whether by way of migration or through electronic mediation, they can also scale up, reaching divergent social strata and multiple locales. "The East Is Red," in linking Party Central to peasants and Peking to Paris (along with any number of other places), resonated in parallel in several circuits at once, with a simultaneity that was very much of its moment.

**The Sea Change**

Yet songs, as Bruno Nettl has reminded us, are "the most indefatigable tourists," traveling not only across radically different media circuits but also through historical time.⁵² "The East Is Red" is a case in point, and its odyssey into outer space reveals much about the maritime origins of pre-revolutionary Chinese popular music and its new trajectory after 1949. Its stirring melody, broadcast by satellite in 1970, had humble origins in the poverty-stricken Shaanbei 陝北 plateau of northwest China as a "mountain song" 山歌, a generic category for folk songs, based on a limited set of tune types, of unknown authorship and subject to improvisation or modification, performed unaccompanied in the open air by nonprofessionals and itinerant musicians alike, and revolving around themes of courtship or erotic longing. In its earliest known iteration, the song, as mountain songs often do, hinged on a graphic double entendre:

> Sesame oil, heart of the cabbage
> If you want to eat the bean, pull off the string
> After three days I miss that man so
> Hu'er hai'yo! Oh my Third Brother⁵³

How did this particular song move so quickly from an old, slow, and extremely circumscribed folk circuit in remote Jia County 葭縣 to national prominence? And how did one distinctly regional sound come to be privileged as representing the nation, over and above the plethora of folk forms across a vast and variegated Chinese countryside? By dint of historical accident, in part. In 1935, the Communist Party had established a mountain stronghold in nearby Yan'an at the conclusion of its epic Long March in retreat from pursuit by Nationalist forces. In Yan'an, Mao and his lieutenants began to formulate a new cultural policy predicated on a "mass line." Art would henceforth speak directly to the peasant populations in which the Red Army was embedded but also educate its own cultural workers, many of whom were idealistic foreign-trained urbanites, in the language of the masses. Chairman Mao most forcefully articulated these ideas—neatly summed up by the slogan "from the masses, to the masses"—in his 1942 "Talks at the Yan'an Forum on Art and Literature," a policy document that came to dominate the artistic life of the nation in the ensuing decades.⁵⁴ As early as 1938, the Party had established a department of music at the Lu Xun Academy of Art committed to gathering, studying, and collating folk music ("from the masses"). Lü Ji 呂驥 (1909–2002), the Hunanese musician and cadre responsible for the Academy's "Society for the Study of Chinese Folk Music," had by 1943 overseen the collection of more than two thousand folk songs from the regions surrounding Yan'an. He and his colleagues used a selection of these transcriptions as the basis for new revolutionary anthems, overwriting their original lyrics with the imperatives and ideals of revolution and disseminating them within the Communist ranks and back to the surrounding rural area by way of newspapers, mimeographed songbooks, and collective singing sessions at mass meetings ("to the masses").[55] It was through this circuitous process that a bawdy mountain song like "Sesame Oil" 芝麻油, originally collected in western Shanxi 晉西, was given a topical slant by Communist cultural cadres and reined in for the task of recruiting soldiers for the anti-Japanese war effort:

> Riding a white horse, carrying a foreign weapon
> Third Brother's eating Eighth Route Army rations
> Even if he wants to come see me
> Hu'er hai'yo! He's too busy fighting the Japanese
> Dressed in a uniform all in gray
> Gun slung over his shoulder
> Ever since Big Brother's become a soldier
> Hu'er hai'yo! He's left behind this little sister[56]

A third but by no means final transformation took place in 1944, when a new riff on "Riding a White Horse" 騎白馬 appeared for the first time in print in the *Liberation Daily* 解放日報. Now a "Migration Song" 移民歌, the melody was marshaled to urge peasants to take part in a larger campaign to relocate to areas like the Northeast, where their labor was most needed. It was in this version that reference to Chairman Mao as the rising sun was first made. That image has traditionally been attributed to a poor peasant named Li Youyuan 李有源, who was working in the Jia County People's Government and who, in his undying gratitude to Chairman Mao, came up with the lines one morning in 1942 as he watched the sun rise on his way to work.[57] The actual textual record is more nuanced, as renditions of both "Riding a White Horse" and the "Migration Song," along with a third and closely related tune called "Visiting Family" 探家, all appear in an official Party publication in 1945, edited by the noted poet He Qifang 何其芳 with Zhang Songru 張松如 and titled *Selected Shaanbei Folk Songs* 陝北民歌選.[58] There remains a great deal of contention related to the authorship of the song, with some attributions pointing to Li Youyuan's nephew, a gifted folk singer named Li Zengzheng 李增正, and other accounts crediting a relatively unknown Communist Party functionary and schoolteacher named Li Jinqi 李錦旗.[59] This historical noise is perhaps symptomatic, for the very essence of the mass line was the notion of a collective authorship blurring the boundary between where the folk ends and the Party begins. What is clear is that the mediation of the Party apparatus was more crucial than any particular individual. "The East Is Red" in its canonical incarnation crossed the threshold to nationwide circulation only after the victory of the Communist Party through its amplification in official print media. In 1949, just after Chairman Mao seized victory on the battlefields of Manchuria, a new edition of He Qifang's *Selected Shaanbei Folk Songs* was published by the New China Press 新華書店, and various versions of the song were widely reprinted in songbooks and in newspapers across the country.[60]

A further, and crucial, moment in the song's canonization was its crossover from printed to phonographic form. By the early 1950s, "The East Is Red" began for the first time to reverberate across a nascent national radio broadcasting network. Indeed, "The East Is Red" was among the very first recordings made and manufactured by the fledgling socialist state. This historic sound engineering project represented an epochal sea change in the development of Chinese music. For it was in 1950 that the most storied and significant producer of Chinese popular music of the first half of the twentieth century, Pathé Records 百代唱片公司, abandoned its premises in Shanghai and relocated to Hong Kong. With Pathé's departure, mainland Chinese music was shunted from one historical circuit, oriented around the trans-Pacific circulation of a cosmopolitan popular music, to another model entirely, one predicated on a Soviet-style construction of a new mass music for the vast rural interior. By the early 1950s, the jazz-inflected "modern songs" 時代曲 of the Shanghai era had been proscribed, reviled as "yellow" or sensuously off-color music, and relegated to the ash heap of history as the colonial off-scourings of a decadent capitalist culture.[61] While successors to this Shanghai sound like Grace Chang went on to thrive in the Mandarin entertainment industry headquartered in Hong Kong, the music would not return to the mainland until the late 1970s, when the ballads of its Taiwanese torchbearer Teresa Teng, many of them covers of "modern songs" from the 1930s and 1940s, plugged mainland Chinese listeners back into the open circuit of commercial popular song.[62]

That earlier circuit, as Michael Denning has brilliantly shown, was maritime in nature, knitted into distinct musical networks by migrants, itinerant musicians, and gramophone records traveling transoceanic steamship lines. For Denning, Shanghai was just one city along an "archipelago of colonial ports" in which a worldwide musical revolution took place in the interwar years:

> In a few short years between the introduction of electrical recording in 1925 and the onset of the worldwide depression of the 1930s, a noise uprising occurred in a series of relatively unnoticed recording sessions. In port cities from Havana to Honolulu, Cairo to Jakarta, New Orleans to Rio de Janeiro, commercial recording companies brought hundreds of unknown musicians into makeshift studios to record local musics. Thousands of inexpensive discs made from shellac (a resin secreted by

the female lac bug, a colonial product harvested in the forests of South Asia) were released, disseminating musical idioms which have since reverberated around the globe under a riot of new names: son, rumba, tango, jazz, calypso, beguine, fado, flamenco, tzigane, rebetika, tarab, marabi, kroncong, hula.... These recording sessions ... stand out in the history of music like a range of volcanic peaks, the dormant but not extinct remains of a series of eruptions caused by the shifting of the tectonic plates of the world's musical continents. For five years, more or less, these eruptions took place as the gramophone and phonograph companies fought with each other to capture the world's vernacular musics through the new electrical microphones and to play them back through the new electrical loudspeakers.[63]

Denning's map of vernacular genres follows the contours of a "maritime network" linking the metropoles with the colonial ports through which the agricultural and mineral resources of the world's rural hinterlands were extracted, sending rubber, sugar, grain, timber, and other tropical commodities to distant markets. These coastal administrative and trading centers grew rapidly between 1910 and 1930. Shanghai's population nearly tripled in two decades, swelling from 523,000 to 1,607,000, and the ports of call by which it was connected to the west coast of the United States by trans-Pacific steamship lines, such as Honolulu, Yokohama, and Singapore, witnessed comparably dizzying growth.[64] New, combinatory musical logics arose out of the rough-and-tumble entertainments of working-class districts in these settlements, as newly proletarianized rural migrants mixed with educated local elites, tramp steamers expedited the flow of merchants, seamen, and soldiers, and diverse linguistic and ethnic groups moved and mixed in promiscuous proximity.[65]

In this sense, Denning's "noise uprising" might be read as a kind of overture to the upheavals of the Jamesonian 1960s that I discussed earlier. On one hand, the steamship was the primary agent of a "worldwide 'enclosure' of the commons," by which indigenous land and its productive capacity were beginning to be brought into the ambit of a world market.[66] That process, as we have seen, accelerated in the 1960s with not only the advent of the Green Revolution but also the expansion of civil aviation enabled by the jetliner and the institution of intermodal containerized shipping, for which a global standard was first established in 1961, linking railways seamlessly with freighters and tying the world's supply regions even more tightly to global markets.[67] The emergence of new musical vernaculars is thus part and parcel of colonial modernity: driven by the profit seeking of multinational companies such as EMI (Electrical and Musical Industries, of which Pathé was a subsidiary) and piggybacking on colonial trade networks. On the other hand, Denning hears in these mongrel musical genres "a somatic decolonization, a decolonization of the ear and the dancing body" that helped to displace the dominance of European musical models and served, albeit in complex and sometimes compromised ways, as a harbinger of the political movements for formal decolonization and self-determination that followed in the postwar period.[68]

Shanghai's music scene in the interwar years amply instantiates these antinomies. The city's International Settlement and French Concessions, administered by a consortium of colonial powers, was the first and most important beachhead for the incursion into China of the American culture industry. First-run theaters hawked Hollywood films and the Tin Pan Alley screen songs that accompanied them. Music retailers sold a steady stream of Victrolas and gramophone records to the local middle classes and colonial elites, proffering not only the operatic arias of Caruso or the latest Paul Whiteman foxtrot but also placing far-flung genres like the rumba or the tango alongside recordings of Peking opera and *pingtan* 平潭 ballads from neighboring Suzhou. A thriving cabaret and dancehall culture, meanwhile, placed the city firmly on a steamship-borne musical entertainment circuit that ran from the west coast of the United States to Honolulu and then splayed out across Asia, with ports of call in Yokohama, Manila, Singapore, Penang, and even Calcutta.[69] Along these routes traveled not only African American jazz musicians like Buck Clayton and Valaida Snow but also hardworking Filipino dance bands out of Manila and Hawai'ian musicians like Ernest Ka'ai's Royal Hawaiian Troubadours and the steel guitarist Tau Moe.[70] Shanghai was thus firmly situated on what the American correspondent Burnet Hershey called in 1922 the "jazz latitude," a musical route "marked as indelibly on the globe as the heavy line of the equator . . . [and running] from Broadway along Main Street to San Francisco to the Hawaiian islands, which had lyricized it to fame," and proceeding from Japan, the Philippines, and China to the rest of the globe.[71]

Amid this cacophony, Pathé Records, with its proprietary studio and pressing plant located on Ziccawei Road in the French Concession, emerged as the epicenter of the Chinese recording industry, eclipsing rivals such as the U.S.-based Victor, the German Beka, and a local concern called Great China Records 大中華.[72] Beginning with its initial incorporation as Pathé Asia in 1908 and on through its later merger with EMI in 1930, the company recorded a massive inventory of local music, including many genres of Chinese opera 戲曲, as well as an impressive array of folk forms. What truly distinguished the company, however, was its stable of starlets, developed in close cooperation with the city's tabloid illustrated press, radio broadcasting stations, and a film industry that was growing by leaps and bounds by the early 1930s in terms of both production capacity and the aesthetic quality of its increasingly topical and politically engaged cinema. By the late 1930s, Pathé's house band, composed of an amalgam of Chinese musicians and Russian exiles, was churning out a new and sophisticated modern vernacular music in which Chinese folk melody, jazz, rumba, and Tin Pan Alley pop commingled. In the wake of the Battle of Shanghai in January 1932, when much of the working-class quarter of the city was decimated by the Japanese Imperial Army in an augury of the full-scale war to come in 1937, Pathé, controlled by a managerial class from abroad, increasingly became the preserve of a cadre of young, leftist intellectuals, eager to harness the mass media toward the ends of anticolonial agitation. Indeed, it was in 1935 that the company released a song, taken from the final scene of a film called *Children of the Storm* 風雲兒女, about a group of urbanites who heed the call to take up arms in the anti-Japanese cause. This anthem, which reworked the melody of "La Marseillaise" into a stirring, pentatonic anthem in martial duple meter, was by a young composer and vociferous critic of "modern songs" called Nie Er 聶耳 and titled "March of the Volunteers" 義勇軍進行曲. As if to confirm Denning's thesis, the song not only provided accompaniment for the long fight for decolonization that ensued but was also designated the national anthem after 1949—only to be briefly supplanted by "The East Is Red" in the 1960s when its lyricist, the stalwart leftist writer Tian Han 田漢, was denounced as a rightist during the Cultural Revolution.[73]

It is in one of the less stirring, yet far more typically commercial Pathé records of the era, however, that we can hear sonic traces of the East Asian maritime network out of which these "modern songs" were produced. Yao Lee 姚莉 is a central figure in the history of Chinese popular music. She was discovered at age thirteen by the greatest pop diva of the day, Pathé's legendary "golden voice" Zhou Xuan 周璇, and became her "silver-voiced" protégé. Her brother Yao Min 姚敏 penned many of Pathé's greatest hits, and, after the company's removal to Hong Kong, Yao Lee went on to a nearly four-decade career, first as a singer and then as a producer and manager. Her song "We're Separated by Myriad Mountains" 人隔萬重山 was recorded in Shanghai and released in late 1947, only two years after the armistice that ended Japanese aggression, bringing the KMT government, along with hundreds of thousands of refugees, back to China's eastern seaboard from their enforced exile in the remote interior. That fall, after a decade of unremitting warfare, the Communist Red Army had launched a ferocious offensive in the Northeast, killing nearly seventy thousand Nationalist troops. So it is perhaps not far-fetched to read the song's lyrical lament, written by Dong Sun 楝蓀 in the quasi-classical demotic typical of "modern songs," in light of the traumatic separations of the recent past and the geopolitical struggle that would continue to rend the country apart:

> Impossible to meet, I weep bitterly alone,
> Looking longingly into the distance all day long
> As I lean on the painted balustrade
> My gaze crosses autumn waters, all waiting in vain
> Resenting the east wind, blowing in gusts
> But it can't blow the sadness filling my breast away
> We're separated by myriad mountain ranges
> Can you recall those years past, and the vow we took under the moon
> How could you betray me, can it be that you've forgotten so soon?
> Not a word of news gets across, my heart might break in two,
> Was the happy laughter of the past just a dream now lost?
> Once you departed, you've sunk like a stone in the sea
> We're separated by a myriad of mountain peaks[74]

While the lack of "news" 音訊 may allude to an indigenous poetic trope of loved ones separated by the battle lines, dating back at least to Du Fu 杜甫 and the catastrophic eighth-century rebellion against the Tang court, the soundscape of the song is built around more exotic sounds: a jazzy 4/4 walking bass line, the steady ukulele-like strum of an acoustic guitar, and the lilt of a Hawai'ian pedal steel guitar that states the main melody and punctuates each of Yao Lee's phrases throughout the song. Its evanescent and eerily reverberant sound not only indexes the maritime traffic that connected the popular music of Shanghai to the South Pacific but also registers in sonic terms the vastness of the spaces that the singer will need to traverse in order to reach her absent lover. For listeners in the wake of the Cold War divide—which included the total prohibition of travel and postal communication between the two Chinas—the song's myriad mountains would have rung even more poignantly. By the early 1950s, "modern songs" had been proscribed, as the mainland disconnected from the littoral circuit and began to construct a new musical infrastructure.

The expulsion of Pathé was part of that process, but it also presented the new People's Republic with a difficult technical challenge: how to mass-produce music for the masses? Not surprisingly, the company had transported much of its personnel (including Yao Lee and many other recording artists), expertise, and equipment to Hong Kong. The first records to be made in the new China, a series of paeans to the victory of the revolution, were pressed at the requisitioned Great China Records plant within months of the city's changing hands in May 1949 but could be produced in only limited quantities.[75] "The East Is Red," in an arrangement by the prominent composer He Lüting 賀綠汀, was among these first recordings.⁷⁶ In 1951, the state embarked on a new record-making venture. Yan Heming 顏鶴鳴, a pioneering cinematic sound engineer and technician who had been closely involved in the making of China's first color film, was pressed into service by Premier Zhou Enlai 周恩來 to aid in the establishment of a new public–private venture, called the Shanghai Record Manufacturing Company 上海唱片製造公司, and tasked with the mission of releasing a set of songs in time to commemorate the second anniversary of the revolution, in October 1951.⁷⁷ Yan Heming assembled a contingent of laid-off workers from the former Pathé and American Victor plants, as well as salvaged recording equipment, lathes, and pressing machines. With no access to high-quality Indian shellac, Yan purchased bulk shellac used as a stiffener from a hatmaker on Nanjing Road and substituted a coarse iron oxide for the fine graphite powder customarily used in the electroplating process. These impurities resulted in a great deal of surface noise and made for records that very quickly wore through the very needles used to play them.⁷⁸ Appropriately enough, given the reddish hue of the wax masters, the company chose to market their products as "Red Records" 紅唱片.

Beyond these technical travails, the task of recording "The East Is Red" and other revolutionary anthems presented a momentous aesthetic and formal problem. What would this new circuit sound like? How could a ten-inch record sound massive enough to represent the masses to themselves? The musical director for these early recordings, He Lüting, had long since been engaged in an effort to fit folk melodies to Western harmonic structures as a way to orchestrate a distinctly modern Chinese music, ample enough for the purposes of constructing a new nation.⁷⁹ Trained in Western classical music in Shanghai under the composer Huang Zi 黃自, he had been recognized for his compositional genius by the Russian pianist Alexander Tcherepnin in the early 1930s. After a prolific stint as a composer of film music and popular songs for the Shanghai cinema (many of which were released by Pathé Records), he fled to the interior during the war and joined the Communist cause. In his wartime years in Yan'an, he led a Soviet-style chorus in singing his own arrangements of revolutionary songs, including one of the precursors of "The East Is Red," "The Migration Song."⁸⁰ He Lüting returned to Shanghai in the late 1940s and was named president of the prestigious Shanghai Conservatory of Music in the watershed year of 1949. He published soon thereafter a score for "The East Is Red" arranged for a choral group, and this cantata was almost certainly the basis for the initial recording by the Shanghai Broadcast Ensemble 上海廣播樂團.⁸¹ The makeshift recording studios in which the earliest examples of mass music were being made, however, were too small to accommodate the masses.⁸² And thus He Lüting was forced to experiment with novel recording techniques, for it was only by separating the musicians and the members of the chorus and threading multiple microphones to many different rooms at once that he could cover the entire acoustic range and patch together an adequately expansive sound.⁸³ The sound of the masses was, from the very start, a network effect.

He Lüting was savagely denounced in 1966 for having had the bourgeois temerity to place his own name on a song that was understood to have been written by a peasant and for imposing European harmonies on a folk melody and, in so doing, defusing its revolutionary spirit.⁸⁴ It is thus no small irony that his arrangements of the song were the foundation for several later recordings of the song released by the state-run China Records 中國唱片 and the basis of its mass-mediated ubiquity during the Cultural Revolution. In underscoring the collective voice with swelling orchestral harmonies, moreover, he seems to have anticipated the song's epic apotheosis in 1964 in the Great Hall of the People: a mountain song made massive enough to move mountains. In 1970, when "The East Is Red 1" lifted off into outer space, however, that was not the version that it broadcast back to the earth. Lacking the analog equipment necessary to play back any of the previous recordings, the satellite's oscillator circuit instead generated a lonely series of tones, warbling the melody of what had once been a love song out into the anechoic expanses of space, like a cosmic come-on.⁸⁵ The song had once again suffered a sea change, transformed into something "rich and strange," sounding the knell of a tempestuous age.⁸⁶ Twenty days later, "The East Is Red 1" fell silent.

CHAPTER ONE

# Circuit Listening at the Dawn of the Chinese 1960s

I want to fly up to the blue sky, fly the blue sky!
我要飛上青天，上青天！

—Grace Chang, "I Want to Fly up to the Blue Sky," 1960

I think the difference is in the mechanical sounds of our time. Like the sound of the airplane in the Forties was a rrrrrrrrooooooaaaaaaaahhhhhhhh sound and Sinatra and other people sang like that with those sort of overtones. Now we've got the krrrriiiisssssssshhhhhhhh jet sound, and the kids are singing up in there now. It's the mechanical sounds of the era: the sounds are different and so the music is different.

—Roger McGuinn of the Byrds, *Mr. Tambourine Man* LP liner notes, 1965

This chapter listens to Chinese-language musicals from Hong Kong and Taiwan, produced on the front lines of the Cold War in the early 1960s and emerging from a moment in which these regions were poised for takeoff into the upper strata of the global manufacturing economy. Well known throughout the Chinese speaking world yet largely unheard in the metropolitan West, their soundtracks participate fully and creatively in globally circulating popular cultures, engaging in particular with Afro-Caribbean-derived popular genres such as mambo and calypso. I contend here that they may help us to think our way into, if not out of, two key questions in popular music criticism.

The first is the question of historicism. What allows us to say that a song or a style is "of its time"? Conversely, is it possible to bring sounds of radically different provenance into critical conjunction just because they happen to have been produced at the same time? In other words, what might we gain from listening synchronically to music made at the same time in different social or geographical locales? Can a certain year or a particular decade serve as a meaningful framing device in narratives of musical historiography? Even more specifically, I am interested in the question of whether we can usefully identify something like a global 1960s in music. To what extent would such a formulation need to rely—as in the evocative epigraph from Roger McGuinn of the southern Californian folk-rock pioneers the Byrds—on an account, deterministic or otherwise, of technological change, from the emergence of the jet plane and the concomitant boom in civil aviation to the worldwide dissemination of television and transistorized electronics?[1] I try to open up these questions by way of engaging with the emergence of a distinctive "period style" at the dawn of the Chinese 1960s. How did this music sound, why did it sound that way, and what can it tell us about the 1960s we thought we already knew?

A second and closely related question has to do with the question of genre in recorded music—or, more precisely, the kinds of ideological work we perform when we attempt to name, identify, or substantiate generic divisions, particularly when they get mixed up with troublesome and ideologically freighted categories such as folk music versus popular music. I am interested in this chapter in thinking about not how a particular genre can be described in a constative sense but what genre formations can *do* and what sorts of transactions they began to enable, especially with the increasingly global reach of mass media in the immediate postwar period. How are genres launched into global circulation? Is "genre" itself a kind of "portmanteau" or shipping container that allows music to become globally portable? Can we think of genres neither as essences nor even as particular repertoires but as vernacular modulations of globally circulating forms, resonating within migratory and mass-mediated circuits? How do we listen for and trace the architecture of such circuits, and what might they tell us about the mobility of musical forms in an era of recorded and increasingly portable sound? Might it be that the increasingly globalized diffusion of certain genres—and thus their fungibility as mass-mediated commodities—is an important harbinger of the musical 1960s?

My inquiry into these questions takes off from the music of Hong Kong's celebrated pop diva, movie actress, and "mambo girl," Grace Chang.[2] But I will also take a circuitous detour into the somewhat lesser-known and far less high-flying world of Taiwanese-language musicals of the same era, before coming to a hard landing at the end. Along the way, we will hear how various genres—from Afro-Caribbean-derived musics such as mambo, cha-cha, and calypso to rhythm and blues and country and western, as well as Japanese *enka* 演歌—circulate within the musicals of the period and how these musicals serve as vehicles for the circulation and rearticulation of these forms well beyond their putative places of origin. How do those sounds travel, what happens to them in the process, and how might the routes they take help us map the hard contours and lingering musical aftereffects of empire in East Asia, be it British, American, or Japanese?

Let's begin with a scene from Grace Chang's 1963 star vehicle, *Because of Her* 教我如何不想她, produced, like all of her late 1950s and early 1960s musicals, by the chief competitor of Hong Kong's famed Shaw Brothers film studios, the ambitiously multinational Singapore-based Cathay Organisation. Owned by Loke Wan Tho 陸運濤, a dashing and determinedly modern scion of a Malaysian mining, rubber, and real estate magnate, Cathay had by 1963 parlayed its real estate holdings into a circuit of first-run cinemas throughout Southeast Asia.[3] Its subsidiary, the Hong Kong–based Motion Picture and General Investment ("MP&GI" or Dianmao 電懋) studio, in turn, supplied Cathay's theaters with feature films. Both MP&GI and the Shaw Brothers, finally, maintained a cozy and mutually profitable relationship with EMI's Hong Kong subsidiary, Pathé Records, hence the prevalence in this era of musical pictures built primarily around the performances of songstresses in the Pathé stable.[4]

In the case of *Because of Her*, the title song comes early on in the picture, when Grace Chang's character, devastated because her musician boyfriend has departed from Hong Kong's Kai Tak Airport to study in Japan, decides to try out for a role in a musical. Accompanied by an older pianist and dressed rather primly in a blue frock, Grace is tightly framed by the camera as she begins what appears to be a rather staid recital of a *lied*-like song. After a few measures, however, with an infectiously mischievous grin and an irreverent snap of her fingers, she and the song are utterly transformed. The camera pulls back to reveal a room full of brightly clad bobbysoxers in miniskirts. A young man with pomaded hair holding a solid-body electric guitar suddenly starts to play a crude rock and roll riff, and Grace's body begins to sway and twist to the rhythm. With a portable tape recorder placed conspicuously in the foreground, the directors of the troupe watch in amazement as Chang belts out the rest of the song's lyrics (see Figure 1.1).

It is an astonishing performance, not only because of Grace Chang's newfangled dance steps but also because it stages what we might call a musical great leap forward. It would not have been lost on contemporary audiences that the title song is one of the monuments of the early assimilation of Western musical forms into a new modern Chinese art-song vernacular: the great linguist and May 4th-era scholar Y. R. Chao's 趙元任 1926 composition "How Could I Not Miss Her" 教我如何不想她. Chao's use of parallel fifths to sound out on the piano "sinified harmonies"—even within the realm of what he called "world music" (by which he meant what appeared to his generation as an unquestionably "universal" Western music)—is matched by the deliberate delicacy with which the melody is

Figure 1.1. Grace Chang in *Because of Her*, 1963.

made to mirror the tonality of the mandarin Chinese lyrics.[5] These delicacies are precisely what are lost in the leap from vocal art song to rock and roll, from the high-minded literary youth culture of the May 4th movement of the 1920s and its efforts to forge a modern Chinese vernacular to the Cold War–era ascendancy of U.S. mass culture to the status of a global vernacular. And yet, despite this disjunction, both the original composition and its makeover represent self-consciously localized inflections of globally circulating musical idioms.

The scene also plugs into what was still an emergent mode of musical production in the early 1960s—the new availability of portable, relatively inexpensive means of musical production and reproduction enabled by transistorized solid-state electronics, as exemplified by mass-produced and mass-marketed electric guitars, transistor radios, tape recorders, and, eventually, televisions, many of which had already begun to be made in Japan for global consumers.[6] The ability of such music to fly free of generational and geographical moorings seems to be figured in the film by the effortless riffing of the guitarist, who barely seems to be plugged in at all. As the scene progresses, the increasing disparity between the soundtrack (which begins with piano and voice but finishes with the brassy flourishes of a fully orchestrated yet invisible big band) and the diegetic space of the rehearsal room onscreen might well remind us of the extent to which this mobility was itself largely a cinematic fantasy.

Grace Chang was herself the most celebrated cinematic embodiment of mobility in the Hong Kong cinema of the early 1960s. In a literal sense, she was famed for her prowess as a dancer and performer in a range of different styles, from the mambo to more traditional modes such as Peking opera. Her life story, as reported in newspapers and glossy magazines such as MP&GI's own *International Screen* 國際電影, reflected the dislocations of the postwar period. Her father, an official in the Ministry of Transport in Nanjing under Nationalist (KMT) rule, had her educated in a Catholic school in Shanghai, before the family emigrated to Hong Kong in advance of the Communist victory in 1949.[7] Grace Chang's own path followed that of the prerevolutionary Shanghai music and film industries to Hong Kong. It is thus no accident that she recorded for Pathé-EMI, one of the most important corporate refugees from the colonial era in Shanghai, and that many of her biggest hits were penned by prominent popular composers from the heyday of Shanghai modern songs, such as Yao Min and the Japanese film composer Hattori Ryōichi 服部良一.[8] Chang's star image, as several critics have noted, was also deeply entwined with the projection of an ideal of postwar social and class mobility, as even a cursory look at the titles of some of her films reveals, from *Our Dream Car* (香車美人, 1959) to *Air Hostess* (空中小姐, directed by Evan Yang/Yi Wen 易文, also from 1959), of which more later.[9]

The same year Grace Chang made these two films, she herself took flight, visiting the studios of NBC television in Los Angeles in late October to appear on a "Pacific Festival" edition of *The Dinah Shore Show*, alongside the Japanese diva Yukiji Asaoka 朝丘雪路 as well as dance revues from the Philippines and Korea.[10] In addition to performing an adaptation of a Shanghai-era song penned by Yao Min, "The Autumn Song" 秋之歌, Chang joined Asaoka and Shore in singing a version of "Getting to Know You" from the 1957 Rodgers and Hammerstein blockbuster *The King and I*—an apt choice given the orientalist and pedagogical overtones of the original musical.[11]

This 1959 appearance on U.S. television—a first in the annals of Chinese popular music history, as the breathless coverage in the Chinese language press emphasized time and again—also led to the release in 1961 of a long-playing record in Capitol Records' "Capitol of the World" series (see Figure 1.2).[12]

This series was one of the ways in which Capitol took advantage of the global reach of its parent company, EMI, which had purchased the upstart West Coast record label in 1955.[13] The producer, Dave Dexter Jr., who

Figure 1.2. Grace Chang on *The Dinah Shore Show* as featured in *International Screen*, 1959. Courtesy of Soft Film.

would go on to notoriety as the man who supervised the Beatles' introduction into the U.S. market, should be seen as a crucial figure in the invention *avant la lettre* of "world music" as a marketing category in the United States, for, not unlike recording industry pioneers at the dawn of the twentieth century such as Fred Gaisberg, he spent the late 1950s traveling the globe (including a visit to Hong Kong) in search of acts that could be repackaged for U.S. audiences. Dexter's greatest, albeit more or less accidental, triumph was his decision to repackage and release the Japanese crooner Kyu Sakamoto's 坂本九 1963 hit "I Look Up as I Walk" 上を向いて歩こ, retitled for the U.S. market as "Sukiyaki."[14]

In this light, *Because of Her* might be seen as a recapitulation of a leap Grace Chang had already achieved, moving from Y. R. Chao's conception of "world music" as a universal idiom to a very different sort of "world music," one ethnically marked yet manufactured by the far-reaching recording and televisual networks of corporate giants like EMI and NBC. In her brief yet charming segment on *The Dinah Shore Show*, Grace Chang is introduced (in a characteristically Cold War circumlocution) as "China's loveliest motion picture star." The cover of the Capitol long-player bills her as "Hong Kong's Grace Chang" and "The Nightingale of the Orient." What I hope to suggest in this chapter, however, is that these attempts to *locate* Grace Chang and her music (which can veer from swing to cha-cha to calypso to Shanghai "modern songs" and ersatz orchestral Chinese folk within the space of a single record or even a single cinematic sequence) obscure the fact that Grace Chang cannot be adequately understood as the product of a singular place. Instead, we might well listen to her work as embedded in a complex and multiply mediated circuit, one that (to name just the most important coordinates) stretches from colonial Shanghai to Hong Kong, from Hong Kong to diasporic Chinese settlements in Southeast Asia and to Taiwan, across the Pacific to Hollywood and Tin Pan Alley, and from New York City to Caribbean islands such as Cuba, Trinidad, and Jamaica from which so much of the material for her music was drawn. And from the Anglophone Caribbean, of course, we might even circle back to London, the headquarters of EMI and of the proprietors of the British crown colony of Hong Kong (see Figure 1.3).

What kinds of analytical gains might come of this kind of "circuit listening"? All local musics—particularly in the modern era of commercial sound recording—are constituted by (and need to be historicized in terms of) the particular circuits of media and migration in which they are embedded. Circuit listening may help us to avoid falling into models of musical interpretation that rely on vague attributions of one-sided and seemingly inevitable influence, while at the same time opening our ears to the agency, irreducible dynamism, and complexity of any local mediation of "global" cultures. It is not so much that Grace Chang successfully mimicked an originary mambo in her 1957 blockbuster, *Mambo Girl* 曼波女郎, for instance, but rather that she and her collaborators participated in a circuit, routed by way of Havana, Mexico City, New York, Hollywood to Hong Kong, that reproduced "mambo" as a global vernacular.

We also need to be able to differentiate between different sorts of musical circuits. There are old, "slow," and vastly consequential circuits, such

Figure 1.3. Cover art for Grace Chang's Capitol Records release, *Hong Kong's Grace Chang*, Capitol Records T 10272, 1961.

as the enduring musical pathways linking the west coast of Africa with the islands of the Caribbean and with Brazil, connected in turn to metropoles such as New Orleans, New York, London, and Lisbon, tracing a "Black Atlantic" network that has left an indelible imprint on global popular musical practices.[15] By the early 1900s, a maritime circuit linking the west coast of the United States with Hawai'i, Japan, and the colonial treaty ports of East and Southeast Asia had also taken shape in tandem with transpacific steamship lines, leaving its traces on modern musical genres throughout the region. There are also shorter and less consequential circuits, flashes in the pan like Kyu Sakamoto's "Sukiyaki," novelty acts that cross over, blow up, but never come to constitute a real musical system. There are rural circuits in which musical performance and reception remain largely if not entirely local. This is perhaps the realm of what we think of as "indigenous music" or "folk music." Most indigenous musics, however, tend to emerge from out of long historical circuits and migratory movements, and many had been brought into regional, national, and even global circuits by the twentieth century. The Mississippi Delta blues and *huangmeidiao* 黃梅調 or "yellow plum" opera of Anhui province in China are just two examples of local forms that entered into transnational circulation in the 1960s.

There are open circuits characterized by a high degree of circulation and turnover and closed circuits bound by topographical, ethnolinguistic, political, economic, infrastructural, and other sorts of constraints. It should go without saying that not all circuits are born equal, nor are they able to run on the same power sources. Their routes have been traced by histories of colonial domination and reflect unequal global, national, and regional divisions of labor. Indeed, we need to understand circuits not merely as routes that enable circulation but also (and often simultaneously) as containment structures put in place so as to segregate sociomusical space, protect markets, or prevent unsanctioned movement(s). Different musical locales, finally, may be mapped in terms of the multiple musical circuits in which they are simultaneously embedded, and those maps will inevitably give us a sense not only of their distinctive historical pathways but also of the ways in which any given historical moment is a palimpsest of overlapping but not always contiguous or contemporaneous circuits. The sort of "circuit listening" I am proposing, then, is inevitably also a kind of historical cartography, a reconstruction of the mediated spaces and sedimented temporalities out of which musical sounds emerge.

In some ways, Grace Chang's "Capitol of the World" release might seem like a failed attempt to leap from one circuit—Mandarin popular music—to the global entertainment circuit that bears the shorthand designation "Hollywood." The record's polished arrangements of "a worldwide variety of styles" failed to chart in the United States, and Grace Chang never became a crossover success.[16] Barriers (linguistic and otherwise) were still in place, despite the optimistic take of the record's liner notes, which tout Hong Kong as a desirable destination for musical tourism and as an open switch on a global circuit: "The colorful port of Hong Kong, one of the busiest in the world, is a melting pot of music from all over the world. Businessmen, travelers, immigrants, students, sailors—everybody brings his music (or musical preferences) when he comes to Hong Kong—and the result is a free exchange unmatched anywhere else." The blurb, perhaps unsurprisingly given its intended audience, blithely disregards the existence of long-standing and defiantly local circuits of musical production such as Cantonese opera (*yueju*). Nor does it acknowledge that those forms had long since traveled out to the world, circulating throughout Cantonese-speaking communities in southern China, Southeast Asia, and up and down the west coast of the United States.[17] The record's imagined audience was not to be grounded in any one linguistic community.

Grace Chang's MP&GI films invoke a similar sort of promotional rhetoric, in which the port as a figure looms much larger than the particularity of the city of which it is part. *Because of Her* and *Air Hostess* are thus profoundly self-reflexive productions. Their primary object of representation is precisely the circuit along which Grace Chang, her music, and the cinema itself as a commodity are imagined to travel. *Because of Her* features a particularly bravura example. After Grace Chang's character joins the song and dance revue for which she has auditioned, we are treated to a lengthy musical-stage sequence documenting—or perhaps merely envisioning—a triumphal world tour. (It is not clear whether the troupe ever leaves Hong Kong.) The sequence begins as Grace Chang sings a big-band cha-cha number called "Muchacha" (penned by Hattori Ryuichi) in front of a pastoral "Chinese" backdrop, complete with a painted pagoda. Suddenly, and in tandem with the lyrics of the song, Chang is foregrounded against a map of the world, with each country depicted as a bordered two-dimensional plane—not unlike a series of blank television screens—into which Chang is able to enter and through which she and the stage itself are transported someplace else. What ensues is a whirlwind fantasia of international stereotypes, from Hawaiian hula dancers to Japanese geishas to New York swing dancers to Venetian gondoliers and Latin boleros, each with generically correct music and scenery to match. The sequence concludes with a triumphant mise-en-scène in which all of the dancers are united in front of what appears to be a giant roulette wheel, as if to emphasize the circular logic of the sequence and its circumnavigation of what the film scholar Brian Hu has termed the "world stage" of MP&GI's backstage musicals (see Figure 1.4).[18]

In *Air Hostess* as well, the plot is largely a pretext for the cinematic staging of Grace Chang's peregrinations. Filmed on location in Taiwan, Singapore, and Thailand in Eastman color, the film follows the trials and trajectory of a character named Lin Keping as she learns how to be an effective airline stewardess, while at the same time falling for her taciturn pilot, played by Roy Chiao 喬宏. Keping's gendered desire for modernity and mobility beyond the constraints of the bourgeois family is figured by the opening musical sequence, "I Want to Fly up to the Blue Sky" 我要飛上青天, in which Grace Chang, pointedly dressed up as the gender mold-breaking martial-arts heroine Shisan Mei 十三妹, performs to a stylishly attired in-crowd at a masquerade ball.

Figure 1.4. Grace Chang's world map in *Because of Her*, 1963.

Yet, as more than a few critics complained at the time of its release, the film often seems less like a story of emancipation than like an advertisement for the fledgling civil aviation and tourism industries. As Poshek Fu has pointed out, the film foregrounds "the airline business as an incubator for a new transnational capitalist corporate culture."[19] This agenda hardly seems surprising given that Loke Wan Tho doubled as chairman of the board at Malaysian Airways. Closer to home, Cathay Pacific (whose facilities are on display in the film) had in July 1959 swallowed its closest competitor, Hong Kong Airways, and was poised to enter a period of annual growth in the double digits throughout the 1960s.[20]

The film's narrative itinerary traces a Southeast Asia–bound, Chinese diasporic (Nanyang) circuit that of necessity excludes "Red China."[21] Grace Chang's ports of call are, in fact, exactly coterminous with the territories and terminals along Cathay Pacific's route map, the Cathay Organization's exhibition circuit, and Pathé-EMI's principal markets for Mandarin pop records. By the late 1950s, the Cathay Organization had already secured affiliation with fifty-seven movie theaters in Taiwan alone, with a network of more than two hundred venues in Singapore, Malaysia, and Borneo. In addition, the organization had distribution agents in Hong Kong, Taiwan, the Philippines, Vietnam, Thailand, Cambodia, and Burma.[22] Not surprisingly, given Loke Wan Tho's avowedly anticommunist politics, as well as the manifest importance of its market, Taiwan rates an extended sequence, during which Grace Chang goes sightseeing around Taipei.[23] Her day ends with a performance in the ballroom of the Grand Hotel, a landmark highrise constructed by the KMT government in high-orientalist imitation of the palaces of the Forbidden City, of an ersatz folk number called "Taiwan Melody" 台灣調, composed by Yao Min with no reference to local musical traditions and set to a swaying, mock-mambo beat.[24] The lyrics extol the beauty, bounty, strategic military position, social harmony, and infrastructural accessibility of the island nation:

> I love to sing a Taiwan song
> It's where the coast is long and the mountains high
> With glorious harbors everywhere and roads in every direction
> Railroad lines running from the north to the south
> It's the frontline of the Pacific Ocean, Taiwan, the treasure island!
> A wonderland with harvests all year round
> The villages are full of joy, profiting from sugar and tea
> Every household has plenty to eat
> Pineapples, watermelons, and bananas are our special treats
> Everyone praises the island, from long-term locals to new arrivals[25]

A contemporary review of the film in Hong Kong's pro-Communist daily, the *Ta Kung Pao* 大公報, took particular issue with these claims, arguing that MP&GI was merely in the business of whitewashing U.S. clientelism in Taiwan. Nor did this particular critic miss the fact that the film is "less a story, than a documentary" designed to prime the pump of the tourist economy.[26] *Air Hostess* is, in other words, an advertisement for itself, promoting both the musical numbers that are performed at each stop along MP&GI and EMI's distribution networks and the developmental aspirations and diasporic circuits of capital that constitute a "free China" at the dawn of the 1960s.

We are told in great detail how it is that Grace Chang moves across this space: the movie includes what seem now to be quite superfluous primers on subjects like passport control, customs regulations, catering arrangements, and the like. What is left unspoken but everywhere assumed, however, is the ease with which global pop genres are translated into Chinese and reproduced in each of Grace Chang's tropical ports of call. What sort of media allow for this movement, in addition to material substrates such as celluloid and vinyl? Perhaps the most crucial passport for Grace Chang's music is that it functions as a *vernacular*, both linguistically and musically.

It is precisely Grace Chang's use of Mandarin Chinese that allows her music to fly free of Hong Kong and of the patchwork of mutually unintelligible languages and dialects (Cantonese, Hokkien, Hakka, Wu, and many variants) that divides Chinese diasporic space. My argument here rests on the notion that a vernacular (or what is referred to as *baihua* 白話 in Chinese) is always an intermediary form, located above a panoply of local languages but still subsidiary to a cosmopolitan or imperial language such as English.[27] The vernacular Chinese promoted by Y. R. Chao and the May 4th generation of Chinese intellectuals, in this view, did not so much vernacularize classical Chinese as re-create Chinese as a vernacular in the image of cosmopolitan national languages such as English and French—languages that were themselves once vernaculars of Latin. Vernaculars, in other words, are precisely those languages that circulate widely enough to be appropriated for local use. And for that reason, somewhat counterintuitively, they also open up the possibility of local inflections of what had seemed to be a universal standard. In this sense, the Hong Kong mandarin musical itself is an example of what the late, great film scholar Miriam Hansen referred to as a "vernacular modernism": a globally circulating form, able to technologically mediate the pleasures and terrors of a universal modernity, yet also subject to local conditions and articulations.[28]

Globally circulating genres such as mambo and calypso arguably function in a similar register. They are musical vernaculars, emerging from particular (and often marginalized) cultural circuits and serving as a common language between an imperial dominant and local particulars. Yet, as Gustavo Perez Firmat, writing about the history of the mambo, brings to our attention, this process of "vernacularization" often involves a kind of hollowing out of the history of a musical form, the elimination of those aspects of the music's particularity that cannot easily be translated.[29] Mambo, itself a fusion (or perhaps a reduction in the culinary sense) of bop and the rhythmic breakdown of the Cuban *charanga*, traveled so well, Perez Firmat argues, because it was "logoclassic," reducing lyrics to sonorous fragments and articulate speech to rhythmic bursts of sound, as in Perez Prado's trademark grunts.[30]

Typically, the world-beating mambos of the mid-1950s by Perez Prado and Tito Puente laconically announced themselves as mambos ("Que rico el mambo"; "Mambo No. 8"; Puente's "Hong Kong Mambo" likely inspired by his 1962 concert tour to Asia).[31] These titles are performatives, packages that stage the song as a kind of container for the genre, prior to the music itself. This musical cargo was in turn distributed not only through records but also by Hollywood films such as RKO's 1955 *Underwater!*, which brought Prado's "Cherry Pink and Apple Blossom White" to acclaim in Japan and throughout East Asia, spawning numerous local adaptations and articulations of the mambo rhythm.[32] Sometimes these cinematic routes were more circuitous, even bypassing Hollywood altogether. The popularity of Perez Prado's music in South Korea, for instance, is usually attributed to the screening in Seoul of the Mexican *cabaretera* films for which Perez had provided his signature sound and the subsequent borrowing of the mambo for Han Hyung-mo's blockbuster melodrama, *Madame Freedom* (1956).[33] In the case of Grace Chang's own breakout performance in *Mambo Girl*, sources of inspiration were a 1954 Italian-American co-production, *Mambo* (directed by Robert Rossen), and Rosemary Clooney's number one hit of the same year, "Mambo Italiano," as taught to Grace Chang by a Filipino percussionist and dance instructor named Ollie Delfino.[34]

A similar hollowing took place in the case of calypso, which, according to contemporary accounts, reached Hong Kong largely on the wings of Harry Belafonte's appropriation of the form for his eponymous 1956 gold record for RCA-Victor. Local film buffs were apparently made aware of the early roots of the form in Trinidad and Afro-Caribbean culture, as indicated by a capsule history provided in Chinese and English by MP&GI's house publication, *International Screen* from 1957:

> Calypso craze is sweeping the entire world like a full-force hurricane brushing aside the once popular Rock and Roll and Cha Cha. Calypso is by no means a new dance or music. According to the dictionary, the definition of Calypso is: lively, rhythmic, topical ballad improvised and sung by natives of Trinidad. It is characterized by wrenched syllabic stress and loose rhythms.
>
> Its history dates back to the 18th century when slavery was still in practice in Trinidad of the British West Indies. The negro slaves, after a day's work, amused themselves by singing songs and executing dances. This kind of dance and music is called calypso.
>
> Its revival today is attributed to American negroes.
>
> Calypso dance is easy to learn. Anyone who knows Latin American dance will be able to learn in half and hour.[35]

In practice, however, the form was appropriated almost entirely as a rhythm and as a dance step through which the company (and Grace Chang) might perform their own familiarity with global trends. Grace Chang's performance of "I Love Calypso" 我愛卡力蘇 (also composed by Yao Min), staged in an appropriately tropical nightclub setting in Singapore, reduces the rich verbal humor and caustic commentary for which the genre was originally known to an almost incantatory and self-reflexive refrain—"Oh calypso, oh calypso, I love swaying back and forth to the calypso." The orchestration of the recording featured on the Capitol Records release bears little relation to the music of Trinidadian calypsonians—the strummed guitars and double bass pulse characteristic of the genre are enveloped within a smooth, nearly frictionless, arrangement, featuring an ostinato figure played on marimba, decorously muted trumpet, and busy, stepwise melodic embellishments sounded out in unison on the flute. The film's mise-en-scène allows for but a single musical instrument, despite the off-screen presence of a big band: a close-up of the bongos, focusing our visual attention on the rhythmic pulse assumed to be the fundamental syntax of the genre. This is calypso in name only perhaps, but calypso is as calypso does, and the packaging allows the music to fly free of provenance.

If Hong Kong in the early 1960s appeared to be an open switch, linked directly if slightly belatedly to the latest dance crazes in the United States and elsewhere, Taiwan seemed to belong to a subsidiary circuit. The mambo, or so the legend goes, was transmitted to Taiwan by Grace Chang herself, when she sparked a craze for the unfamiliar genre after a command performance for Nationalist troops during a promotional visit to the KMT-controlled island in the late 1950s. There may be some truth to these stories. One of the earliest songs to self-consciously take on the "mambo" mantle in Taiwan, "Shandong Mambo" 山東曼波 was written by Wang Fei 王菲 in 1957 as a result of his exposure to Grace Chang's performances when he was serving in the military, and it was first recorded in 1960. The tune was subsequently cut in at least one other version in the mid-1960s and covered many years later by the legendary performer Teresa Teng. Wang, referencing his own origins in China by parodically playing up the "down-home" Shandong accent typical of many mainlander refugees who fled to Taiwan in the wake of the KMT's defeat, also folds into its lyrics an ingenious and disingenuously naïve linguistic commentary on the assimilation of a foreign genre to local tastes:

> Speaking of "mambo," talking about "mambo"
> We [Shandong people] don't really know what is the "mambo"
> Is it "*mantou*" [Chinese steamed buns]?
> Or is it "*mianbao*" [Western bread]?
> Can anyone tell us what you all know?[36]

Wang Fei's recording is for the most part a mambo in name only, constructed around a standard 4/4 "go-go" beat, punctuated by an elementary electric guitar riff, with only the vaguely "Latin" opening fanfare on the trumpet alluding to its supposed Caribbean origins.

Wang Fei's appropriation of the "mambo" from Grace Chang, however, only hints at some of the complexities of Taiwan's position within global musical circuits. As C. S. Stone Shih reminds us, the trajectory of Taiwanese popular music should not be reduced to a unidirectional movement in which Mandarin popular music is transmitted, via Hong Kong, to the cabarets of Taipei. Instead, there has been a rich history of reciprocal musical flows moving between Taipei and Shanghai since at least the interwar period, as well as a complex interpenetration of local Taiwanese-language popular balladry 歌謠 with Japanese, American, Chinese, and other musical cultures.[37]

The presence of Latin music in postwar Taipei, dating to well before Grace Chang's star turn, is a case in point. As early as 1949, members of Shanghai's Peace Hotel jazz band had arrived on the island, bringing with them a working knowledge of prewar rumbas.[38] Even more significant, a local textiles manufacturer and amateur musician named Hsieh T'eng-hui 謝騰輝, inspired by a performance in Taiwan by the Filipino Air Force Band, founded in 1953 a Latin-tinged big band called the Taiwan Cuban Boys. Working from swing and rumba charts he had learned in Thailand, Hsieh and his collaborators also studied with Filipino musicians headlining at nightclubs and cabarets in Taipei, as well as cribbing compositions from visiting U.S. and Japanese tourists and functionaries. While the band was asked to efface its Cuban inspiration by no less a personage than President Chiang Kai-shek after Castro's revolution in 1959, the renamed Kupa Orchestra (鼓霸樂隊 literally the "Drum Kings") went on to become the house band at Taipei's Ambassador Hotel for more than a quarter of a century.[39] It was in the early 1960s, with the civil aviation boom and the concomitant growth of Taiwan's tourist trade, that the Kupa Orchestra really hit its stride, with four offshoots working various hotels and, after 1962, regular appearances on the newly established TTV television station.[40] The band's popularity was no doubt also aided by the widespread circulation of pirate records of the latest compositions by Perez Prado and other prominent bandleaders.[41]

It was also in 1962, seven years after the height of Perez Prado's popularity and five years after Grace Chang's *Mambo Girl* had lit up screens across the Chinese-speaking world, that the legendary singer Hong Yifeng released a now classic emblem of a bygone era in Taiwanese-language popular music called "Formosa Mambo."[42] The very rhetoric of the song's title seems to indicate the ease with which an adjectivally modified "mambo" might circulate in a vernacular mode, serving simultaneously as a signifier of local identity and as a token of transnational engagement. But the ease with which this cross-border transaction was linguistically effected masks a rather more complicated story about a different kind of Chinese 1960s. Hong Yifeng hailed originally from the southern city of Tainan, beginning his musical life in the late 1940s as an accordionist in a *nakasi* 流し trio (a Japanese-derived genre, performed by itinerant performers at working-class cafes and teahouses). By the mid-1950s, he had made the leap to performing live on the island's increasingly prolific radio stations. The notoriety gained from these broadcasts, in turn, led to a successful touring revue beginning in the late 1950s, augmented by a string of successful records he cut with Taiwan's most successful purveyor of Taiwanese-language ballads, the Tainan-based Asia Records (of which more in chapter 3). By the early 1960s, however, Hong Yifeng, like Grace Chang, had come to rely on the musical cinema for his popularity. Unlike Grace Chang, who had the wind of Cathay's considerable market capitalization in her sails, Hong Yifeng had access to a far more limited production and exhibition circuit. Even more crucially, as a Taiwanese Hokkien speaker, he lacked the linguistic "passport" that would allow his work to travel as fluidly as Grace Chang's across national borders. While the production of Amoy-dialect (Xiayu, referring to the closely related dialect of the Fujianese city of Xiamen, across the strait from Taiwan) films had emerged as early as the 1950s in Hong Kong, this transnational circuit, encompassing audiences across Hong Kong, Southeast Asia, and Taiwan, remained poorly funded and burdened by a reputation for "shoddiness" and productions that were baldly derivative of their Mandarin and Cantonese counterparts.[43] Hokkien, in short, inhabited an altogether different circuit, marginalized with respect to the Mandarin vernacular and permanently restricted to a regional (if also transnational), rather than nominally national, ambit. Its situation in this sense resembled the restricted market for Cantonese music as well.[44] For Hong Yifeng to represent "Free China" to American audiences on *The Dinah Shore Show* would have been unthinkable.

By the early 1960s, with Fujian province behind the bamboo curtain and Hokkien audiences a minority market in Hong Kong and Singapore, most production shifted to what was by far the largest Hokkien-speaking market in the world, Taiwan. As a result, Taiwanese Hokkien films and popular music grew "increasingly local" in character.[45] After 1962, with the burgeoning importance of television as a conduit for popular music promotion, Hokkien music was further marginalized by strict KMT restrictions on broadcasting in "dialect," rather than Mandarin Chinese.[46] These restrictions did not apply to live performance, records, or theatrical screenings, and Hokkien cultural production continued to survive and to thrive in these venues until the late 1960s, albeit within an increasingly narrow and undercapitalized sector. Many films, funded by fly-by-night production companies, have been lost, in part because so few prints were struck in the first place.⁴⁷

What have come to be called "*Taiyu*" 台語 or "Taiwanese-language" musicals had at least two more strikes against them. Within Taiwan, they were often associated, especially by mainlander émigrés, with all that was local, low class, and lumpen. They were at the same time ideologically tainted in eyes of the Nationalist government by what Hong Guo-juin has called their "unclean severance" from the specter of Japan's half-century of colonial rule in Taiwan and its lingering linguistic and cultural influence.⁴⁸

Taiwanese ballads and *Taiyu* musicals throughout the 1960s situated themselves quite squarely within a circuit in which Japan remained a crucial point of reference. The "mixed-blood" 混血歌曲 songs of Hong Yifeng and performers like Wen Shia (of whom more in chapter 3), pressed in local plants in the industrial Taipei suburb of Sanchung-pu 三重埔 where migrant workers from the rural south tended to cluster, often directly adapted the melodies of the latest Japanese *enka*, with the addition of Taiwanese lyrics.⁴⁹ Even local compositions by composers such as Hong Yifeng and his collaborator and lyricist Ye Junlin 葉俊麟, while keen to incorporate some of the rhythm and blues and country and western styles emanating from U.S. Armed Forces radio in Taiwan and Japan, tended to adopt vocal styles and melodic profiles reminiscent of *enka* and other Japanese pop styles. In some cases, these "mixed-blood songs" represented a compensatory measure in that the direct importation of Japanese records, for which there remained an enthusiastic following among Taiwanese who had been educated during the colonial era, had been restricted since the 1950s. The link to Japan, moreover, was not only a question of listening to smuggled or pirated *enka* records. As part of his apprenticeship in the entertainment business, for example, Hong spent a year in Japan, learning his craft at a revue theater affiliated with Toho Film Studios before returning to Taiwan in the early 1960s. For Hokkien speakers, "mixed-blood" music was, to all intents and purposes, the Taiwanese mainstream.

Yet there may have been a foreboding sense, even in 1962, that the Taiwanese musical cinema was a dead end, a closing circuit. The runaway success of Hong Kong's Shaw Brothers' Technicolor production of the operatic story of star-crossed and cross-dressed lovers in *Love Eterne* (梁山伯與祝英台, 1962, starring Ivy Ling Bo 凌波) that same year heralded the emergence of a glossy pop aesthetic predicated on standard vernacular Chinese. Shaw's *huangmeidiao* musicals, loosely based on a folk form from Anhui province but colorfully packaged with the aid of EMI Records as a linguistically standardized cross-platform media spectacle, came to dominate the pan-Chinese screen and radio airtime for the rest of the decade. By the mid-1960s, as a result of KMT direct investment in the development of what was dubbed a cinema of "healthy realism" at its Central Motion Picture Company (CMPC) studio, the monochrome products of the *Taiyu* cinema began to sputter, and by the early 1970s it had essentially succumbed, a victim of strict political controls over the media (which banned Japanese imports and suppressed non-Mandarin media), as well as market forces.

For these reasons, the *Taiyu* films of the early 1960s—black and white in an era in which MP&GI had already begun to film in Eastman color—seem to cast a lingering look back toward an idealized rural and Japanese colonial past, while registering the parallel anxieties of Taiwan's rapid urbanization. Hong Yifeng's first (and only remaining) feature is typical in this regard. Titled *Lingering Lost Love* 舊情綿綿, the film tells the melodramatic tale of a schoolteacher and amateur composer named Hong Yifeng who is assigned to work in a rural area in the agricultural heartland of southern Taiwan. Hong quickly falls in love with a local betel-nut beauty, but her father, who has already arranged for her to be given to his boss in return for a better position, objects. The two lovers elope, fleeing to a mountain retreat in Alishan, but are separated once more by gangsters dispatched by her father to bring her back home. Our heroine is eventually forced into a loveless marriage in Taipei. Hong, heartbroken, also moves to Taipei, becoming a renowned balladeer. In a scene that reflects on the ascendancy of the novel technology of television, Hong's lover chances to tune in a radio broadcast of the title song. Tearfully, she watches as a spectral image of Hong is superimposed over the speaker of the old-fashioned tabletop wireless, as if to compensate for the device's lack of televisual presence, and the radio announcer finishes the broadcast by promoting an upcoming concert appearance at a local dancehall. She and their illegitimate daughter (who had for a time fended for herself as a street urchin lost in the big city) are reunited when Hong Yifeng appears on stage (see Figure 1.5).

What is fascinating about the film, and many others of its ilk, is the extent to which its narrative is structured around the north-south railway network constructed under Japanese colonial rule (and mentioned approvingly in Grace Chang's "Taiwan Melody"). In films like *Lingering Lost Love*, however, the railway figures not so much as a symbol of Taiwan's infrastructural advantages as much as a reminder of the powerful and ongoing cultural and economic disparities between urban Taipei, with its high concentrations of mainlander émigrés and its links to global capitalism, and the agricultural supply regions to the south. This topographical

Figure 1.5. Hong Yifeng in *Lingering Lost Love*, 1962.

divide is traversed over and over again in these films, providing a frame for their melodramatic plots of country lovers torn apart in the crucible of the capitalist city, and is even inscribed in their titles, redolent of missed opportunities and fateful separations, from *The Last Train from Kaohsiung* 高雄發的尾班車 (1963) to *The Early Train from Taipei* 台北發的早車 (1964). Both the title sequence and the climactic sequence of *Lingering Lost Love*, set to the title track and filmed along the outmoded narrow-gauge colonial railway constructed by Japan to log the giant cypresses that used to cover the slopes of Alishan, seem to present a highly kinetic and cinematographic vision of the machinations and forking paths of fate, of the belated and backward circuit in which both the characters and the film itself are trapped. In a series of mesmerizing tracking shots, the camera repeatedly casts a backwards gaze at the rails as the train itself glides steadily forward, across precipitous bridges, through dark tunnels, and across railroad switches. Meanwhile, the music, a distinctive fusion of *enka* melody and jazz instrumentation, anchored by Hong Yifeng's baritone vocals, tracks the movement of the train by way of the steady rhythm and blues-style comping of a piano (see Figure 1.6).[50]

When airplanes, the figure of modern mobility par excellence in the MP&GI musicals, come up at all in the films of this era, they appear as

Figure 1.6. Title sequence of *Lingering Lost Love*, 1962.

harbingers of a terrifying accident of fate. A sequence from a 1968 melodrama called *Hot Meat Rolls* 燒肉粽 (*shao rouzong*, meaning a kind of Taiwanese tamale, wrapped in banana leaves) is a salient example. Focused on a middle-class father who has lost everything as a result of his own extramarital folly, the film serves as a reminder of the precariousness of Taiwan's economic development. In an early scene, the father figure, having finally located a job as a sign painter and settled down in humble and broken-down working-class lodgings in Taipei, delivers a homily over the dinner table about class mobility to his two children. Suddenly, we cut to an image of a massive jet plane, its engines screaming directly overhead. This sudden, shatteringly loud, and seemingly unmotivated interruption is followed by a shot in which we learn from the family's kindly neighbors that the father has tumbled from his perch atop a signboard he was in the process of painting and shattered his arm. Perhaps the appearance here of a jet airplane was an accident, an artifact of the film being made just underneath the approach to Taipei's Songshan Airport. But it is quite deliberately retained as a means of signifying the shock of the father's own catastrophic accident. The tumble leaves him permanently disabled, and his daughter is left to fend for herself and the family by selling the *shao rouzong* of the film's title on the streets of Taipei (see Figure 1.7).

Figure 1.7. The roar of the jet plane in *Hot Meat Rolls*, 1968.

The contrast with a film like *Air Hostess* could not be more clear—one film presents the view from above, the other resolutely from below, as modernity leaves a disenfranchised working class behind. And yet, even as *Air Hostess* shows off its mastery of the global vernacular, emblematizing the free flow of people, capital, cultures, and goods, its narrative is also troubled by the space between its fantasies of mobility and the dangers of unfettered circulation. For, as part of Keping's induction into her role as a stewardess, she is convinced by a customer to carry, unbeknown to her, what turns out to be a parcel containing smuggled counterfeit jewelry. It is a minor subplot but nonetheless quite significant within the overall narrative and ideological economy of the film. Might the musical genres Grace Chang delivers so frictionlessly across national borders also be mere packages, even counterfeit goods?

This parallel between the film's plot and the transnational traffic in music is not so outlandish as it may seem. In fact, Taiwan's substantial production of pirated copies of both Western and Hong Kong–produced Mandarin popular music, which I explore further in chapter 4, flourished in tandem with commercial aviation. By the mid-1960s, Taiwanese factories were churning out at least thirty-five thousand (and by some estimates many more) such pirate records per month, catering to U.S. GIs on "rest and relaxation" leave from the escalating conflict in Vietnam and to budget-conscious music fans in Hong Kong and Southeast Asia, as well as to local aficionados of the U.S. and U.K. chart hits, or what was referred to in Taiwan as "hit music" (literally, "hot music" 熱門音樂).[51] This trade in counterfeit pressings was quite lucrative, fetching up to ten times their original price in Hong Kong, and its primary victims were "The Shaw

Brothers' stable of stars ... and England's the Beatles."[52] A newspaper report from 1968 about a young Hong Kong man detained at customs in Taipei for attempting to smuggle more than nine hundred such records on his flight home only hints at the scale of this sort of illegal traffic and its modal reliance on civil aviation and the tourist trade.[53] Even more interesting for our purposes, industry insiders attest that Taiwanese record companies often pressed stewardesses flying routes between Taipei, Hong Kong, and the west coast of the United States into service as couriers of the latest long-playing records, which could then be smuggled to Taiwanese factories and quickly reproduced as pirated discs.[54]

Perhaps another parallel with real-life events is presented in the denouement of the film with which I began this chapter, *Because of Her*. When we left Grace Chang last, she was triumphantly touring the world in the wake of the departure of her boyfriend for Japan. She is soon forced to reveal that she is pregnant with his child—a condition with dire economic consequences for the troupe, which is entirely reliant on her star power. (This plot perhaps prefigures Grace Chang's real-life marriage, maternity, and departure from the cinema a year later.) The manager of the troupe agrees to marry her and to pretend the child is his own. But just when their act is reestablished at a high-class nightclub and the couple have settled into a comfortable bourgeois existence, the prodigal boyfriend touches down once again at Kai Tak Airport and is hired by the troupe. At the climax of an elaborate restaging of Y. R. Chao's title song in a classic Hollywood mode, Grace Chang is compelled to perform along with her ex-lover, elevated together by means of a stage pulley into the cloud-dappled empyrean of an ersatz blue sky, as her husband directs the orchestral rendition of the song from the orchestra pit below. As her erstwhile leading man leans in to kiss her, Grace Chang glances anxiously toward the orchestra and her husband, who is utterly absorbed in the performance. This moment of misgiving proves fatal. Suddenly losing her footing on the narrow, pulley-suspended platform atop which she is perched, she plummets into the pit below the stage. The film ends with an aerial shot of her limp body, a livid red trickle of blood running across her white dress. This terrifying fall from grace, of course, is the stuff of bad dreams and bad melodrama but also a reminder of the gravity with which even entertainment films represented the developmental aspirations of the Chinese 1960s.

The scene also proved to be one of Grace Chang's last appearances on screen. Just months after the film's premier, she announced her final departure from the world of filmmaking in favor of married life and, in doing so, dealt a serious blow to MP&GI's hopes of competing with its rival in the film business, the Shaw Brothers. In June 1964, the Cathay Organization's owner and principal impresario, Loke Wan Tho, traveled to Taiwan to attend the Asian Film Festival, to explore the possibility of expanding the company's extensive film exhibition circuit in Taiwan, and to indulge his passion for bird-watching.[55] On a lark, Loke arranged an afternoon sightseeing trip to the city of Taichung on a chartered C-46 transport.[56] The flight foundered en route, and all fifty-nine passengers perished in the crash.

CHAPTER TWO

# Quotation Songs

## Media Infrastructure and Pop Song Form in Mao's China

The Chinese 1960s of high revolutionary aspiration arguably came to an end on September 13, 1971, when Lin Biao 林彪, grand marshal of the People's Liberation Army and right-hand man of Chairman Mao, was found dead in the twisted fuselage of a Hawker Trident airplane on the Mongolian steppes. While much about the crash remains enigmatic even now, the official account holds that Lin Biao was fleeing Beijing in the wake of a failed coup d'état. What is clear is that his death and his apparent betrayal of Mao—whose mass-mediated cult of personality Lin himself had helped to engineer—was for many believers a devastating revelation of the duplicitous machinery behind the revolutionary façade. The news of Lin Biao's fall from revolutionary probity to disgrace was relayed by way of an extensive media network that functioned largely as a closed circuit, monopolized by the Party itself and impervious to the music discussed in the previous chapter. Indeed, the apparent isolation of this circuit not only is indexical of the Cold War division of the 1960s but also raises once again a series of questions about the self-sameness of a historical moment and the degree to which the sound of an era is determined by the technology with which it is afforded. The People's Republic, while poor, was not necessarily technologically backward, and indeed, the products of its media system had by the end of the 1960s become au courant as emblems of utopian radical possibility in locales as diverse as Paris, Tokyo, and Mexico City. New technological possibilities, moreover, did not result in unilinear or predetermined outcomes. Transistors, for instance, were as instrumental to socialist media circuit as they were to the infrastructure of information dissemination and cultural products beyond the borders of the People's Republic. Yet the complex material and social contingencies of rural construction and revolutionary political action in China resulted in a radically different media topology. In what follows, I listen to the distinctive "sound" of the Cultural Revolution in order to show the ways in which the popular song of this period, even at the level of formal structure, was part and parcel of this transistorized media landscape.

This story about popular music, oddly enough, also begins with Lin Biao—in his capacity as the editor of one of the most iconic products of the 1960s, *The Quotations of Chairman Mao*, famed worldwide as the "Little Red Book." At the Ninth National Congress of the Communist Party of China in April 1969, Chairman Mao's wife, Jiang Qing 江青, issued a surprising broadside against a form of music that had once seemed to embody the political passions of the Great Proletarian Cultural Revolution: the quotation song. These songs, which had been promoted nationwide since September 1966, set the Chairman's maxims to music and were deliberately conceived as a musical analogue and mnemonic device for *The Quotations*. Upon watching a televised song and dance program extolling the Chairman, Jiang Qing is reported to have said: "Don't you believe that they are singing about Mao Zedong Thought—that's not really what it is at all. It's yellow music. We've already dealt a blow to the emperors and feudal lords, and now they're doing this sort of thing? In future, we need to get rid of folk tunes, we need to be rid of this swing music 搖擺音樂. They say they're eliminating the old and ringing in the new. What's new here? Some of their movements are based entirely on swing dancing."[1] She continued, "They're wearing red stars and waving red flags, but they're swing dancing. They may as well be naked."[2]

We may surmise that Jiang Qing's ire had something to do with the fact that these enormously popular songs were one of the few forms of mass-produced culture not yet under her direct control. Yet it would be a mistake to dismiss these comments wholesale. Indeed, I argue that Jiang Qing's tirade—which drew on a long tradition of leftist critique of popular music in China and not incidentally led to the immediate proscription of quotation songs throughout the country—may not only help us understand quotation songs as a form of popular music but also pose new questions about the relation between musical aesthetics, technology, and media culture in the Chinese 1960s.[3] In this chapter, I show how this new genre emerged out of the political exigencies and limitations of a socialist media circuit constructed around a nationwide network of wired (as opposed to wireless) broadcasting stations. This vast infrastructure, constructed over the course of the 1950s and 1960s and extending deep into rural China, brought the singular voice of the state to the people. Yet, with the advent and spread of transistor electronics in China and in the nearly simultaneous (if only temporarily countenanced) frenzy of youthful political participation of the late 1960s we see portents of a more portable and perhaps authentically "popular" musical culture, one neither fixed in geographical place nor moored as closely to the semantic certainties of state propaganda.

Quotation songs existed in an ambiguous grey zone between disparate media regimes. They were, of course, designed and promulgated by the socialist state and disseminated by its proprietary media networks. This is why, at first blush, Jiang Qing's identification of "quotation songs" as "yellow," or off-color, jazz seems unlikely in the extreme. What could possibly be promiscuous or even pleasurable about a choral march in duple meter titled—to cite just one of the more than one hundred such compositions that were published and recorded between 1966 and 1969—"Ensure That Literature and Art Operate as Powerful Weapons for Exterminating the Enemy" 要使文藝成為消滅敵人的有力的武器?[4] Yet part of the underlying affinity may lie not just in the ecstatic movement that sometimes accompanied the performance of such music but also in the deliberate promiscuity of their *form*. By form, I indicate not only their musical, lyrical, and ideological characteristics but also the way in which these qualities made use of the new technological possibilities and ever-expanding reach of the socialist mass media in the 1960s. Quotation songs, in a manner not radically different from popular music in the same years in the West, were designed for promiscuous movement, for effortless portability. And as with the mass-mediated pop songs of the 1960s in the United States and Europe, the revolutionary songs of the 1960s owed their popularity in part to the self-conscious crafting of a "hook"—a melodic figure, catchphrase, or distinctive sound that rendered a song not only instantly recognizable as it leapt from a loudspeaker but also easily replicable in disparate media and contexts. In fact, the use of melodic hooks drawn from the urban folk song 小調 tradition to ensnare Chinese listeners is precisely what incensed Jiang Qing about the performances to which she and other Party activists were privy at the Ninth Party Congress.[5] Her sense of the affinity of such music with Western pop may well have extended to the linguistic qualities and rhetorical mode of these songs, in that the quotation song did in fact lend itself uniquely well to the performative and citational logic on which pop songs are premised and by which they are able to circulate.

This portability, as envisioned by those who originally promoted these songs at the very height of the Red Guard movement of September 1966 in the pages of *People's Daily*, would not only annihilate spatial and temporal limitations but also penetrate psychological barriers as well: "We believe that with the hard work of musical workers, the sound of songs of Chairman Mao's quotations will resonate across the entire country. This will make the thought of Chairman Mao penetrate ever deeper into people's hearts, so as to forever radiate its brilliance."[6] Interestingly enough, this description, in its emphasis on the ability of these songs to record, broadcast, and enable Mao Zedong Thought to saturate social, somatic, and psychological space, reads almost uncannily like an account of the ethereal yet ubiquitous powers of mass media itself. This is not merely a rhetorical accident. The ubiquity of quotation songs was in fact the product and the logical conclusion of a broadcasting network designed to resonate across the boundary between Chinese cities and their rural hinterlands. This electrical-acoustic network, moreover, was part and parcel of a system of cultural production marked by a high degree of what we might now call "media interactivity," "intermediality," or, even more anachronistically, "cross-platform marketing."[7] The power of the quotation songs was premised on the ease with which they traveled across different media, from print to live performance, from records to radio broadcasting, from poster art to the revolutionary postures of the "loyalty dance" 忠字舞.[8]

### The "Little Red Book"

In the beginning, or so the story goes, there was the "Little Red Book." Compiled at the behest of then Minister of Defense Lin Biao, as part of a larger effort to promote Mao Zedong Thought, the volume in its final form brought together 427 excerpts from Chairman Mao's published writings and speeches, organized under thirty-three thematic rubrics, and was first published in April 1964 by the General Political Department of the People's Liberation Army. As such, the work was originally conceived as a kind of standard-issue ideological "field manual" for PLA soldiers, and this accounts for its handy, durable design and water- and wear-resistant red vinyl cover. With the explosion of the popularity of the *Quotations* after 1966, this emphasis on pocket-size portability was taken to almost fetishistic extremes: one edition squeezed not only the *Quotations* but also the Chairman's regulated verse and *ci* lyrics and the "Five Works" 五篇著作 into a single—and no doubt nearly illegible—matchbox-size edition of 256 *kai* (開), measuring one by one and a half inches. The quantities in which the book was produced during the high tide of the Cultural Revolution are equally staggering: by 1967, 628 million copies were in circulation, and by the end of the following decade, the official figure (not counting offprints and unauthorized copies) had swollen to 1.5 billion. Yet the question remains: how can we understand this phenomenon in the context of the socialist media system? Was the book sufficient unto itself, or was it in some sense an intermedial event, its ubiquity an ancillary effect of its recitation and replication in visual, electro-acoustic, and other forms?

One clue to this question may lie in its formal properties as a text. The portability (and perhaps even the talismanic character) of the material object itself represented in some sense an extension of the underlying logic of the quotation as a literary genre. For what is the function of the quotation, if not to remove a textual extract from its original context and allow it to *circulate* beyond the original and particular historical circumstances in which it was produced, rendering it available for reuse, recitation, and recontextualization? The *Quotations* achieve precisely this function, bringing together words spoken or written from the mid-1920s to the mid-1960s, torn from the often quite specific and complex tactical situations for which they were crafted and offered instead as transhistorical scripts for revolutionary praxis, organized under abstract rubrics such as "Classes and Class Struggle," "War and Peace," "Women," or simply "Study." The "catchiest" of these catchphrases, injunctions, and maxims, moreover, often detach themselves even from the longer quotation of which they were originally a part, traveling seemingly without effort across linguistic and temporal boundaries and attaining (like the "Little Red Book" itself) iconic status: "Revolution is not a dinner party"; "It's right to rebel"; "All reactionaries are paper tigers"; "Political power grows out of the barrel of a gun."

Quotations, in short, are made by their medium, and, once mediated, they take on an itinerant life of their own.[9] In the case of the *Quotations*, that life is indelibly politicized. It is perhaps symptomatic of the quotation's function as what we would now call a "viral" linguistic medium that Lin Biao, in his oft-quoted introduction to the 1966 edition of the *Quotations* (which was itself later set to music as quotation song), emphasizes the bringing to life of Chairman Mao's word through repetition, memorization, and "live application" 活用: "In studying Chairman Mao's work, we need to learn through problem-solving, through live study and live application活學活用, uniting the two together, learning what is of urgent use, so that the results are immediately visible, always putting fierce emphasis on the character for 'use.' In order to really put Mao Zedong Thought to hand, we need to repeatedly study Chairman Mao's many fundamental standpoints, and preferably memorize some of his maxims, repeatedly studying them, and repeatedly using them."[10] With repetition comes mastery, and with mastery, Lin famously concludes, Mao Zedong Thought will be mobilized as "a spiritual atom bomb" 精神原子彈 against the enemies of the revolution.[11] The metaphor speaks directly to the Cold War context in which this mobilization took place, as well as to the centrality of such metaphors in effecting what Lin calls the "weaponization of the minds of the people of the entire nation" 武裝全國人民的頭腦.[12]

In practice, this weaponization was brought about by way of the unprecedented integration, centralization, and degree of saturation of everyday life by the socialist mass media by the mid-1960s. The words in the book rapidly replicated across different media—recited as part of schoolroom and workplace rituals, chalked on bulletin boards, engraved on everyday objects, printed on posters and mastheads and title pages, projected on cinema screens at the beginning of each and every film, and rendered as song. The official "roll-out" of the quotation song as a new genre is itself a primary case in point. A suite of ten "quotation songs," set to music by the prominent leftist composer and head of the Shenyang Conservatory Li Jiefu 李劫夫 (1913–1976), was introduced on the pages of the *People's Daily* a little more than a month after the first of the massive Red Guard rallies on Tiananmen Square which marked the beginning of the high tide of the Cultural Revolution.[13] Released on September 30, 1966, the melodies were provided in simplified notation and accompanied by an introduction.[14] This style of presentation deliberately mirrored the sequencing of the "Little Red Book" itself, by citing the aforementioned quotation from the Lin Biao preface to the *Quotations*, before presenting the very first entry in the *Quotations*, "The Force at the Core Leading Our Cause Forward is the Chinese Communist Party" 領導我們事業的核心力量是中國共產黨 in musical form.

To some extent, quotation songs partook of a long and ongoing tradition of quotation literature 語錄 in China, one whose genealogy might be said to include not only the Confucian *Analects*, Buddhist hagiographies dating back to the Tang, as well as Republican-era compilations of the sayings of prominent political leaders such as Sun Yat-sen 孫中山. Perhaps more relevant to the emergence of the form was the practice of exhortatory choral singing that, having been introduced by Christian missionaries in the nineteenth century, had gone on to become a staple of Chinese school life and political ritual in the early decades of the twentieth century.[15] Yet, as Liang Maochun points out, the appearance of the songs was accompanied by a "theoretical" apparatus—outlined in a series of articles in prominent publications—that insisted (as the *People's Daily* put it) on the unprecedented "novelty of the form" 嶄新的形式.[16]

To the extent that "quotation songs" were designed from the start as modular participants in an integrated national media landscape, this was undoubtedly true. This initial fusillade of songs, released on the day before

National Day, was followed by a barrage of follow-up reports in the print media, which were disseminated through a variety of visual and aural media, including but not limited to neighborhood and work unit bulletin and chalk boards, paintings, posters, study sessions, and public readings of newspapers and official reports.[17]

These forms of dissemination were reinforced by the printing not only of a series of songbooks that allowed for public singing but also by monaural vinyl records (in both seven- and ten-inch formats) of orchestrated choral performances produced by China Records. The packaging of these products, moreover, was to a large degree standardized across different media: song books also sported red vinyl covers, while the covers of the records featured much the same layout and typography as the "Little Red Book" itself. Vinyl long-playing records of the quotation songs, moreover, were exported with bilingual sleeves by the China Publications Centre 國際書店.[18]

Because home ownership of phonographs remained relatively rare in the 1960s, especially in rural areas, quotation songs largely reached listeners across the country by way of radio broadcasts.[19] By October 1, 1966—the day after the song texts were published by the *People's Daily*—Radio Shanghai had already begun FM band wireless transmission of the songs, accompanied by tutorials. Far more widely heard were broadcasts of the same type transmitted across the country by China's extensive rediffusion network. By the early 1970s, this wired or in-line (as opposed to wireless) system, radiating from Radio Peking at the center, routed through various provincial and county-level relays and penetrating deep into the interior, broadcast to (by one estimate) more than 140 million loudspeakers, mounted on utility poles and streetlight standards in urban streets, schools, train and bus stations, army barracks and factory floors, and even rural fields and village lanes.[20] By the late 1960s and early 1970s, many rural homes were also wired for sound, for which no "off" switch was provided.[21] When the *People's Daily* breathlessly reported on October 25, 1966, that "the sound of the singing of quotation songs is ringing out across the nation, from the interior to the borderlands, from country to city, in factories and fields, from barracks to schools," reality had in fact already overtaken rhetoric.[22]

**Rural Radio**

The establishment of a wired rediffusion network was the culmination of a 1955 decision by the CCP to radically expand the reach of the mass media into the countryside.[23] In the first five years of CCP rule, an extensive system of monitored "radio listening stations" had been set up for collective listening, often using commandeered preliberation radio sets and largely reliant on wireless broadcasts (see Figure 2.1).

Wired broadcasting networks, through which local relay stations could pick up broadcasts from the center wirelessly and then rediffuse the signal across a wired network of loudspeakers offered several advantages. First, they were less costly to establish and maintain. Rudimentary moving iron cone loudspeakers (referred to as "tongue and groove speakers" or 舌簧喇叭 in Chinese) were more efficient and easier to manufacture than wireless receivers. Rural broadcasting systems, moreover, were often engineered to piggyback atop existing electrical and telephone lines, further reducing installation costs and labor.[24] Second, they controlled the flow of information by preventing individuals from using radio receiving sets to access shortwave broadcasts from abroad or from simply turning off the radio. Third, they allowed authorities a limited ability to customize broadcasts, inserting directives, announcements, and information pertaining to local conditions and interests. As *Wired Broadcasting* 有線廣播, an authoritative manual for cadres and technicians looking to set up rural broadcast stations, emphasized, wireless radio would never reach the more than 80 percent of the population domiciled in rural areas. Wired networks would not only "expand coverage" of rural areas but also "limit the scope of radio reception" and also guarantee a high degree of "secrecy" for intra-Party communications.[25]

The wired radio network grew hand in hand with the establishment of rural communes in the late 1950s. Indeed, such networks must be seen as integral to the state's efforts to modernize, reorganize, and regulate rural space and the temporal rhythms of rural life (see Figure 2.2 and Plate 2). As contemporary accounts emphasize, programming was keyed to Beijing time, often crackling to life well before dawn, and included morning calisthenics, news, political propaganda, and entertainment accompanying labor. What may have first seemed like an imposition came eventually to function like a clock, imposing order and a reliable aural time stamp on the agrarian working day (see Figure 2.3).[26]

The "broadcasting network" 廣播網, as it was referred to from its inception, also imposed a new spatial logic on the countryside, not merely by way of the serried rows of utility poles and wires strung across the landscape but through lateral connections with adjacent communities and hierarchical links to the center (see Figure 2.4).

Finally, the network not only forged a new topography but also introduced a new Marxist-Leninist political vocabulary and (to many provincial ears) unfamiliar tonality, that of standard official Chinese. The network

Figure 2.1. "Collective Listening," cover image of *Wireless* 1 (1956).

Figure 2.2. "Wired Broadcasting Is Developing Rapidly in the Countryside." *Wireless* 1 (1955).

Figure 2.3. Broadcasting agrarian life. Wu Bozhen 伍伯蓁, *Radio in the Fields* 田間廣播 (Beijing: Posts & Telecom Press, 1958).

grew rapidly. By the time of the Great Leap Forward, in 1959, 9,435 commune-level and 1,689 county-level wired relay stations had been established, linked to an estimated 4,570,000 in-line loudspeakers; that number had increased to 6,000,000 by 1964.[27]

While there is no way to verify the accuracy of these figures, this was by any standard a monumental achievement. By deliberate policy design, much of the installation was conducted at the local level, largely unfunded by the central government and achieved by way of thrift, ingenuity, and what one manual described as "down-to-earth" or "local" solutions 土辦法.[28] Even more astounding—and this point cannot be emphasized enough—the construction of broadcast networks often proceeded in the absence of rural electrification. At the dawn of the decade that the Canadian media theorist Marshall McLuhan famously proclaimed as heralding a "global village" of "electronic interdependence," the majority of Chinese villages lacked any electrical power.[29] While urban power grids were administered by the central government, the provision of power in the countryside was a piecemeal affair, overseen at the county level. Even in those areas that had developed generation capacity, usually through the construction of local hydropower stations, supplies were unreliable at best.[30] In the late

# 一、农村有线广播是党的重要宣传工具

什么是农村有线广播？一般地说，就是在县市城镇或公社成立一个有线广播站，安装上有线广播设备，在生产大队、生产队办公室或者农民住房里安装广播喇叭，并通过广播线路把广播站和用户喇叭联接起来，如图1.1。当广播站里的扩音机转播中央人民广播电台和省、市人民广播电台的重要节目或播送本地自办的节目时，不管是住在广阔的平原地区，还是住在浓密的森林里或崎岖的山区里，凡是有广播喇叭的地方，都可以收听到广播站播送出来的各种节目。

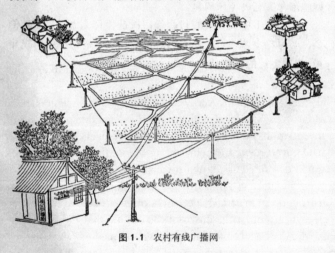

图1.1 农村有线广播网

Figure 2.4. "Wired Village Networks." Fan Dunxing 范敦行, *General Knowledge on Rural Wired Radio* 農村有線廣播常識 (Shanghai: Shanghai People's Publishing House, 1971), 1.

1950s, rural China accounted for less than 1 percent of total national consumption; even after another two decades of steady development, during which approximately ninety thousand small-scale hydropower stations were built at the local level by rural counties and communes, 37 percent of the peasantry had yet to be plugged in by 1979.[31]

Localities, faced with the imperative of extending the reach of the voice of the central state, yet lacking funds and resources, improvised "local solutions" that in many ways seem to cast into question familiar linear narratives of technological progress whereby newer and more efficient technologies inevitably supersede the old. A circuit schematic for rural broadcasting stations in northeastern Liaoning province, for instance, has at its center not sophisticated machinery but a donkey (see Figure 2.5). The TY5725 wired broadcasting system, invented by engineers at the provincial radio station specifically for remote rural villages, featured a twenty-five-watt tube amplifier powered by livestock yoked to a rudimentary pulley and crankshaft generator. This treadmill system, while theoretically allowing for several hours of uninterrupted airtime, was not "without certain unavoidable problems and drawbacks, for instance, livestock defecating and urinating as they work."[32]

Another how-to manual warns peasants not to tether livestock to electrical utility poles, for fear that the animals would bolt and bring high-tension wires toppling to the ground.[33] Animals did not pose the only risk to these ferrous tentacles of modernization; villagers also had to be discouraged from using the wires to hang their laundry out to dry (see Figure 2.6).[34]

From the outset, lack of power and resources in the countryside necessitated counterintuitive engineering decisions. Rural broadcasting stations were encouraged to install moving iron cone speakers, a technology that had been largely outmoded as early as 1925 with the invention of dynamic moving coil transducers.[35] Also known as "balanced armature" speakers, this design had been widely adopted for use in public address systems in the early twentieth century. The principle of operation is simple: when a current is passed through a permanent magnet inside a coil, a fixed metal reed (the armature) responds to variations in the resulting current, vibrating the paper cone. The virtue of this design lies in its compact size and affordability; its vice is poor reliability, an inability to reproduce bass notes, and limited frequency response above the midrange. Despite their notoriously crackly sound quality, moving iron speakers were extremely easy to drive, requiring just one-tenth of a watt to produce adequate volumes. In other words, a single donkey fueling a twenty-five-watt amplifier would theoretically have been able to power no fewer than 250 loudspeakers, handily

## 編者的話

辽宁人民广播电台試制成的 TY5725 型有綫广播設备，对目前还缺乏电源的农村建立乡社放大站是有現实意义的。它虽然还存在电力小、設备成本較高等缺点，但我們相信只要各地在运用时繼續加以改进，这些問題是可以得到解决的。

## 一、概述

甲、TY5725 型有綫广播設备系利用畜力驅动一台齿輪傳动式变速机，帶动一直流發电机，供給一台輸出功率为25瓦的扩音机。

Figure 2.5. Donkey Radio. Liaoning People's Radio Station, *Wired Radio Facilities That Use Animal Power for Electrical Generation* 利用畜力發電的有線廣播設備 (Beijing: Posts & Telecom Press, 1958), 3.

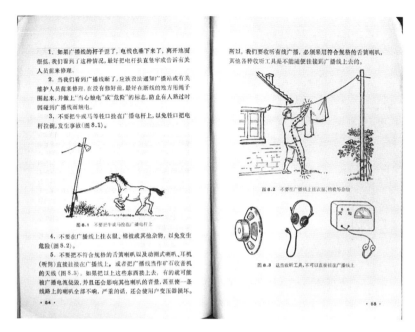

Figure 2.6. Rural Electrification and Its Discontents. Fan Dunxing 范敦行, *General Knowledge on Rural Wired Radio* 農村有線廣播常識 (Shanghai: Shanghai People's Publishing House, 1971), 54-55.

supplying an entire village and its cultivated lands with radio programming. In suburban areas or relatively prosperous communes with good connections to the electrical grid, a broadcast station equipped with a five-hundred-watt dual mono tube amplifier would be able to power an array of several thousand such speakers, although large distances and the poor conductivity of the relatively inexpensive galvanized iron wire commonly in use at the time inevitably resulted in a certain degree of line loss.[36]

Other innovations designed to electrify the countryside during this period also tend to confound conventional ideas about the unidirectionality of technological advance. One appliance introduced at the height of the Great Leap Forward, for instance, utilized one of the most revolutionary technologies of the time, solid state semiconductor transistors, to eke enough voltage from an old-fashioned oil lamp to power a radio set.[37] While this particular thermocouple generator remained too inefficient to be widely adopted, transistors would eventually transform the sonic and social landscape in China in the wake of their introduction in the late 1950s, sometimes in surprising ways. Transistors—first invented at Bell Labs in 1947—were not only smaller and more durable than the vacuum tube technology they replaced but also far more energy efficient. This fact was of crucial importance to the expansion of rural mass media in China, because electrical mains power supplies remained in many areas insufficient, unreliable, or simply nonexistent. Transistor devices could be run far more effectively from batteries than their tubed counterparts and provided far more volume than crystal sets. By 1957, China had already begun to produce transistorized sound equipment, most notably in the East German–designed factory complex in Beijing that has now become globally famous in its repurposed form as the 798 arts district. In fact, the same factory, North China Radio Equipment Factory 華北無線電器器材廠, designed, produced, and installed on the occasion of the tenth anniversary of the revolution in 1959 the loudspeaker systems for Beijing's Chang'an Avenue, as well as the wired "sound columns" 音柱 that continue to define Tiananmen Square as a politically and socially resonant space. Its sister factory, the Beijing Radio Equipment Factory 北京無線電器器材廠, began to manufacture battery-powered transistor radios under its Peony 牡丹 brand imprint as early as 1958, just one year after an upstart Japanese manufacturer called Sony stormed the U.S. market with its "shirt-pocket" TR-63 model.[38]

Transistor radios were marketed in China, if "marketed" is the correct term, explicitly in terms of their convenience for rural users who lacked access to electrical mains. A Shanghai Radio Equipment Factory advertisement in the March 1, 1958, edition of the *People's Daily*, for instance, announced the advent of portable radios able to run on both DC batteries and AC mains (unlike its tubed counterparts).[39] By the time of the Cultural Revolution, eight years later, battery-powered portable transistor radios, microphones, portable public announcement systems, and self-powered loudspeakers not only were widely available but also had reached remote rural areas. This was a matter of deliberate policy, in that transistors allowed the revolution to reach areas remote from or insufficiently supplied by electric mains services.[40] In Anita Chan, Richard Madsen, and Jonathan Unger's classic account of an isolated and impoverished settlement in Guangdong province, *Chen Village*, the installation of a broadcast network takes place precisely in 1966, in the immediate wake of rural electrification and the beginning of an intensive campaign to promote Mao Zedong Thought among the villagers: "The system consisted of thirty loudspeakers positioned throughout the village, with four large ones installed in the village's main meeting places. The volume was tuned loud enough that even while indoors people could hear the announcements."[41]

In the context of a village in which clocks were not yet common, the loudspeaker system provided the villagers with a newly regimented sense of "industrial" time.⁴² Operated by a single sent-down youth named Ao, the system served as a "mouthpiece" for the movement, providing not only music and reports from the provincial broadcast station but also customized political admonitions targeted toward specific villagers.⁴³

The internal migration of urban educated youth to ever more remote areas in the years after the tamping down of the Red Guard movement in the cities seems to have resulted in some tellingly anachronistic technological innovations as well. While most established broadcasting stations, constructed before or in the immediate wake of the Great Leap of the late 1950s, were built around tube amplifiers and linked arrays of moving iron speakers, the remote areas to which many educated youths were sent lacked these amenities entirely. Thus, as Laurence Coderre has noted, factories like Beijing's Peony and Nanjing's Panda brand, which had specialized in console record players and table-top tube radios for domestic use in the early 1960s, began to focus on portable transistorized models by the end of the decade.⁴⁴ The Beijing Radio Equipment's popular "East Is Red 101" 東方紅101, introduced in 1968, is a fascinatingly hybrid case in point. A hand-cranked record player, reminiscent of the portable Victrolas of the 1930s and 1940s, the "East Is Red" was also equipped with a battery-powered amplifier and transistor radio. From an engineering standpoint, the combination makes very little sense; yet form here follows social function, in that these units would have served as the perfect accoutrement for rusticated youth in the hinterlands, allowing them to play the feather-light vinyl flexi-discs of revolutionary music that were also the rage during this period, while doubling as the nucleus for portable, outdoor broadcasting "booths" in remote and mountainous areas where the fixed networks of the state had as yet failed to penetrate.⁴⁵

Transistorized electronics, as these examples suggest, had begun to enable new kinds of traffic between urban and rural areas and to quicken the transformation of rural soundscapes in the late 1960s. And while their development emerged from the imperatives of the state, they were not entirely circumscribed by them. While technological change must be understood in dynamic and rigorously historicized relation to its sociopolitical context, it is difficult to escape the conclusion that the transistor—termed a "revolution in miniature" for its capacity to make formerly clunky consumer goods mobile—also "miniaturized" the revolution and, in doing so, mobilized new forms of social action. In urban areas, battery-powered portable transistor radios, microphones, portable public announcement systems, sound trucks, and, above all, battery-powered loudspeakers opened up the possibility of a newly mobile and even interactive media landscape (see Figure 2.7).

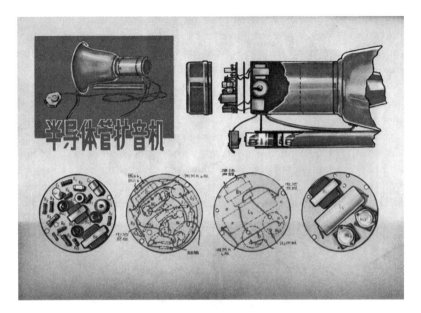

Figure 2.7. "Transistorized Loudspeaker Schematic." *Wireless* 1 (1966).

Designed to mobilize the masses, these devices were quickly commandeered by Red Guard activists and pressed into the service of a new kind of direct politics, one directly at odds with the Party apparatus, in the streets and squares of Beijing and other cities. In a poster produced in the fall of 1966 in the wake of Chairman Mao's exhortation to the Red Guard insurgents to "Bombard the Headquarters!" and thus escalate the scope and scale of the Cultural Revolution, for instance, we see Mao's broadside, visualized as a kind of free-standing column or billboard, presiding over a kind of frenzy of revolutionary representation. Insurgents write and paste "big-character posters" 大字报 on a wall, as if in response to Mao's words, perhaps reinforcing Mao's sense that his own sloganeering was itself a "dazibao": an unofficial, insurrectionary, temporary, portable text-event, directed against his own Party apparatus. A worker speaks animatedly to his cohorts through a PA system. Wind-blown red banners blazoned with slogans form phalanxes above the crowd. A truck, wired for sound with a set of battery-powered loudspeakers, presumably blares out more messages or perhaps music, its sonic barrage aimed at the ubiquitous wired loudspeakers mounted on the wall directly opposite (see Plate 3).

Such an image suggests how transistorized and portable media might have begun by the late 1960s to challenge the fixed networks of the party-state, threatening to surround and thus displace the "headquarters" by way of a new cultural logic, predicated on rapid action, impromptu demonstrations, and the temporary occupation of positions, both spatial and ideological. Indeed, the mimeographed broadsides and flyers, rough-and-ready cartoons and caricatures, and ever-shifting displays of big-character posters so crucial to the Red Guard repertoire suggests the transposition of a "transistorized" aesthetic onto the landscape of a print culture, commandeering territory that had been heretofore monopolized by state presses.

### Mao as Media-Effect

Even so, the ubiquity of portable media could not and was never intended to displace Mao himself as the "master" or "transcendent signifier" of the media system. Indeed, as the image on the cover of the October 1966 issue of *Wireless Magazine* 無線電 illustrates, that relation was seen—and practiced—as a kind of "closed circuit." We see workers reading and reciting from Chairman Mao's *Quotations* as part of the production process of manufacturing solid-state transistor circuits—circuits that will no doubt power the radios and loudspeakers broadcasting vocal as well as musical renditions of the *Quotations of Chairman Mao* (see Plate 4). What this sort of circuitous loop suggests is that "Mao" himself becomes a kind of "media effect," a product of his constant citation as text and as image.

Another way to approach this idea is through what the French philosopher Jacques Derrida called "iterability." Language, Derrida tells us in his essay "Signature Event Context" (written in 1971 as the Cultural Revolution continued to smolder in China), works because each of our speech acts is a kind of "citation" of the speech acts of everyone else.[46] When I say "Mao," I am citing previous usages of the term, not merely creating the term out of nowhere. I am "reiterating" the word "Mao." But its iterability in the first place is a function of having been constantly repeated. So, how is it possible to speak of a real Mao? Is his presence (and his power) merely an effect of linguistic or other types of mediation? What Derrida wants to get at here is an interesting contradiction, and he uses the example of a signature to further underline the problem. A signature is supposed to be the unique possession of its owner—the legal mark of his or her individuality. But in order to function, the signature must be consistently replicable, it has to proliferate, to be used and reused in multiple contexts; thus, by definition, what initially looked like the guarantor of individual identity is not and cannot be unique. In other words, a signature must be replicable to be authentic. And if a signature is replicable, it can also be forged. For Derrida, citation is like a signature: when we quote someone, we both invoke and displace the original source, so that the words can take on a promiscuous life of their own.

This may be why the phenomenon of quotation songs was often accompanied by a persistent and perhaps compensatory trope of presence. Over and over in the news media from this period, citizens are quoted as celebrating the way in which the *Quotations* have rendered Chairman Mao himself portable: "Chairman Mao's book speaks for us poor and middle peasants. Reading Chairman Mao's book every day is like seeing Chairman Mao himself every day," begins one such ventriloquized report.[47] Editorializing on the activities of the "little generals" leading the revolutionary charge, another article captures the extent to which the very act of citation in song was seen as transformative: "[The Red Guards] sing the *Quotations of Chairman Mao*, and they are imprinted upon their hearts . . . they say 'we love most of all to sing and to listen to Chairman Mao's quotations. Singing Chairman Mao's quotation songs, we think of Chairman Mao; singing Chairman Mao's quotation songs, we remember Chairman Mao's instructions, singing Chairman Mao's quotation songs, it's as if Chairman Mao himself is by our side.'"[48] Here, not only does the song effect the Chairman's teleportation but also the body of the singer itself becomes a resonant medium upon which the quotation is printed.

How, then, is this rhetoric of mass-mediated intimacy—one that repeatedly evokes the spiritual *and* somatic effects of song—registered in the compositions themselves and their recorded renditions? How do we account for the undeniable popularity of this music? Part of the answer lies, as Jiang Qing herself suggested, in the effects generated by listening and singing in unison with loud (and especially amplified) music. As Liang Maochun has noted, the distinct musical aesthetics of the Cultural Revolution have been characterized as "high, fast, hard, and loud" 高快硬響.[49] This phrase, of course, could almost as easily be applied to rock and roll, and for reasons that are not entirely coincidental. For when one turns to the recorded versions of the quotation songs released by China Records in 1966, it is immediately apparent that the music has been engineered so as to wring the maximum aural impact from limited technical means. The production is perfectly suited to unison singing, melding choral voices and orchestral accompaniment into a monophonic wall of sound, one pitched high enough and with enough amplitude to penetrate the public spaces in which these songs were usually broadcast.

By the summer of 1966, moving iron cones had rapidly begun to be superseded by horn reflex loudspeakers, especially in squares, streets, schools, open fields, and other outdoor spaces.[50] Such systems, write the authors of *Wired Broadcasting*, have "sprung up across the country like bamboo shoots after the rain during the Great Proletarian Cultural Revolution."[51] While considerably more power-hungry, these directional devices, constructed entirely of metal, were more weather-resistant and, above all, much *louder*, capable of piercing even the din of an urban market or factory floor and clearly audible across a half-kilometer of countryside.[52] Their designation in Chinese, high-frequency loudspeaker or 高音喇叭, was also entirely appropriate, for they emphasized treble to the detriment of all else. The shrillness of the music, with its tendency to emphasize the frequencies well above the midrange, almost certainly reflects the inability of both moving iron and horn reflex systems to reproduce the low-frequency band with any degree of fidelity. The lack of stereo separation and internal space between instruments or individual voices is also an artifact of this technology. The resultant block-like solidity of the sound, coupled with duple, marching rhythms, serves as an aural analogue of their ideological insistence on the collectivity. The consistently "overdriven" timbres of climactic vocal phrases (perhaps an artifact of the soft-clipping of tubed recording equipment) seem to emulate the high pitch to which revolutionary energy was driven in this moment of self-conscious historical emergency.[53] In many of these songs, finally, the choral harmonies are punctuated by a fanfare in brass, serving perhaps as heralds of the arrival of the revolutionary army or of Chairman Mao himself.

Before these technical constraints, of course, came the compositional and political challenge of setting Chairman Mao's words to music. Certain keywords (the "Communist Party of China," for instance) had to be sung at a higher pitch in order to underscore their sacred position in the political lexicon. Melodies, in turn, needed not only to be limited in terms of range (to facilitate mass singing) but also to be structured around preexisting and not always terribly melodious or even metrical prose. The most obvious consequence of this particular constraint is that a composer like Li Jiefu deftly selected for adaptation just those quotations that were the most portable, quotations that on account of their brevity and rhetorical nicety traveled most readily across media. A singular and self-reflexive example is his setting of "We Should Support Whatever the Enemy Opposes and Oppose Whatever the Enemy Supports" 凡是敵人反對的我們就要擁護，凡是敵人擁護的我們就要反對 as a choral round, in which the chiasmus of the original phrase is mirrored by a catchily chiastic melodic line.

Quotation songs—not unlike their contemporary pop musical counterparts in the West—exploited both formal limitations and new technological possibilities in order to forge a new musical language, one predicated on the power of the "hook." A hook is usually defined as the musical or lyrical phrase, particular rhythmic figure, harmonic modulation, or timbral effect that catches the listener's attention and lodges a song in his or her memory.⁵⁴ One example might be the rhythmic flurry of eighth notes we hear in the fanfare-like introduction to "The Force at the Core Leading Our Cause Forward Is the Chinese Communist Party" 領導我們事業的核心力量. The hook is also sometimes referred to as an "earworm"—a metaphor that captures quite nicely the invasive quality of the process, the way pop music has the power to make its way into our heads and to reshape our subjectivities. The hook, finally, having been internalized as memory, often comes to stand in for the song itself, functioning as a kind of sonic synecdoche or self-reflexive citation. In this sense, we might see the quotation song as pop music in its purest most politically effective form. Citational from the very start, the typical quotation song is short, seldom extending much beyond a single minute, brutally repetitive, and compressed to the point that nothing is left *except* the hook itself.

And yet, as Derrida seems to augur, citation is not as stable as it may seem. The very portability of the Chairman's words, of his ideological signature—across time, topography, and different sorts of media—may allow for the possibility of new sorts of semantic promiscuity. In his provocative study of Soviet culture, *Everything Was Forever, Until It Was No More*, the anthropologist Alexei Yurchak makes just such a claim, arguing that the increasingly rigid formalization of socialist language and visual iconography effected what he calls a "performative shift" after Stalin's death.⁵⁵ The more that Soviet citizens internalized propaganda as repetitive ritual formulae that needed to be performed, the less their "original" constative meaning—the signature, if you will—mattered. Indeed, the meaning of icons or slogans or ritual behaviors gradually became "open-ended, indeterminate, or simply irrelevant."⁵⁶ More interestingly, they also became subject to resignification and reinterpretation, to a kind of performative drift.

The Chinese literary critic Huang Ziping, in a memoir about everyday language in the early 1970s, gives us an interesting example of this sort of drift. Remembering his years as a sent-down youth on Hainan island, he cites a love letter written by a friend who was trying to seduce a young woman. The letter consisted of three lines of text, each of which is quoted verbatim from Chairman Mao's "Quotations" and "Highest Directives" 最高指示:

1. Hailing from the five lakes and the four seas, for a common revolutionary aim, we come together.
2. We must share information.
3. We must first have a firm grasp, and secondly be attentive to politics.⁵⁷

As Huang Ziping points out, this is a fine example of Lin Biao's notion of the "live study and live application" of Maoist dicta through their recontexualization and reuse in daily life.[58] Is there a "common revolutionary aim" 共同的革命目標? In order to find out, the lovers will need to share "information" 情報—which, in a clever play on words, can also be understood as a "declaration of love." Having understood each other, they can hold tight to each other with a "firm grasp" 抓緊, an embrace that trumps the business of politics, thereby (in a phrase that has been expediently clipped from the original directive) "cleansing the class ranks."

In this light, Jiang Qing's worries about the promiscuity of the quotation song form were not entirely unjustified. But what of her sense that quotation songs resembled Western pop music? I hope I have successfully suggested some of the underlying formal similarities between the two. I want to end this chapter by noting that quotation songs and the youth culture with which they were associated, despite the enormous gulf separating China from the capitalist West, were very much participants in what we usually understand as the global 1960s. This contemporaneity is most easily illuminated by looking at some of the pathways along which Chairman Mao—as citation, signature, and song—journeyed to the West in those same years. The global diffusion of the "Little Red Book"—translated into more than sixty-five languages by one count—is well known, as is its iconic status as a handbook for activists in locales as far-flung as Paris, Prague, Mexico City, and Berkeley. In the United States and Western Europe in particular, Maoism exercised a magnetic appeal as an alternative ideological system to capitalism. The China of the Cultural Revolution was read as a radically "other" and potentially utopian life-world. But that life-world reached the West largely by way of mass-mediated products for overseas markets distributed by Beijing's China Publications Center: the "Little Red Book," ten-inch long-playing records of revolutionary music, including "quotation songs," pictorial magazines such as *China Reconstructs*, and iconic posters of Chairman Mao.

John Lennon of the Beatles was famously dismissive of the hollowness of such radical chic in his 1968 anthem "Revolution," singing, "But if you go carrying pictures of Chairman Mao, you ain't gonna make it with anyone anyhow." It was Jean-Luc Godard, however, who sensed an underlying formal promiscuity linking Maoist iconography and late 1960s pop culture, between quotation songs and the Beatles-esque music known as "yé-yé" in French. In his prophetic 1967 film about a failed assassination plot perpetrated by an underground cell of self-styled Maoist revolutionaries in Paris, *La Chinoise*, Godard meticulously works to situate these aspiring insurgents within the cultural products they avidly consume. Whether posed in front of Chinese revolutionary posters, assiduously taking notes as they listen to the broadcasts of Radio Peking, foregrounded against shelves of European novels from Goethe's *Wilhelm Meister* to Dostoevsky's *The Possessed*, intercut with imagery from American comic books, replicating laundry detergent commercials, modeling the latest fashions, or unwittingly replaying the plot structures of Hollywood thrillers, these characters do not so much inhabit a world as a global media landscape in which revolution (and, indeed, social reality) is always already misrecognized as a form of citation, a performance.

The point is driven home in an early scene with which I will conclude this chapter. Here, Godard gives us a quotation song of his own, as performed in a distinctly "high, fast, hard, and loud" electric guitar–driven idiom by the yé-yé singer Claude Channes. As the scene begins, cued by an intertitle reading "Deuxieme Mouvement du Filme," and the song suffuses the soundtrack, the face of one of Godard's stylish would-be revolutionaries, played by Anne Wiazemski, is tightly framed in close-up, distractedly worrying a red pen. She is foregrounded against a bookshelf containing a few copies of the "Little Red Book," arranged beside an assortment of hard-bound tomes, French paperbacks, and a blurred photograph of the Chairman himself. With each successive cut, keyed to the frenetic tempo of the song, the camera shifts backward to reveal more of the room.

These are not conventional edits, however, in that with each successive cut, we cannot help but notice marked discontinuities in the mise-en-scène, as the occupants, contents, and composition of the room shift. This time, we can see the table at which the young woman and a male companion are sitting, smoking, and taking notes of Maoist dicta. To their left sits a portable phonograph—the same device the group also uses to listen to Chinese records—which is now revealed to be the source of the rock song playing in the background. On the shelves, we see the same photograph of the Chairman, but this time, a tape transcription machine looms above the image, and the other books have been pushed aside by rows of the bright red, vinyl-clad *Quotations*. In a third and final tableau, the camera draws back even further, to a medium shot in which the shelves are suddenly overwhelmed by monumental and utterly superfluous stacks of identical little red books. All the while, our heroine (who sports a different color sweater and a new hair style in each shot) and a female companion drink tea, unconscious of the seemingly uncontrollable proliferation of books behind her (see Figure 2.8).

Channes's rapid-fire lyrics echo the reduplicative logic and parodic intent of Godard's carefully constructed series of images:

Figure 2.8. *La Chinoise*, 1967.

Vietnam burns and I spurn Mao Mao . . .
Imperialism lays down the law, "revolution is not a dinner party"[59]

Mao's name and Mao's words have quite literally become the hooks in this uneasy fusion of revolutionary ethos and pop art, ideological purity and the au courant, the austerity of dogma and the pleasure of primary colors. It is the redness of the book (*le petit livre rouge*) that chimes in the song's chorus with "making it all move" (*qui fait que tout enfin bouge*), and Channes's increasingly absurd invocations of "Mao Mao" serve as an incongruously catchy sonic refrain. Mao is thus the means by which Godard reflects on the complex interactions between print, mediated sound, and the photographic image, not only in his own cinematic art but also in the unfolding of a particular historical mo(ve)ment. And Mao is also the hook with which Godard skewers his own formal contradictions, along with the utopian longings of his generation of intellectuals. Yet on this same hook hangs the possibility of a politics beyond the merely performative.

CHAPTER THREE

# Fugitive Sounds of the Taiwanese Musical Cinema

History, even the quite recent history of the 1960s, can sometimes seem fugitive, eluding our grasp and defying understanding. So I begin this chapter by considering a rare aural and material artifact of a bygone era. Plucked from amid a pile of records in a cluttered basement shop on Roosevelt Road in Taipei, it is a ten-inch LP by Kang Ding 康丁, originally released around 1967 by Wulong Records 五龍唱片, pressed in transparent red vinyl and titled *Kang Ding's Tale of Heartbreak* 康丁失戀記. There is no official archive for artifacts of this sort, only private collections, online auctions, and the rare record store or junk shop still willing to stock the material traces of an outmoded musical culture. In Taiwan, the continued existence of such ephemera is complicated by a number of factors, not least an unrelentingly humid, subtropical climate that renders the preservation of cardstock and vinyl difficult in the extreme. More important are the disregard and, sometimes, contempt to which such records—produced in the local Taiwanese language, unabashedly vulgar, comical, and sentimental, and obviously derivative of musical models imported from Japan and the United States—were subject in the years after their release.

This record has much to tell us about the relation between local cultural production and global historical moment, precisely because it seems so out of phase with the era from which it emerged. Kang Ding's record stands in for a particular moment in the late 1960s when the Taiwanese entertainment circuit I introduced in the first chapter—after a decade of prosperity—came face to face with its own mortality as a cultural form. Despite its status as the first language of the majority of the population, Taiwanese was increasingly marginalized in this period as a result of the political suppression of local culture in favor of a hegemonic Mandarin Chinese minority. Its economic viability was threatened by shifts in the pan-Chinese film market and by the rise of television as a major medium of cultural dissemination. Indeed, as we have already seen in the case of Hong Yifeng, Taiwanese pop music and cinema, produced and performed within an intermedial complex of small-scale record studios and pressing plants, poorly capitalized film production companies, local radio broadcasting stations, and cinemas, constituted something of a cottage industry, selling ephemeral pleasures on a shoestring. For this reason, the industry also relied surprisingly heavily on an island-wide circuit (in the old-fashioned sense) of live venues, through which stars like Hong Yifeng were directly patched to their public, setting up a kind of intimate feedback loop between them. By the early 1970s, however, this circuit suddenly and irrevocably shorted out, rendered obsolete by an emergent Mandarin media landscape in which television and transistorized consumer electronics, often enjoyed privately within domestic contexts, took pride of place.

In this chapter, I ask what happened when these productions began to reflect on their own imminent expiration, on their status as a fugitive cultural form. How do we make sense of the fact that the music and the movies of this period seem oddly anachronistic, even in their own time? Why is it that in watching a film from 1969 like Wen Shia's *Goodbye, Taipei*—in many ways the cinematic swan song of this cultural moment— we are almost irresistibly reminded not of the 1960s but of the "cinema of attractions" of the early twentieth century? In an age of Technicolor films, *Goodbye, Taipei* is black and white. In the absence of "classical Hollywood"-style narrative continuity, the film is constructed around a supercharged series of kinetic but essentially unmotivated Keystone Kop–style chase scenes. Characters within the diegetic space break through the fourth wall to address audiences directly with alarming and unself-conscious regularity. There are Taiwanese-style sandwich men performing Punch and Judy shows and sequences of scatological slapstick complete with low-budget special effects. This comedic business, finally, is punctuated by performances of pop songs by the male lead, the greatest pop star of the era, Wen Shia, with his all-girl band, the Four Sisters.[1] Following Evelyn Shih, I suggest that this strange and seemingly outmoded aesthetic was not so much an index of the "'failure' of the film to attain classical form" as a self-conscious affirmation of its difference from the Mandarin mainstream and of the embattled solidarity of its increasingly marginalized audiences.[2]

A deeper mystery adheres to the question of how we might read such a film (and listen to its eclectic soundtrack) against the backdrop of the global 1960s. Do these temporal anomalies reflect, following Ernst Bloch's description of uneven development in capitalist modernity, a kind of nonsimultaneity of the simultaneous?[3] The movie—and the local circuit of which it was a part—is saturated by what we now would take to be signifiers of the incandescent flash of youth cultural exuberance we tend to associate with those years. The girls in Wen Shia's band play electric guitars and wear miniskirts and pile into a minibus in hot pursuit of the bad guys. And the soundtrack fairly overflows with instrumental covers of the very latest Anglo-American pop songs, from the Beatles' "Hey Jude" and Percy Sledge's "When a Man Loves a Woman" to Blue Cheer's psychedelic rendition of "Summertime Blues." Chase scenes are propelled by the manic rhythms of surf rock and the syncopations of Memphis-style soul music and punctuated by set pieces in which the band performs Wen Shia's own renditions of the latest in Japanese *kayōkyoku* pop 歌謡曲.[4]

Yet these eclectic traces of the contemporary soundscape—transported to Taiwan by transistor radios and long-playing records—seem somewhat out of place in the context of the political and social realities of the Taiwanese 1960s. Captive to a Cold War logic that designated the island as a front line in the containment of communism and subject to the harsh authoritarian rule of the Nationalist Party, the 1960s of student movements, street protest, and antisystemic politics passed Taiwan by almost entirely. The decolonization struggles that characterized the 1960s were in Taiwan obviated by the island's decoupling from the Japanese empire by way of Taiwan's retrocession to Chinese rule in 1945. The U.S. military and economic presence in East Asia—which in Japan became the target of a vociferous popular movement throughout these years—was by and large welcomed in Taiwan as the guarantor of the island-nation's status as the bulwark of a nominal "Free China." Even rock music—often supposed to be the soundtrack of the era—arrived on the island largely as an aftereffect of the presence of U.S. military personnel in transit to the battlefields of Vietnam—as I discuss in detail in the next chapter. In other words, a notional 1960s of youth revolt and anti-imperialist struggle never took place in Taiwan. In the absence of these familiar interpretative frameworks, how should we understand the presence of the sounds of the 1960s in Taiwan's local soundscapes? Were Taiwanese-language movies (*Taiyu pian* 台語片) struggling (and failing) to catch up to the 1960s? Or was it precisely the 1960s of Cold War containment and developmental aspirations, of Green Revolution leading to rapid modernization and convulsive urbanization, of Technicolor, transistors, and television, that condemned the Taiwanese cinema to obsolescence?

How, finally, is this contradictory temporality registered in formal terms in a film like *Goodbye, Taipei*? Is the movie merely a belated or secondhand "cover" version, a second-rate imitation of globally circulating metropolitan pop cultural motifs? How do we read its reliance on outdated cinematic tropes such as the chase scene or the indiscriminate proliferation of pop tunes from Japan and the West on its soundtrack—a piracy so pervasive that not a single song can be identified as wholly "original"? I argue here that this reliance on the cover song was part and parcel of a larger cultural logic, that for stars like Wen Shia, Kang Ding, and the audiences to whom their work was addressed, any articulation of the local was of necessity global: to be Taiwanese meant to cover. The *Taiyu* films of this era self-consciously, even gleefully, turn our ready distinctions between original and copy, anterior and posterior, the pursued and pursuer, performer and public, upside down. Their fugitive sounds are not so much evidence of Taiwan's backwardness vis-à-vis a global 1960s, then, as a limit case through which we can discern Taiwan's position within the hard-wired circuitry of the Cold War order in East Asia. These short-lived cultural productions show us the "flip side" of the metropolitan 1960s, refracting its usual image in a funhouse mirror and suggesting that, contrary to the popular adage, you *can* tell a lot about a record by its cover(s).

Let's return then to the cover of *Kang Ding's Tale of Heartbreak* (see Plate 5). The image may strike us as unaccountably strange—the residue of another, indefinable time. Indeed, Kang Ding himself looks here like a kind of refugee from a familiar yet oddly illegible scenario. It's tempting and perhaps not completely off base to want to read the cover as camp—as a deliberately ridiculous or even cacophonous rifling through and recombination of a variety of period styles and cultural codes: a sombrero and a rose, cobwebs and cranes, gold lamé and electric guitar, moustache and mole. What would have united these disparate elements for a contemporary listener was Kang Ding's own persona and, in particular, his stage name. Born Zhang Xigui 張錫圭 in the southern coastal town of Lugang 鹿港 during the Japanese colonial era and schooled in the traditional Taiwanese musical form called *beiguan* 北管, Kang Ding got his start playing percussion for a local radio station but had made his way by the late 1950s into the burgeoning local film industry. There Kang Ding was christened by the first film director with whom he worked in honor of the so-called Charlie Chaplin of Mexican cinema, Cantinflas康丁法拉斯. Cantinflas was famed for playing the underdog *analfabeto* (peasant illiterate) or *pelado* (slum dweller), who despite his ignorance and bumbling demeanor invariably triumphed over adversity in the metropolis by way of his dazzlingly nonsensical and idiosyncratic verbal wit.[5]

Cantinflas's breakthrough role in Hollywood was as David Niven's comic sidekick in the 1956 blockbuster *Around the World in Eighty Days*. Playing Passepartout was also his passport to global fame, and presumably to Taiwanese screens as well.[6] While the reasoning behind Kang Ding's adoption of this persona remains shrouded in mystery, its logic, beyond the mere fact of physical resemblance, seems clear enough (see Figure 3.1). Throughout his career as a recording artist and onstage and onscreen comedian, Kang Ding played the country bumpkin from the rural south, making his way as an itinerant migrant worker in Taipei. In this, he embodied the dominant problematic of Taiwanese cultural production itself, inscribed within the persistent socioeconomic divide between the rapidly developing metropolitan north, former seat of Japanese colonial rule and since 1945 the center of Chinese Nationalist power, and the supply regions to the south, which produced rice, sugar, pineapples, camphor, timber, and other commodities for metropolitan markets. This divide, traversed over and over again in films like *Lingering Lost Love*, was also linguistic, separating an increasingly hegemonic Mandarin Chinese from the Taiwanese majority. This north–south divide was further nested within a set of seemingly intractable geopolitical divisions: not only the Cold War contest between the United States and "Red China," for which Taiwan was a militarized staging area and direct proxy, but also the KMT assertion of a muscular Chinese nationalism on an island whose modernization had come under the aegis of fifty years of Japanese colonialism. For many Taiwanese born before 1945, Japanese had been their first language of formal instruction, and, despite tight government controls on the importation of Japanese films and popular music, local cultural production continued to reflect that heritage and bear its stigmatized mark.[7]

In the realm of music, this stigma was common throughout the postwar period. As early as 1946, all writing and publication and instruction in Japanese had been halted by government decree, and listening to Japanese records was summarily banned (even if such bans were in practice unenforceable). As part of a larger campaign to promote the hegemony of Mandarin Chinese, moreover, policies were instituted to ban songbooks (1953) and Bibles Romanized in local idioms (1957) and to make even the casual or conversational use of any nonstandard speech—not only Hoklo Taiwanese but also Hakka, as well as Japanese and various aboriginal languages—in schools or in public settings a punishable offense (1956). The importation of Japanese films was subject to strict censorship, quotas, and regulation beginning in 1950 and outright proscription throughout the 1970s in the wake of the break in diplomatic relations between Japan and the Republic of China in 1972.[8] In the realm of music, the stigma took on additional weight with the advent of a KMT-sponsored "Movement for a Chinese Cultural Renaissance" in the late 1960s, conceived as a counterweight to the perceived desecration of tradition in the mainland as a result of the Great Proletarian Cultural Revolution.

Figure 3.1. (*Top*) Advertisement for a screening of Cantinflas's *El Analfabeto*, Taipei, 1967. Photograph by Tom Davenport. Courtesy of the C. V. Starr East Asian Library, University of California, Berkeley; (*bottom*) cover image of "Kang Ding's Chinese New Year Celebration" 康丁拜年, Wulong Records WL-1034, 1968.

Against this larger backdrop, the composer Huang Guolong 黃國隆 included a telling interview on the topic of popular music with the prominent French-trained musicologist Hsu Tsang-Houei in a 1969 book-length survey of the musical scene in Taiwan.[9] Hsu Tsang-Houei—who only two years previously had rediscovered what he saw as the lost "root" of Chinese folk musical culture in the figure of an impoverished *yueqin* player named Chen Da in southern Taiwan—roundly attacked the lingering taint of Japanese influence:

> The prevalence of Japanese popular song and of Japanese melodies set to Chinese lyrics must be understood as an impediment to developing a healthy Chinese national psychology. Many Japanese melodies have Japanese cultural elements as their foundation, and Japan at one time occupied Taiwan for fifty years, such that Japanese popular song already has a historical precedent here. . . . As opportunists set Japanese songs to Chinese lyrics, audiences will come to be unable to distinguish Japanese songs from songs in the national language, with the result that Taiwan province will become a "colony" for Japanese songs.[10]

In fact, Hsu Tsang-Houei's fears had already been amply realized as a result of the rapid expansion of the local record and film industries in the 1960s, and it was only in the early 1970s that a more thorough "decolonization" was enacted by heightened vigilance against Japanese imports, as well as the imposition of onerous restrictions on both live and televised performances of popular song in Hoklo, Hakka, and other "nonstandard" languages.[11]

Another representative piece of pop ephemera—a record sleeve dating from the early 1960s—speaks to the lingering hold and the hybrid cultural horizons of the linguistic practices that Hsu so deplores. Until the second half of the 1960s, the record industry in Taiwan was still a home-grown affair, geared in large part toward the production of pirated records from abroad, and most companies lacked a dedicated design or marketing department that might individuate each release. Thus many Taiwanese records were marketed in interchangeable sleeves branded not by way of a particular artist or song but by the record company's own logo. The standard sleeve for the most important record company to emerge from the pop boom of the period, Asia Records 亞洲唱片, is a case in point.[12] Asia Records was officially incorporated in 1957 in the southern city of Tainan, the antipode of Taipei and a region often understood as the traditional bastion of local culture. Its stable of stars included Wen Shia and Hong Yifeng, the two most important icons of the Taiwanese-language musical cinema, and its signature style, in large part because of Wen Shia's own efforts, evolved toward a localized fusion of melodic profiles derived from Japanese pop, Hawaiian steel guitar, horn charts reminiscent of American swing, undergirded by foxtrots, cha-chas, mambos, and other Afro-Caribbean dance rhythms, as well as the occasional local folk melody.[13]

A second and perhaps even more significant aspect of the Asia Records "sound" was an artifact of its history and its unique approach to recording practice. The company had begun as a "pirate" plant, pressing copies of Western classical and "light music" LPs. When the young proprietor of the label, a Tainan native named Cai Wenhua 蔡文華 who had a good command of technical English, decided to make the move into recording his own repertoire along with Wen Shia, the company spent the better part of a year researching the available technical literature on recording practice. Its first records, recorded on tubed equipment imported from the United States, were made in the dead of night in Cai's living room, acoustically treated by curtains, not only to improve the sound but also to ensure that no stray noises from the streets found their way inside. With the success of Wen Shia's first single, "Hawaiian Nights," Cai invested the proceeds in the construction of a dedicated recording studio.[14]

The results of this self-taught artistry are impressive indeed, reflecting an aesthetic interest in replicating through the recording medium an immediacy of connection between the singing voice and the audience. The voices of singers like Wen Shia and his label-mate Hong Yifeng are tracked front and center, in single takes without overdubs or mixing, using an RCA ribbon microphone, widely used in broadcasting since the 1930s and famous for its rich tone and almost syrupy warmth of its midrange. Ribbon microphones also benefit by the bidirectionality of their pick-up pattern, allowing them to register the relative position of various instruments and the acoustic character of the room in which they are played.[15] In Wen Shia's recordings, for this reason, Hawaiian guitar runs and the occasional trumpet solo emerge with a palpable presence and clarity, while the rest of the ten-piece band is rendered in the space behind the singers with holographic precision, reproducing the intimate spatial character of the small cabaret and theater settings in which these stars tended to perform for local audiences. In a practice long obsolete in the United States and Europe, finally, each disc was audio-captioned at the end of each side by a female voice announcing the name of the company in Taiwanese, "Asia Records," just before the needle hit the run-out grooves.

The company's reliance on the latest recording technology from the United States finds an indirect echo in its visual trademark (see Plate 6). The presence of the postwar American ascendancy is inescapable here, in the pirated image of a blonde American pinup girl playing a violin, as well

Plate 1. "March with Chairman Mao's Culture Line to Victory," 1968. Courtesy of the Ann Tompkins and Lincoln Cushing Chinese Poster Collection, C. V. Starr East Asian Library, University of California, Berkeley. Digital image courtesy of Lincoln Cushing/Docs Populi.

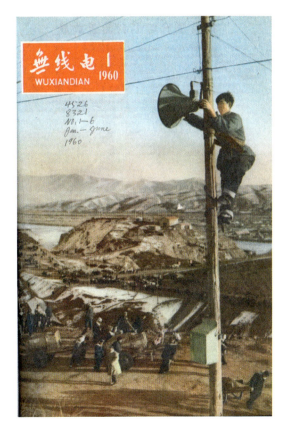

Plate 2. Installation of loudspeakers. *Wireless* 無線電 1 (1960).

Plate 3. "Bombard the Capitalist Headquarters!" Collection Stefan R. Landsberger, International Institute of Social History, Amsterdam, call nr. BG E15/125.

Plate 4: Closed circuits: Cover image from *Wireless* 無線電 10 (1966).

Plate 5. *Kang Ding's Tale of Heartbreak* 康丁失戀記, Wulong Records 009, 1967.

Plate 6. Asia Records sleeve, AL-127, 1958.

Plate 7. "Sgt Peppep's Loney Hearts Club Band" [sic] on Black Cat Records, Black Cat Record BO-4113, 1967.

Plate 8. Chen Da and Hsu Tsang-Houei circa 1970. Digital image courtesy of the Hsu Tsang-Houei Foundation.

Plate 9. Chen Da performing in September 1967. Photograph by Tom Davenport. Courtesy of the C. V. Starr East Asian Library, University of California, Berkeley.

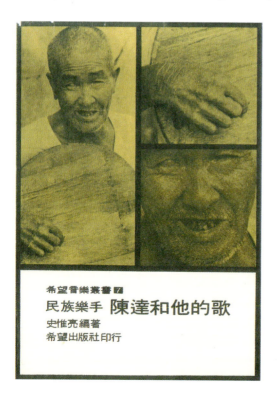

Plate 10. Cover art for the book and long-playing record *Musician of the Nation: Chen Da and his Songs* 民族樂手：陳達和他的歌 (Taipei: Hope Publishing, 1971).

Plate 11. Rural wedding, Pingtung County, September 1967. Photograph by Tom Davenport. Courtesy of the C. V. Starr East Asian Library, University of California, Berkeley.

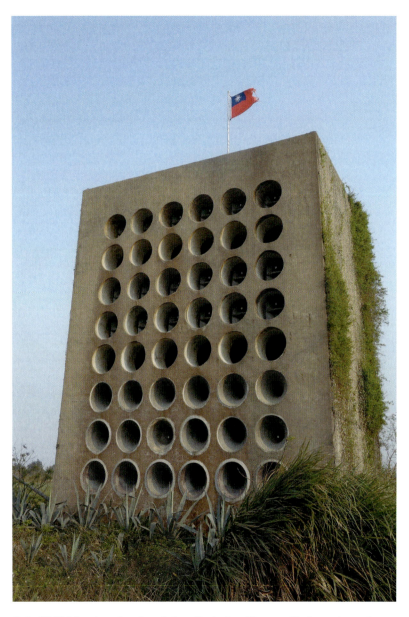

Plate 12. Beishan broadcasting station, Kuningtou, Quemoy. Photograph courtesy of the author.

as the framing of the company logo itself within an anglicized "Asian" frame. The record itself, an excellent stereo recording of the music of Wen Shia and the songstress Chi Lu-Shyia 紀露霞, however, reveals a different sort of heritage, in that seven or eight of the songs are what came to be known (and frequently attacked in the official press) as "mixed-blood music": cover versions of Japanese pop records in a mixed *enka* idiom, rewritten with Taiwanese lyrics.[16]

This idiom was a product of Wen Shia's own social provenance and musical milieu. Well off and fashion-forward, Wen Shia grew up in Tainan as the privileged scion of a prosperous tailor shop and fashion retailer, the Wenhua Fashion Store (文化洋裝店, literally "Culture Foreign Fashions"). The shop, located on Honmachi 本町(present-day Minch'uan Road 民權路), was something of a local institution, from which Wen Shia, born Wang Ruihe 王瑞河 in 1928, took his stage name, Wen Shia (read Bûn Hā in Taiyu). The moniker is a bilingual pun (in Taiyu and Japanese) on how he was addressed around town as a child—"the kid from Wen Hua," or "Bûn Hua-e" 文化へ—and the Japanese word for "culture": *bunka*. The second character in his name, "Ha" 夏, may also allude to another important aspect of his musical lineage, for as a teenager studying music in Ueno High School in Tokyo under the tutelage of Miyashita Tsuneo 宮下常雄 between 1943 and Japan's defeat in 1945, he was enraptured by the music of Hawai'i 夏威夷 and took up Hawai'ian steel guitar and ukulele. Indeed, in his first performances upon his return to Taiwan after retrocession, broadcast locally in Tainan, and later across the island, his ensemble was billed as the Bûn Hā Hawai'ian Band, and the string of successful records that followed his first release with Asia Records in 1955 included a quartet of Hawai'ian-themed ballads, shimmering with the sounds of the steel guitar: "Hawai'ian Nights" and "Hawai'ian Nocturne," "Love Longing on the Passage to Hawai'i," and "Airmail Letter from Hawai'i." The first of these records was, in fact, a faithful cover of the title track, "Hawai'i Nights" ハワイイの夜, of an eponymous 1953 Tōho 東宝 film starring the popular Japanese actor and singer Tsuruta Kōji 鶴田浩二, on whom Wen Shia seems also to have based aspects of his star image, record sleeves, and label designs, as well as his melismatic style of singing (see Figures 3.2 and 3.3).[17]

Wen Shia's Hawai'i was, of course, an imagined space, evoking not so much the tropics themselves as the prewar trans-Pacific popular musical circuit, routed through Japan, that had dominated his childhood years in colonial-era Taiwan and that continued to inform Taiwanese sensibilities even in the wake of KMT efforts to proscribe Japanese language and culture and re-sinify the island. Wen Shia's lyrical preoccupations are similarly

Figure 3.2. Cover versions: (*top*) Tsuruta Koji's 1953 "Hawai'ian Nights" ハワイの夜 on Victor, Victor V-40950; (*bottom*) Wen Shia's first 78-rpm recording for Asia Records, an original called "Drifting Girl" 飄浪之女, Asia Records A-140, 1956.

Figure 3.3. Cover versions: (*top*) Wen Shia's *Hawaiian Nights* 夏威夷之夜, Asia Records AL-116 (1957); (*bottom*) Tsuruta Kōji on the cover of *Star* magazine in 1953.

evocative of the years before civil aviation began to reroute popular music pathways. His songs are replete with steamships and passages by sea ("Darling Sailor," "The Happy Sailor," "The Sailor's Love Song," "Wen Shia's Sailor"), quay-side farewells ("First Love by the Harbor Side," "Bottoms Up by the Harbor Side," "Song of Longing by the Harbor Side"), and the mournful ambiance of rainy nights in seaport towns ("Rainy Harbor Love Song").[18] The vast majority of these compositions, moreover, are set to Japanese melodies, some dating to before the war.[19] By the late 1950s, Wen Shia had also begun to explicitly model his image after contemporary Japanese pop stars such as Kobayashi Akira 小林旭, the celebrated "guitar-toting wanderer" and husband of *enka* star Misora Hibari 美空ひばり, and the matinee idol Ishihara Yujiro 石原裕次郎.[20] Of the 202 sides Wen Shia released for Asia Records, at least 96 (and likely many more) can be confirmed as "mixed-blood" covers of Japanese songs with Taiwanese lyrics.[21] He was also responsible, under cover of his pen name Chouren 愁人 ("The Melancholic"), for composing Taiwanese lyrics for more than three hundred more "mixed-blood" songs. The insistently Japanese tinge of his music—and perhaps its implicit nostalgia for the departed colonizers—earned him the distinction of being targeted more than any other single performer for censorship by the KMT authorities. According to one study by Kuncheng Li, for instance, of the 930 songs banned over a period of nine years between 1973 and 1982 by the Government Information Office of the Executive Yuan (GIO), 99 songs were by Wen Shia (see Figure 3.4).[22]

By the late 1950s, the U.S. military presence in Taiwan was increasingly palpable as a result of the conflict on the Korean peninsula, when the island was pressed into service as an "unsinkable aircraft carrier" in the fight to contain communism in East Asia. The popularity of Wen Shia's Hawai'ian excursions were, in this sense, temporally overdetermined, evoking simultaneously nostalgia for prewar Japan and the burgeoning postwar U.S. presence. The Hawai'ian revival in the United States turned equally on the pivot of the war, driven by the servicemen who had been stationed in the Pacific theater and who brought their enthusiasm for Hawai'ian sounds and for ready-to-wear aloha shirts back to the mainland. Equally important was the concomitant postwar boom in civil aviation and jet-age tourism, especially after Hawai'i attained statehood in 1959.[23] Another sort of Pacific theater, Rodgers and Hammerstein's 1948 Broadway smash *South Pacific* (made into a blockbuster Hollywood film in 1958), also helped to spark a stateside ukulele revival, made possible by the mass marketing of inexpensively molded plastic instruments.[24]

Figure 3.4. Cover versions: (*top*) Wen Shia's *The Sailor* 文夏的行船人, Asia Records ATS-132, 1969; (*bottom*) Kobayashi Akira's *Guitar in Hand* ギター片手に, Crown Records CW-642, 1967.

Taiwan's ambiguous positioning between a new imperial formation (the United States) and its vanquished antecedent (Japan) is evident on another early Asia Records release from 1961. Amid a group of seven songs based on Japanese melodies is an exception to the mixed-blood rule: Wen Shia's crooning rendition in English and Taiwanese of "Wooden Heart," a 1960 Elvis Presley hit.[25] Originally adapted from a Swabian folk song titled "Muss I Denn" and performed partly in German, the song appears in the Technicolor musical "G.I. Blues" in which Presley plays a U.S. Occupation Duty serviceman in a defeated West Germany.[26] The popularity of the song in Taiwan was perhaps a reminder that one of the primary conduits for the entry of U.S. music was the syndication of Armed Forces Network radio in Taiwan, as well as screenings of Hollywood fare such as "G.I. Blues" and its 1961 follow-up, "Blue Hawai'i." Yet Wen Shia's cover may not be so much an homage to the "King of Cats," as Elvis was known in Chinese, as a nod to his Japanese rockabilly disciple, Sakamoto Kyu, whose cover of "G.I. Blues" lit up the Japanese charts in 1961.[27] "Wooden Heart," in this sense, was a cover of a cover of a cover.

It is in this light, perhaps, that Kang Ding's doubling of Cantinflas models something of the logic of local cultural production. Kang Ding's persona is deliberately derivative, a secondhand retailing of a Mexican *campesino* who has reached Taiwan only by virtue of his migration north to Hollywood and his concomitant entrance into its transnational distribution circuit. "Cantinflas" allows Kang Ding to move from margin to center while at the same time maintaining his marginality vis-à-vis Hollywood or, for that matter, Tokyo. He becomes a sidekick without a master, a *ronin*, or drifter 流浪漢, *Kang Ding Adrift in Taipei* 康丁遊台北, as in the title of his 1969 cinematic debut, the "global positioning" of his persona serving only to enhance the comic effect of his real calling card among Taiwanese audiences: the humorous lilt and insistently local musicality of his small-town Lugang accent.

### Goodbye, Taipei

I turn now to one of the most remarkable documents of Taiwanese film culture in the 1960s, in which Kang Ding plays a key role. Titled *Goodbye, Taipei*, the screenplay was written by Wen Shia himself, as the last of an almost decade-long series of ten films that spanned the 1960s heyday of *Taiyu pian* cinema and are collectively referred to as "Wen Shia's Drifter Chronicles" 文夏流浪記. Like each of its predecessors, the film features Wen Shia, inhabiting a persona deeply informed by the modern look and the cool sensibility of Nikkatsu Studios 日活 screen idols/pop stars such as Kobayashi Akira and Ishihara Yujiro, known for their roles as so-called Sun Tribe (太陽族) teenage rebels, yakuza fugitives, or existential wanderers (流れ者).[28] Wen Shia was accompanied in each film by a diminutive sidekick, Xiao Wang 小王, and Wen Shia's Four Sisters 文夏四姊妹, an outfit he had himself cultivated, since the early 1960s as an essential part of his repertoire and with whom he relentlessly toured the island in his trademark British-made white Ford Consul Mk. II convertible.[29] One of these young women, Wen Xiang 文香, famously became his wife, while the others—Wen Feng 文鳳, Wen Que 文雀, and Wen Ying 文鶯—went by variations of his stage name.

*Goodbye, Taipei*, as the Taiwanese scholar Liao Jinfeng has pointed out, might be said to play a pivotal role in the historiography of Taiwanese-language cinema, for it stands at the end of a remarkable run of creativity and box-office success that began in the early 1960s and came to a sudden and shocking halt by the beginning of the 1970s.[30] In 1969, 119 *Taiyu* films were produced, all in black and white, by a variety of private firms. By 1972, the figure was zero. What happened? For Liao Jinfeng, the turning point was the 1969 release of *Home Sweet Home* (literally, "At Home in Taipei" 家在台北), a splashy Technicolor film by the Italian-trained mainlander filmmaker Pai Ching-jui 白景瑞, lavishly funded by the KMT government-backed Central Motion Picture Corporation (CMPC), and touting foreign-educated, Mandarin-speaking returnees who have come back to the country from abroad to build a new export-driven developmentalism with Chinese characteristics.[31] The opening scene of *Home Sweet Home*, in which its principal characters swoop down to Songshan Airport in an airliner, seemed a symbolic swerve, wherein local, privately made films about working-class folks from the country making their way to Taipei by train or by foot are superseded by official blockbusters about a well-educated Mandarin elite, and the north-south locomotive imagery of an earlier era gives way to Taiwan's economic liftoff, buoyed by the East–West traffic of the jet age.

*Home Sweet Home* signaled not only the obsolescence of the *Taiyu* cinema but also, and perhaps more important, the consolidation of a new Mandarin circuit. In October 1969 the newly established China Television Company began to broadcast island-wide, all day long, and, for the first time, in full color, pushing black-and-white film production even further into the margins. It is important to emphasize that this obsolescence was *planned*: China Television was owned and operated by the KMT party-state, which ensured its role as a linguistic and ideological gatekeeper in the entertainment realm. These changes only brought into greater relief the undercapitalization of "dialect" cinema and its concomitant failure to make the transition to color film even as late as 1969, ten years after Grace Chang's Eastman color *Air Hostess* and six years after Hong Kong's Shaw Brothers proclaimed that Mandarin films had entered the "Color Age."[32] Production companies were unable to construct dedicated production facilities, were effectively prevented from importing color equipment and film stock from abroad, and lacked the sort of vertical integration along an industrial model that had rendered outfits like Hong Kong's Shaw Brothers Studio such a threat to local production.[33]

Perhaps most crippling, they lacked linguistic capital. For the Shaw Brothers studio, production in Mandarin became a means of expanding its transnational distribution network into Taiwan and Southeast Asia.[34] CMPC was also a participant in this Mandarin circuit, conceived by the party-state as a counterweight to compete with the Hong Kong studio at home and abroad.[35] *Taiyu* films, however, had already largely withdrawn from the (already very limited) Hokkien niche market in places like Hong Kong and Singapore and remained cut off from potential audiences in Minnanese-speaking Fujian by the Bamboo Curtain.

In short, *Taiyu pian* had begun to look like an antiquated black-and-white industry in a Technicolor world. In 1968, four local companies, including Yongxin 永新, the production company behind *Goodbye, Taipei*, put forward a proposal to join forces so as to solve the problem of vertical integration, but nothing seems to have come of the venture.[36] They were simply too far behind, in a race that was fixed from the very start. *Taiyu pian*, often seen as seedy, shoddy, and second-rate, not only were excluded from government subsidies and televisual promotion but also faced increasing scrutiny, censorship, and regulation for infractions of the official codes pertaining to motion pictures. In early 1969, theaters in more than sixteen locales were fined or shut down by authorities for screening films that had bypassed the censors by avoiding or even fabricating official permission for exhibition.[37] Kang Ding himself was charged and eventually acquitted for public indecency for a comic scene in which he was accused of playing doctor with an actress in a state of undress.[38] By April 1970, with market share waning, there was not a single cinema in Taipei showing first-run Taiwanese films.[39] *Goodbye, Taipei* indeed. In the ensuing years, the stars of *Taiyu pian* cinema were forced to make a living on the stage (despite frequently encountering difficulties securing performance permits) or to cross over into a different linguistic circuit, whether in Mandarin-language cinema or on TV.[40]

For all of these reasons, it would not be far-fetched to say that a film like *Goodbye, Taipei* was aware of its own status as an increasingly fugitive form of culture, a lowbrow form of filmmaking that was never meant to last.⁴¹ In *Goodbye, Taipei*, a frankly derivative reliance on generic conventions from elsewhere, in defiance of copyright laws and the embargo on Japanese imports, vernacularized within a distinctly local aesthetic, results in a wildly syncretic and distinctly slapstick mode of articulation.

The Taiwanese scholar Lu Feiyi has postulated a *Taiyu pian* "comedy boom" that began in 1966 and came to an end only with the senescence of nonstandard cinema itself.⁴² For Evelyn Shih, this boom provided *Taiyu pian* with a "strategy of distinction" from its Mandarin and Hollywood competitors, capitalizing on the linguistic affinities and localized knowledge of a particular audience niche to create a powerful, if also embattled, sense of in-group affiliation.⁴³ Central to this strategy, as Shih shows in a close reading of another 1969 film called *Zhang Di Seeks A-Zu*, is a campy tendency toward "crossing" or 反串 as "a mode of cinematic address"— understood not just in its original sense of female-to-male cross-dressing in traditional operatic genres such as *koa-a-hi* 歌仔戲 but also as a knowing transgression of the boundaries between the diegetic world within the film and the social world outside it.⁴⁴ In casting the *koa-a-hi* opera star Yang Lihua 楊麗花, famed for playing male roles on the stage as a country girl, and the stylish Mandarin dance hall performer Zhang Di 張帝 against type (as a country girl and a *Taiyu* troubadour, respectively) and across genres, the film generates a campy self-consciousness among audiences familiar with the extra-diegetic world the film overturns. In other words, these crossings create a sense of being in on the joke together. Often, this form of cinematic address crosses not just boundaries of language, genre, and gender but also the line between performers and spectators so crucial to the generic conventions of classical Hollywood cinema. *Zhang Di Seeks A-Zu* 張帝找阿珠 ends as the reunited lovers break the fourth wall, waving goodbye to their audience as they move across the frame on a motorcycle.⁴⁵

*Goodbye, Taipei* opens with a similar scene, one that brings irresistibly to mind Tom Gunning's oft-invoked notion of the cinematic "attraction." What Gunning has in mind is how early cinema often called direct and insistent attention to its own magic as a medium, rather than allowing spectators to lose themselves in the narrative continuity of an immaculately constructed diegetic world. This foregrounding of the film's visibility as film is achieved through the "recurring look at the camera by the actors . . . establishing contact with the audience."⁴⁶ In *Goodbye, Taipei*, after an initial tableau in which we are invited to watch from an oblique angle as Wen Shia plays his guitar in a pastoral setting, we cut to a tightly framed, full-frontal shot as he gazes back at us and begins to speak: "Ladies and gentlemen, I am Wen Shia. Thank you for coming to see my movie today. . . . This is my tenth film." What follows is a ten-minute-long sequence in which Wen Shia offers his viewers a lengthy summary of each of his preceding nine films. What is particularly interesting about this sequence and its formal construction is the way in which Wen Shia has pressed the film into service as a kind of intermedial archive. With the introduction of each film, beginning in 1962 with his first production, *Taipei Nights* 台北之夜, and onto the movie he claims as the first "*Taiyu* western," *High Plains Drifter* 高原遊俠 (1963), the camera lingers over a series of paper ephemera: production stills, newspaper clippings, posters, and snapshots from Wen Shia's personal collection.[47] There is even, in the case of his *Taiyu* take on the martial arts genre, *Drifter with a Sword* 流浪劍王子 (1967), an embedded clip from the original film, showing to spectacular effect the kaleidoscopic camera tricks used in the shooting of its climactic sword battle. This is cinema serving self-consciously as a scrapbook or even a shrine, a display of mediated memories shared between an embattled industry and its increasingly marginalized audience, suspending fragments of earlier films and, with them, a fleeting cultural moment in celluloid amber. And while Wen Shia could not possibly have known this at the time of production, *Goodbye, Taipei* was in fact the only film of the ten destined to survive.

We owe the making of this extraordinary sequence to the fact that the original running time of *Goodbye, Taipei* was ten minutes short.[48] Its survival was also serendipitous: a fire tore through the warehouse in which the masters for the first nine films were stored, but, happily, a different company had been responsible for striking release prints of *Goodbye, Taipei*. In another sense, however, the loss of the earlier films was not accidental at all. It was instead linked to the shoestring economics and limited scale of the *Taiyu pian* circuit and the particularities of its exhibition practices. At any given time, only two or three prints of Wen Shia's films would be in circulation. Damaged prints were discarded; new copies struck only as needed. And very few were needed, because Wen Shia and the Four Sisters appeared live in concert *as part of each and every screening of the film*. This promotional ploy meant that with the release of each film, Wen Shia and his entourage would go on tour, circling the island to visit the cinemas that made up the exhibition circuit for *Taiyu pian*. In Taipei, their daily itinerary resembled nothing so much as a mad relay race. As Wen Shia took the stage to greet his fans after a matinee at the Da Guangming Theater 大光明戲院 in the old-town district of Dadaocheng 大稻埕, for instance, a second print would be dispatched to the Daguan Theater 大觀戲院 in neighboring Bangka 艋舺. Wen Shia and the band would then hop into his Consul convertible—equipped with a portable loudspeaker to advertise the film along the way—and set up just in time to perform between screenings. As they played live versions of several songs from the soundtrack, the print would be dispatched to its next destination, the Jianguo Theater 建國戲院 in the industrial suburb of Sanchongpu, to which Wen Shia would be obliged once again to hasten in time for the next show. And because each of the three theaters ran six daily screenings, Wen Shia would run this steeplechase from morning until night, sometimes playing more than a dozen times a day.[49]

This exhibition practice—referred to in Chinese as "running the venues" 跑場 and not uncommon on the *Taiyu pian* circuit, although Wen Shia seems to have pioneered its use—seems at first blush to stand Gunning's "cinema of attractions" on its head. Wen Shia's presence itself became the "real" attraction, drawing spectators into the public space of the cinema. This reversal, in which the cinematic image was not only supplemented but in some sense superseded by the physicality of a live performer, seems to echo the role of the *benshi* 弁士 or film narrator in the silent era in Japan and colonial Taiwan.[50] *Benshi* served not only as commentators but also as linguistic and cultural mediators, translating Hollywood slapstick and Japanese melodrama alike into local idioms and mute images into audible verbal commentary and sound effects. As Wen Shia himself has attested—he was an inveterate filmgoer during the colonial era, enamored of Charlie Chaplin and Laurel and Hardy—the *benshi*'s performance not infrequently became the main attraction, insistently calling attention to its own ingenuity and affective power.[51] Doubling as a modern-day *benshi* in the course of these promotional appearances, Wen Shia also became, in effect, a doppelganger of his cinematic self. The cinematic Wen Shia, in turn, alluded to Wen Shia's imminent presence in the theater by deliberately breaking through the barrier of the screen, thus setting into motion a knowingly recursive feedback loop that, in the end, could only amplify his intimacy with the audience in the theater.

Wen Shia's breathless steeplechase through the streets of Taipei, in turn, is replicated by the funny, frenetic, and relentlessly kinetic series of musical interludes, comic pratfalls, and chase sequences that unfold onscreen. While the opening sequence meditatively catches the audience up with Wen Shia's cinematic past, the film that follows hardly seems able to catch up to itself. The plot, such as it is, lends itself well to this fugitive temporality. Wen Shia and the diminutive Xiao Wang, arriving on foot in metropolitan Taipei from the countryside, come across a newspaper ad promising a reward for locating Ah-Mei, the long-lost granddaughter of a dying tycoon, played by an incongruously youthful Kang Ding. Wandering the city, they rescue a young shoeshine boy called Tailong 泰隆 from a group of bullies. Tailong begins to tag along. Xiao Wang catches sight of a girl selling flowers in front of the newly built high-rise Hotel Hawaii. She's a dead ringer for the missing granddaughter. When Wen Shia steps out to buy her a new dress in preparation to claiming the NT$500,000 reward, the little group is abducted by a pair of comic sandwich men who are also out for the money. A series of antics and extended chase scenes follows. First, Xiao Wang and Tailong manage to give their captors the slip by crowning one of them with a chamber pot and wind up playing a game of cat-and-mouse with their pursuers in a factory warehouse piled high with sacks of cement. Later, Wen Shia and his retinue engage in a high-octane, high-speed automotive chase down a country road in pursuit of the sandwich men, who still have Ah-Mei (and thus the promise of the coveted $500,000 reward) in their custody. Ditching their respective vehicles by a riverside, the Four Sisters, in matching white miniskirts, proceed to pelt and be pelted by the bad guys with a spectacular barrage of mud balls until victors and vanquished alike dissolve into good-natured laughter, along with any pretense that the pursuit was in any way necessary to the narrative continuity of the film. And soon after Ah-Mei has been "rescued," we are given a final revelation. As the street urchin Tailong readies himself for bed and Xiao Wang secretly looks on, we see his face framed from behind in the bathroom mirror. He takes off the Tokyo Giants cap that has been his visual trademark throughout, alluding not only to Wen Shia's Japanese affinities but also to a surreptitious cross-lingual pun: what sounds like Tailong in Mandarin is actually Tailang 太郎 in Taiwanese, or Taro, *the* archetypal Japanese boy's name, popular in the prewar period but later proscribed.[52] We soon learn that Taro, whose long hair proceeds to tumble out from under the cap, is actually a girl. In a further revelation, she takes off her shirt, exposing an oval birthmark on her back, shaped a little like the island of Taiwan, which identifies her as the real Ah-Mei. In a final close-up, she turns, winks, and smiles conspiratorially directly at the camera, without the mediation of the mirror (or, by implication, the cinematic apparatus), simultaneously acknowledging our voyeurism and the audience's complicity in her secret identity (see Figure 3.5).

At this point, of course, we realize that we have been chasing the wrong girl all along and that the movie has been chasing its own tail. The prominence of the chase sequences in the film is yet another way in which it resembles the early cinema of attractions, in that the chase allowed filmmakers to show off the kinetic quality of the medium. As the film historian Jonathan Auerbach has argued, the chase film became one of the earliest cinematic genres in the first decade of the twentieth century, characterized by a "self-conscious emptying of content in order to foreground sheer

Figure 3.5. Taro's true identity revealed. Stills from *Goodbye, Taipei*, 1969.

motion."⁵³ In a 1903 film like the Biograph production *The Escaped Lunatic*, the repetitive motion of the lunatic and his pursuers across eight minutes of unremitting action ultimately proves futile in narrative terms. The lunatic returns unharmed to his cell of his own volition, and we realize that the film's only rationale is to show "bodies in motion," bodies that analogize the constant motion of the cinematic mechanism itself.⁵⁴ Chase scenes, in crosscutting between the pursuer and the pursued, keep the narrative engine going, regardless of the destination.⁵⁵

In the context of *Taiyu pian*, the forward motion of the mechanism is not merely self-reflexive. Instead, it must be read in terms of questions of social and geographic mobility, be it up or down.⁵⁶ This, of course, is also the case in early cinema and American melodrama, as Ben Singer reminds us. For Singer, the chase, with its antic movement across busy urban streetscapes fraught with danger for fragile human bodies, replicates in haptic terms the sensations and the shock of modern city life.⁵⁷ Here, Singer draws directly on the insights of Walter Benjamin in his "On Some Motifs in Baudelaire":

> Moving through traffic involves the individual in a series of shocks and collisions. At dangerous intersections, nervous impulses flow through him in rapid succession, like the energy from a battery. . . . Whereas Poe's passers-by cast glances in all directions which still appeared to be aimless, today's pedestrians are obliged to do so in order to keep abreast of traffic signals. Thus technology has subjected the human sensorium to a complex kind of training. There came a day when a new and urgent need for stimuli was met by the film. In a film, perception in the form of shocks was established as a formal principle. That which determines the rhythm of production on a conveyor belt is the basis of the rhythm of reception in a film.⁵⁸

The "day" of which Benjamin writes was precisely a moment of transition in which formerly rural populations arrived in the city, acclimatizing themselves to its routines of industrial labor, to the spills of street life and the thrills of commodified urban leisure. This transit was precarious, of course. The body is vulnerable. What goes up must come down, and the cinematic gag, often premised on the implacable working of gravity, mirthfully figured the body's subjection to the "crazy machine" of modern life.⁵⁹ Money is the best guarantor of upward mobility and the best cushion in case of a fall. It is hardly an accident, as Singer argues, that the plots that fueled early melodramatic serials were organized almost exclusively around the manic and competitive pursuit of profit, in the form of a "coveted material object," prize, reward, or some other sort of windfall.⁶⁰

Similarly, the chase scenes in *Goodbye, Taipei*—the very title of which anxiously invokes Taiwan's urban-rural divide—revolve around the coveted figure of Ah-Mei, whose birthmark promises a substantial financial reward. The constant motion of Wen Shia and his associates across the thoroughfares of a city, then in the midst of convulsive growth, also suggest the immediacy of metropolitan life, as well as its cinematic mediation. In one sequence, starting twenty-five minutes into the action, we follow Wen Shia for two and a half minutes as he goes in search of his fortune, from the rapidly developing east side to the west. The sequence begins as Wen Shia, his guitar slung behind his back like a sword, strolls down a newly constructed and eerily empty boulevard toward the bustling Taipei Station, where we see new arrivals disgorged from the exits and into the perilous automotive gyre of a traffic circle. As Wen Shia proceeds to climb the steps of a pedestrian overpass, the camera zooms out into a high-angle long shot from below, so that he and Xiao Wang are suddenly dwarfed by the enormous movie posters that dominate the marquee behind them. Arriving at Hsimenting 西門町, the center of Taipei's cinema-going and cabaret culture since the Japanese colonial era, the camera suddenly cranes skyward, tracking the constant flow of pedestrians in the street from a vantage point several stories up and flattening the picture plane so that Wen Shia and Xiao Wang are lost in the crowd.

The mournfully old-fashioned foxtrot on the soundtrack, Wen Shia's "The Lost Girl" 流浪的小姐, simultaneously inscribes these seemingly unmotivated city scenes within the plot of the film and situates its melodramatic plot within a larger social frame, that of rural–urban migration:

> Wandering night after night across the lonely streets
> Only in search of that girl from the south
> Although I don't even know her name
> Her smile lingers in my heart
> Ah! That girl for whom I'm longing
> Ah! That dear Taiwanese girl

Migrancy here is denoted by the Chinese word for "drifting" or 流浪—a complex term that connotes both an unmooring from the matrix of family and native place and an adventurous yet perilous navigation across a wider world—the "rivers and lakes" of the martial arts mythos. It is a word that frames Wen Shia's ten-part cinematic project as a whole, "Wen Shia's Drifter Chronicles," and makes countless appearances in his lyrics. In this sense, it is difficult not to see this sequence as a kind of cipher of a historically specific lyricism, compounded in equal parts of aspiration, alienation, loss, and a nameless longing and projected onto the urban space of

Taipei. Wen Shia's drifter, like the urban scene itself, is self-consciously cinematic, unmistakably echoing Chaplin's Tramp, while transposing the generic conventions of the swordsman film onto the experience of the new arrivals from the rural South.

This pursuit through "lonely streets" inevitably involves a sense of loss and anteriority. Were the rural and working-class drifters to whom the film was pitched forever playing a futile game of catch-up? It is certainly suggestive that the film's action is initiated by another long walk: a three-and-a-half-minute sequence during which we amble along with Wen Shia and his sidekick down a country road on their way to the city. The sequence culminates with a close-up of the sign marking the city limits of "Taipei," where the iconic (and now rebuilt) Taipei Bridge crosses the Tamsui River into town. This is, of course, a route that mimics that of hundreds of thousands of rural–urban migrants who poured into the city's shanties and industrial suburbs throughout the 1960s.[61] The final shot of the film? To the accompaniment of "Wen Shia's Whirlwind," a song about a drifter making his way through the world with only the guitar on his back and a dream, Wen Shia and Xiao Wang walk down the median, precariously stranded between two speeding lanes of automobile traffic, and, in a provisional moment of triumph, wave good-bye not only to their viewers but to the titular city itself (see Figure 3.6).

### Fugitive Sounds

This sense of always playing catch-up extends to the formal logic of the soundtrack, which sounds at first blush like an outdated hodgepodge of foreign covers. Close listening, however, reveals a telling division of musical labor throughout the film, one that limns the geopolitical position of Taiwanese music in the 1960s. The nondiegetic music is entirely of Anglo-American origin, while the set pieces in which Wen Shia and the Four Sisters perform at regular intervals are Taiwanese covers of the latest and grooviest numbers from the Japanese hit parade. This is unsurprising given Wen Shia's fluency in Japanese: he made a career of precisely this sort of transposition of the latest Japanese styles into the local pop scene.

The consequences of this division for our reading of the film, however, are far-reaching. The Anglo-American numbers that saturate the film and lend it a sense of period atmosphere are exclusively instrumentals. Even when the soundtrack follows the contours and psychedelic timbres of the original records quite closely, such as in the rendition of Blue Cheer's "Summertime Blues" that drives an extended chase scene in a cement factory warehouse, the vocal parts have been excised. These songs, moreover,

Figure 3.6. *Goodbye, Taipei*, 1969.

drift free of their semantic content and even of the generic associations, ideological underpinnings, and geographical moorings (soul and African American city life, surf music and southern California, psychedelia and San Francisco) that bind them to their original context. The Ventures' "Mexico" accompanies a brisk walk down a Taipei boulevard; an ersatz version of "Hey Jude" backgrounds a scene in a café—yet neither title seems to have any relation to the narrative situation onscreen. They are quotations taken out of context, fugitive soundscapes signifying nothing. Characteristically, these songs were dubbed onto the soundtrack not from the original records and not from live performances in the studio but from Taiwanese "light music" 輕音樂 records on which they had been covered as instrumentals. Wen Shia's Four Sisters, in turn, would learn to cover these covers note for note from the records so that they could perform them in the process of promoting the film.[62]

For a viewer familiar with this repertoire, the effect is jarring, even a little uncanny. For contemporary *Taiyu pian* audiences, however, the vast majority of whom would not have been proficient in English, these non-diegetic and extra-linguistic sounds functioned as another kind of "attraction," keyed precisely and with premeditation to the tempo of the action on screen, mimicking the motion of the actor's bodies and modeling the kinds of affect they evoke. As Scott Curtis has suggested, this "close matching of sound and image," sometimes referred to as "mickey-mouseing" because of its origins in Disney cartoons, can be understood as a kind of isomorphism.[63] Sound and image take on the same rhythmic shape, and onscreen objects appear to "'come alive' to the beat of the music"—hence the association between isomorphic sound and animation.[64] The manic guitar fills of the Ventures' "Pipeline" become an analogue to the quick crosscuts of the car chase, while the syncopated strut of the Bar-Kays' 1966 "Soul-finger" precisely matches both the loping gait and the cool self-regard with which Wen Shia and Xiao Wang stroll into the city in the opening minutes of the film.[65] Anglo-American pop music, in this sense, animates Wen Shia, lending live action a certain cartoon-like affect, while bringing local cinema into close synchrony with metropolitan rhythms.

If Anglo-American covers function outside the linguistic realm, Wen Shia's covers of Japanese pop songs are pointedly, even poignantly, semantic. Indeed, these hybrid songs work as meta-commentary not only on the unfolding of the film's plot but also on the position of Taiwanese cultural production vis-à-vis the metropole. This meta-commentary, moreover, is accessible only to an in-group aware of the provenance of the music. The first hint of this semantic function comes soon after we have been introduced to Tailong/Taro but before he has been revealed, in a plot twist playing on the gender-bending typical of Taiwanese *koa-a-hi* opera, to be a "she" who has cleverly concealed her long hair beneath a hat. In the following scene, Wen Shia returns to his studio just as the Four Sisters are performing a cover of "The Season of Love" 恋の季節, a one-hit wonder by a band called Pinky and Killers that topped the Japanese charts for seventeen weeks in 1968. What is significant about this choice is that Pinky was famous for performing the song on Japanese television—fetchingly cross-dressed in a black suit and a bowler hat, backed by an all-male band in matching attire (see Figure 3.7).[66]

This cover of "The Season of Love" not only draws on the audience's extra-cinematic knowledge of the Japanese pop scene, foreshadowing the revelation that Taro has been covering up her true identity, but also adumbrates the logic of the film's denouement. As you may recall, Tailong/Taro bears the birthmark that identifies her as the "real" Ah-Mei. Yet, when the two young women are presented to an ailing Kang Ding by the rival claimants to the reward, we realize that they are, in fact, identical twins. Kang

Figure 3.7. "The Season of Love" 恋の季節, King Records BS-865, 1968.

Ding, leaping from his deathbed, enfolds them both in a greedy embrace and leers directly at the camera. What is interesting here—besides the rather characteristic tonal uncertainty, in which filial piety and a family reunion are played for laughs in a manner dangerously suggestive of lechery and even incest—is the film's ultimate lack of interest in separating the real girl from the fake. As with Kang Ding's own dual persona, the distinction between the cross-dressing granddaughter and her doppelganger collapses. Indeed, this uncanny proliferation of doubles and a gleeful failure to distinguish between real and fake, authentic and counterfeit, original and cover, is central to film's aesthetic and its embrace of its own marginality. Wen Shia is replicated by his sidekick in a matching suit jacket, Xiao Wang. Wen Shia's "four sisters"—who aren't really his sisters—come in two neatly matched pairs. The sandwich men who compete with Wen Shia

Figure 3.8. "A World Just for the Two of Us" 世界は二人のために, Victor Records SV-568, 1967.

Figure 3.9. "A World Just for the Two of Us." Stills from *Goodbye, Taipei*, 1969.

for the prize, played by the comedic duo Tuo Xian 脫線 and Qiu Wangshe 邱罔舍, are dead ringers for each other and hardly seem like villains at all. Xiao Wang, played by a dwarf, looks like a child, while Kang Ding, a young man, is made into a doddering old codger. The two Ah-Meis, finally, are played by a pop duo called the Phoenix Sisters 雙鳳姊妹, identical twins whose presence in Wen Shia's entourage inspired the plot in the first place.[67]

In the penultimate sequence, immediately after Kang Ding has adopted both of the young women into his own fictive family, we are regaled with a musical coda in which all of these duplications and duplicities are simultaneously put on display and dissolved. Shot in Wen Shia's living room at home in Tainan, the sequence features a cover of Sagara Naomi's 佐良直美 1967 hit, "A World Just for the Two of Us" 世界は二人のために, with its melodic hook played on a Hawaiian lap steel guitar.[68] This selection, of all songs, represents yet another doubling and, as such, a knowing nod at his audience. For Sagara Naomi, a fixture in the Japanese pop firmament, was famed not only for her richly expressive voice but for her tomboyish looks and her tendency to dress in drag (see Figure 3.8).[69]

As we reach the song's refrain, the camera lingers over the twins, now unmistakably feminine in matching miniskirts, as they strum their electric guitars. The image seems to imply that they are the pair to whom "the world" of the lyric has been promised. Soon the camera tracks across the room, pausing for close-ups of Wen Shia and the Four Sisters, who smile directly into the lens. As the camera pulls out for a shot deep enough to include the whole room, Kang Ding and Xiao Wang start to dance and clown for the camera, the band dissolves into laughter, and we realize that the song's lyrical address is, after all, collective — that the fleeting world being celebrated belongs not only to Wen Shia's little band of outsiders and misfits but to its dispossessed Taiwanese audiences as well (see Figure 3.9).

CHAPTER FOUR

# Pirates of the China Seas

Vinyl Records and the Military Circuit

Perhaps no film captures the contradictions of Taiwan's Cold War culture better than director Pai Ching-jui's 白景瑞 1972 Mandarin melodrama, *Love in a Cabin* 白屋之戀. A cannily commercial film produced by the state-sponsored Central Motion Picture Corporation (CMPC), the film is shot through with the sounds, stylized emblems, and emancipatory aspirations of the youth culture of the 1960s. Its story of a young and independent woman's innocent and ill-fated rebellion against "square" society is suffused by an almost palpable euphoria, a utopian sense of sexual and social liberation for which the pop records suffusing the soundtrack become both an adjunct and a kind of analogy. Yet the film as a whole is also notable for its persistently dysphoric undertone of dread and paranoia, amply borne out by its violent denouement, in which our heroine, having been tricked by her own family into marrying her vindictive and conniving cousin, is beaten, bound, and gagged for her refusal to repudiate her true love and abort the illegitimate baby she's bearing. Her lover, in despair and unaware that she's being held captive against her will, crashes his motorcycle into the side of the cabin they had once shared.

*Love in a Cabin* was a major success, inaugurating a series of over-the-top melodramas—most adapted from the romance fiction of the best-selling author Chiung Yao 瓊瑤—pitting star-crossed lovers against the cruelty of an unreasoning patriarchy. How might we read a film like *Love in a Cabin*, insistently pitched on a domestic and romantic register, in terms of the larger geopolitical fractures of the Cold War–era out of which the film emerged? Do the social strictures against which our young lovers struggle analogize a more pervasive logic of containment? How do the nominal 1960s—that chimerical decade of generational revolt, of antisystemic and anticolonial protest, of mass movements and mass media, play out on an island at the periphery of the world-system and yet smack on the front lines of the Cold War contest in East Asia? What conditions of possibility allowed the flotsam of 1960s youth culture to wash up on Taiwan's shores, and how were these fragments salvaged, reproduced, redistributed, remade, and refracted through the particularity of its position in global circuits? How do the notional 1960s come to inhabit (or even haunt) a film like *Love in a Cabin*, and might it be possible to read their traces as more than merely phantasmal, incidental, or derivative?

In some sense, these questions are counterintuitive, precisely because the 1960s as they are usually narrated never happened in Taiwan. By August 1972, when *Love in a Cabin* was released to screens in Taipei, Chiang Ching-kuo 蔣經國, the Soviet-trained architect of the Republic of China's extensive and fiercely repressive security apparatus, had just assumed a position as premier of the Republic. Martial law, first imposed in the wake of the February 28, 1947, insurgency against Chinese Nationalist carpetbagging and misrule, continued unabated, underwritten by the ongoing "emergency" of Taiwan's proximity to "Red China" and its status as a bulwark of the U.S. security umbrella in East Asia. The political mobilization and revolutionary enthusiasms of the Red Guard movement just across the Taiwan straits were equally anathema. As Ma Shih-fang has argued, Taiwan seemed in the late 1960s to exist at an unfathomably distant remove from these hot spots across the sea; Taipei teenagers might listen to Simon and Garfunkel's "The Sound of Silence" on their transistor radios but remained voiceless.[1] Street protests were an impossibility; discursive boundaries were carefully policed through state censorship of print and other media, and the question of decolonization (whether directed toward U.S. neocolonial clientelism or against the political, economic, and cultural dominance of the KMT in Taiwan) was taboo. Even the external signifiers of 1960s style were targeted by the state: beginning in 1966, police officers were empowered to trim the locks of long-haired youth enamored of the Beatlesesque "a-go-go" sound, and even as late as 1973 the international airport reportedly sported a banner proclaiming that the Republic of China did not welcome hippies.[2]

Small wonder, then, that the space of emancipation in *Love in a Cabin* is limited to the realm of the apolitical and the personal. Indeed, the titular wooden hillside "cabin" 白屋 that is home to our young heroine, an aspiring entertainment correspondent named Cheng Ling (played by Chen Chen 甄珍), is an almost entirely fanciful space, an impossible luxury for an unmarried young woman at the time, located at an unspecified and rustic remove from both socioeconomic exigency and the dense social and architectural fabric of the then rapidly modernizing city of Taipei. The defiantly free-spirited Cheng Ling's improbable room of her own is endowed by the film's set designers with a certain rough-hewn hippie charm. Iconic images of James Dean and Brigitte Bardot adorn the walls next to cut-out collages of images from American magazines, patterned textiles, and primitive, hand-carved folkloric statuettes. Modern appliances (including a miniature transistor TV set and a refrigerator stocked with Coca-Cola) are arranged atop hand-painted cinderblocks. It is here that Cheng Ling brings the handsome Taekwondo competitor and National Taiwan University student Chung Ing-ssu (played by the Hong Kong heartthrob Alan Tang 鄧光榮), several years her junior, after they meet by fortuitous accident outside a movie theater and here that they flirt and fall in love.

At the heart of the cabin, on a wooden loft above the main room, is a record player, and next to the record player are several shelves of LPs. The film foregrounds the stereo system repeatedly, almost as if to say: if music is the medium of love, then the material substrate of courtship is vinyl. During Chung's first visit to the cabin, Cheng Ling plays him her "favorite record"—and the camera allows us visual access to an eclectic selection of titles, from Johnny Cash's "A Man in Black," to easy-listening orchestral pop covers of contemporary hits by Ray Conniff ("Bridge over Troubled Water," 1970) and The Percy Faith Strings ("Today's Themes for Young Lovers," 1967), to Cream's 1967 psych-rock classic "Disraeli Gears" (see Figure 4.1). The consummation of their mutual passion is propelled by a record as well: a proto-disco cover version of the Spanish beat band Los Bravos' 1967 global hit, "Black Is Black," to which the candle-lit pair dance with a physicality and a sensual abandon seldom seen in the Chinese-language cinema of that era. The ensemble of techniques Pai utilizes in this scene—including handheld camera, soft focus, psychedelic color filters, and a slow-motion, extreme low-angle shot of their leap into each other's embrace—not only registers the contemporaneity of Pai's period style but also serves to immerse the audience in an affective, kinetic, and erotic "high."

The Italian-trained Pai, a cinéaste whose tendency toward self-reflexive formal experimentation with technique often ran up against the constraints of the officially sanctioned "healthy realist" style of the CMPC studios, was acutely aware of contemporary developments beyond Taiwan.[3] In what comes to read as a portent of Chung's fate, the film begins *in media res* with a series of rapid-fire grainy images of the now famous chase scene from *The French Connection*, in which Gene Hackman (playing an amoral narcotics detective named "Popeye" Doyle) careens through the gritty streets of Brooklyn in pursuit of a heroin smuggler escaping on an out-of-control elevated subway train. Hackman's car smashes recklessly through a series

Figure 4.1. *Love in a Cabin*, 1972.

of street-level obstacles; meanwhile, the French heroin smuggler mercilessly opens fire on a transit officer in the subway train above. Suddenly, we cut to Cheng Ling, whose enjoyment of the film, much to her annoyance, is interrupted at just this crucial moment by a visual paging system, common in Taiwanese theaters at the time, advising her that someone is waiting for her outside the auditorium.[4] Chung, it turns out, has attempted to page a male friend who shares the same name as our heroine, and this fortuitous coincidence sets their romance into motion.

Pai's framing of his own melodramatic material in terms of *The French Connection* is self-reflexive in a number of ways, for it not only adumbrates the film's violent denouement but also suggests the way in which it—like the profoundly nihilist *policier The French Connection*—will end up playing against generic type. For much as *The French Connection* relentlessly undermines the ethical distinction between cops and criminals, Pai subverts the patriarchal order so central to previous CMPC romantic dramas, revealing the Confucian family as, quite literally, a space of bondage and violent domination. Even more interesting, this gritty window onto another filmic world throws into immediate relief Taiwan's distance from Hollywood and U.S. popular culture, as well as the authoritarian restrictions under which local cinema labored. The film that *The French Connection* bested in 1971 for Best Picture honors at the Academy Awards, Stanley Kubrick's *A Clockwork Orange*, was banned in Taiwan because of its portrayal of youthful "ultra violence."[5] Nor did *The French Connection* arrive in Taipei untouched by censorious scissors. As one commentator reported, not without irony, local filmgoers questioned how the film could have won an Academy Award for best editing, since the copy shown in Taipei had been edited such that "the gaps left the audience unable to grasp the development of the narrative, even to the point of perplexity."[6] If, the article continues, films must be "repaired" to conform with "our national conditions," such emendations should be carried out artfully and particularly skillful censors recognized with an Oscar for "Best Cutting"! Pai, in this sense, has artfully "smuggled" a glimpse of another kind of filmic pleasure into his own melodramatic star vehicle, at the same time sardonically reminding Taiwanese spectators that the world outside can be apprehended only secondhand, in mediated fragments, and in forms neither authentic, uninterrupted, nor uncut.

Just as these opening shots are a kind of self-conscious reflection on the contraband character of globally circulating popular culture in the context of an authoritarian Taiwan, the records shown in the film are also clearly pirated. Cheng Ling's extensive collection bears all the marks of the ubiquitous local copies of vinyl long-playing records that, by the late 1960s, had rendered the island notorious as a safe harbor for copyright scofflaws. As Cheng Ling selects a record, we see behind her an example of the tinted vinyl favored by many of the island's forty-five some-odd pirate pressing plants, as well as a variety of mimeographed covers, locally rebranded and wrapped in clear plastic sleeves. We can even hear the pops and clicks typical of second-generation copies of American originals as Cheng Ling drops the needle onto her favorite song.

Just as *Love in a Cabin* occludes, of commercial and ideological necessity, the larger political situation of authoritarianism in which its drama is nested, we can read pirate records as material ciphers of the Cold War circuitry out of which they were produced. On one level, as Cheng Ling's portable record player attests, Taiwan's industrial economy had already begun to move up the import substitution ladder by the late 1960s, becoming a major site for original equipment manufacturers (OEM) of transistorized electronics for U.S. and Japanese firms, as well as developing its own branded consumer appliances. The development of Taiwan's pirate record industry, as I will expand upon later, was also crucial to this developmental process. Indeed, "piracy," although routinely stigmatized by recording industry associations, copyright watchdogs, lawmakers, and music critics both in Taiwan and abroad, was the very condition of possibility for the development of not only Taiwan's industrial capacity but also a consumer market for locally produced popular music. And without pirate records, the pop genres that emerged in Taiwan in the late 1970s, particularly campus folk, with its epochal and anticolonial call to "sing our own songs," would have been unthinkable.

**Pirate History**

"To write a complete history of piracy from its earliest days would be an impossible undertaking," Phillip Gosse reminds us in his pioneering 1932 account of buccaneers, corsairs, and maritime marauders, for "it would begin to resemble a maritime history of the world."[7] Tracing the history of Taiwanese pirate records is a similarly quixotic task, in that it encompasses a complex industrial history dating back to the Japanese colonial era and extending into the postwar period.[8] That local story, moreover, must also be apprehended in its global dimensions. Piracy, by definition, shadows above-board in-state and interstate commerce, mimics prevalent modes of production, moves opportunistically along existing trade routes, and trespasses geopolitical borders to exploit their loopholes and profit from their gradients.

More daunting still, as Gosse rather dryly points out, the "great difficulty which confronts the pirate historian is the diffidence shown by his heroes in recording their own deeds."[9] Documentation of industrial processes and distribution networks is hard to come by, informal, and incomplete—especially for a sector for which the "primitive accumulation" of capital and technical know-how was tightly linked to what are often seen as nefarious practices of questionable legality. Even more interesting for the purposes of this chapter, the proximate cause of record piracy, not only in Taiwan but also in locales such as South Korea, was the massive presence of U.S. military installations dedicated to the containment of communism in East and Southeast Asia.[10] In Taiwan, piracy emerged as a direct response to the presence of U.S. servicemen either stationed on the island or passing through on rest-and-relaxation (R&R) furloughs from the front lines of combat in Vietnam. These GIs served both as an important vector for sourcing original LPs from the United States and as an important and ready-made market for cut-rate copies.[11] Servicemen also provided Taiwanese record producers with an informal distribution circuit that stretched up and down the "archipelago" of U.S. military installations, from the DMZ on the borders of North Korea to the airbases and port facilities of Kyushu, Okinawa, Taiwan, and the Philippines.[12] Local economies of pop music consumption—and the affective and libidinal economies they engendered—relied on this military infrastructure, including the nightlife and retail districts that sprang up around U.S. bases, as well as the syndication of the Armed Forces Network radio. A chronicle of Taiwanese pirate records, it turns out, "resembles" not so much a "maritime history" or a merely industrial trajectory but rather an imperial chronicle, one that of necessity retraces the circuitry of the Cold War in East Asia.[13]

**Circuits**

What does it mean to speak of a popular musical circuit in this context? Since the early nineteenth century, the term has been used to denote a fixed itinerary of live-performance venues along which itinerant musicians regularly traveled, as in the "Vaudeville circuit."[14] Recent scholarly usage, especially in the context of discussion of the globalization of music, has tended toward a far more open-ended (and sometimes celebratory) evocation of the transnational paths along which migrants, media, and music flow within and across geographical borders. For the purposes of this chapter, I would like to stake out a somewhat more precise and delimited sense of what a circuit does and how it may serve as a compelling metaphor and hermeneutical device in our efforts to map out the geopolitical disposition of Taiwanese and East Asian popular music in the postwar period.

First, in invoking popular musical *circuits* I deliberately invoke electronic circuitry, both as a metaphor and as arguably the most important musical medium (in the broadest sense) of the postwar years. As I discussed in the introduction, the invention in 1947 at Bell Labs of the transistor was one of the signal events of twentieth-century technological innovation. The transistor's commercial application in any number of audiovisual devices—from portable radios to stereo amplifiers and turntables and cassette players and television sets—transformed the distribution, consumption, and, perhaps most important, the *sound* of popular music beginning in the late 1950s. This "revolution in miniature" exponentially increased the electrical efficiency and reduced the cost of consumer electronics, enabling an unprecedented saturation of everyday life by mass-mediated sounds.[15] In many ways, East Asia was ground zero for this revolution. Although pocket-size transistor radios were first prototyped and produced in the United States (the Regency TR-1 of 1955 was the first of its kind), Japanese companies such as Sony and Toshiba had by 1959 exported more than six million transistor radios to the United States alone and came to play a formidable role in the market.[16] By the early 1970s, Taiwan had also become an important site for the manufacture and assembly of consumer electronics, and it began to establish itself as a global leader in the fabrication of integrated circuits in the 1980s.

The power of a transistor lies in its ability to exponentially amplify an electrical current as it runs across a threshold from one terminal (the "base") and through the semiconductor "emitter" to a second terminal, referred to as the "collector." Crucially, this increase in voltage ("gain") can be achieved only when minute impurities have been introduced (in a process known as "doping") into a semiconductor material such as germanium (as in the case of the earliest Bell Labs prototype) or silicon. The transistor also functions as a switch, and in this capacity, semiconductors not only expedite but also direct, regulate, and *restrict* the unidirectional flow of electrical "traffic" through a given circuit. Circuits, in other words, not only expedite but also route and control flows of power and information.

The wide availability of transistor radios and other electroacoustic devices in Taiwan in the 1960s and 1970s was instrumental in allowing local people to tune into the musical signals coming across the Pacific and to play back the electroacoustical patterns embedded in microgroove long-playing records. What I want to suggest here is that U.S. military bases functioned as a "semiconductor" in this particular musical circuit, serving as the decisive gating mechanism or switch through which the currents of

Anglo-American music became widely audible in Taiwan. These bases were perceived and sometimes resented as a source of (racial, cultural, and sexual) impurity, as emblems of an economically and militarily superior neocolonial presence. The presence of this impurity (spatially concretized by the red-light districts adjacent to U.S. bases) was the "doping agent" that allowed for an exponential "gain," as the sounds they emitted were eventually assimilated into emergent local circuits of production and consumption, often in surprising and creative ways. As pirate records, originally marketed to U.S. servicemen, circulated beyond this military niche and were "smuggled" into local circuits, they enabled a concomitant efflorescence of a youth culture centered around Anglophone "hit music" in the late 1960s and 1970s. That culture, as we have already seen in *Love in a Cabin*, existed at an uneasy geopolitical remove from its source. Finally, in ways that I will outline toward the conclusion of the chapter, the business of piracy helped to subsidize the epochal rediscovery and entry into mass-mediated circuits of a newly valorized Taiwanese folk voice in the 1970s and 1980s.

**Base/Emitter**

The origins and topology of this military circuit follow the contours of the Cold War conflict in East Asia. With their defeat at the hands of the Chinese Communist Party in 1949, Chiang Kai-shek and his Nationalist Party evacuated to the island of Formosa, bringing with them more than two million refugees from the mainland. By 1951, against the backdrop of the conflict on the Korean peninsula, the United States had formally established a Military Assistance Advisory Group (MAAG) in Taipei to provide training, technical assistance, and matériel to the armed forces of the Republic of China (ROC) in exile. By December 1954, not coincidentally a mere month after the division of Korea by armistice, President Eisenhower signed the Sino-American Mutual Defense Treaty, which opened up Taiwan as a vital front in the containment of communism. By 1955, a network of U.S. military installations had begun to be established up and down the west coast of Taiwan, often (as in Korea) simply occupying and developing the sites of former Japanese colonial facilities.[17] The headquarters of the U.S. Taiwan Defense Command and MAAG were established in large compounds on Chungshan North Road, near the site of the U.S. embassy to the Republic of Taiwan. The Shulinkou Air Station, located in the mountains sixteen kilometers from the city, was established on the site of a Japanese fighter base as a radar interception and listening post for Chinese Communist radio transmissions almost immediately after the conclusion of the treaty. By 1957, with intense artillery exchanges taking place between Communist and Nationalist forces contending for the offshore islands of Quemoy (Kinmen 金門) and Matsu 馬祖, the Taipei Air Station had opened on Roosevelt Road near the campus of National Taiwan University, and work had begun on expanding USAF air stations in Taoyuan, Tainan, and Taichung, where the sprawling Ching Chuan Kang (CCK) Airbase went on to become an important hub for the repair, maintenance, and overhaul of the C-130 transport planes that moved men and materiél in and out of Vietnam throughout the 1960s and 1970s.[18] As early as 1954, moreover, Kaohsiung port in the far south of the island had begun to function as a fleet landing and repair facility for the U.S. Navy, complemented by a MAAG post in nearby Tsoying 左營. These installations were supported by a network of ancillary institutions, such as the U.S. Navy Hospital, American schools, branches of the military retail network, and officer's clubs.

By 1958, in the wake of the Quemoy crisis, the number of billeted military personnel on Taiwan had grown from just 811 (largely MAAG advisers to the ROC military) to 19,000.[19] This figure stabilized around 13,000 throughout the 1960s but remains misleadingly low, because it includes neither the families of active service members nor an estimated 14,000 U.S. civilians and government functionaries working as ancillary personnel. Even more significant, the number of U.S. servicemen deployed to Vietnam grew steadily by the mid-1960s, peaking at 500,000 in 1968. By 1965, Taiwan had become a popular R&R furlough destination for soldiers fighting in Vietnam; two Pan American World Airways flights arrived at Taipei from the front each day, delivering more than five thousand "war-weary" GIs per month into the neon-lit entertainment quarter that had grown up around the sprawling Taiwan Defense Command and MAAG compounds abutting Chungshan North Road.[20] Kaohsiung also harbored "tens of thousands" of U.S. Navy personnel on shore leave during this period, while the CCK Air Base in Taichung bustled with a population of 4,000 active duty personnel.[21] According to one source, some 210,000 U.S. and Australian soldiers visited Taiwan on R&R between 1967 and 1972, injecting an estimated $52.8 million into the local economy.[22]

Enterprising Taiwanese record pirates capitalized on this military market. Retail outlets for pirate records clustered around establishments catering to the military trade. In Taipei, the intersection of Chungshan North Road and Minzu Road was the epicenter of this business, playing host to numerous hotels (including the Ambassador, the President, and many other less reputable establishments), the Linkou Club (which hosted local and stateside musical acts including the Fifth Dimension and the Silver

Convention), and scores of hostess bars featuring live and recorded music. Indeed, GIs arriving from Vietnam, beginning in 1967, were handed a pamphlet and a map featuring twenty-six such establishments. (See Figure 4.2.)

Just steps from MAAG headquarters, the Linkou Bookstore (among several other establishments) conducted a lively trade in locally produced pirate LPs.[23] Similar outlets clustered around the nightlife districts catering to GIs in Taichung, Tainan, and around the U.S. Navy–administered Sea Dragon Officer's club in Kaohsiung (see Figure 4.3).[24]

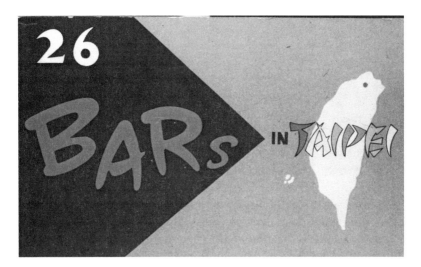

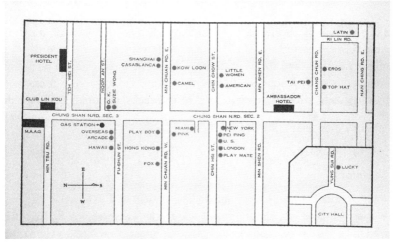

Figure 4.2. "26 Bars in Taipei" (Taipei: Nanhua Publishing, 1970). Digital images courtesy of Doug Price.

Figure 4.3. The Columbia Record Store in Chunghwa market, 1961. Courtesy of the Ministry of Foreign Affairs, Republic of China (Taiwan).

Piracy is often parasitical, piggybacking atop existing transit corridors and trade routes.[25] Retail sites clustered around U.S. military installations served as a gating mechanism, allowing Taiwanese producers access to markets up and down the East Asian "archipelago." Military dependents stationed in Okinawa, for instance, would organize frequent "weekend record buying sprees" to Taipei in order to take advantage of the low prices (usually about one-fifth off retail levels) and easy availability of a variety of Anglo-American titles.[26] The entrance of Taiwanese pirate records into military circuits and their repatriation by soldiers returning home upon completion of their tours of duty, is also amply and materially attested to by their continuing presence in used-record racks and online auctions in the United States and Australia (which supplied a contingent of more than sixty thousand troops to the war effort in Vietnam).

### Collectors

A local record industry had flourished in Taiwan well before the Vietnam War era. Indeed, its history goes back to the Japanese colonial era (in which the Japanese subsidiary of Columbia Records exercised a formative influence on the development of Taiwanese popular music) and extends into the immediate postwar period, with the establishment of eight local recording and pressing facilities by 1958, often with technical aid and cast-off equipment from the China Broadcasting Company 中廣 and the U.S. Armed Forces Network.[27] Among the most prominent of these outfits was Asia Records, based in the southern city of Tainan and an important producer of local Taiwanese-language music by stars such as Hong Yifeng and Wen Shia. As one of the first companies to import automated record-pressing machines into Taiwan, Asia Records also began to produce high-quality copies of Western classical performances and Japanese light music by the early 1960s.[28] Indeed, the growth of the record industry was explosive, with the number of registered manufacturers mushrooming from a handful in 1960 to 116 in 1970—although many of these companies were undercapitalized and transitory in nature.[29] This boom partook of a confluence of factors, from increased purchasing power among Taiwanese consumers (many of whom flocked to retail outlets in Taipei's Chunghwa Market to sample the latest hits, many if not most pirated) to the wider availability of transistorized playback equipment. As portable transistor radio sets became common alongside older vacuum-tube tabletop models, the Armed Forces Radio Network also became a crucial vector for the dissemination of Anglo-American pop beginning in the late 1950s.[30] So popular were these broadcasts of what became known as "hit music" that by the late 1960s, the state-run China Broadcasting Company and other local stations were forced to follow suit, broadcasting seventeen "hit music" programs per week in the Taipei metropolitan area.[31]

But perhaps the most immediate driver of this expansion was an exponential increase in productive capacity, as Taiwanese companies began to upgrade to automated pressing of vinyl records, rather than using manual presses and trimming records by hand.[32] Pirate records, exploiting domestic copyright control loopholes and flouting legislation intended to ban the export of such products, quickly established overseas markets in Hong Kong, Singapore, and other diasporic Chinese communities throughout Southeast Asia.[33] In one widely publicized incident that occurred in January 1968, a Hong Kong smuggler named Liu Zhiming was caught smuggling 910 records, of which 490 were copies of Anglo-American "hit music" such as the Beatles and the rest presumably Mandarin pop and *huangmeidiao* opera from the soundtracks of the widely popular Shaw Brothers costume drama musicals, out of the country.[34] The economics of this trade were quite simple: pirate copies routinely sold for anywhere from five to ten times less than genuine records. Profit margins were thus quite substantial, and all evidence points to the conclusion that pirate records vastly outnumbered their authentic counterparts as a result. Enforcement by customs authorities, moreover, was clearly the exception rather than the rule. As early as 1965, one local commentator estimated that Taiwan was producing some 350,000 pirate records per month, of which 150,000 were being exported to Southeast Asia.[35] A *Billboard* magazine feature five years later (entitled "Orient Pirate Playground") worried that more than 200,000 illegitimate records, churned out by "over forty-five" manufacturers, were flowing out of Taiwan every month.[36] These copies, *Billboard* wryly noted, were exact replicas, down to the inclusion of the "copyright notice."[37]

In sum, it seems clear that while piracy was not the only game in town, it was arguably the dominant model for record production in Taiwan from the early 1960s to the mid-1970s.[38] The U.S. military presence in Taiwan provided much of the initial impetus for Taiwanese pirates, but their products crossed the threshold into wider domestic and international markets precisely because the island's economy and culture were situated at the lower reaches of a precipitous geopolitical incline. David Kaser, writing about the English language books (and particularly textbooks) that were also pirated in staggering numbers throughout the same period, provides a cogent summary of the factors behind Taiwanese copyright infringements. Taiwanese publishers gained access in the 1950s to an exponentially less expensive technology for the reproduction of texts: photo-offset printing. At the same time, English had become the de facto language of imperial power and the *"lingua franca* of the Orient" and, as such, the single most essential conduit for desperately sought "current information," be it language lessons or technical literacy. With U.S. dominance in the region came "hordes of American military and civilian personnel . . . taking up more or less permanent residence" across East Asia, and these officials served as a convenient source for original materials and a ready-made market. Kaser emphasizes the decisive and seemingly insuperable economic gap fueling this trade, resulting from:

> the vast difference in labor and materials cost between the United States and Taiwan. In 1949 per capita income in Taiwan was only $30 per year, whereas in New York it was $1,800. This enormous cost
> differential could be reflected in comparative book prices and appeared to make local reprinting the only viable method of supplying the books needed in Taiwan.[39]

The same logic, of course, applied to records. The gradient between an authorized import of an American or U.K. manufactured vinyl record, which cost $200 NT, and a pirate copy whose price ranged from $12 NT to $30 NT was prohibitive for local consumers. Indeed, for much of the 1960s and 1970s, pay scales in Taiwan ensured that consumers, especially students and intellectuals, would hardly have been able to afford any authentic records at all.[40] As Shao Yiqiang rather poignantly argues in relation to the widespread copying of the European classical repertoire in Taiwan, how could the pirate record trade be accused of stealing profits from the multinationals when their products were simply unattainable for ordinary Taiwanese? Did they not instead perform an invaluable educational service?[41] What is equally apparent, of course, is that Taiwanese manufacturers were able to parlay the steepness of that gradient not only to serve their domestic market but also to find an export-driven path toward import substitution.

As we have seen in *Love in a Cabin*, pirate records and the aura of leisure and fantasy that revolved around their consumption came to saturate daily life, serving as the aural medium for an emergent youth culture, despite the prevailing authoritarian climate. This niche culture, as documented by Tunghung Ho and others, was centered predominantly around Taipei's Chungshan North Road, where local youth could take advantage of the dense concentration of pirate record and book stores to plug into Anglophone youth culture. Strolling the streets adjacent to U.S. military installations offered young flâneurs the thrill of "smuggling" imported styles of dress, music, and affect into the local context and, if only for a moment, leaping across the temporal incline that divided a backward Taiwan from the West:

> Chungshan North Road, for us long-haired youths with jeans, who woke up every morning to the American Radio Station, was the place to derive pleasure from a kind of social smuggling. It was not only an exotic pleasure deriving from the colonial concessions, but it was also the pleasure of rehearsing one's "expectations." Buying western books and pirated records and walking on one of the few shaded boulevards in Taipei among the crowds of foreigners, and feeling jet planes roaring overhead, we were sure that the "future" was here.[42]

A limited number of such flâneurs were able to make lives in the interstices of these "colonial concessions," eking out a living as professional musicians catering to the pub scene in cities like Taipei, Taichung, and Kaohsiung.[43] Amateur college bands also formed in the late 1960s, but their performances were heavily monitored and restricted by campus authorities and the police.[44] But it was the widespread dissemination of Anglophone pirate records into homes and into everyday lives, particularly on campus, that resonated most widely in local circuits. Indeed, one of the most popular and long-running franchises in the pirate-record business in Taiwan was Holy Hawk Records' 神鷹唱片 "The Student Sound" 學生

之音, a taste-making series of compilations of American chart hits. Released monthly from 1968 to the mid-1970s, the "Student Sound" reportedly sold upwards of fifteen thousand copies with each release, a not inconsequential achievement, especially given the mercurial nature of the business. Serving as a sonic window onto other worlds beyond the confines of the island, the "Student Sound" played a pivotal role in introducing folk revivalists such as Bob Dylan, as well as 1970s singer-songwriters such as Joni Mitchell, Cat Stevens, and James Taylor (among many others), onto campus. By the second half of the 1970s, guitar-based campus folk, underwritten by an ideology of authenticity, self-expression, and a burgeoning local consciousness, emerged as a new mainstream in Taiwanese popular music.[45]

The emergence of this local "hit music" circuit was, as Tunghung Ho argues, an "unintended by-product of the expansion of US military imperialism."[46] As such, something as seemingly innocent as buying and playing a pirate record was inevitably nested within larger geopolitical structures. Record collecting ran on differentials of power between the "base" and the "collector." And the new circuits that formed locally around the consumption of pop music tended to flow opportunistically along preexisting paths, often replicating or even amplifying long established social divisions. Circuits, in other words, not only expedite flows of real and symbolic capital but also restrict those flows or direct them toward those with privileged access to the requisite technologies and away from excluded or marginalized groups.[47] The Anglophone "hit music" circuit, for instance, was very much an urban middle-class phenomenon, closely linked to the ascension not only of English as a lingua franca (as opposed to Japanese, the language of Taiwan's former colonizer) but also of the standard Mandarin imposed by the KMT in favor of local idioms such as Taiyu Taiwanese and Hakka. Fans of Anglophone "hit music" tended to be urban youth, often but not exclusively the children of "Mainlander" emigrants associated with the KMT, and relatively well educated and well heeled.[48] Largely excluded from this circle were rural teenagers and speakers of Taiyu Taiwanese and Hakka. The circuit, in other words, plugged directly into existing forms of social inequity. The KMT's aggressive promotion of Mandarin films such as Pai Ching-jui's *Love in a Cabin* (and its alluring promotion of a "coca-colonized" culture of freedom and consumption) coincided with the near-total eclipse of the *Taiyu pian* cinema and the demise of the undercapitalized musical circuit, centered around Taiyu stars such as Wen Shia and Hong Yifeng, with which it was associated, in part because the televisual and radiophonic broadcast of their music was increasingly restricted by the Nationalist party-state in the late 1960s. All circuits are not created equal, nor do they have access to the same power sources.

### First Records: A Case Study

Even within the relatively privileged precincts of Taipei, Anglophone music culture arrived secondhand and in oddly disjunctive fragments. The sound quality of many pirate records was famously poor. Pirates typically would purchase a copy (or copies) of an authentic record and then simply electroplate the vinyl to create new masters, from which stampers could then be fabricated. Properly done, this process could result in acceptable sound quality, but any scratches or residue on the original copy would also be preserved, and impurities or imprecisions in the electroplating process often introduced pitting and other problems. The covers of the records were mimeographed, retouched, hand-colored, rebranded, and reprinted and featured odd and sometimes unintentionally hilarious misprints and translations of English titles into Chinese. The 1967 copy of the Beatles' "Sgt. Pepper's Lonely Hearts Club Band," issued by a long-established local company, Black Cat Record, is a typical example (see Plate 7).

(Mis)translations occasionally rise to the level of quite brilliant translingual malapropisms, as with a pirated edition of John Lennon's 1971 solo record with the Plastic Ono Band from First Records on which the Chinese title for Lennon's dirge "My Mummy's Dead" becomes "The Death of a Mummy" 木乃伊之死. More serious, and more symptomatic of the political tensions attendant upon the movement of the insurgent energies of late-1960s youth culture across the gating mechanism provided by illegitimate record manufacturing, each of the songs on this album is given a Chinese translation, save one: "Working Class Hero" (see Figure 4.4). While there is no way to know whether this omission was enforced by KMT censors or whether it was simply a preemptive move on the part of the record company itself, it is clear that John Lennon's invocation of class consciousness was unacceptable in the ardently anticommunist confines of "Free China."

Pirates are indeed diffident about retelling their exploits, but we can learn quite a lot about the industry from the material artifacts they have left behind. First of all, there was very little lag time between official releases and pirate copies. *John Lennon and the Plastic Ono Band* was released on December 11, 1970, in the United States and the United Kingdom, charting at number six and number eight, respectively, and remaining in the Top 100 for eighteen consecutive weeks. Before that run on the charts was over, the record had been electroplated and mastered directly

Figure 4.4. (*Top*) John Lennon and the Plastic Ono Band, "Working Class Hero," First Records FL-2019-A; (*bottom*) John Lennon and the Plastic Ono Band, "My Mummy's Dead," First Records FL-2019-B.

from a copy transported into Taiwan, perhaps by a U.S. serviceman or, as was sometimes the case, a flight attendant working transpacific routes. The records' provenance is immediately evident, because they still bear the matrix and stamper numbers of the original records from which they were duplicated (SW-2–3372-Z-11 and Z-12), as well as the official logo of the mastering studio ("Bell Sound") in the run-off grooves. Added to these unique identifiers, First Records has also scratched its own matrix number into the groove to identify the record within its sequential catalog of releases as 第一唱片 FL2019A and FL2019B. The label, in line with new regulations passed by censors at the Government Information Office (GIO) 新聞局 in 1968, contains information about the address of the company (No. 9 W. Hsinyi Road, in the industrial suburb of Sanchong, where record-pressing plants tended to cluster), its official publication permit number, and the March 1971 date of release. The plastic-wrapped outside cover, featuring the original image with the addition of the First Records logo, advertises another kind of added value (besides the vastly lower price) provided by local companies: "Lyrics Included," though it is unclear whether they were translated into Chinese (see Figure 4.5).

These details indicate quite clearly that pirate records of this sort operated in a liminal zone of quasi-legitimacy, operating outside the bounds of international copyright convention and yet publishing their wares in compliance with local regulations.[49]

This reflects in part the fact that First Records, unlike many lower-order or illegal pressing plants, was at the forefront of the Taiwanese recording industry and retained that position through the 1990s. Indeed, the story of First Records and its founder, with which I conclude this chapter, opens up several significant dimensions of the story of pirate records, particularly the way in which the U.S. military Cold War circuit I have been at pains to discuss thus far, articulated with and was in some ways complicit with an earlier history of colonization in Taiwan, that of the vanquished Japanese empire that administered the island of Formosa from 1895 to 1945. The story of First Records, moreover, shows the ways in which a circuit founded on the dissemination of Anglophone "hit music" came, by the late 1970s, to subsidize local music.

For even the casual observer or collector of Taiwanese pirate records, the numerical and technical dominance of First Records over and against rivals such as Black Cat, CSJ 中聲, Dragon, Large World 巨世, Leico 麗歌, Liming 麗鳴, Song Jwu 松竹, Sun Shine Record 日新, Union Record 合眾, and many others is fairly clear. As one journalist, evaluating the relative merits of fourteen different pirate labels for prospective record buyers, opined in a music magazine in 1978:

Figure 4.5. *John Lennon/Plastic Ono Band*, First Records FL-2019, 1970.

> First Records: Of all the pirate record companies at present, this is the one operating at the largest scale, and with the highest quality, and what's more, they quite boldly print their covers just like the originals with the imprint "First Records original sound records," to good effect in the marketplace. What's more, they have put out albums in a great number of genres. So, if any of our readers buy records only infrequently, but want to procure some "quality music" on pirated records, it's fair to say that First Records should be your first choice.[50]

First Records released hundreds and perhaps as many as two thousand Anglophone titles, judging by its sequential release numbers (beginning from FL-1000), while the quality of their pirate pressings seems to have surpassed that of almost any other producer save Haishan 海山, another established player in the business.[51] This should not be surprising, because the owner and founder of First Records, Ye Jintai 葉進泰, is a well-nigh legendary figure in the technological development of the Taiwanese record industry. Appropriately enough, Ye Jintai's company is credited with many "firsts" beginning from the 1950s, and many of these achievements involve the resourceful recycling of imperial waste products to local and highly profitable ends. Ye Jintai was born into poverty in 1928 and managed to gain admission to the Taipei Polytechnical School 台北工業學校. After serving as a "student-soldier" for Japan during the war, Ye Jintai was assigned as a machinist to the Japanese colonial–era mining complex at Shifenliao 十分寮, on the island's northeast corner, subsequent to Taiwan's "retrocession" to Chinese Nationalist rule. Perusing castoff Japanese scientific texts in his spare time, he quickly realized that the waste products in the phenols and formaline tailings from the mine could easily be recycled and used to manufacture bakelite. Ye Jintai quickly established himself in the bakelite business, manufacturing light bulb ballasts and dielectric fittings for Taiwan's power grid, as well as cigarette cases and milk bottles made of the newly invented PE (polyethylene) plastics.

It was his interest in plastics, not music, that led to a career in the record industry. Having purchased a secondhand electroplating machine from Japan for prototyping die molds, he soon realized its application to the production of acetate masters for use by CBC Radio. In 1957, he partnered with Wu Sanlian 吳三連 to establish Mingfeng Records 鳴鳳唱片 and, using equipment abandoned by the Japanese military, began to record local popular singers, as well as pioneering a burgeoning market for English-language instructional discs. In 1962, Ye Jintai worked closely with Formosa Plastics to invent a formula for the domestic production of PVC vinyl, a crucial step that emancipated local record manufacturers from their former reliance on outdated shellac or expensive imported materials. The following year, he engineered his own patented "stereomono" system by tinkering with existing monophonic equipment inherited from U.S. Armed Forces Radio, pioneering the production of Taiwan's first stereo microgroove records. Other advances for which Ye was responsible included Taiwan's first multitrack recording studio, established in 1981 with equipment imported from Switzerland and technical assistance from Japan. But perhaps the coup de grâce of his long and storied career was his establishment, in 1988, of a hugely capital intensive venture called Ritek 錸德科技, dedicated to the manufacture of CDs and other optical media. Ritek quickly became one of the leading fabricators of CDs, DVDs, and CD-Rs in the world, producing in quantity for the major multinationals, with a fully automated plant capable of churning out an astounding 200 million units per month. By the 1990s, Taiwan, once a pirate haven, had become a global leader in the production of "digital storage media."[52] Symptomatically, the accounts of Ye Jintai's career from which I have drawn to construct this account are predictably silent about the role of piracy in the company's "primitive accumulation" of capital and expertise and the decidedly analog origins of its leap into the transnational circuit of the digital era.[53]

**Love in a Cabin, Redux**

In 1979, with the enactment of the Taiwan Relations Act, the United States under President Jimmy Carter made the epochal decision to sever diplomatic relations with Taiwan in favor of a formal alliance with the People's Republic. A complete withdrawal of all U.S. military forces across the island had been effected by later that year. It was the end of a significant epoch in the Cold War, a momentous turning point in Taiwan's history, and an uneasy reminder of the precariousness and intractability of the island nation's geopolitical predicament. The withdrawal of U.S. forces, of course, also signaled the breaking up of the Cold War circuit that Taiwanese record pirates had exploited for almost two decades. Ye Jintai, shrewd businessman that he was, had no doubt already seen the handwriting on the wall. By the late 1970s, he was already laying out plans to upgrade First Records' studio facilities to concentrate on the production and promotion of the local guitar-driven Mandarin popular music, springing from the campus folk movement, that would by the late 1980s ensure Taiwan's musical dominance even in mainland China markets.

That same year, Ye Jintai attended a lecture at the Rotary Club in Sanchong, near the First Records factory at the gritty working-class epicenter of Taiwan's music industry. The speaker was one of Taiwan's most distinguished and impassioned professional musicologists and composers, Hsu Tsang-Houei. Hsu, having returned from his studies in Paris, had spent the late 1960s preparing to survey the rugged terrain of the island in search of the folk "roots" of Chinese musical culture—roots he believed were in danger of being irrevocably severed by an influx into Taiwan of commodified popular tunes and "hit music" from abroad. In July 1967, having nearly reached the end of his quest and fearing that the music he was in search of had already been lost forever, Hsu stumbled upon a grizzled, half-blind moon lute (*yueqin*) player named "Red-Eye" Chen Da in a broken-down little cabin on a hill perched on the windswept reaches of the far south of the island. Almost as soon as Chen Da began to play, Hsu burst into tears of gratitude and exaltation. As he wrote in his diary entry for that same day, this was the very music—untouched by the "curse" of modern media and urban life—for which he had been searching:

> Today, in the barren and remote mountains of the Hengchun peninsula 恆春半島, five hundred kilometers away from Taipei, I was moved to tears by a poverty-stricken old man dressed in tattered clothes . . . he's sixty two years old . . . with neither kith nor kin, living all alone in a cabin that is hardly habitable (if you could call it a house at all). The four walls are constructed of clay bricks, with no windows, and a single hole (it couldn't really be called a door) through which you need to bend down as you go in or out. The roof is rigged up with bamboo poles as beams, which are covered with rough thatch.
>
> At four o'clock on a summer's afternoon, as soon as I entered, I felt a palpable darkness and suffocating heat. I slowly began to be able to make out some bedding and a broken old stove on the ground, and last of all, I recognized a *yueqin* hanging on the wall. This was the sum total of Red-Eye Da's 紅目達仔 worldly possessions. A dark, poor, and lonely world, living with only a battered old *yueqin* by his side—the atmosphere alone was enough to make one feel a heavy grief. And yet when he took up the *yueqin* and began to sing along with that mournful sound, I began to understand that this world, this world of Red-Eye Da which has already been forgotten and left behind by city folks, was full of truth."[54]

Hsu's speech at the Rotary Club, delivered twelve years after this revelatory experience, was a bitter lament about the inattention shown to Chen Da's music and to Taiwan's plethora of indigenous folk sounds, which Hsu Tsang-Houei had continued to meticulously document and record for posterity. Part of the problem, he asserted, was his inability to find an outlet willing to make high-quality field recordings of this heritage available to a wider public.[55] Moved—and perhaps sensing an opportunity to burnish his company's reputation as well—Ye Jintai initiated a collaboration whereby, over the course of the following three years, First Records worked with Hsu to release a series of twenty-one long-playing records, with deluxe gatefold packaging on heavy card stock and extensive liner notes—altogether different from the flimsy paper sleeves of pirate records—comprehensively documenting Taiwan's musical traditions. Not unlike Harry Smith's 1955 *Anthology of American Folk Music* on Folkways Records, the resultant *Anthology of Chinese Folk Music* 中國民俗音樂專集 was commercially unsuccessful but deeply influential, helping to catapult Chen Da toward his current status as an indelible icon of Taiwanese music and to consolidate a new folk-revivalist circuit that was to have profound musical, cultural, and political resonance in the ensuing years.[56]

CHAPTER FIVE

# Folk Circuits

Discovering Chen Da

In 1959, the aspiring composer Hsu Tsang-Houei, recently returned from a five-year sojourn at the University of Paris, set out to "listen to the streets of Taipei . . . for one day from dawn to dusk."[1] The resulting essay is a rare document of the city's soundscape at midcentury and a pioneering attempt at a kind of acoustic sociology. As Hsu makes a circuit of the city, noting what he hears, its various districts, idioms, and class divisions take shape as an audible map, one organized around a hierarchy of musical genres. In the modern and high-class entertainment districts around Hsimenting and Chunghwa Market 中華商場, the latest American mambo and cha-cha rhythms sound out from record shops and cinemas, mingled with Mandarin pop from Hong Kong. In the narrow lanes closer to the river and the city's traditional center of spiritual gravity at Longshan Temple, Taiwanese-language ballads set to Japanese melodies suffuse the air. It is only on the margins, where working men or recent migrants from the countryside congregate, that traces of the musical past, in the form of *koa-a-hi* 歌仔戲 opera or folk songs from localities far beyond the capital, can still be heard.

Hsu's acoustic map, while accurate, is less objective than prescriptive. From the moment Hsu wakes to the "sickening" sound of his neighbors' gramophone blaring Japanese music to the late-night "assault" on his ears by foreign popular music streaming out from speakers along Nanking Road, he is appalled by what he hears. His visceral revulsion is prompted not only by his distaste for popular music but also by his conviction that foreign sounds have invaded Chinese territory. Worse still, authentic folk music is almost nowhere to be heard. The underlying difficulty, which Hsu fails to identify explicitly, although it is everywhere in evidence, is that he has gone out in search of voices raised in song and found for the most part only recorded sound. The musical soundscape Hsu surveys, in other words, is already an almost entirely "acousmatic" environment. This term, championed by Pierre Schaeffer, refers to the separation of sound from its immediate source as enabled by technologies for the recording and playback of sound.² Something of the perceived violence and disorientation of this sundering of music from the time and place of its enunciation and of the voice from its anchorage in the human body is registered by another, more derogatory term invented in the late 1960s by the Canadian composer and acoustic ecologist R. Murray Schaefer, for the same condition: "schizophonia."³ Although Hsu's essay was written well before Schaefer began to critique the noise pollution of the modern soundscape, his essay reflects a similar sense of unease. It is titled "Listening to Songs in the Streets of Taipei," but it could just as accurately be rendered as "Listening *for* Songs in the Streets of Taipei" ... and for the most part not finding them. What Hsu encounters instead is the seemingly ubiquitous presence of amplified sound, streaming from record players, radios, and loudspeakers, whether in domestic spaces, in stores, or in the streets.

Over the course of the day, Hsu hears actual, as opposed to electronically mediated, song just three times. The first instance comes as he cycles to his morning class at the National Taiwan Normal University. Schoolchildren sing the national anthem, and from behind the wall of an adjacent military barracks emerges the sound of official anthems extolling the "anti-communist, resist the Soviets" 反共抗俄 cause championed by the KMT authorities. Hsu wryly dismisses these performances as rote; he's interested instead in the spontaneous expression of feeling, in the folk songs that he remembers filling the evening air in the European towns of his student sojourn. It is only late in the evening, when he is on the brink of despair, that he stumbles upon the "depressing" sight of a laborer, sitting on a stool in front of a dimly lit and dilapidated row of tumbledown shacks, "singing hoarsely in the tearful style of Taiwanese *koa-a-hi*" opera and accompanying himself on a crudely fashioned *huqin* 胡琴.⁴ The pathos of this scene and its contrast with the rich, spontaneous musical life he has witnessed in Europe prompt Hsu to question whether China has "any folk songs" of its own.⁵ After two more fruitless hours, during which he's pursued by the constant sound of "amplified foreign pop," Hsu finally finds an indication of where he might find the folk music for which he is searching, and it is with this moment of grace, fragile and contingent, that the essay concludes:

> On the way home, I walked along Hsinsheng North Road as it skirts the river. By that time, it was already after ten o'clock. Pedestrians were few and far between, and the stars were twinkling soundlessly in the

sky. By the pedicab stand next to the Taipei Bridge near Chang'an East Road, I heard a porter softly humming a folk tune from his home village.⁶

This moment may well have pointed out Hsu's direction "home." By the summer of 1967, leading a contingent of ethnographers and enthusiasts, Hsu had begun to comb the rural soundscape for traces of a heritage that he believed had been submerged, not only in Taipei but across the island, in a deluge of commercial pop music. And it was on a hillside, at the furthest remove from Taipei that the island afforded, that he made his epochal discovery of a man he construed as a kind of musical missing link: a living embodiment of an endangered folk lineage. The man was named Chen Da: an itinerant, toothless, and nearly blind sixty-one-year-old. Chen Da's encounter with Hsu Tsang-Houei eventually transformed him into an icon of Taiwanese folk, one whose rural music came to emblematize a newly emergent sense of Taiwanese local identity in the late 1970s (see Plate 8).

This chapter revolves around this oft-retold story but rereads the discovery of Chen Da in the light of the ongoing transformation of the media environment that was already distressingly apparent to Hsu Tsang-Houei in 1959.⁷ In a very real sense, the Chen Da that we know today was a product of that environment. Hsu and his fellow musicologist and folk preservationist Shih Wei-liang were of necessity deeply complicit with the schizophonic logic of the postwar musical economy, even as (or precisely because) they valiantly resisted its power and insisted on the authenticity of what had come before. If Chen Da represented a precious "recording" of the tradition, imprinted upon the flawed—because fungible—medium of the human body, he needed to be preserved, to be remade as an artifact that could stand the test of time. More important, if Chen Da (and the marginalized class and rural culture for which he became a metonym) was to speak to the times, he needed to travel to Taipei. In order to preserve his voice and render it portable, in other words, he needed to be recorded, and those recordings, pressed into long-playing records or broadcast on television, would have to circulate within or even open up new urban media circuits. Chen Da's migration from the Hengchun peninsula to Taipei, in person and in electronically mediated forms, was a pivotal (if not decisive) moment in the inception of the Taiwanese modern folk song movement and its anticolonial injunction to "sing our own songs." That movement, in turn, sparked the explosive growth of a new pop genre, "campus folk," and, with it, of the Taiwanese commercial music industry, enabling its eventual expansion into mainland Chinese markets in the late 1970s and 1980s.

This chapter also asks how Chen Da's story—playing out at the juncture of the Green Revolution, rural-urban migration, technological miniaturization, and decolonization, speaks to the global conjuncture of the long 1960s. One of the musical hallmarks of that decade is the nearly simultaneous efflorescence and proliferation of (often highly politicized) folk revivals across a stunningly diverse range of locales, irrespective of all the usual East–West and North–South divides, from the folk explosion in the United States and Great Britain to Chile's antiauthoritarian *nueva cancion* and from folk song festivals in Czechoslovakia and Poland and the newfound popularity of folk singers in Korea and Japan to the marshaling of indigenous musical traditions to the task of nation building in newly decolonized states such as Ghana and Mali. Equally integral to the popular musical history of the era was the simultaneous and nearly ubiquitous emergence of newly electrified musical genres (often viewed with contempt by folk purists) that transported folk idioms into urban circuits by electrifying and resculpting their sonic profiles in the recording studio. The emergence of folk rock and the hippie-pastoral mode in Anglo-American pop in the wake of Bob Dylan's electric apostasy at the 1965 Newport Folk Festival is just one such example, but others abound, from the *Tropicália* movement in Brazil to roots reggae in Jamaica or the propulsive electric guitar–driven sound of Nigerian highlife in the 1970s.

Taiwanese "campus folk" was just one of many newly emergent genres in this period, the development of which was directly informed by the circulation of countercultural ideas, especially via pirate records, to the island. Neither its popularity nor the earlier efforts of Hsu Tsang-Houei to revive the folk tradition, however, can be readily read in terms of American influence. Clearly, Chen Da's story presents certain inescapable analogies with the American folk revival of the late 1950s and 1960s. It would be easy to liken Chen Da to Leadbelly or Mississippi John Hurt or Furry Lewis or any of the many other largely African American blues artists who, having recorded extensively in the golden era of "race records" in the late 1920s and early 1930s, had been forgotten, only to be rediscovered by left-wing activists, oddball enthusiasts, 78-rpm record collectors, and musicologists in the 1950s, finally to be appropriated by the rock and roll counterculture of the late 1960s.[8] Hsu Tsang-Houei and Shih Wei-liang, who embarked on an arduous effort to locate, record, study, and promote the folk musical cultures of Taiwan in the late 1960s, could in this light be read as Taiwanese versions of pioneering field recordists and scholars such as John and Alan Lomax. And it is true that their work unfolded in a rarified artistic and intellectual milieu in which the music of Bob Dylan and Joan Baez, as well as some of the political ideas and styles associated with the counterculture, had already begun to circulate, if only in attenuated forms.

Yet, as I will explore here, the analogy is inexact, not least because of the specificities of Taiwan's colonial history and its position on the fault lines of the Cold War. Many questions about the movement remain relatively unexplored. How and why did a folk circuit come into being in the late 1960s? How did it correlate with Taiwan's prevailing linguistic and urban–rural divides? How were the discovery and eventual dissemination of folk and its popular derivatives reliant upon the concurrent boom of the island's consumer electronics industry? The fascination for the folk on the part of urbanites in Taipei, as elsewhere in the world, emerges as a dialectical product of these ever-accelerating processes of modernization. Is it possible to observe these developments not only through an urban lens but also from the perspective of a rural Taiwanese circuit in which industrial Taipei loomed ever larger as a magnet for migrants, agriculture was increasingly industrialized, and everyday life punctuated by the presence of transistorized music?

One point of entry into these questions is aesthetic. How did the music of the Taiwanese folk revival sound, and why did it sound that way? In recent years, critics have begun to ask why a genre of music that emerged from the combatively anticolonial calls of musicians like Li Shuangze to "sing our own songs" was so sonically wan, so lacking in local character?[9] Why does campus folk—performed in standard Chinese by singer-songwriters with predictable harmonic structures, simple arpeggiated chords played on acoustic guitar, and light pop arrangements—pale in comparison to the rough-hewn, rhythmically rich, improvisatory power of Chen Da singing in his inimitably archaic Taiwanese to the accompaniment of a two-stringed *yueqin* (moon lute)? Why did it prove so difficult for Chen Da's "country blues" to be emulated in the city? And how did a movement that began its life with explicitly nationalist calls for a decolonized musicality come to adopt the harmonic norms and instrumental forms of a globally circulating Anglo-American pop sound?

The solution to this enigma, I argue here, has to do with questions of pop song form. How do certain sounds adapt (or prove to be maladapted) to prevailing media environments? What formal characteristics allow music to travel within certain circuits? What sonic shapes lend themselves to passing through the gating mechanisms of a given media topology, and which fail to cross over? Proponents of the folk revival, none more so than Hsu Tsang-Houei and Shih Wei-liang, defined their venture in vehement opposition to the colonization of Taiwan's auditory space by the sounds of commercial music, be it ersatz mambo, Mandarin musicals imported from Hong Kong, "mixed-blood" Taiwanese balladry, or Anglo-American "hit music." Instead, they championed a vision, derived in part from May 4th-era calls for the modernization of Chinese musical life, that looked to the ways in which composers like Debussy and Bartok had alchemically turned what conservatory-trained musicians may have heard as the harmonic instabilities and tonal irregularities of folk music to hand as materials for a locally inflected modernist idiom. In transporting Chen Da's music via field recordings from the far southern reaches of the island and releasing them in the form of long-playing records, Hsu and Shih recast Chen Da as an artifact. Paradoxically, however, it was largely by way of the acousmatic landscape of commercial pop music of which Hsu and Shih despaired that Chen Da's singular musical legacy began to proliferate and take on a new and unexpected afterlife of its own. Even more surprising, this process had been set in motion two decades before Hsu Tsang-Houei ever set foot in Chen Da's hut in the hills above Hengchun, by musicians and listeners largely outside the purview of the urban circuits of the folk revival movement. Chen Da and his signature song, "Sixiang qi" (Remember when), it turns out, had been *covered*, long before he was *dis*covered.

**Folk Modernism**

On July 21, 1967, the Folk Song Collection Movement 民歌採集運動 began in earnest as a group of scholars and enthusiasts affiliated with the newly founded Center for Research in Chinese National Music 中國民族音樂研究中心 set off in high spirits from Taipei. Divided into two teams of researchers, one covering the sheer mountains of the east coast and the other the more settled agricultural floodplains to the west, the group made a ten-day circuit of the island, collecting, documenting, and recording more than two thousand folk songs in each of the principal local languages, Hoklo Taiwanese and Hakka, as well as the many diverse languages of Taiwan's indigenous peoples. Funded by a businessman and patron of the arts named Fan Jiyun, the venture was spearheaded by Hsu Tsang-Houei and Shih Wei-liang. The two men were somewhat unlikely comrades. Hsu Tsang-Houei (born 1929) hailed from the village of Hemei 和美 in Changhua 彰化 county, where his father, a prominent physician, ran a private clinic. Like many native Taiwanese of means in the colonial period, he was sent as a boy to be educated in Japan, and he spent the war years learning violin before returning to the island in 1946. Also as was the case for many others of his generation, his inability to speak or to understand Mandarin Chinese was initially an impediment to his continuing education upon the island's return to Chinese rule in 1945. He was active, if only peripherally and without serious consequence, in the island-wide unrest following the February 28, 1947, uprising against the KMT authorities. His political sympathies, to the extremely limited extent that he was able to voice them in the repressive years following the subsequent imposition of martial law, were progressive, fostered in part by his readings in Russian literature, French philosophy and poetry, and left-wing realist Chinese literature from authors such as Lu Xun 魯迅.[10] He entered the Department of Music at what is now the National Taiwan Normal University in 1949 and six years later, in the wake of the death of his father, wagered his inheritance on pursuing advanced training in Paris.

Shih Wei-liang (1925–1977), in contrast, had spent the war years as an underground resistance fighter for the KMT against the Japanese occupation in his native Manchurian province of Liaoning. In 1947, he began to study with the Taiwanese composer Jiang Wenye 江文也 at the Peking Academy of Arts 北平藝專 and arrived in Taiwan in 1949 as a refugee. He continued his musical education there, also enrolling at the National Taiwan Normal University. He was a staunch nationalist and was associated throughout his musical career with the KMT state apparatus and its China Youth Corps (or the "China Youth National Salvation Corps" 救國團, as it was known in Chinese), for which he penned "anticommunist" choral anthems of the sort Hsu Tsang-Houei reported hearing emanating from the barracks.[11] Although they were classmates in the Department of Music at the same university, the two men traveled in different social and linguistic circles.

What brought them together was the experience of studying music in Europe. Hsu spent over six years in France, between 1955 and 1962, when he studied with Jacques Chailley and André Jolivet at Paris–Sorbonne, attended lectures on musical analysis with the visionary modernist composer Olivier Messiaen at the Paris Conservatoire, and wrote his doctoral thesis on the music of Debussy. Shih travelled to Madrid to study at the National Academy of Music on a government scholarship in 1958 and transferred to the Conservatory in Vienna two years later. Supporting himself with stints as a coal miner in Huelva and as a worker in an electronics factory in Germany, while at the conservatory in Stuttgart Shih began to write his first monograph, on the music of Belá Bartok, and this work was published upon his return to Taiwan in 1965.[12] The choice of composer was telling in both cases. Bartok's field recordings of Hungarian folk music in the Carpathian mountains in the first years of the twentieth century allowed him to hear, with x-ray-like precision, microtones and harmonic intervals that could not be accounted for by standard written notation.

These folk "deviations" from the hegemony of Western European musical practice became the basis for his articulation of a radically modern, yet also insistently national musical language. Debussy, renowned for his interest in the pentatonicism and non-Western tonalities of the Javanese music he had first encountered at the World Exposition in Paris in 1889, developed a progressive, yet still characteristically French musical language.

Bartok and Debussy, in short, offered the possibility of a new Chinese music that was both idiomatic and modern and a methodology through which the raw resources for such compositions might be found among the folk. Both men also emerged from their immersion in Europe as ardent nationalists and anticolonialists, driven partly by a sense of Chinese inadequacy on the world musical stage and partly by a sense of urgency with respect to the vast, vulnerable, and untapped potential of a traditional music culture. Shih Wei-liang's admiring account of Bartok's achievements, *On Folk Song*, published nearly simultaneously with the Folk Song Collection Movement itself, reads very much like an account of his own aspirations. In Shih's account, Bartok throws off the shackles of his training in German music, challenges the political dominion of the Austro-Hungarian empire, and learns to "accept the musical thought of the world, and still love that of his own country even more."[13] Hsu, upon his return to Taiwan, had clearly begun to come to similar conclusions. Hsu and Shih began to correspond after Hsu read an open letter Shih had penned in Vienna and published in the *United Daily News* in which he fiercely lamented the lack of a Chinese national music and concluded with a question that was to be echoed by the proponents of the modern folk song movement of the 1970s: "Do we need a music of our own?"[14]

Hsu and Shih did not, of course, need to rely exclusively on the example of Bartok. They were both deeply cognizant of a long tradition of musical practice and exegesis, dating back at least to the Han scholiasts' consolidation of the Confucian textual legacy and deriving from the Zhou court (eleventh to seventh centuries BCE), in which the collection, compilation, and performance of folk songs was seen as an essential aspect of statecraft.[15] Indeed, the epigraph for Hsu's essay is the third-century BCE text "Record of Music" 樂記, in which sound is seen as a barometer of the times and social temper and its regulation the linchpin of moral governance:

> Therefore with music of weak purpose and garbled notes, the people will be fretful and sad; with music that is spacious, harmonious, slow and easy, its embellishments emerging from a clear structure, the people will be happy; with music of coarse vitality, rapid attacks and distinct cadence, and a bright, resonant sound, the people will be strong and

resolute; with music that is direct, righteous, and truthful, the people will be serious and respectful; with music that is rich, broad, allowing for voices to blend smoothly and bodies to move in resonance, the people will be loving and kind; with music that runs to extremes or tends toward dissipation and is overwhelmed by disorderly changes, the people will be depraved.[16]

As much as the Confucian legacy and its fretful disdain for the decadent sounds 靡靡之音 of popular song may have resonated with their contemporary concerns, Hsu and Shih also had far more proximate influences from which to draw. Fred Chiu 丘延亮, an anthropologist and former student of Hsu Tsang-Houei who participated in the Folk Song Collection Movement, cites a rich slate of intellectual precedents, from the Russian *narodniks* of the nineteenth century to liberal-leftist intellectuals in Taisho Japan in the Shirakaba group 白樺派, including Mushanokōji Saneatsu 武者小路実篤, whose New Village movement left a lasting imprint on May 4th-era Chinese intellectuals such as Zhou Zuoren 周作人 and Lu Xun.[17] Zhou Zuoren was himself at the epicenter of a folk song collection movement centered around Peking University in the early 1920s that was dedicated to gathering the raw materials for a new Chinese vernacular literature. Also arising out of this milieu was the Sichuanese activist and musician Wang Guangqi 王光祈 (1892–1936), who studied music in Germany and whose series of comparative musicological studies was formative for both Hsu and Shih in their affirmative stance toward indigenous traditions. Yang Yinliu 楊蔭瀏 (1899–1984), whose recordings and transcriptions of a blind singer named Abing 阿炳 in his native Wuxi became central to the post-1949 canonization of folk music in the music pedagogy of the People's Republic, was also an influence.[18] There was, finally, a rich tradition of field recording and ethnomusicological study of the indigenous populations of Taiwan, carried out under the auspices of the colonial Japanese regime by recordists such as Kurosawa Takatomo 黑澤隆超, although it is not clear to what extent these materials would have been available in the 1960s.[19]

The immediate catalyst for the expedition, however, was directly political, for with the advent of the launch of the KMT's "Movement for a Chinese Cultural Renaissance" 中華文藝復興, Chiu argues, Hsu and Shih found an expediently amorphous banner (and the necessary financial support) with which to undertake their ethnomusicological work—work that, in demanding that urbanites listen to the marginalized voices of rural folks who had been left behind by the KMT's developmentalist ethos, carried with it an unmistakably subversive undertone.[20] Ironically in this regard, given that the "Renaissance" was conceived of as a counterweight to the Great Proletarian Cultural Revolution, Chiu recalls listening surreptitiously to proscribed shortwave mainland Chinese broadcasts from Radio Peking and taking inspiration from the Maoist injunction to go down to the countryside and learn revolution at the source: from the Chinese peasantry.[21]

These transmissions from the People's Republic were, however, overmatched by the currency of American youth culture among youthful literary circles in Taipei and its environs.[22] This potent conjuncture of suppressed left-wing and anticolonial sentiment, a nascent nativist modernism, and the allure of Cold War–era counterculture is materially registered in the pages of the November 1967 issue of one of the most significant avant-garde journals of the period, the *Literature Quarterly* 文學季刊. Alongside poetry by Yu Guangzhong 余光中 (who would go on to fame as a lyricist in the modern folk song movement of the 1970s), short fiction by the modernist provocateur Qideng Sheng 七等生, and early work by a luminary of Taiwan's native soil fiction movement, Huang Chunming 黃春明, we find an advertisement for Barbarian 野人, a Taipei coffee house featuring "Brazilian coffee, jazz music, an underground atmosphere, and all the sensations of the heat of youth." Crucially, the issue also features a transcript of a long and lively forum, "The Song of the Soil" 大地之歌, presided over by the prominent dissident writer Chen Yingzhen 陳映真, who would be arrested and jailed the following year on charges of subversion.[23] In a shockingly freewheeling conversation about the history and contemporary meanings of American folk music, a visiting American student of Chinese literature, Douglas A. White, and a young photographer working on assignment in Taiwan for *National Geographic*, Tom Davenport, discourse on the Popular Front and protest music, the roots of Bob Dylan's music in the folk revival, the field recordings of Alan Lomax, leftist currents and the Little Theater, race relations, drug culture, hippie self-realization as imagined in Eric Berne's *The Games People Play*, free love, and LSD. The forum, in other words, presents readers with a litany of late 1960s countercultural concerns, routed through the particular nexus of folk songs and antiauthoritarian politics. And it is surely no accident that the article preceding this piece is a report in diary form, authored by Hsu Tsang-Houei, on the folk song collection expedition he had only just recently completed, the centerpiece and climactic moment of which is his discovery of Chen Da.[24]

## Recording Chen Da

Hsu's account, in some sense, grounds the intellectual crosscurrents and political energies of the forum in the soil of southern Taiwan. At the same time, Hsu himself becomes the live wire that sets up a circuit between a disappearing rural past and a restive urban modernity. Indeed, it is precisely the temporal disjunction between these dipoles that renders the connection so poignant. Mary Beth Hamilton has written insightfully of the "primitivist" desire of folk revivalists like Alan Lomax "to be deeply moved by manifestations of inner feeling . . . to dissolve boundaries, renounce autonomy, merge with the wellsprings of life."²⁵ Hsu Tsang-Houei's diary entries are suffused with these sorts of moments, of which his lachrymose encounter with Chen Da is only the last and most consequential. Hsu describes the performance of a song by a villager nicknamed Hogtail 豚尾仔 earlier the same day, for instance, as "desolate, sorrowful, melancholy, pulling profoundly at the heartstrings, such that all of us who were listening sank deep into thought, and I could not help but to shed tears."²⁶ The melancholy is perhaps as much a product of Hsu's sense of an irreparable cultural loss as of any intrinsic quality of Hogtail's performance:

> Oh! At that moment the monophonic melody of this Hengchun ballad, "Niuwei bai" 牛尾擺 surpassed even the grand scale of a symphonic composition by Beethoven. Because it had circulated for hundreds of years in the bloodstream of our ancestors. Because it was the naked expression of authentic feeling. No decoration, no technique, no pretense—it seemed to bypass thought on its way to striking my soul.²⁷

Hsu's modernist aesthetic, of course, in which a primitive, rough-hewn lack of sophistication takes precedence over polish, is predicated on a particular and quite sophisticated kind of thinking. For as much as he lauds its simplicity, a song is never just a singular folk song. Instead, it stands in for the repertoire as a whole, while the moment of its performance serves to instantiate and bring to presence the centuries that preceded it. A particular locality in Taiwan, in turn, must stand in for China as a whole, while a mere mortal becomes a living embodiment of a dying tradition, a kind of fragile catchment point for the lifeblood of a national culture.

Perhaps this is also why there is a great deal of attention paid in Hsu's field diaries to dilapidation and disrepair, not only of the houses he visits but also of the very bodies of the men and women he records.²⁸ Many of his encounters with those who are willing to sing for him seem to take on an almost allegorical valence. In the features of an eighty-one-year-old singer reduced to living in a mean hovel in Changhua, Hsu discerns the traces of the beauty of her youth. And in the sorrowful timbre of her voice is preserved not only the popular tunes of the late Qing and early Republican entertainment quarters but also the very "sound of courtesans in ancient times." Chen Da, in his early sixties at the time, is described in terms of the misery of his hovel, his damaged and diseased eyes, his betelnut-stained and missing teeth. His body is marked by years of poverty, thus serving all the more poignantly as a fragile repository, a medium on which the racial past is inscribed. Old age becomes a synecdoche for the onrush of historical time and of the relentless displacement of the past in modernity. This logic is brought home by a curious rhetorical turn. At the moment when, with a gush of tears, Hsu realizes that he has finally discovered "the spirit of Chinese folk music" for which he has searched for so long, Chen Da's apotheosis from a man to something much larger is realized in graphic terms, as the personal pronoun "he" 他 is displaced by the identically pronounced third-person singular "it" 它.[29]

In pointing out the power of this kind of rhetoric, I do not intend to belittle Hsu's visionary work. What interests me is how the imperative of preservation exists in a tense and mutually complicit relation with the very culture of schizophonia that threatens to inundate its object. To preserve Chen Da beyond his inevitable expiration, his voice needed to become an object, a recorded artifact.[30] Indeed, one of the most important functions of the Folk Song Collection Movement lay precisely in the creation of what Bruno Latour has called in another context "immutable mobiles." Latour's evocative phrase was originally intended as a description of the ways in which the production of bureaucratic paperwork condenses a messy and many-faceted world into a standardized, scalable, portable, and archivable form of knowledge.[31] "Immutable mutables" permit knowledge to be transported from the field to centers of learning and control such as universities and government ministries. They allow scholars and bureaucrats easy, indexed access to this stockpile of information and facilitate their efforts to understand and administer the worlds to which the documents refer. Yet they also flatten and limit our vision, for, in selecting some significant objects for preservation but not others, they not only maintain but also come to constitute the historical record.

The methodology of the Folk Song Collection Movement, as set out by Fred Chiu in his report on their activities, involved meticulous written records of members' activities, as well as the transcription and musical notation of the songs they collected.[32] The archivists arrived in the field with preprinted forms for each piece of music to be collected, with a standardized grid on which the particulars of geography, ethnicity, song title, as well as the coordinates of the performer and the performance, could be duly noted.[33] The work of putting the songs on paper in notated form, however, was largely done after the fact and relied on audio recordings, especially given the difficulty of rendering Taiwan's panoply of local languages and dialects into standard Chinese. An even more implacable problem, of which both Hsu and Shih were deeply cognizant, was that of performance style.[34] Much of what made the music they were hearing irreplaceable and worth preservation—what made folk music folksy—were parameters such as vocal and instrumental timbre, microtonal fluctuation, metric and rhythmic variations, and other acoustic accidents and irregularities, all of which lay beyond the purview of standard notation.

The problem was perhaps especially acute in Chen Da's case. In Chen Da, Hsu Tsang-Houei believed he heard a particular sound that elevated his music above that of the many other musicians he had encountered along the way.[35] Much of Chen's appeal lay in his ability to spontaneously improvise new and occasional lyrics atop the eight major tune types 調 that constituted the folk repertoire on the Hengchun peninsula. No performance, in other words, was definitive; no two were even alike. Indeed, Chen Da frequently moved freely between tune types over the course of narrating a particular story or even in the course of single song. The strings of his *yueqin* were made of nylon or fishing line, often very loosely wound at low tension and strummed with a plectrum fashioned of tree bark or "fish-thatch" 魚藤 (trifoliate jewelvine), allowing for free and irregular rhythms, sudden stops and starts, and variations in tempo, followed by flurries of plucked eighth or sixteenth notes.[36] Nor were the plaintive timbre of his voice and his phrasing reducible to notation. As Shih Wei-liang, writing in the booklet that accompanied Chen Da's first album, put it in the course of discussing the problem of notating his signature tune, "Sixiang qi" (Remember when):

> "Sixiang qi" has been one of the best known and most familiar folk songs for quite some time, and had long since been transcribed. Yet sung by Chen Da, the song has a special sound that no one else can touch. First of all, he has shattered the strophic form of the song, so that even the appearance of "Remember when," the fixed first line of each verse, is always in flux. . . . Moreover, Chen Da's rendition of "Sixiang qi" is full of flourishes and embellishments, parts of which we have tried to preserve to the extent possible as we transcribed. Yet if you tried to approach Chen Da's song simply on the basis on the notation, without actually listening to him sing, I'm afraid you could never understand the appeal of his distinctive cadence. In much the same way, what you get when a folk song's been notated by a musician, and then performed by another musician on the basis of the notation, will be very far from the "original."[37]

For all of these reasons, audio recordings—as a less compromised form of documentation of the "original" performance—were perhaps the most valuable sort of "immutable mobile" to be produced by the expedition. The relatively recent invention of portable reel-to-reel magnetic tape recorders was thus a huge boon for Hsu and his colleagues. In the immediate postwar period, Tokyo Communications Manufacturing 東京通信工業, the forerunner of the world-beating Sony Corporation, had begun to specialize in tape recording devices.[38] As early as 1953, Ibuka Masaru 井深大 traveled to the United States, signing a licensing agreement for transistor technology with Bell Labs that would eventually propel his company, and Japan, to the forefront of the consumer electronics business.[39] By the 1960s, Sony—along with other Japanese firms such as Sanyo 三洋, Asahi 朝日, and Akai 赤井, as well as the Swiss firm Revox—had brought a plethora of relatively lightweight transistorized tape recorders to the global market. In Cold War–era Taiwan, however, the importation of these devices was strictly regulated by the Central Bureau of Investigation, and each unit had to be registered with the central government because of the potential for unauthorized recording and reproduction of privileged information or Communist propaganda.[40] Recorders and high-quality microphones thus remained hugely expensive and difficult to procure in the late 1960s, and supplies of magnetic tape were scarce.[41] Hsu and his colleagues were extremely parsimonious with the supply they brought to the field, recording on slow-running 1-7/8 inch reels better suited to voice annotation than the transcription of music and using each side of a reel as a separate track, rather than recording in stereo (see Figure 5.1).[42]

Despite these difficulties, the tapes, many of which were later transferred to cassette by Hsu Tsang-Houei for use in the classroom, remain a richly polyphonic document, registering not only the music but also the protocol utilized in the recording process itself.[43] On one hand, the tapes provide an accidental window onto the rural world in which they were recorded, as crowing roosters, seagulls, casual conversation, and children at play seep into the audio field.[44] There are occasional microphone glitches, as well as the crackle and hiss of tape degradation. Most significant, each performance is preceded by a spoken audio-caption, providing in standard Mandarin Chinese the name of the performer and the title of the song, along with any other relevant information. The songs themselves, however, are never sung in Mandarin, and the contrast clearly signals the status of these tapes as a kind of "mobile" gating mechanism, making the music "immutable" at the same time that it propels it from one linguistic realm and order of knowledge to another. This is an order of knowledge, finally, in which the song itself as a discrete object of study is privileged over the quite different temporal rhythms of a story cycle or an impromptu live performance.

Figure 5.1. Fred Chiu with portable tape recorder, 1967.

## Chen Da and the LP Format

In 1971, three years after his initial discovery, Shih Wei-liang brought Chen Da to Taipei, inviting him into the recording studio to make an album of his songs under the auspices of the modest publishing enterprise called Hope 希望, which he had established in hope of promoting musical literacy in Taiwan.[45] The resulting long-playing record, accompanied by a booklet by Shih himself, represented a concerted attempt to transport an itinerant rural voice into urban living rooms. Could Chen Da cross over into a market made up of ardent consumers of American "hit music"? Might his record stand next to those of Bob Dylan or the Beatles on record store displays or even initiate new forms of musical commensurability and cross-fertilization between the two? Probably not. Despite its later significance as a cultural touchstone, the record was initially a commercial flop, and very few copies remain extant. Yet the album—from its provenance to its packaging and its paratextual apparatus—represents a complex and important attempt to open a portal between the "modern world" and its putative rural past. Yet, despite Shih's efforts to cast Chen Da as a mythic voice of a timeless Chinese tradition, *Musician of Our Nation: Chen Da and His Songs* 民族樂手陳達和他的歌 also provides startling insight into the historical and geographical contingencies of the distinctly Taiwanese and ineluctably modern folk circuit from which Chen Da had emerged.

Chen Da's record was recorded and pressed by Huimei Records 惠美唱片 in Sanchung-pu, an industrial suburb just across the Tamsui River via the Taipei Bridge that had become by the mid-1960s the center of the island's record manufacturing industry, accounting for some 70 percent of production. The densely populated streets of Sanchung played host not only to Huimei Records but also to First Records, Mingfeng Records, Wulong Records, RingRing Records 鈴鈴唱片, and King Records 大王唱片. These companies not only specialized in pirate pressings but also worked in symbiosis with the local cinema industry, pressing Taiwanese Hoklo and even popular music in a variety of aboriginal Formosan languages for listeners across the island.[46] The population in Sanchung itself represented an ethnic and linguistic patchwork of newcomers from rural areas. Arriving by rail from the agricultural south, these migrants were part of larger wave of urbanization that saw the percentage of the population living in urban areas island-wide mushroom from just 24 percent in 1950 to 60.7 percent in 1976.[47] The population of the Taipei metropolitan area nearly doubled between 1961 and 1981, from 3.5 to 6.2 million.[48]

If Sanchung provided much of the "software" for the record industry, the hardware came from a formerly rural village just across the Xindian River from Taipei called Zhonghe 中和. Hong Jianquan 洪建全 (1913–1987), the son of a coal miner, had grown up in the area under Japanese colonial rule, learning as a youth to repair radios and getting started in business as an importer of electronic components. Hong eventually founded one of Taiwan's most successful electronics manufacturers, National 國際牌, as a joint investment partnership with Japan's Matsushita Electric Industrial Company. When Hong sited its first manufacturing facility there in 1962, the workshops were surrounded by open fields.[49] By 1970, Zhonghe was among the most densely populated neighborhoods on the island, and National was a humming engine of import substitution, churning out everything from transistor radios and television sets to record players and home stereo equipment, as well as refrigerators and rice cookers. Chunghwa Market, a modern complex of eight low-slung concrete blocks built in 1961 and extending for nearly a mile along the railroad tracks in the heart of Taipei, served as the premier retail outlet for the city's burgeoning audio and electronics industry. Chen Da, arriving in the city by rail in 1971, would have surely have spotted National's iconic four-story neon ziggurat, anchoring the market's rows of record stores and radio shops and towering over Taipei's cinema and nightlife district, Hsimenting (see Figure 5.2).

Figure 5.2. Chunghwa Market in the 1960s. Photograph by Tom Davenport. Courtesy of the C. V. Starr East Asian Library, University of California, Berkeley.

The record Chen Da cut in Taipei, however, was utterly unlike the kinds of music blaring from market stalls onto the sidewalks of the market. This was not merely a question of its sound but also one of format. The accompanying booklet provided both transcriptions of the songs and translations of their lyrics into standard Chinese, as well as an introductory essay arguing for Chen's status as living repository of national culture and analyzing his grounding in the tradition. Shih's text brings this point home by recounting his own journey to Chen Da's home village as a kind of time travel:

> May. In the baking sun of southern Taiwan, the soil exudes a rich aroma replete with a feeling of fertility. It's only a five-minute taxi ride from the town of Hengchun to the village of Daguangli 大光里. Modern civilization has compressed time and space, and like a typhoon, will strip away and obliterate what remains of the order of agrarian society of days past. Yet Daguangli in large part retains the tranquility of a country village. It's not that civilization isn't capable of destroying it—just that the centrality of modern civilization has yet to establish itself here.[50]

Having introduced the story of Chen Da's life as a hardscrabble farm hand, migrant laborer, and itinerant storyteller and musician, Shih not only brings urban listeners along with him to the country but also transports Chen Da to the city and into commensurability with its "electrical" acoustic environment:

> Chen Da seems to have been born to preserve the lifeline of our national music. He's never married, never had a career, and his life has been spent in poverty and hard labor, but he's never put aside his *yueqin*, never ceased to perform, and this is the reason we can now say that he concentrates the essence of Chinese music in his playing, that his music is an encouraging ray of hope in a time of transition, for it is in him that we can see our true selves. Listening to his songs, we feel that we have finally found what we have been searching for all these years. Listening to his songs, any modern person with real musical feeling in their blood will be jolted by an electrical shock of recognition, will be moved, and transported, like a Beatles fan, by wave after wave of ecstatic feelings.[51]

The comparison to the Beatles, for Shih, springs from Chen Da's improvisatory lyrics, which reveal him not only as a practitioner in the tradition but also as an original artist and folk poet. The Beatles, he continues, have impressed urban dwellers as "wandering minstrels" 唱遊詩人, but Chen Da is every bit their equal in this regard, and even if his music does not play to the demands of the "modern sensorium" 現代感官, its authenticity might serve as the wellspring of a new modern sensibility.[52]

The modernist aesthetic of the album's cover art of the record also positions Chen Da on the cusp between the rustic and the contemporary. An original photograph of Chen Da by Tom Davenport is tinted bright yellow, tightly cropped to remove the spatial context of his performance as well as those who are listening to his recital. In the original photo, a trio of barefoot children surrounds Chen Da, listening raptly to his performance. A farmer sits to his left, and a man whose leather shoes likely identify him as a local official looks back at the camera. On the cover, however, Chen Da is flattened, isolated as a singular, even iconic, figure, rather than being seen as a member of a community. The image is broken up, moreover, into a geometric grid. On the left side, we see Chen Da's oval face looming above the circular expanse of the sounding board of his *yueqin*. The right side is divided into two quadrants: a blowup of his hand on the wooden sounding board of the instrument is placed above a close-up of his mouth as he sings. This disaggregation is clearly meant to suggest in visual terms the elemental quality of the music, its basis in wood and wind. Yet it is also a visual provocation. One of his eyes is badly damaged, either filmed over by scar tissue or perhaps even missing altogether. The few teeth that remain are crooked and stained. In Shih's accompanying text,

Chen Da is likened to a "mirror" for modern listeners in search of their roots.[53] Here we are invited to gaze closely at his unseeing face, perhaps with a mingled sense of discomfort and recognition. The close cropping and planar geometric pattern, in denying us any sense of spatial depth, emphasize rough-hewn textures: a crack running down an adobe wall, the patched and uneven grain of paulownia wood, the lines scored by time across the skin of Chen Da's fingers and forehead. These echoes not only fuse Chen Da with his instrument but also infuse the image with an organic sense of the tenacious historicity of his music (see Plates 9 and 10).

It is important to emphasize the extent to which this rhetoric of rusticity militated against the direction of the mainstream of the late 1960s. The culture, as we have seen in the case of Wen Shia, was captivated by the figure of the drifter 流浪 making his way in Taipei, not the rural remnant.[54] As the cultural critic Li Zhiming recalls, one of the sonic touchstones of his youth in Sanchung was a 1964 "mixed-blood" *Taiyu* pop song set to a Japanese melody, "Country Boy" 田莊兄哥 by Huang Xitian 黃西田.[55] Beginning with the blast of a train whistle and the call of a vendor selling a bento box lunch for the trip north and followed by a refrain that mimics the rocking motion of a locomotive, the song follows a young migrant, sick of the "smell of soil" and "the sound of croaking frogs," on his journey to new economic opportunities in Taipei. The cover art for the soundtrack album to the accompanying film, *Drifting into Taipei* 流浪到台北, shows Huang not as a "country boy" but as a young man who has already arrived, in both senses of the word, decked out in a stylishly cut white suit and a red pocket square, looking toward an offscreen television set, alongside a pretty young woman with a sleeveless dress and bobbed hair sitting by his side (see Figure 5.3).[56]

These sorts of sounds and images, moreover, were not restricted to urban circuits. The traffic flowed in both directions and even catered to rural markets. The island's electronics industry had increased its output by more than 280 percent in the 1960s and was producing U.S. $1.3 billion worth of goods by 1970.[57] By 1967, according to contemporary accounts, radios and record players were within the economic reach of most rural households.[58] Television had rapidly expanded since the launch of Taiwan TV in 1962, especially with the establishment of a nationwide color network, China TV 中視, in 1968.[59] With the opening of these media circuits came new kinds of urban–rural traffic and new musical forms. Tom Davenport, on his way south to photograph Chen Da in September 1967, attended a rural wedding in Jiuru Village 九如, Pingtung county 屏東縣, at which a local band, the Southern Sound Light Music Troupe 南聲輕音樂團, complete with a drum set, electric guitars, and a horn section, played

Figure 5.3. Huang Xitian, *Drifting into Taipei* 流浪到台北, Wulong Records FT-349.

the "beat music" known in the Chinese-speaking world as "a-go-go" 阿哥哥, as dancers in paisley, sleeveless dresses, and miniskirts celebrated the occasion (see Figures 5.4 and 5.5 and Plate 11). Indeed, it was precisely the sudden ubiquity of this new musical culture, which Davenport's informants rightly attributed to the "TV decade," that had provoked the ire and urgency of the Folk Song Collection Movement in the first place.[60] As early as 1962, with the initial broadcasts of Taiwan TV, "hit music" had been a prominently featured part of the programming mix, and by the late 1960s China TV regularly featured electric guitar-based a-go-go acts such as the Tel-Star Band, as well as the Mandarin pop stylings of up-and-coming singers such as Judy Ongg 翁倩玉 and Teresa Teng.[61]

Against this backdrop, Shih Wei-liang's insistence on Chen Da's timelessness makes a certain rough-and-ready sense. Yet close listening to Chen Da's recordings and close attention to the contextual information provided

Figure 5.4. A-go-go dancers, rural Pingtung county, September 1967. Photograph by Tom Davenport. Courtesy of the C. V. Starr East Asian Library, University of California, Berkeley.

by Shih Wei-liang himself reveal not a reified folk essence but the provenance of his music in an older but also distinctly modern folk circuit. For, not unlike the *Taiyu* pop of the 1960s, Chen Da's music arose from the exigencies of migrant labor and reflected the colonial history and cultural cross-pollination of his island home. Chen Da, born in 1906, hailed from the Hengchun peninsula, a region in which Chinese settlers had since their arrival in the late 1600s contended and intermingled with the indigenous peoples of the region. Chen Da's own grandmother was an indigene, and he insisted to a somewhat skeptical Shih Wei-liang that several of the songs in his repertoire partook of that same heritage.[62] By the first decade of the twentieth century, the Japanese colonial authorities had begun to develop the eastern coast of the island, still largely untouched by Chinese settlements, planting large tracts of sugarcane. By 1918, the Taitō Sugar

Figure 5.5. Rural wedding, Pingtung County, September 1967. Photograph by Tom Davenport. Courtesy of the C. V. Starr East Asian Library, University of California, Berkeley.

Company 台東糖廠 had constructed a railway linking Taitung 台東 to the rice-growing region of Chih-shang 池上 in the north. The peninsula, lacking extensive tracts of arable land, remained largely undeveloped. By age twelve, Chen Da had made the arduous overnight journey by sea from the Japanese whaling port of Hengchun to Beinan 卑南 in Taitung county to work in the sugarcane fields alongside relatives who had left home for economic opportunity.[63]

It was in Beinan that Chen Da first began to pick up the *yueqin*, and it was from the indigenous Puyuma melodies of that region—closed to Chinese settlement in the nineteenth century under Qing rule—that some of his repertoire also derived.⁶⁴ His performance on *Musician of Our Nation* is suffused with indigenous melody, and his improvised lyrics return again and again to memories of his participation in this colonial labor circuit. In his rendition of "Wukong Tune" 五空小調 he laments the shortchanging of laborers working under a burning sun by mean-spirited Japanese overseers. Another performance to the tune of "Spring the Year Round" 四季春 portrays his journey to the east on the Japanese steamer Fushun, in enigmatic, lyrical, and darkly cautionary terms:

> Passing the cape of Eluanbi
> Sea water sparkling gold
> Keen to leave and see the sights of the world
> I observe the black coral fish feeding on the little fish called parasols⁶⁵

**On the Impossibility of Campus "Folk"**

Ultimately, *Musician of the Nation: Chen Da and His Songs* was unable to cross over, resonating with neither rural fans of mixed-blood Taiwanese pop nor urban aficionados of Mandarin pop and the Anglo-American hit parade. Indeed, there is little evidence that the record circulated beyond a small coterie of intellectuals in Taipei, and Chen Da never performed for the sorts of audiences who might show up to watch a film by Wen Shia. For urban pop music devotees, even those who enjoyed Bob Dylan and the Beatles, Chen Da's linguistic idiom and the cumbersome apparatus devoted to its explication may well have been an impediment to acceptance. A deeper problem, and one that I explore in greater detail in this section, had to do with musical form—and what Shih Wei-liang referred to as the "modern sensorium." The handful of "tune types" in the Hengchun folk repertoire, each consisting of a repeated melodic line that a performer might improvise upon or embellish, do not necessarily lend themselves to the logic of modern pop song form or to the sequencing necessitated by the LP format. *Musician of the Nation: Chen Da and His Songs* consists of ten tracks, across which Chen Da plays five tune types. These tunes, however, do not function as discrete compositions. In the course of telling a single story of eloping lovers across eight verses, for instance, Chen roves across the boundary of two "tune types," "Sixiang qi" and "Wukong Tune." The selections presented on the album, moreover, radically fragment and abridge the original performance by reducing them to two tracks. In any context but the recording studio, Chen Da would have extended and elaborated a strophic narrative of this sort indefinitely, as song and spoken phrases alternated with riff-like melodic refrains strummed on his *yueqin*. A given narrative could certainly run much longer than the eighteen minutes per side of a standard long-playing record. And the long-playing record represented the best-case scenario for Chen Da in an acousmatic environment: his digressive improvisations were even less well suited to the rapid, regulated, time-slotted, and formatted temporal flow of radio and television broadcasting. The acoustic profile of his music, with its relatively limited dynamic range, also failed to approximate to the "modern sensorium" of electronically amplified music. Even more problematic was the fact that Chen Da could not play guitar, in an era in which that instrument emerged not just as an emblem of youth culture but also as the basis of popular musical syntax and thus acted as the guarantor of the transmissibility of any given song. Chen Da became an icon of a nascent folk revivalism, but, for all of these reasons, he could not serve as its musical model.

Ironically, Chen Da's gradual transformation into a mediated "spectacle" for urban intellectuals and aspiring folkies, as Wen-Shu Juan has shown, stemmed from the failure of his record to cross over.[66] By 1972, Chen Da had disappeared so completely from the public eye that Chang Chao-Tang 張照堂, an art photographer and music journalist then working as a producer for China Television, felt compelled to travel to Hengchun and film him at home in Daguangli for a segment of a news digest program called *60 Minutes* 新聞集錦.[67] In September 1973, Chen Da appeared briefly on television a second time, in connection with his participation in a Christian charity program called "Grandpa and Grandma Travel to Taipei" 阿公阿婆遊台北 that brought more than one hundred impoverished rural seniors to see the wonders of the modernizing capital city.[68]

Televisual clips, however, were even less suited to Chen Da's long-form balladry than long-playing records. In this sense, only live performance could bring Chen Da to the attention of urban listeners. In late 1976, it was again Chang Chao-Tang, an influential figure among the circle of rock and folk aficionados in Taipei, who helped bring Chen Da back to the city for an extended engagement.[69] Chang had already hosted a series of "Rock Dinners" 搖滾大餐, complete with a printed and fully annotated "menu" of the Anglo-American records he had curated for these occasions. He had also published a series of influential profiles of Bob Dylan, Joni Mitchell, and Van Morrison in a new glossy magazine, *Music and Stereo* 音樂與音響, a forum predicated on the mutual imbrication of music connoisseurship and the hi-fi industry.[70] As Chang wrote in the preface to one of his "Rock Dinner" menus, the superiority of music as a "medium of communication" lay in its ability to transport other worlds into one's living room via the simple act of "switching on a tiny transistor circuit, and playing a $15 record."[71] In order to argue for an analogy between Chen Da and the

Anglo-American singer-songwriters he had championed, Chang brought about another, even more dramatic sort of transportation. Working with a friend and fellow Dylan fan, the manager of the Scarecrow Restaurant 稻草人, Hsiang Tzu-long 向子龍, Chang brought Chen Da to Taipei for an extended engagement.[72] The resultant media coverage, orchestrated by Chang himself, led to a repeat billing at the club in 1977, as well as Chen Da's brief but significant presence within the ambit of a nascent "modern folk songs" and campus folk movement.

The story of the emergence of campus folk is complex and richly documented and has already been told elsewhere.[73] What I would like to emphasize here is its reliance on the transistor circuit. What the small circle of musicians, poets, and critics involved in launching Taiwan's "modern folk song" movement had in common was their acousmatic engagement—primarily via pirate records—with the guitar-driven folk revivalist sounds of Bob Dylan, Joan Baez, and Donovan. This was as much the case for an older and established poet like Yu Guangzhong (who had made a name for himself in the modernist literary ferment of the 1960s) as for youthful outsiders such as Hu Defu 胡德夫, a college student and aspiring singer of indigenous Paiwan heritage who had encountered counterparts such as Yang Xian 楊弦 and T. C. Yang 楊祖珺 on Taipei's coffeehouse scene in the early 1970s. Their music, moreover, was not only fueled by "tiny transistor circuits" but also subsidized by the island's burgeoning electronics industry. The first long-playing record to emerge from the movement, *A Collection of Modern Chinese Folksongs* 中國現代民歌集, presented Yang Xian's adaptation to the guitar-folk idiom of a collection of nine poems by Yu Guangzhong and was released in 1975 by none other than the Hong Jianquan Foundation 洪建全教育基金會, an organization established in 1970 by the founder of the National brand of consumer appliances to promote the arts and culture in Taiwan.[74] It was also to the Hong Jianquan Foundation that Shih Wei-liang, terminally ill with lung cancer in 1977 and concerned about the legacy and the livelihood of the singer he and Hsu Tsang-Houei had discovered, entrusted the re-release of *Musician of Our Nation: Chen Da and His Songs*. And the same foundation provided the seed funding for what remains Taiwan's most globally renowned modern-dance troupe, choreographer Lin Hwai-min's 林懷民 Cloud Gate 雲門, whose epic 1978 production, *Legacy* 薪傳—premiering on the very day that the United States broke off diplomatic relations with Taiwan in favor of the People's Republic—portrayed the migration of settlers to Taiwan since the seventeenth century. The soundtrack of that production was provided by Chen Da's balladry and opened with an epic song-story of Hokkien migration across the darkling waters to the island of Formosa, set to the tune "Sixiang qi." This momentous geopolitical event—Taiwan's unceremonious fall from its Cold War grace as the guarantor of a "Free China"—cemented the folk singer's status as a local icon. Delegitimated as the political representative of China proper, Taiwan would increasingly face inward and explore its own distinctive historical trajectory, with Chen Da serving as a portal into the island's "native soil."[75]

Even before this dramatic and, for many, traumatic political rupture, the rise of a local folk revivalism had been informed in complex and contradictory ways by nationalist and anticolonial currents. The defining incident in the historiography of the movement—one that has taken on a legendary status analogous to that of Bob Dylan's electrifying apostasy against folk ideals at the 1965 Newport Folk Festival—was the call one evening in December 1976 by Li Shuangze, then a student at Tamkang University, for the Chinese people to "sing our own songs" 唱自己的歌. Known as the "Coca-Cola incident" because of the bottle Li reportedly brandished (and perhaps even dashed to the floor of the stage) as he admonished his peers for mindlessly mimicking the Anglo-American pop brought to the island by pirate records, the event became a flashpoint, illuminating new possibilities for a locally produced and explicitly politicized folk song movement.[76] In some sense, Li Shuangze's exhortations were hardly new—merely answering in an emphatic affirmative the fervently anticolonial question Hsu Tsang-Houei and Shih Wei-liang had posed at the dawn of the 1960s: "Do we need our own music?"[77] Li's performance of this imperative, however, was hampered by the limitations of his generation's musical repertoire. After working his way on acoustic guitar through a selection of three songs in Taiwanese (including the classic 1930s popular ballad "Rainy Night Flower" 雨夜花) and a patriotic song in Mandarin (Li Jinhui's 黎錦暉 "Elegy for Sun Yat-sen, Father of Our Country" 國父紀念歌) to mixed cheers and jeers, his encore tune was less a definitive answer than a lingering question: Bob Dylan's "Blowin' in the Wind."

Li Shuangze, then twenty-seven years old and recently returned from a sojourn in the United States and the Philippines, was well aware of the internal contradictions of an anticolonial advocacy so deeply indebted to the norms and forms of the U.S. counterculture. That same night, in conversation with the MC for the evening, the popular radio DJ Tau Hsiao-ch'ing 陶曉清, Li quoted approvingly from the preface of a folk song book published just months before, in April 1976, and compiled by one of the leading writers of the emergent Native Soil literary movement, Huang Chunming: "Before we have the wherewithal to write our own songs, we should keep on singing the songs of our ancestors, singing them until we can write our songs."[78] Li himself would go on to write several of the classic protest anthems to come out of the folk song movement, including "Young China" 少年中國 and "Formosa" 美麗島, just before his untimely death by drowning the following year.

The cover of the first edition of the songbook, *Suite of Our Native Soil: A Selection of Taiwan's Folk Songs* 鄉土組曲: 台灣民謠精選, from which Li Shuangze had drawn inspiration, featured a color photograph of none other than Chen Da (see Figure 5.6). It seems natural, then, that Chen Da would also preside over the first major folk concert in the wake of the Coca-Cola incident, billed as an "Evening of Chinese Folk Ballads" 中國民俗歌謠之夜 and held at Tamkang's outdoor roller-skating rink on March 31, 1977. His improvisatory prowess left a deep impression on T. C. Yang and other young folkies in attendance. And yet, as Yang and other attendees that night have noted, Chen Da struck most of the college-age audience, having already assimilated the rhythmic norms of Anglo-American pop and unable to understand his speech, as something of an antique or an oddity.[79] As his performance went on, Yang recalls, many of the students "drifted away to talk among themselves under the stars," and the master of ceremonies eventually managed to convince Chen Da to cut his performance short.[80]

**Disparate Circuits**

Despite Chen Da's *visibility* as a kind of tutelary figure within the folk song movement, in other words, his musical aesthetic remained barely audible in its musical output. Why not? In the ensuing years, folk music took the island by storm. As Chang Chao-wei has emphasized, the left wing of the movement associated with Li Shuangze and T. C. Yang and the dissident journal *Xiachao* 夏潮 (Summer tide) was deeply committed to a populist notion of a politically engaged folk music, one indebted to the examples of Woody Guthrie and Pete Seeger and dedicated to the construction of community, rather than commercial opportunities. Yang, for instance, organized a "Grassroots Folk" 青草地演唱會 concert on September 28, 1978, one year after Li Shuangze's death, as a benefit for disenfranchised sex workers, many of them of indigenous origin. Because of their association with the burgeoning democratization or "Dangwai" 黨外 (extra-party) movement, this sort of folk activism was largely driven underground by the KMT. T. C. Yang's first album, featuring a pop-orchestral arrangement of Li Shuangze's setting of a 1940s poem by Chen Xiuxi 陳秀喜 about the settlement of Taiwan, "Formosa" 美麗島, was banned within weeks of its

Figure 5.6. Chen Da on the cover of Huang Chunming 黃春明, ed., *Suite of Our Native Soil: A Selection of Taiwan's Folk Songs* 鄉土組曲：台灣民謠精選 (Taipei: Yuanliu Publishing, 1976).

release.⁸¹ "Formosa" went on to become an important anthem of the democratic movement in the wake of a crackdown that December on democratic activists in Kaohsiung—whose dissident journal shared with it the same title—and an enduring sonic emblem of Taiwanese localist consciousness.

By the early 1980s, the politically engaged folk that had emerged from Tamkang University had all but been eclipsed by the wide dissemination and commercialization of what came to be referred to as "campus folk." This phenomenon, while informed to some extent by the cachet of a nascent nativism, was rooted in the popularity of American singer-songwriters such as Dylan and Joan Baez but even more closely akin to the appeal of the plangent sort of self-expression identified with 1970s singer-songwriters such as James Taylor, John Denver, and Carole King.⁸² It was spurred, moreover, by the easy availability of pirate records, printed songbooks, and cheap, locally made acoustic guitars (the production of which had begun to be outsourced to Taiwan from Japan). Campus guitar clubs proliferated throughout the 1970s, and aspiring singer-songwriters were snatched up from their midst by local record companies eager to cash in on this new youth market. Shin Lee Records 新格唱片 was the most important of these outfits, presiding over a new "Golden Harmony" contest 金韻獎 for singer-songwriters beginning in June 1977 and releasing "songs from the heart of the youth of a new generation" 由這一代年輕人的心聲 in a series of lavishly produced and best-selling long-playing compilations. Haishan Records, which had been selling Mandarin pop since the 1960s, quickly followed suit with its own "Folk Wind" 民謠風 series, the cover of which featured a pair of young folkies strumming guitars and silhouetted in psychedelic colors, with the legend "Everyone sing your own song!" 大家來唱自己的歌. The subtle modulation away from Li Shuangze's collectivist calls to "Sing our own songs!" to an emphasis on individual self-expression was telling, as was the aesthetic program outlined below the image: "A pure and simple sound—a wayward melody" 純樸的聲音，走調的旋律.⁸³ The competition-winning talents featured on these compilations, including Pao Mei-sheng 包美聖 (then a student in the History Department at National Taiwan University) and Chyi Yu 齊豫, were quickly packaged as the new starlets of campus folk and given their own releases.⁸⁴ Shin Lee also released a pair of long-playing records featuring instrumental arrangements of Taiwanese folk material in an up-to-the-minute Western pop-orchestral idiom, directed by a talented young composer and disciple of Hsu Tsang-Houei, Li Tai-hsiang 李泰祥.⁸⁵ By the early 1980s, the new sound, characterized with very few exceptions by wistful and poetic lyrics, the standard thirty-two-bar verse–chorus popular song form, 4/4 time signatures measured out with a drum kit and electric bass, sweet female voices, gentle guitar arpeggios, sophisticated studio production, string overdubs, and a certain purity of tone, had not only become the mainstream of Mandarin pop music but had helped to kick-start the local music industry. For in providing local content, campus folk also enabled record producers to shift away from the production of pirate records, move up the import substitution chain, and pivot toward positioning themselves as exporters of Chinese-language pop to the mainland.

It was amid this same boom, as we have seen in the preceding chapter, that Hsu Tsang-Houei convinced the founder of First Records to release a treasury of albums documenting Taiwanese folk sounds, starting with a newly recorded album of Chen Da's music, released in 1979.[86] Yet this recording, *Chen Da and Hengchun Tune Minstrelsy* 陳達與恆春調說唱, across the entire length of which Chen Da strung out a single rambling tale of the "miserable" fate of a migrant laborer and his son, shuttling back and forth on the steamship and sugarcane circuit between Hengchun and Taitung, could not have been more at odds with the new campus folk.

Much of the difference had to do with the ideological and logistical centrality of the acoustic guitar to the proliferation of campus folk. What made the guitar compelling—its mass production, its portability, its standardized intervals, and its compatibility with the syntax of Western tonality—also limited its applicability to local sounds. The songbooks on which aspiring folkies relied, from Huang Chunming's *Suite of the Native Soil* 鄉土組曲：台灣民謠精選輯 to later and more comprehensive bestsellers such as *The Key to Folk Guitar* 民謠吉他之鑰, compiled by the National Taiwan University's guitar club, were predicated on simple, easy-to-learn and easy-to-follow simplified notation, in which melodies were indicated by the numbers 1–7 and the accompanying chordal support was indicated by guitar tablature.[87] Time signatures and keys were also fixed within strict and familiar limits, and the alternate and open tunings that might have enabled more flexible approximations of the tonality of traditional instruments such as the *yueqin* were entirely absent. While these songbooks were at pains to transcribe Taiwanese folk tunes into guitar-friendly notation, in other words, making the music easily transmissible and commensurable with globally circulating pop music, their very form compromised and even silenced the musical qualities that made folk sound "folk."

When campus folkies arrived in the recording studio, moreover, their efforts were constrained not only by these musical conventions but also by the commercial demands and technical constraints of popular musical production and its appeal to the "modern sensorium." The cyclical and additive structures of Chen Da's story-telling sessions, with their variable and fluctuating tempi and constant dialogic toggling back and forth between an unaccompanied vocal line and a flourish of notes fluttering out from his *yueqin*, were fundamentally incompatible with the linear harmonies and predictable, evenly measured structures of the pop song. The sonic density of the interplay between his reedy tenor voice and the resonant twang of his instrument, firmly situated in a relatively narrow midrange band, carried well in open air to village audiences. But in an acousmatic listening environment, in which amplified music more often than not was decanted through domestic loudspeakers or blared out of the even smaller transducers built into transistor radios, portable tape players, or TV sets, a wider dynamic range was a prerequisite for a fuller sound. The regular pulse and three-minute pop song had long been integral to the sequencing of the long-playing record, the format of commercial radio, and the programming of televised variety shows.

Small wonder that when guitarists like Li Shuangze—well versed in popular song forms but unschooled in the syntax of indigenous musical practices—wanted to cover folk songs, they turned to transcriptions of this music into the only musical language they could use: pop song form. These transcriptions, as Hsu Tsang-Houei and Shih Wei-liang were already painfully aware in the late 1960s, had circulated in Taiwan for quite some time. "Sixiang qi," the Hengchun melody that has become Chen Da's signature tune and a powerful invitation for nativist nostalgia because of its refrain, "Remember when . . ." 思想起, had "long since been known to housewives and children, and had been transcribed by someone into notation quite early on," as Shih makes clear in his liner notes to *Musician of the Nation: Chen Da and His Songs*. Hsu Tsang-Houei, in a diary entry from the day before his fateful encounter with Chen Da, also commented on this song and its widespread popularity in conspicuously gendered terms:

> This evening in Fenggang 楓港, a poor village four hundred and sixty kilometers removed from Taipei, I encountered for the first time and with great emotion the true face of Hengchun folk tunes. . . . And tonight I want to say that the sins committed by those who in the past transcribed these songs were grave indeed. They dressed "Sixiang qi" up, slathered its face with make-up, and turned it into a "modern" and "civilized" "Sixiang qi" that's neither here nor there, so that it could continue to be popular at tourist venues in Taipei, so that it could continue to be insulted and distorted and suffocated.
>
> I want to plead on behalf of "Sixiang qi," to ask that we restore its freedom, to return it to its natural state, to let it live again![88]

In fact, both Hsu Tsang-Houei and Shih Wei-liang would have been well aware of who had perpetrated this enormity. His name was Hsu Shih 許石.

Born in Tainan in 1919, Hsu Shih, like Hsu Tsang-Houei, was the son of a doctor who had received his musical education in Japan and returned to Taiwan in 1946 to pursue a career as a composer and bandleader. That same year, he organized an island-wide tour, performing his own original compositions and collecting folk songs to adapt to a more modern idiom. By 1953, he had organized a "Taiwanese Native Folk Song Concert" 台灣鄉土民謠演唱會 in Taipei, in close collaboration with Hsu Ping-ting 許丙丁, a poet from the same region. This was the first of a series of similar concerts, held in 1959, 1960, 1962, and 1964, that were designed to promote and revive a tradition that, in Hsu Ping-ting's words on the concert program:

> reveals a sublime national consciousness, yet unfortunately has been trampled upon by the recent popularity of Japanese balladry, and even held in contempt by the upper crust of society, to the extent that we can hardly see it for what it is. What is needed is for all of us to discover, collect, transcribe, study, and cherish this tradition as a source for own creativity.[89]

By 1964, Hsu Shih had completed an orchestral suite based on these collected melodic materials, "Symphonie Folksongs of Taiwan" 台灣鄉土交響曲, which he premiered that year (see Figure 5.7).

What separated Hsu from younger colleagues such as Hsu Tsang-Houei and Shih Wei-liang, despite the manifest similarity of their rhetoric, was that he had also leapt feet first into commercial pop music and lacked their cool, modernist contempt for mass-produced kitsch. He instead authored several of the most enduring and sentimental favorites of the *Taiyu* hit parade of the 1950s and 1960s, including "Anping Reminiscence" 安平追想曲 and "Streetlamp at Midnight" 夜半路燈.[90] As early as 1952, Hsu also established his own recording company, issuing not only his own compositions but also those of prominent songwriters such as Yang Sanlang 楊三郎 under the "King" and "Queen" 女王唱片 labels. Pressings of his *Melodies of Taiwan* collection 台灣鄉土民謠, a series of instrumental adaptations of local folk songs, were a perennial favorite and were widely available in various formats from the 1950s through the early 1970s. He also organized and personally performed with a series of touring cabaret-style revues, such as the China Folksong Troupe 中國民謠合唱團, which he led to Japan in the 1970s, and the "Taiwan Peanuts" 台灣若比娜子, a popular duo composed of his two daughters, Hsu Pi-kui 許碧桂 and Hsu Pi-yun 許碧雲. These performances, which typically combined dance routines with young female musicians in colorful and none-too-authentic

Figure 5.7. Hsu Shih's *Melodies of Taiwan* 台灣鄉土民謠, King Records KLK-66.

native costumes, playing folk melodies on traditional instruments strapped on in the manner of beat bands with electric guitars, and accompanied by Latin rhythms and orchestral flourishes, were wildly syncretic. They were also, doubtless, precisely the sort of "dressed-up" and ersatz folk, played at "tourist venues" for the benefit of urbanites, that had so incensed Hsu Tsang-Houei (see Figure 5.8).

Yet it was precisely Hsu Shih's flair for orchestral arrangements and his facility with the syntax of popular music that allowed him to preserve and even popularize, albeit in altered form, the folk legacy of which Hsu Tsang-Houei had despaired. "Sixiang qi" is perhaps the best example of his success. Hsu Shih's transcription of the Hengchun melody into pop song form, with a delicately poetic lyric about romantic loss in the Taiyu

Figure 5.8. Hsu Shih's Taiwan Peanuts in performance, late 1960s.

vernacular appended by Hsu Ping-ting, was publicly performed as early as 1953 and was featured on his *Melodies of Taiwan* LP in 1962.[91]

The afterlife of the song was even more momentous. For once it had been rendered into an easily transmissible form, it entered into and quickly proliferated within an emergent *Taiyu* pop circuit. A slightly different version, performed by Lan Qian 藍茜 to a cha-cha beat, was released by Asia Records in 1957. Hsieh T'eng-hui's Taiwan Cuban Boys 鼓霸樂隊 reimagined the song as a jazzy big band number in the ballroom of the Taipei Ambassador Hotel.[92] Hsu Shih's student Liu Fuzhu 劉福助 rode another Latin-inflected iteration of the song, titled "Sishuang zhi" 思雙枝, to the top of the charts in 1968.[93] This is also the version employed by the pop idol Teresa Teng, readily identifiable by the sudden lurch into a-go-go–inflected double-time two-thirds of the way through shared by all of these covers of the song — a break we might call a kind of modernization modulation, as the old tune is performatively dragged by a drum kit into a new contemporary currency.

Even more counterintuitively, when the young firebrands of the modern folk song movement who opposed with every fiber of their being the cultural promiscuity of mixed-blood music and cover versions of Anglo-American pop attempted to re-create this crucial part of the folk repertoire, they turned not to Shih Wei-liang or Hsu Tsang-Houei's recordings of Chen Da but to Hsu Shih's cosmetically improved cover. Li Shuangze,

Figure 5.9. Hsu Shih in Hengchun in 1947, moments before his discovery of Chen Da. Photograph by Wen Shia. Image courtesy of Charles Hsu.

in his only recording of the song, left unreleased at the time of his death, relied on Hsu Shih's transcription and Hsu Ping-ting's lyrics.⁹⁴ Li Tai-hsiang's 李泰祥 disco-inflected cover of the song, included on his *Native Soil Folk* album 鄉土民謠, copies almost verbatim the melodic contours and structure of Hsu Shih's transcription, beginning with a reverb-laden statement of the melodic theme on a suitably folksy Chinese flute before finally breaking into the now familiar double-time drumbeat-fueled modernization modulation at its rousing conclusion. Even Chen Ming-chang 陳明章, one of the most serious and creative students of Taiwanese folk to have emerged in the wake of the revival and an ardent admirer of Chen Da, covered Hsu Shih's version in a minor mode, singing Hsu Ping-ting's plaintive verses over an artfully arranged acoustic guitar part.⁹⁵ In the end, then, the iterability of Hsu Shih's transcription and its adaptability to various media environments served as a guarantor of its longevity, over and against the artifactual authenticity of Hsu Tsang-Houei and Shih Wei-liang's singularly beautiful but unreproducible recordings of Chen Da's performances.

Perhaps even more unsettling to our accustomed narratives of the Taiwanese folk revival is the story of how Hsu Shih came to transcribe the song in the first place. In 1947, two full decades before Hsu Tsang-Houei wrote his well-known account of his tearful discovery of a half-blind folksinger in Hengchun and well before the advent of portable magnetic tape recorders, Hsu Shih set off from his hometown of Tainan, where he had recently secured a position as a high school music teacher, on a folk song–collecting expedition. At his side was one of his favorite students, Wen Shia, the scion of a wealthy family, who would go on to a long and storied career in Taiwanese popular music. The two young men disembarked from a bus at a stop on the road that ran along the seashore, took a pair of commemorative photographs, and strolled into the town of Hengchun, inquiring at the local inn as to where they might find someone who could sing folk songs (see Figure 5.9). They were pointed in the direction of the adjoining temple, where, they were told, a man named "A-Da" 阿達 would often perform on his moon lute for passers-by. And so it was that Hsu Shih and Wen Shia requested of the forty-year-old Chen Da a song. He obliged with a rendition of "Sixiang qi," they noted down the melody, and Chen Da's musical afterlife was ensured.⁹⁶ Decades later, in the wake of Taiwan's economic take-off, Chen Da would return to his hometown from the city, blind, destitute, and increasingly mentally disturbed. On April 11, 1981, he was hit by a bus speeding along the same road and died shortly thereafter.

CHAPTER SIX

# Teresa Teng and the Network Trace

Rising like a modernist obelisk on a cliff above the coast of the island of Quemoy (Kinmen) is a curious concrete structure. More than four stories high and symmetrically punctuated by circular portholes, the building looks like nothing so much as gigantic loudspeaker (see Figure 6.1 and Plate 12).

This is precisely what it is—perhaps the world's largest and most imposing sound system, housing an array of forty-eight horn reflex speakers and capable of projecting sound up to twenty-five kilometers away. This particular "wall of sound" 播音牆, built in 1967, is located above a beach in Kuningtou 古寧頭, the site of a hard-fought battle between the

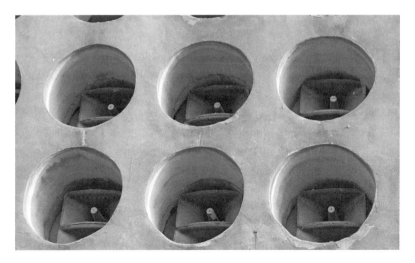

Figure 6.1. Detail of Beishan Broadcasting Station speaker array. Photograph courtesy of the author.

People's Liberation Army and the Nationalist forces of the Republic of China in late 1949, during which an all-out Communist effort to take the island was ultimately repulsed, leading to its continuing position at the front line in the Cold War conflict between the two states. As you look out from this windy bluff, across the narrow six-mile strait separating Quemoy from the Chinese mainland, the skyscrapers and the smog of the city of Xiamen are clearly visible in the distance.

Kuningtou was just one of five such "sloganeering stations" 喊話站 constructed between 1954 and the late 1960s as part of an extensive sonic infrastructure dedicated to waging "psychological warfare" 心戰 through the cross-strait projection of propaganda.[1] The construction of this and other defensive emplacements, as well as the deployment of nearly sixty thousand KMT troops to the island in August 1954, set off the First Taiwan Strait Crisis, during which Quemoy was subject to months of heavy artillery bombardment. When major hostilities were averted in late 1955 by the United States and its threatened deployment of its nuclear arsenal in service of "containment," the conflict switched to a somewhat cooler register. The Republic of China's loudspeakers were countered by rival installations on the mainland side, shouted slogans gradually replaced artillery shells, and each party contended for sonic dominance. The increasingly sonic character of the Cold War is already adumbrated in a propaganda poster from the 1954 crisis, in which Premier Zhou Enlai's pronouncements in protest of American military assistance for Chiang Kai-shek and his regime are imagined as thunderbolts of sound launched by a horn reflex speaker across the Taiwan straits (see Figure 6.2).

While these concrete towers may strike us now with all the pathos of the Easter Island figures—ciphers of an inexplicable and irrational past—they have much to tell us not only about the Cold War but also about the everyday Chinese soundscapes of the late twentieth century. Even before they fell silent, in the 1990s, hard-wired military sound systems of this sort had long since been rendered irrelevant by a stunning development in China's media infrastructure: the widespread diffusion beginning in 1978 of transistorized consumer electronics and, in particular, of inexpensive portable cassette tape recorders. Massive "walls of sound" were supplanted by relatively diminutive "bricks" of sound 磚頭式收錄機, as the "boom box" was called in Chinese. Cassette tape recorders and other domestic appliances had by the mid-1980s rendered the mainland's own massive, nation-wide wired network of more than one hundred million wired public loudspeakers obsolete, ushering in a newly privatized acoustic infrastructure. Kyle Devine, in an essay on the history of the loudspeaker in the twentieth century, suggests that "sound technologies and acoustic subjectivities

Figure 6.2. 1954 poster: "No American war provocation whatsoever can intimidate the Chinese people!" Chinese Posters Foundation, https://chineseposters.net, call nr. PC-1958-017.

consist in their mutual modulation." In this chapter, I explore how the emergence of this new acoustic infrastructure effected just such a modulation, one that produced new sounds, new ways of listening, and new affective interiorities.[2] It was a modulation, moreover, that had far-reaching social, political, and even military consequences, heralding the dissolution of the structures that had sustained the Cold War divide and enabling the advent of new forms of privatization and mobility.

In mainland China, this transistorized transformation of everyday musical life and its structures of feeling is intimately bound up with a singular figure: Teresa Teng. Born in Yunlin 雲林, Taiwan, to a mainland émigré family, Teng remains the single most beloved Chinese-language singer worldwide and an enduring icon of late twentieth-century Chinese media culture. She is also perhaps its most paradoxical. Although she was among the first and most formative figures in a newly transistorized, televisual, and transnational Mandarin pop circuit outside the mainland, her fame in China rests on her role as an avatar of the Chinese popular musical tradition of "modern songs" that had flourished in prerevolutionary Shanghai and postwar Hong Kong before its banishment by the Communist Party in the early 1950s. Her reputation in Taiwan was tightly tied to her televisual image, yet she was in China an ethereal presence: heard but not seen. Her music first began to trickle into the mainland in the 1970s by way of shortwave radio broadcasts. In 1978, with the opening of borders and the beginning of economic reform, that trickle became a wave, as cassette recorders and pirated recordings of her songs began to flow from coastal cities in the south to the rest of the country. By 1983, the extent of the popularity of her music had inspired a government campaign against "yellow music" and its attendant "spiritual pollution."[3] But to no avail— her music had become the unofficial soundtrack of the "new era" of economic liberalization presided over by Communist Party Chairman Deng Xiaoping, giving rise to a new popular adage: "Listen to 'Old Deng' in the daytime, and 'Little Deng' by night" 白天聽老鄧，晚上聽小鄧.[4] The phrase captures not only the contradictions but also the productive collusions enabled by Teresa Teng's music in the 1980s. For just as surely as her songs and the culture of listening that grew up around them radically displaced the centrality of the socialist media networks of the Maoist years, they also underwrote the legitimacy of the post-Mao modernization drive, in which collective aspirations were to be satisfied precisely by the satisfaction of individual desires. Teng's music also had far more material effects on China's modernization drive, for, in helping to bring into being a new domestic market for popular music, it was in no small measure responsible for the convulsive growth of China's consumer electronics industry.

In this chapter, however, my primary concern is in Teresa Teng not so much as an historical personage but as a particular acoustic effect, as an affective affordance, and even as a kind of domestic appliance. At the center of my inquiry is the elusive notion of timbre (or tone-color). How and why do we hear particular timbres as representative of particular historical moments or even as heralds of epochal historical change? Do particular eras really have a signature sound, and, if so, how do we access the musical past and characterize its tone? Is the sound of an era an ontological reality, unfolding in the present, or can it be grasped and narrated only after the fact?

Listening closely for timbre may help us answer some of these questions. Yet timbre is quite a slippery subject, in that it is usually understood as that particular sonority which is *beyond* the descriptive reach of musical notation. As Emily Dolan tells us in *The Orchestral Revolution: Haydn and the Technologies of Timbre*, modern notions of timbre find their headwaters in Johann Gottfried Herder's assertion that "tone-color" is a kind of remainder, "beyond pitch and volume," that allows us to distinguish between various different instrumental sonorities when all other parameters are equal.[5] Timbre can thus be understood in some sense as the particular acoustic trace of the resonating body by which it was produced. If that resonating body happens to be human, timbre is what allows us to identify the "signature" of someone's voice. If the resonating body is instrumental, it is the material trace that allows us to distinguish an acoustic guitar from an electric one, steel strings from nylon, or a kick drum from an 808 synthesizer. Timbre has been understood as "embodied and immediately sensible," a "direct experience" of a tone that resists abstraction into measurable values.[6] Yet timbre is also ineluctably historical, in that particular timbres are understood to be indexically linked to the people, the instruments, or even the locales and moments that produced them. For Dolan, this understanding of timbre as indexical is itself deeply historical, representing the "birth of an aesthetic" constituted around a new kind of attention to "music's immediate sensations and its mediating technologies, its instruments" in the eighteenth century.[7]

With the advent of electrical recording and a worldwide upsurge of vernacular musics in the late 1920s, as Michael Denning has argued, timbre emerged as the sonic signature that distinguished multiple genres from one another:

> [by] their characteristic ensembles, their instruments and voices. It is not surprising that these were heard as noise, because timbre is the product of the specific noise of an instrument: in acoustic terms, timbre consists both of the hard sound of the attack, the first pre-pitched

moment of the sound envelope, and of the peculiar mix of overtones or partials that color the fundamental frequency as the sound resonates and decays. Timbre long seemed an accidental and ephemeral aspect of music, escaping notation and evading the mathematics of harmony and rhythm: but recording gave new substance to timbre, as the sheer noise of voices and instruments reverberated even when the harmonies or rhythms seemed rudimentary.[8]

Denning is surely correct that electroacoustic recording allowed for a new dispensation of sound in which timbre loomed ever larger in musical aesthetics and came to serve as the distinctive metonymic trace of particular musical idioms, as well as of the idiosyncrasies of particular performers. In a subsequent age of multitrack studio recording, and especially in the wake of digital sound engineering, however, it would be naïve to understand timbre merely as a material imprint of the real, a Bazinian fossil form that allows us unmediated access to an historical moment. Much of the work of studio engineers is geared toward the meticulous crafting of specific timbral effects, whether through the selection and placement of microphones; the sculpting of echo, reverb, delay, and gating effects; or the deployment of software modules such as Auto-tune.[9] Recording engineers, in turn, have always been acutely aware of the specifications of the technical systems and the sorts of listeners for which they were designing particular sounds, be it Phil Spector famously crafting a "wall of sound" engineered for the limited frequency range of transistor radios, the Beatles' producer George Martin exploiting the capabilities of domestic hi-fi stereo systems to create new musical spaces and sonorities, or today's R&B producers playing to the particular tonal distribution and frequency specifications of laptops and earbuds.[10] Timbre, in this sense, is not merely a direct transfer or decal of a world but also something like a "network trace," a sonic signature that bears the indexical imprint of its historical moment by registering, in ways both overt and subtle, the mediation of a technologized acoustic environment, as well as diverse listening practices and forms of aesthetic attention associated with that environment. The network, in this sense, is also an "instrument."

We can hear in Teresa Teng's music just such a network trace. In order to explore this idea further, we need to return to the island of Quemoy. The first broadcasting station of its kind to be established was on the mainland side, in Xiangshan 香山, Fujian, in 1953.[11] Because of the geographic proximity of Quemoy and its neighboring islands to the coast, a series of four stations was subsequently constructed on the Taiwan side between 1954 and 1967.[12] In the years that followed, rival sound systems engaged in a high-volume sound clash, sparring with one another through slogans, threats, warnings, persuasion, military music, as well as the occasional pleasantry ("It's about to rain; please take in your wash from the clothesline"). Each station on the Taiwan side could muster 2400 watts of amplification, powering speaker arrays mounted in protective concrete bunkers, and between them, these installations were designed to envelop a broad swathe of the coastline surrounding the city of Xiamen in sound. One of these arrays, located at Guishan 龜山島, was destroyed in the blistering artillery attack launched by the mainland on August 23, 1958, amid the Taiwan straits crisis of the same year.[13]

On both sides of the strait, these acoustic networks were conceived as a weapon working in tandem with more conventional armaments such as artillery. At the height of the hostilities in 1958, for instance, each side attempted to press its advantage by way of a constant and menacing barrage of sound arriving in tandem with live cannon fire.[14] More typically, broadcasting personnel would take advantage of momentary lulls in the fighting, especially in the quiet of night, to press their case.[15] Their operations were also enmeshed with other forms of "psychological warfare," such as the airborne or seaborne dispatch (by way of specially designed artillery shells, helium balloons, and floats) of propaganda leaflets, canned goods and other desirable commodities, and, by the late 1970s, audiocassettes of popular music.[16]

This acoustic network was constituted not only by architectural structures, electrical equipment, and military personnel but also by the topography in which it operated. The network's design and operation, from the very start, needed to take into account the rate at which sound travels over water, as well as climatological conditions such as cloud cover, wind speed, and direction. Broadcasters were quick to identify and exploit ideal conditions under which sound might carry across the straits or to power down when fog or adverse headwinds might render any communications inaudible.[17] They also developed new sorts of diction and new speaking rhythms to adapt to the phase delays attendant on the sheer volume of the amplification and the distances their voices would need to travel:

> since we were transmitting from speakers almost as big as houses, we needed to broadcast one word at a time, so between each character, we needed to insert a two or three second pause, like this: "Dear—main—land—com—patriots. . . ." That's the only way we could be intelligible, and that's why it was called "shouting slogans" 喊話.[18]

Listeners, of course, were an integral if involuntary part of this military communications circuit, and their experiences were similarly shaped by the vagaries of the natural as well as the political climate. In the 1950s and 1960s, many of the broadcasts on both sides were of a belligerent nature, but by the late 1970s, with the slackening of political tensions, the tone softened, and recordings of popular music, especially those of Teresa Teng, became a regular feature of broadcasts emanating from Quemoy and aimed toward the coast.[19] The testimony of a student at Xiamen University provides an evocative sense of how cross-straits broadcasts were perceived in this period:

> What floated over to us from the Quemoy side were things like "Our brothers in the Communist army . . ." "Generalissimo Chiang . . ." "bounty money for defection. . . ." That would have been in 1977. . . . We wouldn't hear it all day long, because the tides and wind direction would have to be just right! I think it had something to do with the moon. When the moon was bright, when the night was quiet, the sound would be quite loud . . . at first we didn't like to listen to those Taiwanese songs, we felt that those were "decadent sounds," but later by the 1980s, when Teresa Teng came out, we started to feel that it sounded quite wonderful.[20]

Unlike other listeners throughout mainland China, local residents on the Fujian coast would have had the opportunity to hear Teresa Teng's voice not just in recorded form but projected live across the straits. She first visited Quemoy to perform for the ROC troops stationed there in 1974 and returned in 1981, in the course of a month-long tour of military installations across Taiwan that was made into a gala two-hour Taiwan TV special called "On the Front Lines with You" 君在前哨.[21] In 1991, she returned to the island, where she spoke directly to listeners across the straits by way of the military broadcasting station at Mashan 馬山. This command performance was also televised nationally in Taiwan and continues to circulate today in various online venues.[22] In the original telecast, a camera captures Teng, situated in front of a microphone in the Mashan broadcast booth, with the Chinese characters for "resonance" 共鳴—a phrase from a slogan on the wall extolling the efficacy of psychological warfare—clearly visible behind her.[23] She is clad in a military uniform and demurely brushes back her hair, before beginning to speak slowly and deliberately into the microphone. "Dear—main—land—com—patriots, this—is—Ter—esa—Teng." The camera cuts to a hazy view of the opposite coastline and then swings back to Teng as she continues:

> I am now—at the Quemoy—broadcasting station, umm, to broadcast—to my—main—land com—patriots. What I want to—say

today—is that I am happy—to stand at the frontline of—our free—
motherland—Quemoy. Umm . . . I feel very happy—very joyful.

Here, Teng's pace begins to quicken appreciably:

I hope—that my mainland compatriots can enjoy that same—
democracy and freedom. It's only with—a free, democratic, and
prosperous life—that individuals have the opportunity—to realize their
ideals. And it's only when—young people—are even more freely
able—to give rein to their intelligence and wisdom—that the future of
the nation—will be full of brightness and—hope.

At this point, the camera cuts away from Teresa Teng, asking us instead to survey the apparatus itself, as it pans across the honeycombed surface of the concrete tower through which her voice is resonating.

What is striking throughout the clip is the incongruity between the sweet sonority and occasional hesitancy of Teng's voice and the military-grade installation by which it is made into an instrument of diplomatic power. That incongruity is made even clearer when the camera cuts from the inside of the studio to the outside, substituting its close-mic'ed, anechoic representation of Teng's anodyne message for an acoustic image of what her voice—massively amplified, altered by electronic delay, and reverberating across open air—might sound like to listeners across the straits. What is dramatized for us here, in other words, is precisely the presence of Teng's voice in the circuitry of a Cold War network *and* the traces that the circuit leaves on her voice. This signal moment, however, came toward the very end of the service life of the broadcasting station. By 1992, the loudspeakers had fallen silent, and the ubiquity of Teresa Teng's voice in the mainland had long since been facilitated by other means.[24]

### Teresa Teng and Mobile Privatization

Teresa Teng was well positioned to play a starring role in the sonic theatrics of the Cold War. Her father was a rock-ribbed ROC military man from Hebei Province, who had arrived on the island as a refugee in the wake of the KMT's defeat. She was tutored in music by an uncle who played in the Unit 93 Military Entertainment Band (93康樂隊). Teng began performing informally at the tender age of six for the Nationalist troops stationed near her home in the Taipei suburb of Luzhou.[25] Yet Teng's later popularity stemmed not so much from her upbringing among KMT loyalists or her later billing as a "soldier's sweetheart" always ready to perform for the troops. Instead, her meteoric rise to prominence in the late

1960s and 1970s was directly tied to the emergence of new forms of transistorized media and transnational mobility. Her first big break came in 1968, just as Taiwan began to move up the import substitution chain as a manufacturer of consumer appliances and electronics. With the establishment of China TV—the island's first full color network—Teng was hired as the youthful host of the primetime variety showcase "A Star a Day" 每日一星, which aired for twenty minutes every night from Tuesday to Sunday beginning at 8:10 in the evening (see Figure 6.3).[26]

Teng had also begun in 1967 to record a series of long-playing albums of "a-go-go" dance tunes, Western pop covers, and ersatz versions of local Taiwanese, Chinese, and Southeast Asian folk numbers for a local company called Yeu Jow Records 宇宙唱片. Yeu Jow—which was also in the business of manufacturing pirated titles by foreign acts, including Nancy Sinatra and the Kinks—turned out long-playing records at a blistering pace: no fewer than thirteen albums were released under Teng's name in 1967 and 1968 alone. Yet it was Teng's association with the new, Mandarin-dominated medium of television, particularly her performance of two hit theme songs for China TV's serialized dramas, "Thanks, Mr. Manager" 謝謝總經理 and "Jing Jing" 晶晶, that catapulted her to national fame.[27] This success came at the same time that television ownership in Taiwan, which had already reached some 350,000 households, was increasing at a brisk clip; the number of sets on the island soared by 25 percent between 1968 and 1969.[28] As K'o Yu-fen has argued, television in the 1960s was not just a means of installing the imperatives of the KMT developmental state into domestic spaces but also an instrument of industrial policy, one that would kick-start a virtuous cycle of economic growth centered around the manufacture and export of consumer appliances.[29] In this sense, it is perhaps not surprising that Teresa Teng's star image—frequently featured on the cover and in the pages of the fledgling network's glossy magazine and program guide—shared space with advertisements for TV sets, stereo components, washing machines, refrigerators, and other trappings of modern domestic life (see Figure 6.4).[30]

Teresa Teng's mastery of standard Mandarin, in turn, was her passport to a wider diasporic market beyond Taiwan. In 1969, Teng relocated to what was still by far the most important global node for the production of Mandarin musicals and popular music, Hong Kong. There, following in the footsteps of Grace Chang and many others, she was featured in a highly self-reflexive film about a teen sensation making her big career move in Hong Kong. It was called *I Want to Sing* 歌迷小姐 (1971) and featured, between a series of staged song-and-dance numbers, a teenaged Teng

Figure 6.3. Teresa Teng featured in the pages of *China TV Weekly* 中國電視週刊 (1969) alongside advertisements for home appliances. Figures 6.3a and c appear in 1969 volume 7; 6.3b appears in volume 16.

Figure 6.4. Album cover for Teresa Teng's 1968 hit "Jing Jing" 晶晶, Yeo Jow Record AWK-010.

(playing a character called Ding Dang 丁鐺) fearlessly presenting herself at the studios of Pathé-EMI Records and winning the affection and respect of an established pop singer (Lan Yun 藍雲, played by Zhang Chong 張沖), who takes her on as a protégé. This Hong Kong sojourn, during which she recorded prolifically in Mandarin, allowed Teng to break into the Southeast Asian diasporic circuit, as her records and her reputation as a rising star spread across Singapore, Malaysia, Thailand, and Indonesia.

Teng's vertiginous takeoff in the 1970s seemed to augur an ever-increasing mobility, as her music began to flow, seemingly without friction, across national and linguistic borders. By 1974, she had parlayed her familiarity with Japanese popular music (to which she had inevitably been exposed growing up in the Taiwan of the 1960s) to break into a new entertainment circuit, winning first prize at the Fuji TV–sponsored Shinjuku Popular

Music Festival and signing with Polydor Records in Japan. Her indicatively titled first hit, "Airport" 空港, an *enka*-styled tune sung in flawless Japanese about the melancholy farewell between a mistress and her married paramour, became immensely successful and inaugurated a run of eight Japanese releases between 1974 and 1985. Transnational distribution of her music by Polydor also helped to introduce her to new markets across Southeast Asia.

In 1981, Teng became the face of a multinational advertising campaign, beamed to television screens across Asia, for Yamaha's new line of motor scooters, the "Passola," on which she zipped around town doing her daily errands, every inch the epitome of the modern, upwardly mobile office lady or happy young housewife. The Passola billed itself as something of a fashion accessory; its brightly painted frame and flatbed footrest made moving around the city easier and more elegant for riders in high heels. Teng's star image, often characterized as epitomizing the innocent "girl next door" or even idealized as a representation of a virtuous yet vivacious "Chinese femininity," thus straddled the space between middle-class domesticity and the accelerating demands of a developing economy (see Figure 6.5).

Despite this increasing currency in the 1980s, however, her crossover into the Japanese and pan-Asian market had not been entirely frictionless, nor had it been unencumbered by the shadow of Cold War division. Two years before her stint as the spokesperson for the Passola, the United States formally broke off diplomatic relations with Taiwan as part of its pivot toward formally recognizing the People's Republic of China, and Japan quickly followed suit. Taiwan, in retaliation, broke briefly with Japan and imposed travel restrictions on its citizens traveling to that country. Fearful of losing her access to the Japanese entertainment circuit, Teng purchased a fraudulent Indonesian passport in Hong Kong for $20,000 to smuggle herself back into the country for a concert tour. Upon her arrival at Haneda Airport in Tokyo, however, she was questioned, detained, and deported.[31] As contemporary news reports seemed to relish pointing out, her ruse was detected because the customs agent was a fan and recognized her right away.

This embarrassing incident ultimately did little to inhibit Teresa Teng's rise to the top of the entertainment firmament. This was in part because her physical presence had already become less instrumental to her success than the cross-border circulation of televisual images and phonographic recordings. Live shows, while remaining part of her portfolio as a performing artist, were increasingly a supplement to her mediated presence. Teresa Teng came to life and was consumed by most of her fans in

Figure 6.5. Taiwanese advertisement for Yamaha's "Passola," early 1980s.

the comfort of their living rooms, whether through a hi-fi stereo console or beamed in by way of an FM or television broadcast. Her popularity in this sense was an artifact of the arrival in East and Southeast Asia of what Raymond Williams identifies as a new form of modern living, predicated on the presence in the home of audiovisual and other appliances:

> By the end of the 1920s the radio industry had become a major sector of industrial production, within a rapid general expansion of the new kinds of machines that were eventually to be called "consumer durables." The complex of developments included the motor-cycle and the motor-car, the box camera and its successors, home electrical appliances, and radio sets. Socially, this complex is characterised by two apparently paradoxical but deeply connected tendencies of modern urban industrial living: on the one hand, mobility, on the other hand the more apparently self-sufficient family home. The earlier period of public technology, best exemplified by railways and city lighting, was being replaced by a kind of technology for which no satisfactory name has yet been found: that which served an at-once mobile and home-centered way of living: mobile privatisation.[32]

Williams's insight is properly dialectical in the sense that in the very moment that household appliances enable the emergence of a mass audience, they also atomize and isolate individuals within the confines of the bourgeois home. While Williams sees the advent of this process in the popularization of radio in the 1920s, it was only with the cost savings enabled by the transistor that mobile privatization as a mode of media consumption began to saturate not only the urban centers of the West but also Japan and its postcolonial peripheries in Taiwan and Korea. Sony, Samsung, and Matsushita (known as National in Taiwan), in this sense, were instrumental to a new wave of capitalist expansion in the 1960s, turning the world outside in. For just as the wider world as mediated through consumer-grade appliances colonized domestic space, those same appliances, manufactured ever more cheaply and in ever greater numbers, began to percolate out from manufacturing centers like Taipei into the rural interior.

In this new dispensation, Quemoy was an anomaly. Because of its proximity to the mainland, the island had long suffered under a state of military siege, becoming, as Michael Szonyi has termed it, "the state of exception within a state of exception" that was the Cold War.[33] The island's wartime footing, involving precautionary measures taken against any form of espionage, had forestalled the advent of "mobile privatization" as a generalized condition for local residents. Quemoy was in fact one of the only places in the Republic of China where transistor radios were entirely banned and televisions tightly controlled for fear that their components could be used to communicate with the mainland or serve as a conduit for locals to listen to "enemy" broadcasts. (Basketballs were also banned, since they could double as a flotation device for would-be defectors.)[34] Rather than listening to portable radios, villagers across Quemoy were entertained and edified by a wired broadcasting network that extended out from the principal township of Jincheng.[35] Residents of the island, in other words, shared with their mainland compatriots of the 1960s and 1970s a reliance on public, fixed, and hard-wired broadcast networks that saturated public space with official programming. Quemoy was, in this sense as well, far closer to the mainland than the rest of Taiwan.

**Ethereal Voices**

The media infrastructure of the Chinese mainland, of course, had been explicitly engineered in the post-1949 period to defeat the very possibility of mobile privatization, favoring instead the mobilization of mass publics through collective listening. Yet, as is widely known, intrepid Chinese listeners had long since learned to bypass the monolithic sonic dominance of the Central People's Broadcasting Station and its extensive wired network of loudspeakers by tuning into shortwave broadcasts from abroad. This surreptitious practice, condemned as "listening to enemy radio," was both dangerous and difficult. Government measures to jam objectionable frequencies meant that reception was sporadic. By the early 1970s, however, rates of radio ownership, especially of cheap and portable transistor models (as opposed to tabletop tube sets), had begun to increase. Even before the end of the Cultural Revolution, it was possible in major cities like Beijing to listen (behind closed doors and shuttered windows) to Taiwanese broadcasts directed at the mainland, as well as to Chinese-language programs offered by the BBC, the Voice of America, and Australian National Radio. These programs featured not only news but also musical programs featuring the songs of Teresa Teng. Anecdotal accounts indicate that the opportunity to hear her music was a primary attraction. A typical account, from a man who was a young police officer in Beijing at the time, describes the sensation of hearing her music for the first time in 1975 as a kind of intoxication 陶醉: even with the sound so low that he and his friends would have to press their ears to the wooden frame of an old shortwave radio, their bodies would begin to tremble in response to the beauty of her songs, in a paroxysm of pleasure but also out of terror of the enormity of the transgression.[36]

For the generation of former Red Guards and "educated youth" that was relocated in vast numbers to isolated rural areas beginning in 1969, listening to "enemy radio" became by the mid- to late 1970s a common, even collective, practice. The writer Ah Cheng's 阿城 account of his internal exile in the mountains of Yunnan is perhaps representative in this regard:

> Yunnan was endowed with a magnificent geographical gift: you could hardly hear Central People's Radio, and the newspaper would take days to make its way into the mountains and then be collected at the Party Secretary's house, where you could ask him to tear off a strip when you wanted to roll up a cigarette. For people who listened to enemy radio, radio from the center or the official newspaper were merely a supplemental reference. But listening to enemy radio was not about political news so much as entertainment. I remember that whenever the Australian National station broadcast a radio play of the Taiwanese film *Story of a Small Town*, everyone would bring their own radio, because the shortwave signal would tend to drift, and that way, we could cover the entire frequency range and make sure we had continuous sound from at least one receiver at a time. The boys and girls sitting around that grass hut would be in tears! Especially when Teresa Teng's voice rang out, emotions would rise to a fever pitch—her voice was to die for.[37]

In this and nearly all accounts of encountering Teresa Teng's music for the first time, there is an extraordinary and almost overwhelming sense of affective intensity.[38] Teng's soft pop stylings—which may register today as pleasantly romantic at best and perhaps syrupy or sentimental at worst—were perceived as nothing short of revelatory, a sound to be savored with a rush of tears. In the popular culture of the post-Mao period, these moments of initial aural encounter, repeatedly evoked in memoir, fiction, and film alike, have often come to serve as a highly compressed synecdoche for the complex personal and collective transformations wrought by the postsocialist transition.[39]

How do we historicize the affective response Teresa Teng's music evoked? For many memoirists in the mainland, Teresa Teng's voice serves as a powerful solvent, disaggregating the socialist past and its soundscapes from all that ensued later on. Where revolutionary songs spoke in strident tones of the collective, Teresa Teng gave voice to a previously proscribed world of private sentiment. In a world of privations that valorized hard proletarian self-denial and steely determination, she represented sensuality, softness, and emotionality. In a brave new world in which traditional feminine differences had been suppressed in favor of a masculinized revolutionary ideal, she embodied the lost graces of an idealized Chinese womanhood. In a drab planned economy, she represented all the flash of consumer goods and the promise of prosperity. She provided, in other words, precisely what the everyday life world of socialism lacked. The literary critic Cai Xiang 蔡翔, in an essay on the Chinese 1970s, echoes many of these notions. Against the prohibitions of an "overly rigid, even prohibitive" system, he asserts, Teresa Teng's music provided a "transgressive thrill" by opening a window to a curious new world beyond socialist normativity.[40] "All it took was one Teresa Teng," he relates having said to a friend, "to bring the 'The East Is Red' to an end."[41]

There is a great deal of truth in all of these ex post facto narratives. Yet they also tend to traffic in starkly binary and therefore suspect categories such as collectivism and individualism, backwardness and modernization, repression and freedom. In this sense, they replicate the very ideologies that underwrote China's postsocialist process of marketization in the first place, without necessarily taking us closer to the specificity of Teresa Teng's sound and its specifications. They also tend to elide and suppress memories of the presence of lyrical sentiment and even the (albeit rare) songs of love in the socialist musical repertoire of the 1950s and early 1960s.[42] Nor do they provide us with a more material understanding of the media infrastructure that shaped how that sound was heard and understood.

Perhaps more telling are those accounts of listening to Teresa Teng that linger a little longer on the surface of the music itself, providing close, even granular, attention to the quality of Teresa Teng's voice. Here is one example, from a blog by the Shanghai-based cultural critic Zhang Hong 張閎:

> One afternoon at the end of the 1970s, a group of college students gathered in a dilapidated bedroom, surrounding a big brick-shaped Sanyo-brand tape recorder. What emerged from the tape was a female voice, cotton-soft, sticky-sweet, by turns crystalline or honeyed, sometimes impassioned and full of heat, sometimes meandering, hesitant, and tinged with melancholy. At certain moments it sounded almost as if she was running out of air, as a fetching kind of breathlessness crept into her voice. I asked timidly: "Who *is* this?" Someone answered by invoking an unfamiliar name that sounded archaic and ethereal to my ears: "Deng Lijun."[43]

Here, once again, we sense a contrast, but it is at first blush a timbral contrast, rather than an immediately ideological one. Teresa Teng sounds soft, even tentative. There are spaces between the notes and subtle microvariations of pitch. There is, above all, a sense of corporeality generated from the breathiness of her performance, from the almost imperceptible intake of air preceding a note, the sibilance of an initial, the vibrato quaver that swells and prolongs a syllable, or the slight nasal sigh with which a melodic phrase trails off toward silence.

All of this, of course, placed her music in direct opposition to the folk-inflected and bel canto vocal styles, insistent duple rhythms, unremitting intensity, and timbral stridency of revolutionary song. To reprise Liang Maochun's concise commentary cited in chapter 2, the musical aesthetics of the 1960s and 1970s were "high, fast, hard, and loud," in part because revolutionary song was deeply imprinted by the features of the wired loudspeaker network through which it was disseminated. Melodic range was limited, not only to facilitate communal singing but also because the frequency range of the ubiquitous horn reflex loudspeakers that made up the wired broadcasting network was extremely restricted, with little or no bass response. The public soundscapes of the Cultural Revolution era, in other words, were canted toward the upper midrange and above. It was also monophonic, meaning that it would have been difficult, if not impossible, to parse out individual voices from within a choral ensemble. Even if that had been possible, voices were almost never close-miked, and the recording practices of the period, geared toward amplitude and intensity, rather than fidelity, tended toward overdriven, grainy, and distorted vocal textures. In a 1966 recording of "Our Hope Is Placed on You" 希望寄託在你們身上—one of the best known of the quotation songs discussed in chapter 2—the timbral surfaces of its chorale sound seem almost to crack under the strain of containing such a large and exuberantly revolutionary sound in such a small acoustic space.[44] That "wall-of-sound" effect would only have been amplified when it was broadcast over a network of tinny, horn-driven speakers mounted on school or factory walls, urban streetlamps, or rural electrical poles.

The socialist soundscape, in other words, bore the traces of its media network. Nowhere was this trace more pronounced than on the human voice. The contemporary critic Wang Min'an 汪民安, in a set of exploratory essays on the aesthetic affordances of household appliances, insists on the primacy, even the nonhuman agency, of the broadcasting network itself, asserting that voices on the radio:

> are a sonic assemblage. Voices are transmitted through the machine, but the machine is not by any means a transparent conduit or pure medium. Is the voice making use of the machine to speak to other

people? Could it be that the voice exists for the sake of the machine? Or that the voice finds itself in the radio, that is, it exists first and foremost for the machine? When the voice speaks, the first listener is the machine. The first objective of the voice is to be heard by the machine. The voice needs to accommodate itself to the machine. Yet the machine is itself like a vocal organ, just as the tongue, the lips, the nasal cavities, and the throat form an assemblage through which the collisions of breath with its surroundings are shaped into sound. The apparatus of the machine, like these bodily organs, alters the tonality of the voice, changes its syntax, and its significance.... Precisely because of the machinic quality of the radio voice, it becomes more serious, firmer, more authoritative, more saturated with the "truth." This kind of voice has a clangorous rhythm, like a machine. In a specific era when the radio was in thrall to politics (during the Cultural Revolution), the sound of the radio (often coming through public address systems) wiped away the contingencies and idiosyncrasies of people's voices, and even wiped away their desires and their genders, until they became components in the coming together of an automated code. This was a man-machine assemblage. In this assemblage, what was speaking was neither the voice of a human being alone, nor the voice of the machine, but a combination. And this is why, under specific historical circumstances, broadcasters are of very little importance, because their systems of articulation have already been rewritten by machinic elements to resemble the apparatus itself, so that their very voices ring with a steel-like sonority.[45]

Wang's account, moreover, stresses the primacy of listening over looking in the media dispensation of the socialist period, arguing that:

People who could talk, and not those who could act, people with nice-sounding voices and not pretty faces—in other words, those who could speak well rather than look good—became for the brief time when radio ruled the real stars. At the same time, because these voices were tightly tied to historical tastes, those voices registered the changes undergone by society and its power structures, and in just such a way, the voice became an ideological machine for the nation, not only shaping the national language, but also through its manner of speaking remolding the manner of speaking of the citizenry.[46]

This insight is borne out by Nicole Huang's revelatory research on the intermediality of popular cultures of the late Mao period, in which access to television was rare, the popularity of radio-plays based on feature films sometimes eclipsed that of the films themselves, and voice actors who dubbed foreign films into Chinese achieved something like a cult status among cinemagoers that far exceeded that of the actors onscreen, precisely because of the exotically foreign inflections of their spoken Chinese.[47] What Huang's research suggests is that audiences in the 1970s, primed by a culture of listening, were already acutely attentive to variations in tonal emphasis and vocal timbre, especially if they diverged from official or local norms.

For these reasons, we should perhaps not be surprised that the now notorious collection of articles issued by the editors of the state-run periodical *People's Music* 人民音樂 to combat the scourge of Teresa Teng's music in the mainland, *How to Distinguish Yellow Songs* 怎麼鑑別黃色歌曲, despite its ideological stridency, registers a sensitivity to the nuances of vocal and instrumental timbre that is equally exquisite, if far less approving, than that of the Ah Cheng and Zhang Hong anecdotes cited earlier, in which small groups of intimates lavish rapt attention on a distant and disembodied voice resonating through a radio receiver. The collection begins with a provocative question: How can music have a "color"?[48] The origins of the term—said to derive from the analogy with the off-color quality of American "yellow journalism"—are initially explained with reference to the history of the origins of the music in the degraded colonial culture of prerevolutionary Shanghai. The author, Wu Yongyi 伍雍誼, is careful and convincing in tracing the music back to its origins in Shanghai's nocturnal economy of dance halls, cabarets, and cathouses. We are provided with taxonomies of the sorts of lyrics of which unsuspecting listeners should be wary and an analysis of how their off-color and objectifying portrayal of romantic love reflects the alienation of human relations in a commodity society.[49]

The problem with yellow music (a category with which contemporary popular musical imports from Hong Kong and Taiwan are conflated), however, is not merely the way in which it shows the distortions of capitalist culture. Worse still, as the next chapter of the collection, "How to View 'Popular Songs' from Hong Kong and Taiwan" explains, those distortions are mirrored in the tone-colors of the music itself.[50] Even a seemingly healthy song like Teresa Teng's cover of the perennial "Village Girl Who Sells Watermelon" 小村姑賣西瓜, which may superficially appear to reflect the struggles of the working-class migrants in the city, conceals a number of musical booby traps, from its toe-tapping rhythm to Teng's "slippery and seductive grace notes and portamento slides," all of which inevitably trivialize their subject.[51]

The essay goes on to an attentive, even lovingly detailed, musical analysis of Teresa Teng's 1976 Polydor release *Island Nation Love, Volume 2* 島國之情歌第二集—although the record, banned at the time, could have reached the author only as a contraband cassette. In fact, the mere mention of Teresa Teng's name is strictly taboo throughout the ten articles and nearly sixty pages of the pamphlet, and she is referred to only obliquely as "a certain singer," even as her presence is felt on nearly every page. The author, Zhou Yinchang 周蔭昌, begins by singling out, in remarkably sexualized terms, the seductive problem of syncopation in Teng's "Night Mist" 夜霧, for which he has helpfully provided a chart in simplified notation:

> Everyone has had the experience of hearing music (particularly music with a strong rhythm) and feeling their body's mechanisms of motion begin to unconsciously change in response, to harmonize with the pulse of the music. These so-called "popular songs," in their continual use of syncopations that evade the strong beats, never allow the body to harmonize with the normal pulse of the music, so that it always falls just short. The music constantly tempts you to become one with it, but won't let you take hold of it, and so you feel its flicker and sway as seductive, all the more so what with the soft and pillowy melodies and sweet and sticky vocal performance.[52]

The "perversity" of the music is compounded by the "special" kinds of sonorities employed by the accompaniment, sonorities so new and strange that they can be described only in phrases that profane ordinary Chinese syntax or even require resort to the realm of graphic illustration of their shapes: "massive wave-like ripple trills, great sighs sounding out husky timbres, and underneath the sighs, sounds that take on the shape of an olive in their enunciation."[53] These instrumental timbres mimic the sounds of the body in the extremities of intoxication, indulgence, and even sickness and cannot but help to stimulate the listener.[54] Yet even more central to the effect of the music is the "delicate and cloyingly feminine" 嬌聲嗲氣 tonality of Teng's voice itself, the qualities of which are elaborated in no fewer than five dimensions and illustrated with musical examples and charts: (1) her use of whispers and the spoken voice, (2) the breathiness of her vocal tone, (3) the beguiling delicacy of her enunciation, (4) her frequent and "seductive" use of glides and quavers, and (5) her use of rhythmic variations such as delay, unexpected pauses, and the reversal of stress on the syllables in a particular phrase.[55]

Significantly, Zhou singles out for mention the often taken-for-granted technology that has rendered these timbral subtleties so distinctly audible: the multitrack recording studio. While he is unimpressed by the instrumental arrangements as such, he is struck by the clarity with which each frequency band is isolated: from the bass guitar at the bottom, to the keyboard and electric guitar in the middle, to the vocals and orchestral embellishments "floating" above the mix.⁵⁶ These aspects of the recording, of course, were unremarkable aspects of international pop recording practice in this period—but were unheard of in China. As such, the care with which Zhou elaborates these aspects of the mix indicates the extent to which his critique also represents an encounter with a different kind of network trace. And while Zhou does not mention the microphone, his fascination with every nuance of Teng's vocal performance not only is enabled by close-miking but also describes exactly the breathily intimate style of crooning that, from the early years of electrical recording in the late 1920s, had developed in symbiosis with the affordances of that technology.⁵⁷ Just as the microphone offers the listener a new kind of proximity to the body of the singer, the amplified audio image of that voice is also located within a spacious stereophonic sound stage. Each instrument has its individual place within that stereo image: the steady tap of the hi-hats on the drum kit, the pillowy warmth of the bass guitar, the arpeggiated chordal support of the rhythm guitar, as well as the occasional orchestral flourishes that swell in the background. Every instrument is cleanly played and recorded, without a hint of harmonic distortion. *Island Nation Love*, like all of the Teng's records from the 1970s, has unmistakably been engineered with the two-channel home stereo system in mind, and thus its acoustic contours fit comfortably into the domestic spaces in which her music would usually have been consumed.⁵⁸ In a very real sense, its sound engineering presupposes the domestic listener as part of a network, one who is encouraged to take up position in what domestic hi-fi enthusiasts call the "sweet spot" where the stereo image converges in front of the speakers.⁵⁹

I began the chapter by suggesting that Teresa Teng might be analyzed as a kind of domestic appliance, one that allows new sorts of affective or even analytical affordances. Zhou's protestations notwithstanding, he is quite clearly in the "sweet spot," perfectly positioned by the network affordances of Teng's transistorized pop to immerse himself in the treacly qualities of her music. How much the more so for ordinary, nonprofessional listeners? In Zhang Hong's memoir of his encounter with that voice, as well as many others, there is almost always a description of not only the listener's position vis-à-vis a transducer (a sound source) but also exactly where he or she happened to be at that moment (a point of audition). The elephant in the room, in other words, is precisely the room—in Zhang Hong's case, the dilapidated but safe space to which he and his intimates retreat in order to listen closely to the music. What renders that room resonant in memory, in turn, is the imported Sanyo tape player that conveys Teresa Teng's "ethereal" voice in from the outside, carrying with it the "archaic" suggestion of a prerevolutionary linguistic habitus and ideological order, that of the exiled KMT.⁶⁰

The Sanyo, in other words, is the gate through which an exotic Teng jumps across a threshold, opening up a new musical circuit and bringing the music of "Free China" back home. In this sense, the portable radio–cassette recorder—first developed in Japan in the mid-1970s—came to occupy a rather different place in China's musical infrastructure than in the developed world. In the United States, these machines were infamously dubbed "boom boxes" or "ghetto blasters," often condemned for bringing popular music out of the home and into urban streets and public spaces.⁶¹ In China, however, they were largely, if not entirely, domestic appliances, serving less as instruments of musical mobility than as tools of musical privatization. The first portable cassette decks arrived in southern China in 1978, followed by a flood of imports and copycat local production. By 1980, according one report, domestic manufacture of these units had already begun, to the tune of nearly 430,000 units—a number dwarfed by the vast quantities of imports manufactured by Japanese brands like Sanyo, Sony, and Aiwa and beggared by seemingly inexhaustible market demand.⁶² One of the contributors to *How to Recognize Yellow Music*, in pointing out the central role played in the music's morally corrosive dissemination among young people by the cassette, claims that, "according to informal surveys, hundreds of thousands of units have found their way into the parts of Guangdong province bordering on Hong Kong and Macau" and that the numbers for Shanghai, Hangzhou, Xiamen, and other coastal cities were equally "startling."⁶³ While exact figures are impossible to come by, it is clear that the portable radio–cassette player quickly became one of a trinity of "must have" consumer durables for the home. The periodical press, responding to demand, also produced numerous guides educating would-be consumers as to the finer distinctions between various models and their features. Was it better to purchase a model with a single deck or one with dual cassette decks? Two or four speakers? And what were the benefits of noise reduction technology?⁶⁴

Cai Xiang's reminiscences of the period, in which China was suddenly flooded with novel consumer products from abroad, from Coca-Cola to Nescafé, are representative in this regard:

> Even later, we got "Sanyo brand" tape recorders, with dual speakers, and also models with four speakers. In my opinion, the historical significance of the tape recorder surpasses that of the television. The programs on TV were still regulated by the state, but cassettes poured in through all kinds of channels like an uncontrollable flood.⁶⁵

The local market for cassette tapes also grew by leaps and bounds, with production shooting from six million in 1982 to seventy million in 1986.[66] These figures, of course, take account of neither the huge influx of illegally imported cassettes nor the primary affordance of the new technology—the ability to quickly and conveniently record or transfer music at home or to cheaply produce multiple copies of a recording for sale in the informal marketplace.[67] As Zhang Hong asserts in another short piece on what he calls an "era of sonic smuggling" 聲音走私的時代, the portable radio–cassette deck had for this reason "revolutionary" significance:

> for it seemed to separate itself from the state broadcasting network as a small, and easily portable source of sound. It was not only a receiver capable of reproducing the sound waves emanating from the center, but was also at the same time an independent piece of equipment that could produce its own sounds. . . . Cassette tapes were easy to carry around, could be played at will, and destroyed the ambience of mystery surrounding the sound of the radio. And the fact that they could be erased and re-recorded made sound into an ordinary object, something that could be revised on demand, and this further broke down the seemingly eternal quality of radio broadcasting. In this process, the public underwent a process of transformation. They were no longer merely cast as receivers and consumers of sound, but could also be producers. As a result the monopoly on sound held by state institutions underwent a fundamental change.[68]

Zhang Hong evokes here what Charles Hirschkind, writing about the religious soundscapes of the Islamic world, calls the "cassette's capillary motion, its ability to proliferate beneath the radar of law enforcement."[69] The radio–cassette recorder may thus have resulted in a kind of epistemological shift, ushering in a new era of technological reproducibility at the level of musical consumption and displacing the sonic obelisks of the state. On a more visceral level, however, the boom box also left an indelible timbral trace on the sound of music. By introducing stereo sound and a wider frequency range, with far fuller bass sound than Chinese listeners had heretofore enjoyed, the music took on new warmth and solidity. Volume and tone controls allowed listeners to adjust the music to their preferences and to the specifications of their domestic spaces. And the relative quiet of enclosed domestic interiors—so different from the cavernous spaces, deafening volumes, limited frequency range, and echoic phase delays of collective listening to a wired broadcast network—allowed for an entirely different distribution of the audible, in which the breathlessness, the hesitations, and the exquisitely close-miked rhythmic and affective fluctuations of Teng's voice could become perceptible to listeners. In that sense, for all that Chinese listeners may have heard Teresa Teng's voice as an emblem of a long-disavowed interior world of sensuality and privatized affect, that timbre was as much a trace of the advent of a new acoustic ecology forged by cassette tapes and portable electronics as it was of the resonating body of Teresa Teng herself.

Despite her ubiquity in the soundscape of her nominal homeland, Teresa Teng never set foot in China. Border crossings, impossible to effect at the height of the Cold War, remained difficult even in the wake of diplomatic détente and China's new era of "reform and opening." Nonetheless, new political and cultural energies unbound by China's partial and often problematic postsocialist reintegration with global capitalist networks accelerated throughout the 1980s. In the spring of 1989, just months before the fall of the Berlin Wall and two years before the walls of sound on Quemoy would fall silent forever, a popular movement for further political reform and against official corruption spilled out from the college campuses of Beijing and into the streets of cities across the country, and its soundtrack featured not only the music of Teresa Teng but also the sounds of an emergent Chinese rock and roll that had been catalyzed by an influx of recorded music on cassette. At the same time, students in Taipei, having only two years earlier helped to put an end to forty years of martial law on the island, rallied repeatedly in a plaza dedicated to the memory of Chiang Kai-shek in support of their mainland peers. The implacable boundaries of the Cold War order seemed to be wavering.

And so it was that on May 5, 1989, Teresa Teng made a rare and unscripted appearance onstage at the racecourse in Hong Kong's Happy Valley in front of an estimated audience of 300,000 supporters of the Tiananmen movement, televised images of which were then transfixing the world. The nostalgic ballad she chose to sing at this open-air "Concert for Democracy in China" 民主歌聲獻中華 represented a sonic crossing of circuits that imbued the moment of performance with a powerful historical charge. "My Home Is on the Other Side of the Mountain" 我的家在山的那一邊, the title of which seemed to gesture toward an expansive sense of pan-Chinese solidarity, had first been recorded under this title in 1958, just two months before the mainland artillery attack on Quemoy that triggered the second Taiwan straits crisis. Composed in Taiwan by the prominent song-writer Zhou Lanping 周藍萍, the song had been featured in a forgettable Mandarin film musical, *Love Story of Uncivilized Girls* 水擺夷之戀, set among the tribal Bayi people 擺夷族 of distant Yunnan province. This exotic locale was merely a commercial veneer, displacing onto an ersatz indigenous village song lyrics that conveyed not only a virulent anti-Communism but also the melancholy of Nationalist refugees stranded on the island of Taiwan:

> My home is on the other side of the mountain
> Uncle Zhang has lost his delight, and Auntie Li put away her smile
> The birds have fled their warm nest, spring has turned to cold winter
> Friends and family have lost their freedom
> and abandoned their beautiful homeland
> Friend, don't pursue the pleasures of a moment
> Friend, don't be greedy for a moment's peace
> Hurry home, and rekindle the torch of liberty
> Don't ever forget where we were raised
> On the other side of the mountain, the other side of the mountain

In an ironic double displacement, the melody and motifs of "My Home Is on the Other Side of the Mountain" were transparently modeled on another song from 1936: the Communist cultural worker Zhang Hanhui's 張寒暉 elegiac and stirring anthem calling for the reclamation of the lost Manchurian territories occupied by the Japanese Imperial Army, "Along the Sungari River" 松花江上. So it was that Teng, in superimposing a martial anthem known across the Chinese mainland with its despairing and even kitschy KMT cover version, had managed the difficult feat of reconciling two bitterly opposed camps under one banner. That banner, in both songs, fluttered over a ruined, even apocryphal map: provinces that had long since fallen, an imaginary tribe, a distant land on the other side of the sea.

The performance, throughout which Teng wore a banner opposing martial law 反對軍管, seems also to have foreshadowed her own displacement and inability to return to a home she had never known, especially in the wake of the violent crackdown on the movement on June 4, 1989. In 1991, Teng traveled for the last time to Quemoy to speak directly to her compatriots across the straits before embarking on an increasingly peripatetic series of journeys across the United States, France, and Southeast Asia. On May 8, 1995, a news flash went out across Chinese-language media circuits around the world. Teresa Teng had died on vacation in Thailand of an attack of asthma. Her voice will continue to echo within that circuit, reaching listeners from the other side.

APPENDIX

# "Listening to Songs in the Streets of Taipei"

Hsu Tsang-Houei

> Therefore with music of weak purpose and garbled notes, the people will be fretful and sad; with music that is spacious, harmonious, slow and easy, its embellishments emerging from a clear structure, the people will be happy; with music of coarse vitality, rapid attacks and distinct cadence, and a bright, resonant sound, the people will be strong and resolute; with music that is direct, righteous, and truthful, the people will be serious and respectful; with music that is rich, broad, allowing for voices to blend smoothly and bodies to move in resonance, the people will be loving and kind; with music that runs to extremes or tends toward dissipation and is overwhelmed by disorderly changes, the people will be depraved.
> 
> —*The Record of Music*

I've been back in Taipei for four months now. One day, out of curiosity and a spirit of inquiry, I listened to the songs I heard in the streets of Taipei (limited of course to those I could walk through) from morning to night. As a worker in music, I should understand the sonic environment around me and then think about how to confront that environment. All right, then, without further ado, let's start to listen to the songs on the streets of Taipei.

    Upon waking in the morning, before I've even completely opened my eyes, I hear the sound of Japanese popular songs, coming from a record player in someone's apartment nearby. Whether it's yellow, red, blue, black, or white, I hate this sort of popular song more than anything else, especially Japanese pop, which makes my hair stand on end and my stomach churn with nausea. Well, then, no choice but to get out of bed. Upon rising, I turn on the radio, but careful now! As soon as you're not paying attention, popular music begins to stream from the radio as well. This time, the songs are sung in Taiwanese, but it's easy enough to tell that the melodies are Japanese. I think to myself: Why should that be the case?

Aha! The government has banned the performance of Japanese songs, so the radio stations, with an eye to business, have come up with this clever workaround. What they seem not to have realized is that in the course of adapting or translating the original lyrics, the songs are now even more sickeningly cloying than before. Hair standing on end, nauseated, and sickened—I don't know how to describe the feeling. My morning vigor and vitality have been laid waste, trampled underfoot. There's no way I could stay at home any longer. I hurriedly wash up, arrange the things in my briefcase, and hop on my bicycle. At the corner of Sungchiang Road and Chungcheng Road I sit down at a restaurant to have a bowl of soy milk and then continue along Hsinsheng South Road. Passing a school, I hear the sound of students singing the national anthem. The national anthem always inspires a solemn feeling and a consciousness of the nation. But there's nothing special about hearing it now, since everyone knows it's a mandatory part of morning roll. I continue along my way, passing a military barrack, from which distantly emerges the sound of voices in unison, singing anti-Communist and Soviet resistance anthems. Right! It's only then that I remember that we're living in an era of anti-Communism and resistance to the Soviets. I turn the corner onto Peace Road East, Section 1, to the Normal University, and go on through the gate to teach my classes.

In the afternoon, I go as usual to the Sichuan place on Roosevelt Road for a bowl of noodles. The sounds in the streets are obviously much more lively than in the morning. I can sit, for instance, in the Sichuan place and hear the sound of radios and record players blaring from the neighboring ice seller, noodle stall, and electrical appliance store, plus the sound of bicycles, carts, trucks, and public buses hurrying past. Even with my eyes closed, I would know that this is the sound of the street at midday. But aside from the sounds coming from all these machines, I don't hear any real singing voices. I think maybe it's because at the busiest time of day, no one has time to sing.

In the afternoon, I need to teach, and classes go on until half past five. Then I ride my bicycle home along the same route as before. Now it's rush hour, and the streets are packed with all kinds of vehicles and pedestrians, and for the sake of my own safety I am not able to pay any attention to the task of surveying the sounds around me.

The best time to survey the songs in Taipei's streets, I think, is between when people have finished their dinner and when they go to bed. This is when people are free to give themselves to a mood of enjoyment, leisure, and rest. Naturally, this is also the time when people would find it easiest to sing. You could also say that the songs that might emerge from this kind of mood are the most natural and authentic. All right—let's go out into the streets and listen.

Around the shops and entertainment districts around Hengyang Street and Hsimenting, there are bright lights and streams of all sorts of passers-by. On Hengyang Street, aside from a few musical teahouses broadcasting light music to sidewalks on speakers, I don't hear anything particular in the way of song. Yet as soon as I pass the train tracks by Chunghwa Road, I hear all kinds of music. From the illegal shop stalls to the side of Chunghwa Road, where I happen to know there are a number of record shops, comes the sound of several different kinds of Japanese popular music. (Japanese pop songs again!) At the same time, emerging from the teahouses on the other side of the Hsimen plaza is the sound of pop songs from Hong Kong and the latest American hits: cha-cha, mambo, and rumba. Yellow music, pink music, grey music . . . and anything else you like. I continue walking, passing by the lobbies of several cinemas, for it goes without saying that this is Taipei's premier entertainment quarter. But the situation is the same. No one is singing; there is only the clamor of popular songs pouring out of amplifiers. Maybe no one else notices, or maybe it makes no difference if they hear it or not. But it grieves me terribly. Even if I dislike pop songs, we need to have our own popular music. How could we allow foreign popular songs to occupy our country? Isn't this a kind of cultural invasion? And an invasion of low-class culture at that?

From Hsimenting, I walk toward Bangka, around Longshan Temple. Everywhere I go, I hear popular music. The only difference is that here, I don't hear Hong Kong or American-style music; instead, there's only Taiwanese and Japanese-style pop. As for the Taiwanese songs, with the exception of *koa-a-hi* opera, all the melodies are Japanese. I have no further interest in what I am hearing, nor do I have the courage to walk any further. Yet, to finish the task I have set myself, I can't give up quite yet. I think to myself that these relatively lively districts don't necessarily represent Taipei as a whole, so I must continue to walk. I walk along the quiet and dimly lit road that runs parallel to the Tamsui River. After ten minutes, I still haven't heard any songs. It's only just after eight in the evening. It couldn't be that everyone has already gone to sleep? Nor is it the dead of winter, when people would be inclined to stay home behind closed doors to ward off the cold. Yet there's definitely no one singing. I walk for a little while more, and suddenly I hear it. In the distance ahead, someone is singing along to the sound of a *huqin*. This time it's actually a real person singing. I approach to take a look. In front of a row of low shanties with tile roofs, resting among a group of men on bamboo stools, there's a middle-aged man, who looks like a laborer, playing a crudely fashioned *huqin* and singing hoarsely in the tearful mode of *koa-a-hi* opera. I found the sight terribly depressing! I stood by him for a few seconds and then left, continuing to walk ahead. As I walked, I wondered to myself. I remember what it was like to walk at night in Europe, especially in Germany, Austria, and Italy. You would hear so many songs. People loved to sing! Better to say that it was simply part of their lives. In church, in the schools, out of doors, walking, during all kinds of gatherings, if they were so moved, they would use song to express their feelings. And the sound of their singing was so fresh, healthy, lively, lovable. . . . The sorts of songs I mean are folk songs, folk music from the treasury of national music, and not pop hits. And now I am back in China. I am in Taipei, capital city of Free China, and I don't hear any folk songs, nor any enthusiastic singing of anthems urging us to resist Communism and take back the mainland. Don't Chinese people like to sing? Is it that they don't have any folk songs? No, it absolutely can't be true! I believe that Chinese people have no less love for music than their foreign counterparts. The boatmen's calls in the reaches of the Yangtze and Yellow Rivers, the climbing songs of Suiyuan, the tea-picking songs of Taiwan's hill districts, mountain songs, and the dance songs of Mongolia and Xinjiang—all of these are folk songs full of character. Chinese folk songs are more rough-hewn than those from abroad, and more distant and profound, and also among the most lovable of folk traditions.

I'm almost to the Taipei Bridge. I turn right past Dihwa Street, Yenping North Road, the Roundabout, and Nanking West Road. All along the way, I hear no more songs. There's only the decadent sound of amplified foreign pop playing from speakers, constantly assaulting my ears. It's not until I get to Nanking East Road that I regain my composure. Now it's time to summarize the day's survey of songs in the streets of Taipei:

1. Districts populated mostly by local Taiwanese are occupied by Japanese-style popular music (including Taiwanese dialect songs).
2. Where there are more mainlanders, the music is mostly Hong Kong–style mandarin pop.
3. American music is the most popular among the so-called higher class of patrons in the prosperous entertainment districts, irrespective of whether they are Taiwanese or mainlanders.
4. In poor districts or where three-wheeled carts are stationed, you can often hear the lovable yet pitiful sound of folk songs.
5. Anti-Communist and anti-Soviet songs sung in chorus are heard only at certain designated places.

On the way home, I walked along Hsinsheng North Road as it skirts the river. By that time, it was already after ten, pedestrians were few and far between, and the stars were twinkling soundlessly in the sky. By the three-wheeled cart stand next to the bridge on Chang'an East Road, I heard a porter softly humming a folk tune from his hometown.

October 20, 1959, in Taipei

*The translation is my own. This piece originally appeared as "Taibei jietou tingge ji," in Hsu Tsang-Houei,* Zhongguo yinyue wang nali qu [Where Is Chinese Music Heading?] (Taipei: Wenxing, 1964).

# NOTES

**Introduction**

Note on the romanization of Chinese terms: throughout the book, I adhere for the most part to the standard Hanyu pinyin romanization system, especially in the book's notes and bibliographic citations, with some significant exceptions. I have chosen in the text proper to render certain proper names, place-names, and descriptive terms in a manner that respects historical conventions in the period under discussion, the specificity of regional as opposed to standard Mandarin Chinese usage, locally prevalent romanization schemes, and the preferences as to nomenclature of the historical figures to whom I am referring, for instance, Hsu Tsang-houei 許常惠 rather than Xu Changhui, Hsimenting 西門町 rather than Ximending, and koa-a-hi 歌仔戲 rather than gezaixi. In these cases, I have supplied Chinese characters so as to eliminate any possible ambiguity.

1. The photograph, taken by astronaut William Anders and credited with catalyzing the growth of the environmental movement and inspiring the first Earth Day, April 22, 1970, also made its mark on the popular music of the era, from the Brazilian *tropicalista* Caetano Veloso's exquisitely lyrical "Terra," written after he came across the picture as a political prisoner inside a jail cell in 1968, to David Bowie's "Space Oddity," released just days before the Apollo 11 mission put a man on the moon for the first time. See Caetano Veloso, *Tropical Truth: A Story about Music and Revolution in Brazil* (New York: Da Capo, 2002), 239.

2. See "Hongse weixing fei changkong, yuzhou xiangche 'Dongfang hong'" [A red satellite flies into Space, and "The East Is Red" rang out across the universe], *Renmin ribao* [People's Daily], April 27, 1970. See also "Wo guo renzao diqiu weixing yunxing qingkuang lianghao, cong kongzhong fahui 'Dongfang hong' yuequ qing xi liaoliang" [Our man-made earth satellite operating well, and its space broadcast of "East Is Red" is loud and clear], *Renmin ribao* [People's Daily], April 26, 1970.

3. All told, the production enlisted the efforts of three thousand performers. *Morning Sun*, a documentary film directed by Carma Hinton, provides a well-documented and amply illustrated history of the film and its music on an informational website. See http://www.morningsun.org/east/index.html. Accessed June 29, 2018. For contemporary accounts of the production and its technical achievements, see Situ Huimin, "Rang zhuangli de geming shishi zai yinmu shang fangda guangcai" [Letting a gorgeous revolutionary epic shine on screen], *Dianying yishu* [Film Art] 5 (1965): 37–42, and Wei Yanbi, "Geming zange de beijing shi zheyang goucheng" [This is how the backgrounds for the revolutionary song of praise were put together], *Kexue dazhong* [Popular Science] 11 (1965): 30–33. For an account of the origins and implementation of the production, see Hon-lun Yang, "Unravelling *The East Is Red* (1964): Socialist Music and Politics in the People's Republic of China," in Esteban Buch, Igor Contreras Zubillaga, and Manuel Deniz Silva, eds., *Composing for the State: Music in Twentieth Century Dictatorships* (New York: Ashgate, 2016), 51–69.

4. *Dongfang hong / Dahai hangxing kao duoshou* [The East Is Red / Sailing the Seas Depends on the Helmsman], China Record Company XM-1031, 1969.

5. See "Haiguan dazhong gaozou geming yuequ 'Dongfang hong'" [The customs house clock tower rings with the revolutionary sounds of "The East Is Red"], *Renmin ribao* [People's Daily], August 29, 1966. See also Chi Ti, "The East Is Red Rings Out over Shanghai," *China Reconstructs* (February 1967), 10.

6. For a classic study of church bells as a technology for territorial and community consolidation, see Alain Corbin, *Village Bells: Sound and Meaning in the Nineteenth Century French Countryside* (London: Macmillan, 1999).

7. Writing in 1970, McLuhan was to intone "Since Sputnik and the satellites, the planet is enclosed in a manmade environment that ends 'Nature' and turns the globe into a repertory theater to be programmed." See Marshall McLuhan and Wilfrid Watson, *From Cliché to Archetype* (New York: Viking Press, 1970), 9. For an analysis of the program as a seminal moment in the globalization of the media, see Lisa Parks, *Cultures in Orbit: Satellites and the Televisual* (Durham, N.C.: Duke University Press, 2005), 21–46.

8. I am following in this reading of the song the train of thought of Richard Poirier, whose essay "Learning from the Beatles" insightfully points to the band's historical depth. See Richard Poirier, "Learning from the Beatles," in Jonathan Eisen, ed., *The Age of Rock: Sounds of the American Cultural Revolution* (New York: Vintage Books, 1969), 177.

9. McLuhan himself glossed the meaning of his appropriately malleable aphorism thus: "This is merely to say that the personal and social consequences of any medium—that is, of any extension of ourselves—result from the new scale that is introduced into our affairs by each extension of ourselves, or by any new technology." See Marshall McLuhan, *Understanding Media: The Extensions of Man* (New York: McGraw-Hill, 1965), 7.

## NOTES TO INTRODUCTION       205

10. Ernest Braun and Stuart Macdonald, *Revolution in Miniature: The History and Impact of Semiconductor Electronics*, 2nd ed. (Cambridge: Cambridge University Press, 1982), 1. For an account of the early development of transistor technology, see Michael Riordan and Lillian Hoddeson, *Crystal Fire: The Invention of the Transistor and the Birth of the Information Age* (New York: W. W. Norton, 1997).

11. For a history of the transistor radio, see Michael Brian Schiffer, *The Portable Radio in American Life* (Tucson and London: University of Arizona Press, 1991). Greg Milner, among many others, points to the studio production work of Joe Meek and Phil Spector as being expressly engineered for the tiny speakers of transistor radios and portable record players. Interestingly, Milner offers Meek's production of the Tornados' instrumental smash hit "Telstar" as a prime example. See Greg Milner, *Perfecting Sound Forever: An Aural History of Recorded Music* (New York: Farrar, Straus and Giroux, 2009), 154.

12. These examples of McLuhan's most celebratory rhetoric derive from his discussion of sound recording and the phonograph in his landmark 1966 study *Understanding Media*. See McLuhan, *Understanding Media*, 283. For an evenhanded and insightful discussion of McLuhan's media theory and how it has been situated within contemporary debates about technological determinism, see John Durham Peters, "'You Mean My Whole Fallacy Is Wrong': On Technological Determinism," *Representations* 140, no. 1 (Fall 2017).

13. McLuhan, *Understanding Media*, 283.

14. Fredric Jameson, "Periodizing the 1960s," *Social Text* 9/10 (Spring–Summer 1984). Christopher Leigh Connery, following Jameson, stirringly addresses the historiography and political implications for the left of the "worlding of the 1960s" in his essay "The World Sixties." See Rob Wilson and Christopher Leigh Connery, eds., *The Worlding Project: Doing Cultural Studies in the Era of Globalization* (Santa Cruz, Calif.: New Pacific Press, 2007).

15. Jameson, "Periodizing the 1960s," 180–81.

16. Jameson, "Periodizing the 1960s," 181.

17. Jameson, "Periodizing the 1960s," 185.

18. Jameson, "Periodizing the 1960s," 208. Perhaps we can grasp this conjunction and how it played out on the ground of everyday life, at least in the United States, by imagining the televisual juxtaposition of the dream worlds of Madison Avenue, hawking the most advanced products and pleasures of industrial civilization, and telecasts of helicopters and raining death on the defoliated jungles of Vietnam.

19. There is an extensive literature on these conjunctions in the United States. For an ambitiously global look at political protest music in the late 1960s, see Beate Kutschke and Barley Norton, eds., *Music and Protest in 1968* (Cambridge: Cambridge University Press, 2013).

20. I am thinking here of the Beatles' dalliances with "eastern" sounds and spirituality, as exemplified by George Harrison's 1965 introduction into their instrumental palette of the sitar, as well as the band's 1968 sojourn in India to commune

with the Maharishi, during which they wrote the majority of the *White Album*. See Jonathan Bellman, "Indian Resonances in the British Invasion, 1965–1968," in Jonathan Bellman, ed., *The Exotic in Western Music* (Boston: Northeastern University Press, 1998), 292–306. One might also point to the avant-folk band the Incredible String Band's gleeful rifling of indigenous musical instruments, among numerous other examples. See Rob Young, *Electric Eden: Unearthing Britain's Visionary Music* (London: Faber, 2010).

21. See for instance, Carl Clements, "John Coltrane and the Integration of Indian Concepts in Jazz Improvisation," *Jazz Research Journal* 2, no. 2 (2008), and Ben Ratliff, *Coltrane: The Story of a Sound* (New York: Picador, 2008).

22. See Michael Denning, *Noise Uprising: The Audiopolitics of a World Musical Revolution* (London: Verso, 2015).

23. For forró and rural migrants, see Jack Draper, *Forró and Redemptive Regionalism from the Brazilian Northeast: Popular Music in a Culture of Migration* (New York: Lang, 2011). The critical literature on reggae is extensive; for an introductory history of the genre, see Lloyd Bradley, *Bass Culture: When Reggae Was King* (London: Penguin, 2000).

24. There has been in recent years a renewed interest in these various postcolonial inflections of rock and roll idioms, resulting in a raft of reissues on specialist labels of "lost" recordings from this era.

25. For a history of the American folk revival, see Benjamin Filene, *Romancing the Folk: Public Memory and American Roots Culture* (Chapel Hill: University of North Carolina Press, 2000). For Dylan's notorious performance at Newport, see Elijah Wald, *Dylan Goes Electric! Newport, Seeger, Dylan, and the Night That Split the Sixties* (New York: HarperCollins, 2015).

26. See Christopher Dunn, *Brutality Garden: Tropicália and the Emergence of a Brazilian Counterculture* (Chapel Hill: University of North Carolina Press, 2001).

27. See Timothy W. Ryback, *Rock around the Bloc: A History of Rock Music in Eastern Europe and the Soviet Union, 1954–1988* (London: Oxford University Press, 1990).

28. For an intimate account of Chilean *nueva cancion*, see Joan Jara, *Victor: The Life and Music of Victor Jara* (London: Bloomsbury, 1988).

29. See John C. Schaefer, "The Trịnh Công Sơn Phenomena," *Journal of Asian Studies* 66, no. 3 (2007), and Barley Norton, "Vietnamese Popular Song in 1968: War, Protest, and Sentimentalism," in Beate Kutschke and Barley Norton, eds., *Music and Protest in 1968* (Cambridge: Cambridge University Press, 2013).

30. For postwar Japanese popular music, see Michael Bourdaghs, *Sayonara Amerika, Sayonara Nippon: A Geopolitical Prehistory of J-Pop* (New York: Columbia University Press, 2012). For protest folk, see Toru Mitsui, "Music and Protest in Japan: The Rise of Underground Folk Song in 1968," in Beate Kutschke and Barley Norton, eds., *Music and Protest in 1968* (Cambridge: Cambridge University Press, 2013).

31. See Pil Ho Kim and Hyunjoon Shin, "The Birth of 'Rok': Cultural Imperialism, Nationalism, and the Glocalization of Rock Music in South Korea, 1964–1975," *Positions: East Asia Cultures Critique* 18 (2010): 199–230. For profiles of individual musicians as well as genres, see also Hyunjoon Shin and Seung-ah Lee, eds., *Made in Korea: Studies in Popular Music* (New York and London: Routledge, 2014).

32. Many of the guitars that fueled this revolution were manufactured in Japan and, later, Taiwan. A local electric guitar boom took off in Japan with the arrival of the Ventures and the Beatles. The export market expanded exponentially in just a few years, as Japan went from producing 20,000 electric guitars in 1962 to a staggering 767,000 in its peak year of production, 1966. See Frank Meyers, *History of Japanese Electric Guitars* (Anaheim Hills, Calif.: Centerstream, 2015), 12.

33. For a study of the Shanghai era in popular music, see Hong Fangyi, *Shanghai liuxing yinyue 1927–1949: zazhong wenhua meixue yu tingjue xiandaixing de jianli* [Shanghai popular music, 1927–1949: Hybrid cultural aesthetics and the establishment of auditory modernity] (Taipei: Chengchi University Press, 2015).

34. For a general history of Taiwan's postwar experience, see Thomas Gold, *State and Society in the Taiwan Miracle* (Oxford and New York: Routledge, 1986).

35. See Lisa Reynolds Wolfe, "Cold War Taiwan's Electronics Industry," *Cold War Magazine*, June 10, 2013. See https://coldwarstudies.com/2013/06/10/cold-war-taiwans-electronic-industry/. Accessed July 8, 2018.

36. For a comprehensive history of Japan's industrial policy in this period and especially its reliance on rural labor, see Simon Partner, *Assembled in Japan: Electrical Goods and the Making of the Japanese Consumer* (Berkeley: University of California Press, 1999).

37. See Wolfe, "Cold War Taiwan's Electronics Industry."

38. See Wolfe, "Cold War Taiwan's Electronics Industry."

39. See Wolfe, "Cold War Taiwan's Electronics Industry."

40. The question of how to refer to nonstandard or regional forms of Chinese is a complex and contentious one. I have chosen to consistently use the term "Taiwanese language" or Taiyu because of its prevalence in daily parlance in Taiwan. There are a number of other overlapping and alternative terms for the idiom—to which I will also occasionally refer throughout the book—each of which reflects a different historical vantage point, contextual nuance, and political position. "Hokkien" loosely refers to a number of closely related idioms deriving from Fujian province, and its use gestures toward the linguistic commonalities among diasporic communities in Taiwan, Hong Kong, Singapore, and throughout Southeast Asia. "Hoklo Taiwanese" is sometimes used to mark the distinct ethnic identity of Taiyu speakers with respect to other communities, such as Hakka or indigenous peoples, within Taiwan itself. "Minnan dialect" insists on the close affiliation of Taiwanese with the Southern Min idiom of Fujian, while emphasizing its status as a "dialect" of a putatively standard Mandarin Chinese. This designation, while not necessarily in accordance with strictly linguistic criterion for the designation of dialects, has

historically been important to the nation-building imperatives and programs of linguistic standardization of both the KMT and the Commmunist party-states.

41. Hsu, 許常惠 (Xu Changhui), customarily romanized his own name using the nonstandard designation Hsu Tsang-Houei.

42. The application of the adjectival "Chinese" to language, music, or other forms of cultural production, it must be said, is admittedly imprecise, as is a more recent and widely used cognate, "sinophone." I am in sympathy with the efforts of Sinophone studies scholars to disaggregate our sense of Chineseness from monolithic conceptions of the nation-state and thus open to scholarly inquiry a range of diverse and diasporic Chinese languages, literatures, cultures, and social formations outside "China proper." The semantic range of this term, however, has yet to stabilize. For some scholars, it may indicate little more than a neutral designation denoting something very like "Chinese" or "Chinese-speaking," while others may be inclined to tie the term to a more systematic set of claims about politics, history, or Chinese identity. For my part, I have tried to avoid anachronistically applying the term "sinophone" to a historical era in which such interventions and arguments were not yet within the realm of the discursively possible. The story of Chen Da that I relate in chapter 5 is a striking example. While Chen Da has long since become an emblem of a resolutely localist Taiwanese national identity, Hsu Tsang-Houei (himself a Japanese-educated scion of the island) understood Chen Da's music as a rare exemplar of a greater Chinese national folk tradition. To collapse that category—which for Hsu was freighted with anticolonial feeling—would be to do violence to the historical specificity of his era. More broadly speaking, the Cold War was a time in which geopolitical conflict between the two "Chinas"—no matter how phantasmal those designations were or remain—was an inescapable presence that shaped politics, economics, cultural production, daily life, and individual fates. Whenever possible, I will foreground local linguistic differences and historical exigencies, while also acknowledging the historical presence and discursive power of "China" as an ideological formation. My hope is that the notion of the circuit itself will allow us to analyze the traffic (military, ideological, musical) that bound these "Chinese" regions together and connected them to many other near and far-flung regions as well. And it is the density of those global connections, I think, that reveals the extent to which the "sinophone" realm was never wholly or exclusively sinophone in the first place. For a collection of essays on these issues, see Shu-Mei Shih and Chien-hsin Tsai, *Sinophone Studies: A Critical Reader* (New York: Columbia University Press, 2013).

43. Nicolai Volland shows quite convincingly the extent to which China participated in a Soviet- and socialist-centered literary network in the seventeen years between 1949 and 1966. That is also true in the musical realm, where the deep traces of Soviet musical practice are easily audible. With the Sino-Soviet split of the early 1960s and especially after advent of the Cultural Revolution, the ambit for such interaction and collaboration narrowed considerably. See Nicolai Volland,

*Socialist Cosmopolitanism: The Chinese Literary Universe, 1949–1965* (New York: Columbia University Press, 2017).

44. See Jason Young, *China's Hukou System: Markets, Migrants, and Institutional Change* (Basingstoke: Palgrave Macmillan, 2013).

45. For a useful collection of studies of the *hukou* system and its implications for internal migration, see Kam Wing Chan, ed., *Urbanization with Chinese Characteristics: The Hukou System and Migration* (London and New York: Routledge, 2017).

46. Sigrid Schmalzer, *Red Revolution, Green Revolution: Scientific Farming in Socialist China* (Chicago: University of Chicago Press, 2016), 2.

47. Schmalzer, *Red Revolution, Green Revolution*, 2–3.

48. Interestingly, one of the most important innovations of Taiwan's Green Revolution, a high-yielding rice variety called IR-8, had reached China by 1967. See Schmalzer, *Red Revolution, Green Revolution*, 11.

49. Brian Larkin, *Signal and Noise: Media, Infrastructure, and Urban Culture in Nigeria* (Durham, N.C., and London: Duke University Press, 2006), 220.

50. Larkin, *Signal and Noise*, 10.

51. For a collection of essays on the worldwide impact of the "Little Red Book," see Alexander C. Cook, ed., *Mao's Little Red Book: A Global History* (Cambridge: Cambridge University Press, 2014).

52. Bruno Nettl, *The Study of Ethnomusicology: Thirty-One Issues and Concepts* (Urbana and Chicago: University of Illinois Press, 2005), 334. Nettl borrows this evocative phrase from the late nineteenth-century work of Wilhelm Tappert on melody.

53. The lyrics can be found on the *Morning Sun* website at "The East Is Red," *Morning Sun*, http://morningsun.org/east/song.swf. Accessed November 2, 2018. The translation is my own.

54. For a full translation of this document, see Mao Zedong, "Talks at the Forum on Art and Literature," in Kirk A. Denton, ed., *Modern Chinese Literary Thought: Writings on Literature, 1893–1945* (Stanford: Stanford University Press, 1995).

55. For an account of this process, see Chang-Tai Hung, "The Politics of Songs: Myths and Symbols in the Chinese Communist War Music, 1937–1949," *Modern Asian Studies* 30, no. 4 (1996): 901–29.

56. The lyrics can be found on the *Morning Sun* website at "The East Is Red," *Morning Sun*, http://morningsun.org/east/song.swf. Accessed November 2, 2018. The translation is my own.

57. A version of this story, probably in part apocryphal, appears in Jian Qihua and Shao Qihua, "Renmin geshou Li Youyuan yu 'Dongfang hong' de dansheng" [The people's singer Li Youyuan and the birth of "The East Is Red"], *Renmin yinyue* [People's Music] 1 (1978): 34–35.

58. See Li Sheng's illuminating essay on the history and meaning of the song: "Sheng zhi xin ming yu yue zhi benshi: 'Dongfang hong' de shidai bianzou yu

yinyue kaogu" [A new sonic fate and its musical sources: The historical modulations of "The East Is Red" and its musical archaeology], *Wenhua yichan* [Cultural Heritage] 1 (2018): 116–25.

59. Li Jinqi, before his death in 1998 claimed that he was inspired to write the song by the presence of visiting revolutionaries from around Asia in Yan'an in those years, for they fueled his conviction that the "East" would indeed go "Red" in time. He suffered punishment and even imprisonment during the Cultural Revolution for belatedly claiming his authorship of the song, and his story did not emerge until 1992. See Wu Zhihui, "'Dongfang hong gequ de dansheng yu zhuanchang de gushi" [The story of the birth and dissemination of "The East Is Red"], *Fujian dangshi yuekan* [Fujian Party History Monthly] 5 (2010): 44–45. Also see Wu Zhihui, "'Dongfang hong' dansheng yu zhuanchang beihou de pushuo mili" [The bewildering back story to the birth and dissemination of "The East Is Red'], *Wenshi jinghua* [Essences of Literature and History] 256 (September 2011): 42–47.

60. In the 1945 edition of the songbook, there are no fewer than twelve songs that utilize the "Riding the White Horse" tune type. See Lu Xun Wenyi Xueyuan, ed., *Shaanbei minge xuan* [Selected Shaanbei folk songs] (Yan'an: Xinhua, 1945). That is also the case for a 1951 edition from Haiyan Books 海燕書店 in Shanghai, which includes the "Migration Song" attributed to Li Zengzheng with the same opening lines as what eventually became "The East Is Red." See He Qifang and Zhang Songru, *Shaanbei minge xuan* [Selected Shaanbei folk songs] (Shanghai: Haiyan shudian, 1951), 245–46.

61. See, for instance, Qian Zhang, "The Conflict between Red Music and Yellow Music during the Anti-Rightist Campaign," in Michael Bourdaghs, Paola Iovene, and Kaley Mason, *Sound Alignments: Pop Music in Asia's Cold Wars* (Durham, N.C.: Duke University Press, forthcoming). For a historical genealogy of the term "yellow music," see Huang Xingtao and Chen Peng, "Jindai Zhongguo 'huangse' ciyu bianqian kaoxi" [A study of the shift in the meaning of the word "yellow" in modern China], *Lishi yanjiu* [History Research] 5 (2010), 83–98.

62. For a study of the emergence of "modern songs" in tandem with modern media culture in interwar Shanghai, see my previous book, *Yellow Music: Media Culture and Colonial Modernity in the Chinese Jazz Age* (Durham, N.C.: Duke University Press, 2001). For a snapshot of the dynamic musical landscape that followed the transformations set into motion by Teresa Teng's "return," including the simultaneous emergence of new forms of state-sponsored pop music along with a new rock and roll underground in the 1980s, see my *Like a Knife: Ideology and Genre in Contemporary Chinese Popular Music* (Ithaca: Cornell East Asian Series, 1992). *Circuit Listening* is chronologically situated between these two earlier studies and stands as the middle term of a trilogy, rounding out an unsystematic history of Chinese popular music in the twentieth century.

63. See Denning, *Noise Uprising*, 40 and 2–3.

64. Denning, *Noise Uprising*, 43.

65. Denning, *Noise Uprising*, 39.

66. Denning, *Noise Uprising*, 41.

67. Both the Boeing 707 and the Douglas DC-8 went into service in 1958, ushering in a golden age of commercial aviation.

68. Denning, *Noise Uprising*, 137.

69. Andrew Field has provided an authoritative history of this lost world of nightlife in his *Shanghai's Dancing World: Cabaret Culture and Urban Politics, 1919–1954* (Hong Kong: Chinese University Press, 2011). Fritz Schenker, in his groundbreaking and deeply researched dissertation, brings to vivid life the nature of this littoral musical circuit in East Asia from the perspective of the Filipino musicians who labored within it. See Fritz Schenker, "Empire of Syncopation: Music, Race, and Labor in Colonial Asia's Jazz Age," doctoral dissertation, University of Wisconsin–Madison, 2016.

70. For the stories of Tau Moe and Ernest Ka'ai, see Lorene Ruymar, ed., *The Hawai'ian Steel Guitar and Its Great Hawai'ian Musicians* (Anaheim Hills, Calif.: Centerstream Publishing, 1994), 31–38. The Shanghai-born Filipino dance band leader Bernardo Endaya's reminiscences in the same collection on the popularity of Hawaii'an music between 1937 and 1949 in that city is worth reproducing here: "Most radio stations played an hour of it every week. We used to listen to the music of Sol Ho'opi'i, Sol K. Bright, Lani and Dick McEntire, Lena Machado, Harry Owens, etc. . . . The night clubs of Shanghai were packed to capacity every night. The Chinese patrons demanded at least one session of Hawaiian music before the night was over." See Lorene Ruymar, *The Hawai'ian Steel Guitar*, 39. For a comprehensive history of how Hawaiian music has traveled globally, see George S. Kanahele, ed., *Hawaiian Music and Musicians: An Illustrated History* (Honolulu: University of Hawa'i Press, 1979), and James Revell Carr, *Hawaiian Music in Motion: Mariners, Missionaries, and Minstrels* (Urbana: University of Illinois, 2014).

71. Burnet Hershey, "Jazz Latitude," *New York Times*, June 25, 1922. Also cited in Denning, *Noise Uprising*, 90–91.

72. For the history of the company and its place within the Shanghai recording industry, see Ge Tao, *Changpian yu jindai Shanghai shehui shenghuo* [Records and life in modern Shanghai society] (Shanghai: Shanghai Cishu chubanshe, 2009), 235–316.

73. For an excellent history of the song and its provenance, see Robert Chi, "The March of the Volunteers: From Movie Theme Song to National Anthem," in Ching-Kwan Lee and Guobin Yang, eds., *Re-Envisioning the Chinese Revolution: The Politics and Poetics of Collective Memories in Reform China* (Stanford: Stanford University Press, 2007). For the ascension of "The East Is Red" to the status of de facto national anthem, see Barbara Mittler, *A Continuous Revolution: Making Sense of Cultural Revolution Culture* (Cambridge, Mass.: Harvard University Asia Center, 2012), 100–111.

74. The song was released by Pathé as catalog number 35667b. The composer of the tune was Yan Zhexi 嚴折西 (Zhuang Hong 庄閎).That the A-side of this

78-rpm record, "Don't Think of It" 不要想 (Pathé 356667a), also by Yan Zhexi, directly addresses the aftermath of eight years of war and its resultant privations reinforces my sense that the record can be read in terms of these larger political upheavals. A slow blues-inflected ballad in a minor key, "Don't Think of It" begins by invoking, in unmistakably melancholic and embittered terms, the return of the KMT from the interior: "Don't think of it, don't think of it / I've waited eight years for your return / and you haven't changed a bit."

75. See Andreas Steen, "Propaganda on Shellac, Vinyl, and Plastic: The Politics of Record Production during the Cultural Revolution in China (1966–1976)," *Journal of Contemporary Chinese Art* 4, nos. 2–3 (2017): 224.

76. A recording issued under catalog number 38217-A is included in a 1954 *Da Zhonghua* catalog, categorized as both "folk" and "revolutionary song," performed by the Shanghai Broadcast Orchestra 上海廣播樂團 and credited to He Lüting. I am grateful to Andreas Steen for sharing this information with me.

77. This story derives from an article by Jiang Yuanzhou, seemingly sourced from Yan Heming's own anecdotal account. See Jiang Yuanzhou, "'Dongfang hong' changpian dansheng ji" [Notes on the birth of the record of "The East Is Red"], *Yinyue shijie* [Music World] (March 15, 1997), 9. The claim, made here, that Yan Heming supervised the *first* recording of "The East Is Red," however, may be problematic. He Lüting's arrangement of the song was issued by Da Zhonghua, perhaps as early as 1949. I have not been able to independently confirm the existence of the "Red Record" version of the song. It is possible that Jiang's account, which I find otherwise credible, conflates the earlier recording session at Da Zhonghua with the later productions made by the Shanghai Record Manufacturing Company. Oddly, Jiang's account of "Red Records" and "The East Is Red" reappears under a different name but with the same title and much the same content in Zhao Zhenyang, "'Dongfang hong' changpian dansheng ji" [Notes on the birth of the record of "The East Is Red"], *Yunnan Dang'an* [Yunnan Archives] 1 (2018): 42–43. A variation on the story is also presented in Zhen Yang, "1951 nian: Zhongguo shizhi chu de hong changpian" [1951: China's experimental production of "Red Records"], *Dang'an Jiyi* [Archival Memories] 4 (2018): 32–33. For a biographical sketch of Yan Heming's career, see Hou Ren and Huang Yiqing, "Zhongguo yousheng dianying yu caise dianying de qianquzhe: Yan Heming" [A pioneer of China's sound and color films: Yan Heming], *Dianying xinzuo* [New Films] 2 (2011): 55–60.

78. These details are provided by Jiang, in "'Dongfang hong' changpian dansheng ji," and echoed in Zhen, "1951 nian: Zhongguo shizhi chu de hong changpian," 32–33.

79. For He Lüting's own views on national form, see He Lüting, *He Lüting yinyue lunwen xuanji* [A selection of He Lüting's musical theses] (Shanghai: Shanghai wenyi chubanshe, 1981).

80. For a detailed and evenhanded summary of He Lüting's storied career, see C. C. Liu, *A Critical History of New Music in China* (Hong Kong: Hong Kong

University Press, 2010). Also see Shi Zhongxing, *He Lüting zhuan* [A biography of He Lüting] (Shanghai: Shanghai wenyi chubanshe, 1989). He is also profiled in Richard Kraus, *Pianos and Politics in China: Middle Class Ambitions and the Struggle over Western Music* (Oxford: Oxford University Press, 1989), 121–23. For his work on the "The Migration Song" in Yan'an, see Han Sanzhou, *Dongdang lishi xia de Zhongguo wenren qinghuai* [Chinese intellectuals in tumultuous times] (Taipei: Xiuwei, 2011), 150.

81. See He Lüting, *Dongfang hong: Shaanbei minge* [The East Is Red: Shaanbei folk song] (Shanghai: Shanghai yinyue chubanshe, 1950). The song was published again under his name in 1951 and 1953 and included in his collected works in 1957.

82. The 78-rpm SP (standard play) format, allowing for only three minutes per side, was also too short to include the more numerous verses included in the song's earlier versions. In a fascinating contribution to the contentious archive about the development and authorship of the song, Gu Zhenyi claims that the lyrics for the second and third verses of the first recording of "The East Is Red" in 1949 were crafted over the course of a single evening by an eighteen-year-old musician named He Bin 何彬, who had been tasked by the director of the newly nationalized China Records, Ji Liankang 吉聯抗, to cut the song short enough to fit into the SP format, without having to change sides. See Gu Zhenyi, "Dongfang hong cizuozhe kaozhen" [A correction as to the real lyricist of "The East Is Red"], *Renmin yinyue* [People's Music] 9 (1993): 30–31.

83. See Jiang, "'Dongfang hong' changpian dansheng ji," 9; Zhen, "1951 nian: Zhongguo shizhi chu de hong changpian," 33.

84. See "Zhuijiu kou zhandou zu" [Struggle group to apprehend thieves], "He Lüting cuangai weida songge 'Dongfang hong' zui gai wansi" [He Lüting should die ten thousand deaths for the crime of appropriating and revising the great praise song "The East Is Red"], in *Xin shangyin* [The new Shanghai conservatory], August 28, 1967. The broadside is reproduced and accessible at http://www.wengewang.org/read.php?tid=7988. Accessed July 19, 2018. For a collection of materials related to his denunciation, see *He Lüting pipan wenti huibian: jizi 1966 quannian Shanghai Wenhui bao* [A compilation of materials on the problem of the criticism of He Lüting from the 1966 run of the Shanghai *Wenhui bao*] (Hong Kong: Yangkai shubao gongying she, 1970).

85. The broadcast is audible at five and a half minutes into a propaganda film called "Yuzhou gaoge Dongfang hong" [The universe sings out "The East Is Red"], made to commemorate the launch. Available at https://www.youtube.com/watch?v=M_g_La6os90&t=25s. Accessed July 20, 2018.

86. I am likening the satellite's aerial song here to "Ariel's Song" in the first act of Shakespeare's *The Tempest*, which hymns the death of Ferdinand's father in a shipwreck and concludes with the hauntingly sonorous lines "Nothing of him that doth fade / But doth suffer a sea-change / Into something rich and strange / Sea-nymphs hourly ring his knell: Ding-dong / Hark! now I hear them—Ding-dong, bell."

## 1. Circuit Listening at the Dawn of the Chinese 1960s

1. As quoted in the liner notes to the Byrds' 1965 Columbia Records debut LP, *Mr. Tambourine Man*. McGuinn, whose band was known as the Jet Set before riding an electrified cover of Bob Dylan's "Mr. Tambourine Man" to the top of the U.S. pop charts, also composed the pioneering 1966 psychedelic single "Eight Miles High," a tune that simultaneously invokes drug-induced euphoria and the experience of air travel, while drawing on timbral and harmonic effects inspired by John Coltrane's modal jazz composition "India." Interestingly, Gene Clark, one of the original members of the Byrds, was forced to resign as a result of his own fear of flying.

2. Jean Ma's exemplary study of the songstress in Chinese cinema provides a full and fascinating discussion of several salient aspects of Grace Chang's cinematic career, including her appropriation of various globally circulating musical vernaculars. See in particular the two-chapter sequence from "The Mambo Girl" to "Carmine, Camille, and the Undoing of Women" in Jean Ma, *Sounding the Modern Woman: The Songstress in Chinese Cinema* (Durham, N.C.: Duke University Press, 2015), 139–212.

3. An important English-language source for Cathay and MP&GI is Ain-ling Wong, ed., *The Cathay Story*, rev. ed. (Hong Kong: Hong Kong Film Archive, 1992). See also Lim Kay Tong and Tiong Chai Yiu, *Cathay: 55 Years of Cinema* (Singapore: Published by Landmark Books Pte. Ltd. for Meileen Choo), 1991.

4. See, for instance, "Pathé Records Nets MP&GI's Flock of Stars / Baidai changpian wangluo Dianmao qunxing," *International Screen* 33 (July 1958): 50–51.

5. See Y. R. Chao, *Xin shige ji* [New poetic song collection] (Shanghai: Commercial Press, 1928), 8–11. The collection and its introductory essays on the question of Chinese and Western music have been translated by Kaelyn Lowmaster with John A. Crespi and published online by the MCLC Resource Publication as "Y. R. Chao and the *New Poetic Songbook*" at http://mclc.osu.edu/rc/pubs/chao.htm. Accessed February 3, 2012.

6. For the history of the transistor radio and other portable radio receivers in American life, see Michael B. Schiffer, *The Portable Radio in American Life* (Tucson: University of Arizona Press, 1992). For a sense of the Japanese contribution to transistor radio production and design, see Roger Handy et al., *Made in Japan: Transistor Radios of the 1950s and 1960s* (San Francisco: Chronicle Books, 1993).

7. For a sketch of Grace Chang's life story, see Guo Shu, "Bu jin yinhe gungun lai—Zhongguo yingxing lishi hua lang" [The silver river rolls on and on: A historical gallery of Chinese film stars], *Dianying huakan* [Film Pictorial], no. 4 (2004): 58–59.

8. As Lily Wong has pointed out, MP&GI often restaged, reinvented, and redistributed the classics of this earlier era across a diasporic "sinophone" network of audiences. See her excellent study of music and affect in the 1959 MP&GI production *Calendar Girl*, "Moving Serenades: Hearing the Sinophonic in MP& GI's

*Longxiang Fengwu,*" *Journal of Chinese Cinemas* 7, no. 3 (2013): 225–40. For a study of the emergence of modern Chinese popular music in the Shanghai of the interwar period and its relation to the transnational recording industry, see my earlier study, *Yellow Music: Media Culture and Colonial Modernity in the Chinese Jazz Age* (Durham, N.C.: Duke University Press, 2001). Hattori began working in the Shanghai film industry during the occupation of that city by Japanese forces during the war and continued to collaborate with Hong Kong studios such as the Shaw Brothers and MP&GI until the late 1960s.

9. See, for instance, Poshek Fu, "Modernity, Diasporic Capital, and 1950s Hong Kong Mandarin Cinema," *Jump Cut*, no. 49 (Spring 2007), and Mary Wong, "Women Who Cross Borders: MP&GI's Modernity Program," in A. Wong, ed., *The Cathay Story*, 85–93.

10. The *New York Times* gives a brief account of her appearance in John B. Shanley, "Bayanihan Troupe," *New York Times*, October 26, 1959, 59.

11. Footage of the performance is available online at www.youtube.com/watch?v=Ib0_rJeDZjw. Many thanks to Durian Dave, author of the Hong Kong and Chinese film history blog, http://softfilm.blogspot.com/, for providing me with the footage. Accessed April 15, 2011.

12. See, for instance, the series of five articles covering her visit to the United States in Taiwan's *Lianhe bao* [United Daily News] from September 24, 1959, to November 21, 1959. Interestingly, her performance in the United States was also rebroadcast in Taiwan by the U.S. Information Service.

13. For an in-house introduction to Capitol Records and its corporate history, see Paul Grein, *Capitol Records: Fiftieth Anniversary, 1942–1992* (Hollywood, Calif.: Capitol Records, 1992).

14. For Dave Dexter's life and work, see his *Playback: A Newsman-Record Producer's Hits and Misses from the Thirties from the Seventies* (New York: Billboard Publications, 1976). The "Capitol of the World" series, which comprised more than four hundred releases, is also profiled in Janet Borgerson and Jonathan Schroeder, *Designed for Hi-Fi Living: The Vinyl LP in Midcentury America* (Cambridge, Mass.: MIT Press, 2017), 299–338. For Gaisberg's memoir of his strikingly similar peregrinations around the globe in search of musical material, see F. W. Gaisberg, *The Music Goes Round* (New York: Macmillan, 1943). Kyu Sakamoto perished en route to Osaka in the crash of Japan Airlines Flight 123 in August 1985.

15. Steven Feld's work on the complex musical, material, and intellectual interactions between musicians in Ghana, the Caribbean, and the United States is an eloquent exposition of this circuit. See *Jazz Cosmopolitanism in Accra: Five Musical Years in Ghana* (Durham, N.C.: Duke University Press, 2012). For a classic formulation of the pan-Atlantic circulation of a black musical modernism, see Paul Gilroy, *The Black Atlantic: Modernity and Double Consciousness* (Cambridge, Mass.: Harvard University Press, 1993). Timothy Brennan has also written persuasively of the webs of cultural and spiritual affiliation linking the musics of West

Africa and Cuba to those of the United States and beyond in his *Secular Devotion: Afro-Latin Music and Imperial Jazz* (London and New York, Verso, 2008).

16. See the liner notes for "Hong Kong's Grace Chang." While there were reports in the Chinese press that the first pressing of the record had "sold out," there is no evidence that the record reached the Billboard charts, and Capitol Records did not opt to release a follow-up. See "'Ge Lan zhi ge' zai Mei da shou huanying" ["Hong Kong's Grace Chang" warmly received in the U.S.], *Lianhe bao* [United Daily News], May 2, 1961.

17. For an authoritative study of the first half-century of recorded Cantonese music and its audiences, see Sai-Shing Yung, *Yueyun liusheng: changpian gongye yu Guangdong quyi, 1903–1953* [Phonographing the Cantonese cadence: The record industry and Cantonese song art] (Hong Kong: Cosmos, 2006). For developments in Cantonese pop after the 1950s, see Helan Yang and Siu-wah Yu, *Yueyu gequ jiedu: tuibian zhong de Xianggang shengyin* [Reading Cantopop: The transformation of the Hong Kong soundscape] (Hong Kong: Wise Publishing, 2013). For an English-language study, see Yiu-wai Chu, *Hong Kong Cantopop: A Concise History* (Hong Kong: Hong Kong University Press, 2017).

18. See Brian Hu, "Star Discourse and the Cosmopolitan Chinese: Linda Lin Dai Takes on the World," *Journal of Chinese Cinemas* 4, no. 3: 185–86.

19. Poshek Fu, "Modernity, Cold War, and Hong Kong Mandarin Cinema," in A. Wong, ed., *The Cathay Story*, 28.

20. See "Cathay Pacific" at http://en.wikipedia.org/wiki/Cathay_Pacific. Accessed February 15, 2012.

21. Brian Bernards traces the history and topology of Nanyang as a literary circuit in his illuminating *Writing the South Seas: Imagining the Nanyang in Chinese and Southeast Asian Literature* (Seattle: University of Washington Press, 2018).

22. See Lim and Tiong, *Cathay: 55 Years of Cinema*, 44, 152.

23. Interestingly, the company was hit by serious labor unrest in 1961 and by a concerted strike led by "leftist activists" in 1963. See Lim and Tiong, *Cathay: 55 Years of Cinema*, 58.

24. Reputedly based on the melody of a Cantonese popular song, the song's bright pentatonic melody and orchestration are also "playful" responses to Hollywood *chinoiserie*, according to Wong Kee-chee. See his "Yao Min's 'MP&GI Style'" in A. Wong, ed., *The Cathay Story*, 148.

25. This last line is a not-so-veiled sop to the social and economic tensions on the island between the largely local Taiwanese-speaking population and the nearly two million refugees from the Chinese mainland who fled to the island in the wake of the defeat of the KMT by the Chinese Communist Party in 1949.

26. See Gao Shanyue, "The Other Agenda of *Air Hostess*" [*Kongzhong xiaojie* bie you yongxin], *Ta Kung Pao*, June 10, 1959, 6.

27. For discussions of the vernacular in history, see Sheldon Pollock, "The Cosmopolitan Vernacular," *Journal of Asian Studies* 57, no. 1 (February 1998) and "Cosmopolitan and Vernacular in History," *Public Culture* 12, no. 3 (2000).

28. See Miriam Bratu Hansen, "Vernacular Modernism: Tracking Cinema on a Global Scale," in Nataša Durovicová and Kathleen Newman, eds., *World Cinemas, Transnational Perspectives* (London and New York: Routledge, 2007), 295. This is one of a series of essays in which Hansen articulated the scope and heuristic consequences of "vernacular modernism." See also "The Mass Production of the Senses: Classical Cinema as Vernacular Modernism," *Modernism/ Modernity* 6, no. 2 (1999): 59–77.

29. See Gustavo Perez-Firmat, *Life on the Hyphen: The Cuban-American Way* (Austin: University of Texas Press, 1994), 87–88.

30. Perez-Firmat, *Life on the Hyphen*, 88.

31. For Puente's tour in Hong Kong, see Carl Myatt, "Tito Puente Dates Boost Latin Music," *Billboard*, November 7, 1962, 33.

32. For contemporary coverage of the mambo craze in Japan and elsewhere in East Asia, see "Music: Mambo-San," *Time*, July 25, 1955. See also Hui, "Pailameng faxing diyi bu manbo yingpian" [Paramount distributes its first mambo movie], *Lianhe fukan* [United Daily News supplement], May 10, 1955, 6.

33. See Kathleen McHugh, "South Korean Film Melodrama: State, Nation, Woman, and the Transnational Familiar," in Kathleen McHugh and Nancy Abelmann, *South Korean Golden Age Melodrama: Gender, Genre, and National Cinema* (Detroit: Wayne State University Press, 2005), 32–33.

34. Sek Kei, "One Big Happy Family: Grace Chang's MP&GI Story," in A. Wong, ed., *The Cathay Story*, 192. *Mambo Girl*, on an initial investment of HK $144,842, brought Cathay box office receipts of HK $300,748 from screens in Singapore, Malaya, Thailand, Vietnam, the Philippines, and Indonesia. See Lim and Tiong, *Cathay: 55 Years of Cinema*, 148. Delfino, an important figure in the dissemination of Latin music in Hong Kong, is also featured in Chang's 1957 *Mambo Girl*.

35. "Calypso Enjoys Worldwide Popularity / Kalisao xianhua," *International Screen* 23 (September 1957). In fairness, the Chinese text of the piece is both more detailed and somewhat more sophisticated than the English summary, acknowledging both the modernity of Trinidadian calypsonians and their "literary" and "harmonic" talent. A nearly verbatim English language description of the new dance step also appears in a second Hong Kong film journal, *Southern Screen*. See "Gelisao yu qiaqia" [Calypso and cha-cha], *Nanguo* [Southern Screen] 3 (October 1958). Thanks to Jean Ma for sharing these materials with me. The notion that calypso was a successor to or even a threat to displace rock and roll was a common one at the time. See Ray Funk and Donald R. Hill, "'Will Calypso Doom Rock'n'Roll?': The U.S. Calypso Craze of 1957," in Garth L. Green and Philip W. Scher, eds., *Trinidad Carnival: The Cultural Politics of a Transnational Festival* (Bloomington: Indiana University Press, 2007): 178–97. For contemporary efforts to define the calypso, see Daniel J. Crowley, "Towards a Definition of the Calypso," *Ethnomusicology* 3, no. 2 (1959): 57–66.

36. Wang Fei's original recording is available on YouTube.com, albeit without any discographic information, at http://www.youtube.com/watch?v=Ts1WrdMO1

Es&feature=related. Accessed on February 8, 2012. I have located a subsequent 33 1/3 LP record from the Black Cat Records (Heimao changpian) label in Taiwan with a cover of the song, unattributed to any particular artist but featuring a rudimentary "Latin" beat played on the bongos. The record (BCL 66 A) can be dated from between 1963, when LPs were first produced in Taiwan, and 1968, when government agencies first required records to be labeled with their date of production. My gratitude to Xu Guolong (K'ho) of Wien Records, Tainan, for his assistance in dating the record. The following blog entry also contains a useful history of the song: http://blog.roodo.com/muzikland/archives/15634765.html. Accessed February 8, 2012.

37. For C. S. Stone Shih's illuminating intervention into prevailing pop musical historiography, see "Taiwan geyao zuowei yizhong 'shidai shengxing qu': yinyue Taibei de Shanghai ji zhu hunxue meiying" [Taiwan ballads as a form of "mainstream popular music": Shanghai and other mixed-blood influences in musical Taipei, 1930–1960], *Taiwan shehui xuekan* [Taiwanese Journal of Sociology] 47 (September 2011): 94–141.

38. C. S. Stone Shih, personal interview, Taipei, December 30, 2011.

39. See David Frazier, "Kupa Big Band: That Old Style Hoklo Swing," *Fountain: Arts and Living* 4 (2010): 30.

40. For an account of the band's origins and activities, see the composer Huang Guolong's *Zhongwai gujin yinyue chaoliu* [Musical currents: Chinese and foreign, ancient and contemporary] (Taipei: Wuzhou chubanshe, 1970), 261–63. Their popularity continued into the late 1960s. They are prominently featured, for instance, in the *China TV Weekly* in 1969. See Zhe Xiong, "Guba yuedui: liuxing yinyue de da jiazu" [Kupa Band: Popular music's big family], *Zhongguo dianshi zhoukan* 13 (January 18–25,1969): 8–12.

41. One such example is an undated stereo pressing from the early 1960s produced by Tainan's Asia Records. The record is an unauthorized pirate copy of The Bay Big Band's long-playing compilation of instrumental Perez Prado covers, "Latin Beat" (Omega Records, 1958, issued as "Pradomania" in the U.K.). Asia Records retitled the work "Mambo in Stereo," perhaps inadvertently reversed Side A and Side B in the process, and issued it as ASL-5, with track listings given in English and Japanese *katakana*, suggesting that this may have been a copy of a Japanese issue of the original record.

42. "Hokkien" is a general term for the language, largely deriving from the Zhangzhou and Quanzhou regions of southern Fujian province, that is widely spoken in Taiwan and across the diaspora.

43. See Jeremy Taylor's groundbreaking critique of nation-centered approaches to Chinese cultural production in "From Transnationalism to Nativism? The Rise, Decline, and Reinvention of a Regional Entertainment Industry," *Inter-Asian Cultural Studies* 9, no. 1 (2008): 5. For a comprehensive study of Hokkien cinema, see Jeremy Taylor, *Rethinking Transnational Chinese Cinemas: The Amoy-Dialect Film Industry in Cold War Asia* (London: Routledge, 2011).

44. The Cantonese record industry, like its counterparts in Taiwan, often survived by covering and in the process creatively inflecting both Mandarin material and songs from abroad. A similar logic also governed the production of Cantonese films. See Hon-Lun Helan Yang's forthcoming essay, "Cosmopolitanism and Sound Alignments: Cantonese Cover Songs from Hong Kong Films of the 1960s," in Michael Bourdaghs, Paola Iovene, and Kaley R. Mason, eds., *Sound Alignments: Popular Music in Asia's Cold Wars* (Durham, N.C.: Duke University Press, forthcoming).

45. Taylor, *Rethinking Transnational Chinese Cinemas*, 8.

46. Taylor, *Rethinking Transnational Chinese Cinemas*, 8. Huang Guolong also cites the years between 1962 and 1967 as the "age of television" in Taiwanese popular musical history, as televised broadcasts eclipsed live performances in cabarets and other venues as the primary means of securing promotional notice and recording contracts. See Huang, *Zhongwai gujin yinyue chaoliu*, 80.

47. Of ten films starring the star Wen Shia, for instance, only his last, *Goodbye, Taipei* (*Zaijian Taibei*, 1969) survives in the Taipei Film Archives. Similarly, only Hong Yifeng's most popular film, *Lingering Lost Love* (*Jiuqing mianmian*, 1962) is still extant.

48. See Guo-Juin Hong, *Taiwan Cinema: A Contested Nation Onscreen* (New York: Palgrave Macmillan, 2011), 7 and 60–62.

49. For an excellent musical analysis of Hong Yifeng's work and its fashioning of a new "baritone" (*diyin*) aesthetic in Taiwanese balladry, see Wan-Ting Chiu, "Baodao diyin gewang zhi lu: Hong Yifeng chuangzuo yu hunxie gequ tantao" [Formosan baritone king: Hong Yifeng's work and the question of mixed-blood songs], master's thesis, Graduate Institute of Musicology, National Taiwan University, 2011. See also her later monograph, *Baodao diyin gewang: yichang qimeng zhi lu* [Formosan baritone king: A journey of musical enlightenment] (Taipei: Tonsan, 2013).

50. Elsewhere in the film, Hong Yifeng's music harks back not only to doo-wop and early rock and roll but also to the yodeling of Jimmie Rodgers.

51. This figure derives from an article by He Fan from 1965, "Taiwan daoyin changpian" [Taiwan's Fake Label Records], *Lianhe bao* [United Daily News], October 27, 1965. Carl Myatt, writing in *Billboard*, reports that the monthly figure for Taiwanese pirate records was much higher: "150,000 LPs . . . leave Taiwan every month," according to an EMI Hong Kong representative. See Carl Myatt, "Pirates Capturing Business," *Billboard*, August 31, 1963, 30.

52. He, "Taiwan daoyin changpian." As quoted in Ye Longyan, *Taiwan changpian sixiang qi, 1895–1999* [Remembering the Taiwanese recording industry, 1895–1999] (Luzhou: Boyang wenhua, 2001), 201–2.

53. See Ye, *Taiwan changpian sixiang qi*, 146–47.

54. Personal interview with Taiwanese music scholar and collector Xu Guolong (Kh'o), Wien Records, Tainan, Taiwan, July 10, 2011.

55. On Cathay's ties with Taiwan, see Emilie Yueh-yu Yeh, "Taiwan: The Transnational Battlefield of Cathay and Shaws," in A. Wong, ed., *The Cathay Story*, 72–76.

56. Loke's ornithological research was published in a monograph titled *The Company of Birds*, and he enjoyed recording bird songs with a portable Nagra and a parabolic reflector. See Lim and Tiong, *Cathay: 55 Years of Cinema*, 6, 17.

## 2. Quotation Songs

1. I am relying here on the account of the incident provided by Liang Maochun in his groundbreaking study of the phenomenon, "Lun 'yulu ge' xianxiang" [On the "quotation songs" phenomenon], *Huangzhong: Wuhan yinyue xueyuan xuebao* 1 [Huangzhong: Journal of Wuhan Music Conservatory] (2003): 46–47. Jiang Qing's comments were made on April 15, 1969.
2. Liang, "Lun 'yulu ge' xianxiang," 46.
3. For the politics of popular music in the pre-1949 era, see Andrew F. Jones, *Yellow Music: Media Culture and Colonial Modernity in the Chinese Jazz Age* (Durham, N.C.: Duke University Press, 2001).
4. This particular composition is included on a seven-inch 45-rpm record released under the title "Wei Mao zhuxi yulu puqu" [Quotations from Chairman Mao set to music]. See China Records S-103, 1966.
5. Her comments of April 15 were followed by an equally vehement summary the following day: "Last night I saw a TV program, watched for the first time in my life, as they adopted unbearably bourgeois techniques to distort the solemnity of the great Ninth Party Congress. What's more, before they played a documentary about the Ninth Party Congress, they inserted some so-called arts programs, which claimed to propagate the thought of Chairman Mao, to praise Chairman Mao. But in reality what they were singing were just popular folk tunes [*minjian de xiaodiao*], vulgar 'yellow' folk songs, tunes that are all about 'my darling man' and 'my little girl.' I have nothing against talking love, but to use these tunes to sing of the Ninth Party Congress, to sing quotations, is not to praise Chairman Mao, it's an insult to the thought of Chairman Mao. And to dance so crazily is actually swing dancing. Playing the flute, blowing on a *suona*, dressed in PLA uniform or worker's clothes, swaying and bobbing their heads. The music lacks a clear rhythm, 'cha cha cha,' just like jazz. The dancing has no shape, no form, they're twisting back and forth, dancing like crazy . . . before the Cultural Revolution, when they wanted to mount an attack on us, they would start from performances and arts reviews, and now they're at it again." See Liang, "Lun 'yulu ge' xianxiang," 47.
6. See "Yiwan renmin qi huan chang, Mao Zedong sixiang fang guangmang" [The multitudes of the People sing joyfully in unison, Chairman Mao's thought radiates brilliance], *Renmin ribao* (People's Daily), September 30, 1966.
7. Steve J. Wurtzler has provided a sustained and thoughtful analysis of the ways in which "electrical-acoustic" technologies such as radio, records, "talkies," and television powered the rise of corporate media in the United States. See *Electric Sounds: Technological Change and the Rise of the Corporate Mass Media* (New York: Columbia University Press, 2007). More directly relevant, Nicole Huang, in

her analysis of radio-plays and their intermedial intertwinement with the cinema in 1970s China, has argued for just such a notion of "cross-platform saturation" as a hallmark of socialist media in that era. See Nicole Huang, "Listening to Films: Politics of the Auditory in 1970s China," *Journal of Chinese Cinemas* 7, no. 3 (2013): 196.

8. Paul Clark makes much the same point in exploring the centrality of the model operas (*yangbanxi*) as a locus of cultural production in forms as diverse as fiction, film painting, sculpture, and so on. See Paul Clark, *The Chinese Cultural Revolution: A History* (Cambridge: Cambridge University Press, 2008), 74.

9. I am deliberately "misquoting" the work of the Bakhtin scholar Gary Paul Morson, who asserts that "Cited expressions become quotations, they are not automatically so. Becoming a quotation is a change in status, which may involve a change in form. When a set of words achieves that status, we typically remember it in its quoted form, which takes on a life of its own." See Morson, "The Quotation and Its Genres," *Sun Yat-sen Journal of Humanities* 21 (Winter 2005): 129.

10. See Lin Biao, "Zaiban qianyan" [Preface to the second edition], in *Mao zhuxi yulu* [Quotations of Chairman Mao] (Guangzhou: Zhongguo renmin jiefang jun zong zhengzhi bu, 1967), 2.

11. Lin, "Zaiban qianyan," 3.

12. Lin, "Zaiban qianyan," 1.

13. Richard Kraus characterizes Li Jiefu as a staunch populist and the opposite number of Shanghai-trained musicians like He Lüting. Formed by his experiences as a cadre in the Yan'an base area, Li Jiefu produced work deeply imprinted by Soviet martial music. He was arrested in the wake of Lin Biao's alleged coup attempt in 1971 and died just before the conclusion of the Cultural Revolution in 1976.

14. For a brief profile of Li Jiefu in relation to his music settings for the quotation songs, see Liang Maochun, "Lun 'yulu ge' xianxiang" [On the quotation songs phenomenon], part two, *Huangzhong: Wuhan yinyue xueyuan xuebao* [Huangzhong: Journal of Wuhan Music Conservatory] 2 (2003): 91–93.

15. For an illuminating history of revolutionary song and its roots in Christian hymnal, see Isabel K. F. Wong, "*Geming gequ*: Songs for the Education of the Masses," in Bonnie Macdougal, ed., *Popular Chinese Culture and Performing Arts in the People's Republic of China, 1949–1979* (Berkeley: University of California Press, 1984).

16. See Liang, "Lun 'yulu ge' xianxiang," part two, 45–46. See also "Lingdao women shiye de hexin liliang sh Zhongguo gongchandang" [The force at the core leading our cause forward is the Communist Party of China], *Renmin ribao* [People's Daily], September 30, 1966.

17. One interesting example of these sorts of visual representations of the *Quotations* was an exhibition of "quotations paintings" held in Shanghai in the summer of 1967. For a contemporary news report, see "'Mao zhuxi yulu huazhan' zai Shanghai zhanchu shoudao relie huanying" [Opening of the "Chairman Mao

quotations paintings" exhibit is warmly welcomed in Shanghai], *Renmin ribao* [People's Daily], June 5, 1967.

18. For the Guoji Shudian's role in the international dissemination of the *Quotations* in this era, see Lanjun Xu, "Translation and Internationalism," in Alexander Cook, ed., *Mao's Little Red Book: A Global History* (New York: Cambridge University Press, 2014).

19. Recordings of quotation songs became more accessible to domestic listeners in 1968, when China Records began to produce inexpensive flexi-discs for the domestic market. Referred to as *baomo changpian*, these records, mostly in the 7-inch format, were pressed on a thin sheet of vinyl. China Records developed their process for manufacturing flexi-discs in house and by 1968 had manufactured 1.8 million such records. For a handy comparative chart of technical developments in the Chinese and Taiwanese record industries, see Xu Guolong (Kh'o), "Ershi shiji er zhan hou liang an leibi changpian fazhan gaiyao" [A summary of the development of analogue records in China and Taiwan after World War II], http://blog.sinaarr.tw/wiwienen/article.php?pbgid=323&entryid=580588. Accessed on July 30, 2012

20. Estimates as to the number of loudspeakers vary and are based of necessity on (not always entirely reliable) official statistics. According to Alan P. Liu, China had installed 6 million loudspeakers by 1964. Andrew Nathan estimates that this figure had mushroomed to 141 million by the mid-1970s, reaching 95 percent of production units and 65 percent of rural homes. See Andrew Nathan, *Chinese Democracy* (London: I. B. Tauris, 1986), 163.

21. For a history and description of this radio network, see Alan Liu, *Communications and National Integration in Communist China* (Berkeley: University of California Press, 1971), 119–29. The penetration of everyday life by this speaker system reached into even the most intimate spaces of the home. As the anthropologist Yan Yunxiang notes in regard to the collectivization of individual space in an agricultural commune, "Wired broadcasting is a typical example. In the early 1970s, Dadui village installed a loudspeaker in every home, typically right above the *kang* bed. The loudspeakers had no on/off switches, and both the content and the schedule of the programming was determined by the county broadcast station. The Dadui station was just a relay for the county broadcast system. And so the villagers had no control over what they could hear or when they would hear it. They were forced to listen every day to official news, political propaganda, speeches by cadres, entertainment programs, and the like. But as time went on, everyone not only got accustomed to the wired broadcasts, but came to depend upon them." See Yan Yunxiang, *Siren shenghuo de bianqe: yige zhongguo cunzhuang li de aiqing, jiating yu qinmi guanxi, 1949–1999* [The transformation of everyday life: Love, family, and intimacy in a Chinese village, 1949–199] (Shanghai: Shanghai shudian, 2006), 41.

22. See "Mao zhuxi de shu shi ti women pinxia zhong nong shuo hua de" [Chairman Mao's book speaks for us poor and middle peasants], *Renmin ribao*

[People's Daily], October 1, 1966. This article appeared, it is worth noting, just the day after the roll-out of the first ten quotation songs on September 30.

23. The policy is laid out in an editorial in *Wuxiandian* (Wireless) titled, "Vigorously Develop the Rural Broadcasting Network" [Dali fazhan nongcun guangbo wang], *Wuxiandian* [Wireless] 2 (1956): 4–5.

24. Detailed guidelines for installation are provided in Fan Dunxing, ed., *Nongcun youxian guangbo changshi* [A guide to rural wired broadcasting] (Shanghai: Renmin chubanshe, 1971). One drawback of exploiting existing telephone lines was that these systems could not be used simultaneously without crosstalk, interference, or the risk of a short circuit because of mismatched impedances.

25. See Chen Yadong, *Youxian guangbo* [Wired broadcasting] (Beijing: Renmin chubanshe, 1968), 1.

26. See Yan, *Siren shenghuo de bianqe*, 41.

27. The numbers are provided in a table titled "Number of Rural Wired Broadcasting Stations and Loudspeakers in China, 1949–1964," compiled by Alan P. Liu and based on various official sources, including Xinhua News and *People's Daily*. See Liu, *Communications and National Integration in Communist China*, 120.

28. Of necessity, these sorts of local solutions had a great deal of currency in the Maoist era, as part of the state's larger effort to promote "local" or "indigenous" science (*tu kexue*) over the remote universalisms of "foreign science" (*yang kexue*). For a thoughtful discussion of this binary and its application to agricultural development in the period, see Sigrid Schmalzer, *Red Revolution, Green Revolution: Scientific Farming in Socialist China* (Chicago: University of Chicago Press, 2016), 34–38. Hu Youren, ed., *Nongcun dianhua he guangbo xianlu shigong zhong de "tu" banfa* [Down-to-earth solutions for working with rural telephone and broadcasting networks] (Beijing; Renmin youdian chubanshe), 1958.

29. See Marshall McLuhan, *Understanding Media: The Extensions of Man* (New York: McGraw-Hill, 1964).

30. For an illustrated introductory pamphlet on rural electrification during the Great Leap Forward, see *Rural Electrification in Rapid Progress* (Peking: Foreign Languages Press, 1958).

31. These statistics derive from Wuyuan Peng and Jiahua Pan, "Rural Electrification in China: History and Institution," *China and World Economy* 14, no. 1 (2006): 74–77.

32. See Liaoning renmin guangbo diantai, ed., *Liyong chuli fadian youxian guangbo de shebei* [Equipment for livestock-powered wired broadcasting] (Beijing: Renmin youdian chubanshe, 1968), 4.

33. Fan, ed., *Nongcun youxian guangbo changshi*, 54.

34. Fan, ed., *Nongcun youxian guangbo changshi*, 55.

35. Dynamic speakers were largely reserved for applications for which sound quality was a paramount consideration, such as indoor public address systems in theaters and auditoriums. For contemporary guidelines as to the various types

of speakers available and their recommended applications, see Chen, *Youxian guangbo*, 35.

36. This, at least, was the ideal configuration suggested by Fan, *Nongcun youxian guangbo changshi*, 4. Despite being far less conductive than copper and considerably less flexible, galvanized iron remained the material of choice in this period because of its low cost. Fan, *Nongcun youxian guangbo changshi*, 18.

37. The lamps were refitted as thermocouple generators. See *Bandaoti fadianqi* [Semiconductor generators] (Beijing: Renmin youdian chubanshe, 1959).

38. For a list of Peony brand models, see this invaluable online resource: http://www.radiomuseum.org/m/beijingref_prc_en_1.html. Accessed July 28, 2015. For Sony and the history of transistor radios in the United States, see Michael Brian Schiffer, *The Portable Radio in America* (Tucson and London: University of Arizona Press, 1995), 202–23.

39. "Xin chanpin: liang zhong shouyin ji, shouti liangyong, chengxiang xianyi" [New products: Two types of radios, dual portable, convenient for town and country]. See *Renmin ribao* [People's Daily], March 1, 1958.

40. A spate of articles on the problem of rural electrification and the expansion of the broadcasting network, as well as how-to guides for local cadres and activists interested in overcoming these difficulties, appears in the pages of *Wuxiandian* (Wireless) throughout 1966. See, for instance, "Tuchu zhengzhi, queli wei nongmin fuwu de sixiang, mianxiang nongcun, sheji wei nongmin huanying de chanpin: jieshao Xiongmao B-302 xing bandaoti shouyin ji" [Emphasize politics, affirm ideology in service of the peasants, face the countryside, and design products that will be welcomed by the peasants: Introducing the Panda brand B-302 semiconductor radio set], *Wuxiandian* [Wireless] 6 (1966): 38–39; "Zenyang xuanze diantai de weizhi" [How to site a relay station], *Wuxiandian* [Wireless] 6 (1966): 42–44; "Jianli fangda zhan de jige jishu wenti" [Some technical problems in setting up a broadcasting station], *Wuxiandian* [Wireless] 9 (1966): 23–24; "Nongcun youxian guangbo yong 500 haowa bandaoti fangda qi" [500 mW transistors for use in rural rediffusion broadcast amplifiers], *Wuxiandian* [Wireless] 10 (1966): 24–25.

41. See Anita Chan, Richard Madsen, and Jonathan Unger, *Chen Village: The Recent History of a Peasant Community in Mao's China* (Berkeley: University of California Press, 1984), 84–85.

42. Chan et al., *Chen Village*, 85.

43. Chan et al., *Chen Village*, 85–86.

44. Laurence Coderre, "Socialist Commodities: Consuming Yangbanxi in the Cultural Revolution," Ph.D. dissertation, University of California, Berkeley, 2015, 73–74.

45. For a brief history of flexi-discs in China, see Coderre, "Socialist Commodities," 74–75.

46. See Jacques Derrida, "Signature Event Context," in Derrida, *Limited Inc.* (Evanston, Ill.: Northwestern University Press, 1988), 1–24. The essay was originally written by Derrida in 1971.

47. See "Mao Zhuxi de shu, shi ti women pinxia zhong nong shuo hua de, tiantian du Mao Zhuxi de shu, jiu haoxing tiantian jiandao Mao Zhuxi" [Chairman Mao's book speaks for us poor and middle peasants. Reading Chairman Mao's book every day is like seeing Chairman Mao himself everyday], *Renmin ribao* [People's Daily], October 1, 1966. The report was produced by the Fuyu County Party Committee, Jilin Province, and covers developments in the Xin'an zhen People's Commune.

48. See "Dangdai zui weida de Malie zhuyizhe Mao zhuxi de yulu pucheng de gequ shi woguo renmin zui xin'ai de geming zhange" [The quotations set to music of the greatest Marxist-Leninist thinker of our time, Chairman Mao, are the most beloved battle hymns of our people], in *Renmin ribao* [People's Daily], September 30, 1967. This article was published exactly one year after the initial introduction of the genre to China's reading public in 1966.

49. Liang, "Lun 'yulu ge' xianxiang," 48.

50. The burgeoning popularity of horn reflex systems for use in open fields is also noted in *Nongcun youxian guangbo changshi*, a manual first published in May 1966. See Fan, *Nongcun youxian guangbo changshi*, 41.

51. Chen, *Youxian guangbo*, 79.

52. A manual for installing broadcasting networks in open fields measures the range of a directional horn reflex speaker running on four watts at two hundred to five hundred meters, depending on wind direction. See Wu Bozhen, *Tianjian guangbo* [Field Broadcasting] (Beijing: Renmin youdian chubanshe, 1958), 14.

53. In the United States, the deliberate use of overdrive distortion was pioneered in the late 1940s and became a staple of popular musical timbre in the 1960s. For a helpful primer on the types and uses of distortion in the recording process, see Jay Hodgson, *Understanding Records: A Field Guide to Recording Practice* (New York: Continuum Books, 2010), 97–116.

54. For an extensive and helpful discussion of how hooks work, see Gary Burns, "A Typology of 'Hooks' in Popular Records," *Popular Music* 6, no. 1 (January 1987): 1–20.

55. See Alexei Yurchak, *Everything Was Forever, Until It Was No More: The Last Soviet Generation* (Princeton: Princeton University Press, 2006), 24–26. My thinking here is indebted to Jason McGrath, who observes a similar phenomenon underlying the increasing formalization of revolutionary realism, as evinced by the model opera films. See his "Cultural Revolution Model Opera Films and the Realist Tradition in Chinese Cinema," *The Opera Quarterly* 26, no. 2–3 (Spring–Summer 2010).

56. Yurchak, *Everything Was Forever*, 26.

57. See Huang Ziping, "Everyday Linguistics in the 1970s" [Qishi niandai richang yuyan xue], in Bei Dao and Li Tuo, eds., *Qishi niandai* [The Seventies] (Beijing: Sanlian, 2009), 324. Huang's essay has been translated by Nick Admussen as "Practical Linguistics of the 1970s" in *Renditions* 75 (Spring 2011).

58. Huang, "Everyday Linguistics in the 1970s."

59. The translation of the song lyrics from the original French is adapted from the Australian DVD edition of the film, released by Madman Cinema.

### 3. Fugitive Sounds of the Taiwanese Musical Cinema

1. A note on nomenclature. Wen Shia's name is rendered as Wen Xia in standard *Hanyu Pinyin* romanization and as Wen Hsia in the Wade-Giles system traditionally used in Taiwan. Here I adhere to Wen Shia's own idiosyncratic spelling, which appears on album covers and other promotional materials throughout his career. In Taiwanese Hoklo, his name is Bûn Hā.

2. See Evelyn Shih, "Getting the Last Laugh: Opera Legacy, Comedy and Camp as Attraction in the Late Years of Taiyupian," *Journal of Chinese Cinemas* 7, no. 3 (2013): 246. Shih's critique is directed in part at Liao Jinfeng's identification of *Taiyu pian* as a "transitional cinema" situated between primitive early cinema and classical form. See Liao Jinfeng, *Xiaoshi de yinxiang: Taiyu pian de dianying zaixian yu wenhua rentong* [The vanished image: Cinematic representation and cultural identity in Taiwanese-language films] (Taipei: Yuanliu, 2001), 136–37. This notion is also echoed in Liao's emphasis on the lack of a realist sound design in the films of the era. See Liao, *Xiaoshi de yinxiang*, 118–22.

3. This particular articulation of the problem of uneven development can be traced back to Bloch's 1932 essay "Nonsynchronism and the Obligation to Its Dialectics," trans. Mark Ritter, *New German Critique* 11 (Spring 1977): 22–38. The notion of uneven development is taken up and developed in the work of a number of Marxist thinkers, including Theodor Adorno, Ernest Mandel, and the world-systems theorist Immanuel Wallerstein, and in Fredric Jameson's work on modernism and postmodernity. See, for instance, Fredric Jameson, *Post-Modernism, or the Cultural Logic of Late Capitalism* (Durham, N.C.: Duke University Press, 1991), 307.

4. The proliferation of pop songs is characteristic not just of Wen Shia's *Goodbye, Taipei* but of late 1960s *Taiyu pian* as a whole. *Dangerous Youth* (*Weixian de qingchun*, 1969, directed by Xing Qi), for instance, features everything from Otis Redding to the theme from the *Valley of the Dolls*. For a discussion of the pop landscape in *Taiyu pian*, see Liao, *Xiaoshi de yinxiang*, 82–86. For a study of the Japanese pop musical landscape in the postwar period, see Michael Bourdaghs, *Sayonara Amerika, Sayonara Nippon: A Geopolitical Prehistory of J-Pop* (New York: Columbia University Press, 2012).

5. Cantinflas, born Fortino Alfonso Moreno Reyes in 1912, is often seen as emblematic of a kind of underdog consciousness, or *rascuachismo*, in Mexican culture. For an insightful introduction to his life, cultural significance, and afterlife in Mexico, see Ilan Stavans, "The Riddle of Cantinflas," in Stavans, *The Riddle of Cantinflas: Essays on Hispanic Popular Culture* (Albuquerque: University of New Mexico Press, 2012), 77–95.

6. Cantinflas is profiled in a *United Daily News* (*Lianhe bao*) piece from 1963, which focuses on the contrast between his pitifully downtrodden persona

and the considerable fame and fortune he derived from his film career. See "Moxige guaijie: Kangdingfalasi" [Mexico's strange knight: Cantinflas], *Lianhe bao*, February 15, 1963. His 1961 film *El Analfabeto* screened at Taipei's Wanguo cinema as late as 1967, billed as *Ah Ding kuxue ji* [The vicissitudes of Ah Ding in school].

7. For language policies under Japanese colonial rule, see E. Patricia Tsurumi, *Japanese Colonial Education in Taiwan, 1895–1945* (Cambridge, Mass.: Harvard University Press, 1977). For postwar developments, see Chen Meiru, *Taiwan yuyan jiaoyu zhengce de huigu yu zhanwang* [Language and educational policy in Taiwan: History and future prospects] (Kaohsiung: Fuwen, 1998). The process whereby the KMT sought to quash the use of Japanese, as well as instituted legal constraints on the public use of Hoklo, Hakka, and other local languages, is documented in an online "Timeline of Taiwan's Linguistic Policies" ("Taiwan yuyan zhengce da shiji") compiled by the National Museum of Taiwan Literature: nmtldig.nmtl.gov.tw/taigi/02sp/04_list.html. Accessed September 9, 2015.

8. See "Taiwan sheng Riwen shukan ji Riyu dianying pian guanzhi banfa" [Procedures for the regulation of Japanese books and periodicals and Japanese-language films], promulgated by the Taiwan Provincial Government in April 1950, as well as "Taiwan sheng Riwen shukan ji Riyu dianying pian shencha hui zuzhi guicheng" [Guidelines for the establishment of a Japanese-language publication and film censorship committee], issued in May 1950. Both documents are accessible at gaz.ncl.edu.tw/detailjsp?sysid=E1045589. Accessed September 10, 2015. Only Japanese films with "significance for 'anti-Communism and resisting the Soviets'" or "scientific education" were permitted entry. The actual implementation of these rules was uneven, as is detailed in Huang Ren, *Riben dianying zai Taiwan* [Japanese films in Taiwan] (Taibei: Xiuwei zixun, 2008).

9. See Huang Guolong, *Zhongwai gujin yinyue chaoliu* [Musical currents, east and west, ancient and modern] (Taipei: Wuzhou wenku, 1969). The book begins with an obligatory encomium to the Cultural Renaissance movement, as well as a treatise on Generalissimo Chiang Kai-shek's views on music.

10. See Huang, *Zhongwai gujin yinyue chaoliu*, 142.

11. The popular press also issued frequent critiques of this phenomenon. See "Riben diao fanlan, fuzhi feng risheng" [Flood of Japanese tunes as the copycat trend gets more common by the day], *Lianhe bao* [United Daily News], August 22, 1966. For an overview of the censorship regime, see Li Kuncheng, *Zaijian! Jinji de Niandai* [Farewell to the era of taboos] (Kaohsiung: Kaohsiung Government Information Office, 2007).

12. For a history of this period, see Ye Longyan, *Taiwan changpian sixiangqi* [Remembering Taiwanese records] (Luzhou: Boyang wenhua, 2001), 133–53.

13. The origins of Wen Shia's collaboration with Cai Wenhua, the founder of Asia Records, and the company's successful entrance into the popular music market are recounted in Wen Shia, *Wen Xia chang(chang)you renjian wuyu* [The story of Wen Shia's song of life], ed. Liu Kuo-wei et al. (Ilan: Huafeng wenhua, 2015), 34–38.

14. See Wen Shia, *Wen Xia chang(chang)you renjian wuyu*, 36–38.

15. This is why two bidirectional ribbon microphones, placed at a ninety-degree angle, were often used to record in stereo. This procedure, called the "Blumlein pair" recording array after its inventor, was published in the *Journal of the Audio Engineering Society* in 1958, just as Cai Wenhua was setting up his studio. See H.A.M. Clark, G. F. Dutton, and P. B. Vanderlyn, "The Stereosonic Recording and Reproducing System: Two Channel Systems for Domestic Tape Records," *Journal of the Audio Engineering Society* 6, no. 2 (February 1958): 102–17.

16. For a major study of Chi Lu-shyia and her contribution to the Taiwanese ballad tradition, see C. S. Stone Shih (Shi Jisheng), *Shidai shengxing qu: Ji Luxia yu Taiwan geyao niandai* [Modern song: Chi Lu-Shyia and the era of the Taiwanese ballad] (Taipei: Tonsan, 2014).

17. The success of Wen Shia's cover of the song is, in fact, singled out for initiating the popularity of "mixed-blood" songs in a 1966 article decrying the phenomenon in the *United Daily News*. See "Riben diao fanlan, fuzhi feng risheng" [Flood of Japanese tunes as the copycat trend gets more common by the day], *Lianhe bao* [United Daily News], August 22, 1966.

18. For a complete list of his compositions and their derivation, see Wen Shia, *Wen Xia chang(chang)you renjian wuyu*, 181–89.

19. Wen Shia was often pictured in promotional materials at this time sporting an appropriately nautical sailor's cap.

20. Like Kobayashi, Wen Shia took to wearing his favorite white Fender acoustic guitar slung over his back. For an introduction to Ishihara and his moment, see Michael Raine, "Ishihara Yujiro: Youth, Celebrity, and the Male Body in Late-1950s Japan," in Dennis Washburn and Carole Cavanaugh, eds., *Word and Image in Japanese Cinema* (Cambridge: Cambridge University Press, 2001).

21. C. S. Stone Shih, "Taiwan geyao zuowei yizhong 'shidai shengxing qu': yinyue Taibei de Shanghai ji zhu hunxue meiying (1930–1960)" [Taiwan ballads as a form of "mainstream modern popular music": Shanghai and other mixed-blood influences in musical Taipei, 1930–1960], *Taiwan shehui xuekan* [Taiwanese Journal of Sociology] 47 (September 2011): 103.

22. Li, *Zaijian! Jinji de Niandai*, 2007.

23. For a sense of the place of Hawai'i in the military propaganda of the war years, see Adria Imada's "The Troops Meet the Troupes: Imperial Hospitality and Military Photography in the Pacific Theater," in Imada, *Aloha America: Hula Circuits through the U.S. Empire* (Durham, N.C.: Duke University Press, 2012), 213–54.

24. See Jim Tranquada and John King, *The 'Ukulele: A History* (Honolulu: University of Hawai'i Press, 2012), 136–52.

25. The song is featured on *Wen Xia Gechang ji* [Wen Shia's Song Collection], Asia Records AL-396. The Taiwanese lyrics of seven of the eight songs, including "Wooden Heart," are attributed to Chou Ren, that is, to Wen Shia himself.

26. The film was screened in Taiwan in January 1961, with Chinese subtitles, as "Junzhong chunxiao" [Spring nights in the barracks], with the tagline "Ten of the latest songs by the 'King of Cats' Presley!" See *Shijie yingxun* [World Cinema Bulletin] 41 (January 15, 1961).

27. This is, of course, the same Sakamoto Kyu whose global smash hit "Sukiyaki," as marketed by Capitol Records, heralded a new sort of "world music." Michael Bourdaghs analyzes Sakamoto's version of the "G.I. Blues" as an oblique meditation on the U.S. occupation of postwar Japan. See Bourdaghs, *Sayonara Amerika*, 96–101.

28. See Mark Schilling, *No Borders, No Limits: Nikkatsu Action Cinema* (London: FAB Press, 2008).

29. For the formation of the "Four Sisters," see Wen Shia, *Wen Xia chang(chang)you renjian wuyu*, 81–87. For a profile of Xiao Wang (Wang Weiming), see "Yongyuan zhang bu da de xiexing" [The comical stars who will never grow up], *Lianhe bao* [United Daily News], June 21, 1967.

30. Liao, *Xiaoshi de yinxiang*, 175–76. For another account of this precipitous decline, see Ye Longyan, *Chunhua menglu: zhengzong Taiyu dianying xingshuai lu* [Spring flowers and illusory dew: The rise and fall of the authentic Taiwanese-language cinema] (Luzhou: Boyang wenhua, 1999).

31. See Liao, *Xiaoshi de yinxiang*, 178–80. Brian Wicks has astutely pointed out that the film's overt emphasis on the priorities and policies of the KMT party-state is to some extent belied by the formal complexity of Pai's filmmaking, a phenomenon I also explore in chapter 4. See Wicks, "Projecting a State That Does Not Exist: Bai Jingrui's *Jia Zai Taibei / Home Sweet Home*," in *Journal of Chinese Cinemas* 4, no. 1 (2010): 15–26.

32. See, for instance, "Yingjie caise dianying de xin shidai" [Mandarin films enter color age], *Nanguo dianying* [Southern Screen] 59 (January 1963). Su Chih-Heng argues that this failure was in some sense hard-wired into the governance and tax structures of the KMT party-state. While producers of *Taiyu* films were able through various loopholes to import black-and-white film stock throughout the 1960s, they were prevented from obtaining the needed expertise and materials to make the transition to color. By 1970, supplies of black-and-white film stock had dried up almost completely, effectively compelling the industry to halt production and cede the market to the state-run Central Motion Picture Corporation and Hong Kong imports. See Su Chih-Heng, "Chongxie Taiyu dianying shi: heibai dipian, caise jishu zhuanxing he dangguo wenhua zhili" [Rewriting the history of Taiwanese vernacular cinema: Black-and-white film stock, the conversion to color film, and party-state cultural governance], master's thesis, Department of Sociology, National Taiwan University, 2015.

33. For a collection of essays on the Shaw Brothers, see Poshek Fu, ed., *China Forever: The Shaw Brothers and Diasporic Cinema* (Urbana: University of Illinois Press).

34. See Sai-shing Yung, "Territorialization and the Entertainment Industry of the Shaw Brothers in Southeast Asia," in Fu, ed., *China Forever*, 133–53.

35. See Guo-Juin Hong, *Taiwan Cinema: A Contested Nation on Screen* (New York: Palgrave Macmillan, 2011), 65–86.

36. See "Sijia zu lianhe gongsi; Wen Xia you pai gechang pian" [Four film companies are organizing a conglomerate; Wen Shia will once again film a musical], *Lianhe bao* [United Daily News], December 16, 1968.

37. See "Shiji bu Taiyu pian qunian weiying yanchu" [More than ten *Taiyu* films illegally screened in the past year], *Lianhe bao* [United Daily News], January 9, 1969.

38. See "Fanghai fenghua: Kang Ding bei su" [Injurious to public morals: Kang Ding is indicted], *Lianhe bao* [United Daily News], June 25, 1971. For news of his later vindication, see "Huangse jingtou an: Kang Ding pan wu zui" [The case of the pornographic shot: Kang Ding not guilty] *Lianhe bao* [United Daily News], October 13, 1971.

39. Ironically, the local industry was also damaged by a temporary relaxation on restrictions on the import of Japanese films in 1970. See "Taiyu pian yu zhen fanli, muqian jin liang bu zai paishe, yanzhi yuan ling mou fazhan" [*Taiyu* films lack the strength to recover; only two films in production, while performers look for other career options], *Lianhe bao* [United Daily News], April 20, 1970.

40. For a discussion of this exodus of performers from the *Taiyu pian* to the Mandarin entertainment circuit, see "Taiyu pian yu zhen fanli, muqian jin liang bu zai paishe, yanzhi yuan ling mou fazhan" [*Taiyu pian* lack the strength to recover; only two films in production, while performers look for other career options], *Lianhe bao* [United Daily News], April 20, 1970. For an account of linguistic policies that resulted in these changes, see A-Chin Hsiau, "Language Ideology in Taiwan: The KMT's Language Policy, the Tai-Yu Language Movement, and Ethnic Politics," *Journal of Multilingual and Multicultural Development* 18, no. 4 (1997): 307–8.

41. Wen Shia has spoken of his "sixth sense," even as he filmed it, that *Goodbye, Taipei* might represent the end of the line. Personal interview, Taipei, December 20, 2014. His wife, Wen Xiang, also states that by 1969 their circle shared a common "sadness and apprehension" about the future of Taiwanese-language entertainment. Wen Shia, finally, has stated that the profusion of bit parts in *Goodbye, Taipei* was a result of their efforts to subsidize a number of entertainers in their circle who were increasingly hard put to support themselves. By 1972, even Wen Shia was forced by economic exigency to take on an engagement as the house band at a hot spring resort in Hakone, Japan, and he continued to tour Japan throughout the decade. Personal interview with Wen Shia and Wen Xiang, June 21, 2014. For his sojourn in Japan, see Wen Shia, *Wen Xia chang(chang)you renjian wuyu*, 154–57.

42. See Lu Feiyi, *Taiwan dianying: zhengzhi, jingji, meixue, 1949–1994* [Taiwan cinema: Politics, economics, aesthetics, 1949–1994] (Taipei: Yuanliu, 1998), cited in Shih, "Getting the Last Laugh," 242.

43. Shih, "Getting the Last Laugh," 242.
44. Shih, "Getting the Last Laugh," 245.
45. Shih, "Getting the Last Laugh," 247.
46. See Tom Gunning, "The Cinema of Attraction: Early Film, Its Spectator, and the Avant-Garde," *Wide Angle* 8, nos. 3–4 (Fall 1986): 64.
47. For a synopsis of each of the films, see Wen Shia, *Wen Xia chang(chang)you renjian wuyu*, 106–51.
48. Personal interview with Wen Shia, June 21, 2014.
49. Personal interview with Wen Shia and Wen Xiang, June 21, 2014. See also Wen Shia, *Wen Xia chang(chang)you renjian wuyu*, 98–105.
50. For a provocative argument on how *benshi* allowed for a distinctively Japanese mode of cinematic articulation, see Noel Burch, *To the Distant Observer* (Ann Arbor: University of Michigan Center for Japanese Studies Publications, 1979). For an account of the film historiography of the *benshi*, see Aaron Gerow, "The Subject of the Text: Benshi, Authors, and Industry," in Gerow, *Visions of Japanese Modernity: Articulations of Cinema, Nation, and Spectatorship, 1895–1925* (Berkeley: University of California Press, 2010), 133–73. For a brief account of the transmission of *benshi* to Taiwan, see Michael Baskett, *The Attractive Empire: Transnational Film Culture in Imperial Japan* (Honolulu: University of Hawai'i Press, 2008), 13–20.
51. According to Wen Shia, in the Tainan of his childhood, after the first two or three screenings of a film, the *benshi* would master a new film and learn how to amplify its drama and pathos to the point that audiences would invariably be left in tears. Sound effects were common: rain suggested by pouring beans into a bowl or the sound of horses' hooves reproduced by a pair of bowls "galloping" across a tabletop. He also suggested (perhaps slightly mischievously) that some *benshi* would even open a steaming hot *bento* lunch box at the very moment the characters onscreen were eating, so as to introduce an olfactory aspect to the moviegoing experience. Personal interview with Wen Shia, December 30, 2014.
52. Personal interview with Wen Shia, December 30, 2014.
53. Jonathan Auerbach, "Chasing Film Narrative: Repetition, Recursion, and the Body in Early Cinema," *Critical Inquiry* 26, no. 4 (Summer 2000): 802.
54. Auerbach, "Chasing Film Narrative," 805.
55. Hence, Tom Gunning's sense that the "gag," which temporarily suspends the headlong forward motion of many early American films through an "explosive counterlogic" by which the body is threatened by the "crazy machine" of modern life, must be analyzed as a distinct category from the chase. See Tom Gunning, "Crazy Machines in the Garden of Forking Paths: Mischief Gags and the Origins of American Film Comedy," in Kristine Brunovska Karnick and Henry Jenkins, eds., *Classical Hollywood Comedy* (London and New York: Routledge, 1995), 87–105.
56. Train platform signage in Taiwan registers this social and political topography quite directly: one can either travel "up North" 北上 to Taipei or return "down South" 南下.

232  NOTES TO CHAPTER 3

57. See Ben Singer, *Melodrama and Modernity* (New York: Columbia University Press, 2002), 93–99.

58. Walter Benjamin, "On Some Motifs in Baudelaire," in Benjamin, *Illuminations*, trans. Harry Zohn (New York: Schocken Books, 1968), 175.

59. See Gunning, "Crazy Machines in the Garden of Forking Paths," 99. In *Goodbye, Taipei* one example of this sort of gag, directly alluding to Laurel and Hardy–style slapstick, takes place thirty-one minutes into the action. When Tuo Xian and his comic sidekick Qiu Wangshe, dressed in the ridiculous flowery suits of sandwich men to advertise the reward for Ah-Mei, sit down on the railing around a roadside median, they both slide helplessly backward and fall to the ground. In a nod to Chaplin, the fall dislodges Tuo Xian's old leather shoe.

60. Singer, *Melodrama and Modernity*, 144–45.

61. This sequence, according to Wen Shia, was actually shot in Houli in central Taiwan.

62. Personal interview with Wen Shia, June 21, 2014.

63. See Scott Curtis, "The Sound of the Early Warner Bros. Cartoons," in Rich Altman, ed., *Sound Theory/Sound Practice* (New York and London: Routledge, 1992), 201.

64. Curtis, "The Sound of the Early Warner Bros. Cartoons," 200.

65. Wen Shia had originally intended to set the sequence to the 1963 folk hit "Washington Square" by the Village Stompers, but he scrapped the idea when he found that "Soulfinger" synchronized more closely with the onscreen action. He covered "Washington Square" in his own song "Happy Life" ("Kuaile rensheng"). Personal interview with Wen Shia, December 30, 2014. Interestingly, the surf-rock of the Ventures, which enjoyed huge popularity and was frequently emulated in Japan, appeared with great frequency on the soundtracks of *Taiyu pian* and later came to be associated in Taiwan with the action scenes in televised *po-te-hi (budaixi)* puppet opera. See Liao, *Xiaoshi de yinxiang*, 120.

66. "Pinky" was, in fact, the renowned actress Yoko Kon.

67. Personal interview with Wen Shia, June 21, 2014.

68. Personal interview with Wen Shia, December 30, 2014.

69. The common denominator in all of these occurrences of drag, according to Wen Shia, was the popularity of the cross-dressing Takarazuka Dance Revue in both Japan and Taiwan. Personal interview with Wen Shia, December 30, 2014.

### 4. Pirates of the China Seas

1. Ma Shih-fang, "Jijing de shengyin, 1966" [The sounds of silence, 1966], in *Dixia xiangchou landiao* [Subterranean Homesick Blues] (Taipei: Shibao wenhua, 2006), 55–63.

2. Tunghung Ho, "The Social Formation of Mandarin Popular Music Industry in Taiwan," Ph.D. dissertation, Lancaster University, 2003, 12. The Central News Agency was reported as issuing a statement that "foreigners arriving in the

country with hippy-style hair or clothes may be deported." See "Taipei Trims Its Hairstyles," *Sydney Morning Herald*, June 30, 1970. In January 1971, the United Daily News reported that more than two hundred "Beatle-cut youths" 披頭髮型的青少年 had been captured, forced to cut their hair, and fined ten dollars. See "Taibei jietou duo pitou, jingcha dongyuan da zhengxiu" [Police mobilize to clean up the many Beatles youth in Taipei's streets], *Lianhe bao* [United Daily News], January 10, 1971.

3. For an analysis of "healthy realism," see Guo-Juin Hong, *Taiwan Cinema: A Contested Nation Screen* (New York: Palgrave Macmillan, 2011), 65–86.

4. The names of theater patrons could be projected to the side of the screen. This practice piggybacked on systems originally developed to project subtitles for foreign films or to allow for instantaneous "translation" between standard Chinese and a variety of local languages..

5. See Liang Liang, *Kan bu dao de dianying: bainian jinpian daguan* [Invisible cinema: A century of forbidden films] (Taipei: Shibao wenhua, 2003). For film censorship codes in the Republic of China, see Zheng Wanxiang, "Taiwan zhanhou dianying guanli tixi zhi yanjiu, 1950–1970" [Research on the postwar film management system in Taiwan, 1950–1970], master's thesis, National Central University, 2001.

6. "Jianji de yishu" [The art of cutting], *Lianhe bao* [United Daily News], April 23, 1972.

7. Phillip Gosse, *The History of Piracy* (London: Longmans, Green and Co., 1932), vii.

8. Gosse, *The History of Piracy*.

9. Gosse, *The History of Piracy*.

10. Korean pirate records, common in urban markets and referred to as *bbaek pan*, played a similarly pivotal role in local popular music history, and their prevalence was also spatially and ideologically linked to U.S. military establishments in Seoul and elsewhere.

11. For a rich document of pop musical consumption and its meanings among American GIs, see Doug Bradley and Craig Werner, *We Gotta Get Out of This Place: The Soundtrack of the Vietnam War* (Amherst and Boston: University of Massachusetts Press, 2015).

12. My invocation of the "archipelago" follows the historian Bruce Cumings, who has written persuasively of a global network of "somewhere between 737 and 860 overseas military installations" that formed a "stealth empire" invisible to most American citizens. As Cumings makes clear, this persistent form of territorial colonization was established in East Asia in the wake of the fall of the Japanese empire in 1945 and the construction of a policy of "containment" as a result of the Korean War. See Bruce Cumings, *Dominion from Sea to Sea: Pacific Ascendency and American Power* (New Haven: Yale University Press, 2009), 393.

13. For a historical analysis of that Cold War backdrop and its differential impact on popular musical development in Taiwan and South Korea, see Shin

Hyunjoon and Tung-hung Ho, "Translation of 'America' during the early Cold War Period: A Comparative Study on the History of Popular Music in South Korea and Taiwan," *Inter-Asia Cultural Studies* 10, no. 1 (2009): 83–102.

14. The Oxford Dictionary of English, for instance, defines the circuit as "a route regularly followed by an itinerant entertainer; a number of places of entertainment (theatres, music-halls, etc.) at which the same productions or entertainers are presented successively; a group or chain of theatres, cinemas, etc., under the control of one person or company."

15. See Ernest Braun and Stuart Macdonald, *Revolution in Miniature: The History and Impact of Semiconductor Electronics* (Cambridge: Cambridge University Press, 1978).

16. See Michael Brian Schiffer, *The Portable Radio in American Life* (Tucson: University of Arizona Press, 1991), 208–9.

17. This is true of U.S. installations in Korea as well as in Taiwan. The most important U.S. base of operations in Seoul, Yongsan Garrison, served as the headquarters of the Japanese Army from 1910 to 1945. In Taiwan, the correspondence is also uncanny. Even the E.M. Navy Club in Kaohsiung, to provide just one example of many, had been used as an Officer's Club under Japanese colonial rule. See http://taipeiairstation.blogspot.tw/2014/05/the-navy-em-club-in-kaohsiung-where.html. Accessed May 28, 2014.

18. The history of many of these installations has been amply and lovingly documented on the World Wide Web by former service members who were stationed in Taiwan. These sites are rich documentary troves, not only for the history of the U.S. military abroad but also for reminiscences, photographs, maps, and other materials that allow a glimpse into daily life in Taiwan from the 1950s through the U.S. military withdrawal from the island in 1979. Notable blogs are devoted to the Shulinkou Air Station (http://shulinkou.tripod.com/Dawg1.html); the U.S. Taiwan Defense Command in Taipei (http://ustdc.blogspot.com/); and the Taipei Air Station in Gongguan (http://taipeiairstation.blogspot.com/).

19. These numbers, culled from the Statistical Information Analysis Division (SIAD) of the Directorate for Information Operations and Reports (DIOR) in the U.S. Department of Defense, are summarized by Tim Kane in his "Global US Troop Deployment, 1950–2003" on the website of the Heritage Foundation. See http://www.heritage.org/research/reports/2004/10/global-us-troop-deployment-1950-2003. Accessed May 23, 2014.

20. See "R&R in Taipei," http://ustdc.blogspot.com/2011/09/r-in-taipei.html. Accessed May 22, 2014. These R&R furloughs in Taipei are documented in what appears to be a 1967 U.S. military informational film titled "Holidays from Hell" and accessible at http://www.youtube.com/watch?v=OwWcPOALoRY. Accessed March 22, 2014.

21. See, for one anecdotal report, "Kaohsiung Sea Dragon Club," http://taipeiairstation.blogspot.com/2014/01/kaohsiung-sea-dragon-club-updated.html. Accessed May 22, 2014.

22. See "R&R in Taipei," http://shulinkou.tripod.com/dawg10a.html. Accessed May 22, 2014.

23. See, for example, "Bootleg Phonograph Records," http://ustdc.blogspot.com/2009/04/bootleg-phonograph-records.html. Accessed May 22, 2014.

24. An image depicting a bootleg record store in Tainan in the late 1960s appears on the Taipei Air Station blog at "More of the US Navy Facility—Det Tango—Tainan Air Base—UPDATED," *Taipei Air Station*, March 27, 2013, http://taipeiairstation.blogspot.com/2013/03/. Accessed December 11, 2018.

25. Brian Larkin's *Signal and Noise* provides a lucid and insightful discussion of the "infrastructure of piracy." See Larkin, *Signal and Noise: Media, Infrastructure, and Urban Culture in Nigeria* (Durham, N.C.: Duke University Press, 2008), 217–41.

26. See "The Mysteries of Taiwanese LPs" from the blog of the National Film and Sound Archive of Australia, http://www.nfsa.gov.au/blog/2010/06/01/the-mysteries-of-taiwanese-lps/. Accessed May 22, 2014.

27. For a comprehensive source on the history of the Taiwanese recording industry, see Ye Longyan, *Taiwan changpian sixiang qi* [Recalling Taiwanese records] (Taipei: Boyang, 2001). Also useful is the composer Lin Liangzhe's meticulously researched and illustrated history of Taiwanese popular music in the colonial era. See Lin Liangzhe, *Taiwan liuxing ge: rizhi shidai zhi* [Taiwan popular song: A chronicle of the Japanese colonial era] (Taizhong: Baixiang wenhua, 2015).

28. See Ye, *Taiwan changpian sixiang qi*, 137. Also see Shao Yiqiang, "Taiwan fanban changpian neimu (shang/xia)" [The inside story of Taiwan's pirate records (section 1 and 2)], *Yinyue yu yinxiang* [Music and Stereo] nos. 1 & 2 (1973): 112–13, 78–79. Shao, a middle school music teacher, was engaged in writing liner notes for these releases and asserts that more than two thousand classical titles had been released by the 1970s. He argues that, despite the murky ethics of copyright violations, pirate records had been instrumental in raising the level of musical appreciation in Taiwan and that the high prices of official releases were prohibitive for local listeners.

29. Ye, *Taiwan changpian sixiang qi*, 141.

30. The Billboard Hot 100 and Wolfman Jack's rock and roll program were widely appreciated. See Ho, "The Social Formation of Mandarin Popular Music Industry in Taiwan," 68. A typical Armed Forces Network Taiwan broadcast, entitled "China Nights," from the evening of June 23, 1968, is available at http://www.ricksworkshop.org/AFNT.html. Accessed May 24, 2014.

31. See Ho, "The Social Formation of Mandarin Popular Music Industry in Taiwan," 62–68. Ma Shih-fang, whose mother was a prominent "hit music" DJ at the time, notes that the poor English skills and lack of due diligence on the part of local disk jockeys resulted in the airing of quite a few notoriously "druggy" anthems that had been banned from broadcast in the United States and the United Kingdom, including the Byrds' "Eight Miles High" and Bob Dylan's "Rainy Day Women #12 and 35." See Ma, "Jijing de shengyin, 1966," 60.

32. An industry observer reported that manufacturing by "hand press" was prevalent in 1960, according to a 1970 *Billboard* report, and this assessment is echoed by Ye Longyan's comprehensive history. See Brian Blevins, "Orient Pirate Playground," *Billboard*, March 14, 1970, 58.

33. Taiwan was throughout the 1960s one of the world's most flagrant centers of book piracy as well. For an overview of copyright law and the illegal reproduction of English-language materials in this period, see David Kaser, *Book Pirating in Taiwan* (Philadelphia: University of Pennsyvania Press, 1969).

34. Liu Zhiming's luggage topped out at a staggering 170 kilograms. See *Lianhe bao* [United Daily News], January 8, 1968.

35. He Fan, "Taiwan daoyin changpian" [Taiwan's fake label records], *Lianhe bao* [United Daily News], October 27, 1965. He Fan's figure may derive from Carl Myatt, writing in *Billboard* in 1963, who echoes an EMI Hong Kong representative claiming that "150,000 lps . . . leave Taiwan every month." See Carl Myatt, "Pirates Capturing Business," *Billboard*, August 31, 1963, 30.

36. Blevins, "Orient Pirate Playground," 58.

37. Blevins, "Orient Pirate Playground," 58.

38. For a discussion of piracy in the mid-1970s from the perspective of record producers, retailers, and consumers, see Peng Yanhua, "Taiwan fanban changpian zongheng tan" [Taiwan's record piracy from all angles], in *Yinyue feng* [Music Trend] 62 (October 10, 1976): 41–45.

39. Kaser, *Book Pirating in Taiwan*, 20–21.

40. Shao, "Taiwan fanban changpian neimu," 78.

41. Shao, "Taiwan fanban changpian neimu," 78.

42. See Chen Chuanxing, "Hengtang de tongtian ta" [The fallen tower], in Yang Ze, ed., *1970 Qianqing lu* [A passionate chronicle of the 1970s] (Taipei: Shibao wenhua, 1994), 32. Cited in Ho, "The Social Formation of Mandarin Popular Music Industry in Taiwan," 79.

43. Ho, "The Social Formation of Mandarin Popular Music Industry in Taiwan," 13, 59–79.

44. For a profile of the emergence of these local rock and roll musicians, see Luo Gejia, "Daji! Daji!" [Hit! Hit!], part of a special suite of features titled "1956–1968 Taiwan remen yinyue fazhan shi" [The development of Taiwan's hit music, 1956–1968], in *Jintian huakan* [Today], October 10, 1968, 48–49.

45. For an authoritative account of this movement and its moment for Taiwanese cultural history, see Zhang Zhaowei, *Shei zai nabian chang ziji de ge* [Who's over there singing their own songs?] (Taipei: Gunshi wenhua, 2003).

46. Ho, "The Social Formation of Mandarin Popular Music Industry in Taiwan," 62.

47. The modernist writer Wang Wen-hsing's early short story "Toy Gun" 玩具手槍 revolves around a particularly harrowing scene of bullying at a party for elite mainlander youth, in which listening to the latest Anglophone pop records features

as a badge of status. See Wang Wen-hsing, *Shiwu pian xiaoshuo* [Fifteen short stories] (Taipei: Hongfan, 1979).

48. Ho, "The Social Formation of Mandarin Popular Music Industry in Taiwan," 72.

49. Copyright controls existed domestically for the Republic of China, but there is some controversy over whether those protections were understood to apply to foreign products as well. Barry Kernfeld, for one, asserts that "the laws and treaties of other Asian countries such as Korea and Taiwan had no provisions at all for protecting foreign recording until well into the 1990s." See Kernfeld, *Pop Song Piracy: Disobedient Music Distribution since 1929* (Chicago: University of Chicago Press, 2011), 187.

50. See Li Caigui, "Changpian xuangou mianmian guan" [Everything about selecting which records to buy], *Aiyue zhi you* [Melody Fan Magazine] 29 (September 1978), 61.

51. An incomplete accounting of 446 pirated titles can be found on the label's page on discogs.com, http://www.discogs.com/label/72896-First-Record. Accessed March 25, 2014.

52. While copyright laws and enforcement were stepped up considerably as Taiwan moved up the global supply chain in the 1990s, scholars of music piracy such as Alex Sayf Cummings report that abuses continued to take place during this period, with legitimate producers frequently dumping surplus product onto markets in the People's Republic of China. See Alex Sayf Cummings, *Democracy of Sound: Music Piracy and the Remaking of American Copyright in the Twentieth Century* (New York: Oxford University Press, 2013).

53. See "Ye Jintai: Taiwan chucun meiti de xianfeng" [Ye Jintai: Taiwan's storage media pioneer], *Xin Taiwan xinwen zhoukan* [New Taiwan] 477 (May 12, 2005), http://www.newtaiwan.com.tw/bulletinview.jsp?bulletinid=21950. Accessed May 25, 2014. For Ye's own account of the development of the industry, see Ye, *Taiwan changpian sixiang qi,* 177–79.

54. Hsu's account of this moment of discovery is included in the liner notes to the CD compilation of Chen Da's music, *Shancheng zouchang: Chen Da, yueqin, Taiwan minge* [Fulao folk songs in Taiwan Island] (Taipei: Wind Music, 2000). For an account of the folk musical fieldwork of Hsu Tsang-Houei and his colleagues and for their sense that modern mass-mediated music is tantamount to a "curse," see Qiu Yanliang, *Jimu tianye* [Fieldwork visions] (Taipei: Mutong, 1978), 237–49.

55. See "Ye Jintai: Taiwan chucun meiti de xianfeng" [Ye Jintai: Taiwan's storage media pioneer], *Xin Taiwan xinwen zhoukan* [New Taiwan] 477 (May 12, 2005), http://www.newtaiwan.com.tw/bulletinview.jsp?bulletinid=21950. Accessed May 25, 2014.

56. The first long-playing release of Chen Da's music had taken place in 1971, accompanied by a book by Hsu's colleage Shi Wei-liang, titled *Minzu yueshou Chen Da he tade ge* [Folk singer Chen Da and his songs]. The LP record was released by the Hong Jianquan Educational Culture Foundation 洪健全教育基金會.

Hong Jianquan, whose foundation maintained a music library and subsidized Hsu Tsang-Houei and Shi Wei-liang's archival research, was one of the founders of Taiwan's consumer electronics industry, heading up the Taiwanese subsidiary of the Japanese corporate giant Matsushita, known worldwide by the brand name adorning their transistor radios, stereo components, and other appliances: Panasonic.

### 5. Folk Circuits

1. See Hsu Tsang-Houei, "Taibei jietou ting ge ji" [Listening to songs in the streets of Taipei], in *Zhongguo yinyue wang nali qu?* [Where is Chinese music heading?] (Taipei: Wenxing, 1964), 49.

2. See Pierre Schaeffer, *Traités des objets musicaux* (Paris: Seuil, 1966). The term has entered into critical parlance largely by way of the work of the film theorist Michel Chion. For his influential treatment of acousmatic sound in cinema, see Michel Chion, *Audio-Vision: Sound on Screen* (New York: Columbia University Press, 1994), 71–73. Hsu, at least by the late 1960s, was clearly aware of and receptive to this electronic landscape and even wrote approvingly of "concrete music" and the use of the tape recorder to capture soundscapes, manipulate existing sounds, and fabricate new musical possibilities. In a fascinating essay called "A Discussion of Devices for the Transmission, Reproduction, and Production of Music, and the Future of Electronic Music," he lays out what he sees as the pros and cons of radio and television broadcasting, tape recording, and hi-fi stereo systems. While acknowledging the valuable applications and profound consequences of these technologies, he also sounds a cautionary note about "canned" music and its potential to cause "mechanical modern music sickness" 機器性的現代音樂病. See Hsu Tsang-Houei, *Xunzhao Zhongguo de yinyue quanyuan* [Tracing the source of Chinese music] (Taipei: Jinxue, 1968), 129–36.

3. See R. Murray Schaefer, *The Soundscape: Our Sonic Environment and the Tuning of the World* (New York: Alfred A. Knopf, 1977), 90–91, 273.

4. Hsu, "Listening," 52.

5. Hsu, "Listening," 51.

6. Hsu, "Listening," 52.

7. The most comprehensive account of campus folk to date is that of Chang Chao-wei, *Shei zai nabian chang ziji de ge: Taiwan xiandai minge yundong shi* [Who's that singing their own songs: A history of the modern folk song movement in Taiwan] (Taipei: Gunshi wenhua, 2004). Liao Pei-ju's study of the Folk Song Collection Movement also provides thorough coverage of its history and of documentary sources for its study. See Liao Pei-ju, "Minge caiji yundong de zai yanjiu" [Revisiting research on the Folk Songs Collection Movement], in *Taiwan yinyue yanjiu* [Formosan journal of music research] 1 (October 2005). Ma Shih-fang has also contributed a great deal to our understanding of this period in Taiwanese musical history in a series of essays scattered across three books. See Ma Shih-fang, *Dixia xiangchou landiao* [Subterranean homesick blues] (Taipei: Shibao chuban,

2006); *Zuori shu* [My back pages] (Taipei: Xin jingdian wenhua, 2010); *Erduo jie wo* [Lend me your ears] (Taipei: Xin jingdian wenhua, 2014).

8. For an account of this process of canonization, see Mary Beth Hamilton, *In Search of the Blues* (New York: Basic Books, 2008).

9. The debate in question, conducted largely via posts on Facebook, constellated around an exchange between the music writer and disk jockey Ma Shih-fang and the cultural and political commentator Chang Tieh-chih in the wake of a concert celebrating the fortieth anniversary of the modern folk song movement. Chang Tieh-chih suggested that the music emerging out of the movement was aesthetically anemic and politically anodyne, especially in comparison with the innovative provocations of the "native soil" fiction and modern dance of the same era. Ma Shih-fang—whose mother, Tau Hsiao-ch'ing (Tao Xiaoqing), was a radio deejay and an important taste-maker and participant in the Taiwanese music scene of the 1970s—took exception to this characterization, arguing that the absence of overt protest songs was less important than the new sensibilities and musical possibilities that had been opened up by adherents of the folk sound. For Ma Shih-fang's defense of the movement, see https://www.facebook.com/permalink.php?story_fbid=10152907156397543&id=680792542. Accessed July 20, 2016. For Chang Tie-chih's position, refer to https://www.facebook.com/tc.chang1/posts/10152829444987391. Accessed July 20, 2016. For an insightful summation of the debate, see Tunghung Ho, "Yinyue de shehui xing meijie: cong Minge 40 de zhenglun tanqi" [Music's social media: Beyond the Folk Song 40 debate], *Gongzhi* [Com Magazine], December 15, 2015, http://commagazine2011.blogspot.com/2015/12/40.html. Accessed July 20, 2016. The movement's fortieth anniversary was celebrated by a series of commemorative exhibitions and activities and by the release of a collection of essays and CDs, edited by Tau Hsiao-ch'ing and Yang Chia. See Tau and Yang, eds., *Minge 40: Zai chang yiduan "sixiangqi"* [Folk at 40: Sing another sound of "remember when"] (Taipei: Locus, 2015).

10. For a biography of Hsu Tsang-Houei, see Qiu Kunliang, *Zuo zi haishang lai: Xu Changhui zhi shengming zhi ge* [From the sea: Hsu Tsang-Houei's song of life] (Taipei: Shibao wenhua, 1997).

11. For a biography of Shih Wei-liang, see Wu Jiayu, *Shi Weiliang: hongchen zhong de kuxing seng* [Shi Weiliang: A wandering monk in the mortal world] (Taipei: Shibao wenhua, 2002).

12. For Shih's years in Europe and his coming to consciousness as a staunch adherent of Chinese musical culture, see Shih Wei-liang, *Yige Zhongguoren zai Ouzhou* [A Chinese in Europe] (Taipei: Wenxing shudian, 1967).

13. See Shih Wei-liang, *Lun minge* [On folk song] (Taipei: Youshi wenhua, 1967), v.

14. See Shih Wei-liang, "Yuefu chunqiu: Weiyena yinyue jie" [Report from the Vienna Music Festival], *Lianhe bao* [United Daily News], June 21, 1962. Hsu responded in the pages of the same newspaper to Shih's question with a resounding affirmation. See Hsu Tsang-Houei, "Women xuyao ziji de yinyue: da Shi Weiliang

xiansheng de gongkai xin" [We need our own music: A reply to Mr. Shi Wei-liang's open letter], *Lianhe bao* [United Daily News], July 10 and 12, 1962.

15. There is an extensive literature on early Chinese musical thought and its relation to poetics. For a useful introduction, see Kenneth Dewoskin, *A Song for One or Two: Music and the Concept of Art in Early China* (Ann Arbor: Michigan Monographs in Chinese Studies, 1982).

16. See Hsu, "Listening," 49. The passage derives from Section 5.1 ("Yueyan" 樂言) of the *Record of Music*. The translation is mine. For a complete annotated translation, see Scott Cook, "Yueji—Record of Music: Introduction, Translation, Notes, and Commentary," *Asian Music* 26, no. 2 (Spring–Summer 1995): 1–96.

17. See Tunghung Ho and Fred Chiu, "Minge caiji yundong yu qingnian xiaxiang: Qiu Yanliang de huiyi diandi" [The folk song collection movement and youth rustification: Qiu Yanliang's reminiscences], in Tunghung Ho, Amy Cheng, and Jeph Lo, eds., *Zaoyin fantu* [Altering nativism: Sound cultures in postwar Taiwan] (Taipei: Lifang wenhua, 2015), 62–63. For the May 4th–era folk song collection movement, see Chang-tai Hung, *Going to the People: Chinese Intellectuals and Folk Literature* (Cambridge, Mass.: Harvard East Asian Monographs, 1984).

18. See Jonathan Stock, *Musical Creativity in Twentieth Century China: Abing, His Music, and its Changing Meanings* (New York: University of Rochester Press, 1996).

19. Fred Chiu does not believe that Kurosawa's work was an important precedent for the movement. See Tung-hung Ho and Fred Chiu, "Minge caiji yundong yu qingnian xiaxiang," 62. For a study of Japanese colonial-era ethnomusicology in Taiwan, see Wang Yingfen, *Tingjian zhimindi: Heize Longchao yu zhanshi Taiwan yinyue diaocha, 1943*) [Listening to the colony: Kurosawa Takatomo and a wartime survey of Taiwan's music, 1943] (Taipei: National Taiwan University Library, 2008).

20. Personal interview with Fred Chiu, Institute of Ethnology, Academia Sinica, Taipei, January 20, 2016.

21. Personal interview with Fred Chiu, Institute of Ethnology, Academia Sinica, Taipei, January 20, 2016.

22. For a nuanced and thoughtful account of this milieu and its historical emergence, see Hong-sheng Zheng, "Chen Yingzhen and Taiwan's 'Sixties': Self-Realization of the Post-war Generation in Taiwan," *Inter-Asia Cultural Studies* 15, no. 3 (2014): 455–76.

23. See "Dadi zhi ge" [Song of the soil], *Wenxue jikan* [Literature Quarterly] 5 (November 1967): 140–59. The dialogue took place on September 16, 1967.

24. Tom Davenport, very likely in conversation with Hsu Tsang-Houei himself, learned of the existence of a kind of "Taiwanese folk troubadour" just around this time. According to his personal diaries of his time in Taiwan, he set off for the south just two days after the forum in search of him. The singer was, of course, Chen Da, and Davenport's photos from their meeting in late September 1967 are among the first known photographs of the singer. One of these photographs was

used as the cover image of the first long-playing album (of which more later) of Chen Da's music, recorded and released by Shih Wei-liang in 1971 with an accompanying essay, lyrics, and notation. Davenport, like many others, was impressed by Chen Da's improvisatory skills. When asked to play, Chen Da improvised a song about the young foreigner who had come from afar to see him, much to the delight and amusement of the children of the village sitting in a circle around the singer. Personal telephone interview with Tom Davenport, February 21, 2016.

25. See Hamilton, *In Search of the Blues*, 243.

26. Hsu's dispatches from the field diary were published in the newspaper immediately in the wake of the folk song collection expedition. See "Minge caiji dui xidui riji" [Diary of the folk song collection group's west team], in *Taiwan Xinsheng bao* [Taiwan New Life News], July 30, 1967. Subsequent entries were published in the same paper on August 4, 22, and 23, 1967. The diary has been reprinted in a number of venues. Here I have relied upon Hsu Tsang-Houei, "Minge caiji riji" [Diary of folk song collection], *Wenxue jikan* [Literature Quarterly] 5 (November 1967): 138. "Niuwei bai" is rendered as "Niumu ban" 牛母伴 in a later reprint collected in Qiu Yanliang (Fred Chiu), *Jimu tianye* [Fieldwork visions] (Taipei, Mutong, 1978), 40.

27. Hsu, "Minge caiji riji," 138.

28. Hsu, "Minge caiji riji," 134.

29. Hsu, "Minge caiji riji," 139.

30. Jonathan Sterne has written eloquently of the ways in which recording technologies have been associated from their inception in the nineteenth century with the problem of preservation, of individuals as well as of indigenous cultures, beyond the moment of their inevitable demise. See his "A Resonant Tomb" in *The Audible Past: Cultural Origins of Sound Reproduction* (Durham, N.C.: Duke University Press, 2003), 287–334.

31. See Bruno Latour, *Science in Action: How to Follow Scientists and Engineers through Society* (Cambridge, Mass.: Harvard University Press, 1987), 227.

32. Qiu Yanliang, "Xian jieduan minge gongzuo de zong baogao" [Comprehensive report on the current stage of folk song work], in *Jimu tianye* [Fieldwork Visions] (Taipei: Mutong, 1978), 52–54.

33. An example of this standardized form, labeled "Zhongguo minjian yinyue yanjiu fayang zhongxin minge jilupu" [Center for the promotion of research on Chinese folk music song reporting form], is included in a 2017 exhibit at the Taiwan Music Institute in Taipei celebrating the fiftieth anniversary of the Folk Song Collection Movement titled "Zhuixun lishi, yuanyin chongxian" (Trace and reveal).

34. Hsu Tsang-Houei addresses the necessity of notation and its limitations at length in his essay "Cong xiyang yinyue shi kan muqian Zhongguo yinyue de jidian wenti" [Looking at several problems in today's Chinese music through the lens of the history of Western music], in *Zhongguo yinyue wang nali qu?* [Where is Chinese music heading?], 13–18. Shih Wei-liang is quite explicit about the inability of notation to capture what's essential about Chen Da's sound. See his *Minzu*

*yueshou Chen Da he tade ge* [Musician of our nation: Chen Da and his songs] (Taipei: Xiwang chubanshe, 1971).

35. According to Professor Wu Rung-shun 吳榮順, many Hengchun locals were perplexed by Hsu Tsang-Houei's high estimation of Chen Da's talents, given his poverty and his eccentricity and the idiosyncrasy of his performances, and they wondered in the local idiom whether Xu's eyes had not been "snail-slimed." Personal interview, Wu Rung-shun, December 22, 2015. Fred Chiu asserts that Hsu's choice to emphasize Chen Da as the single most representative singer stemmed precisely from his poverty and the political charge carried by his utter marginality in the society. Personal interview with Fred Chiu, January 22, 2016.

36. Many thanks to the Taiwanese folk-rock legend and *yueqin* player Lin Sheng-xiang 林生祥 for discussing Chen Da's inimitable approach to the instrument with me. Personal interview with Lin Sheng-xiang, May 1, 2016.

37. Shih, *Minzu yueshou Chen Da he tade ge*, 10.

38. Part of the reason for Japan's prominence in the field was that "one of the core technologies for tape recording—the AC bias recording head—had been patented in Japan before its development in the West." See Simon Partner, *Assembled in Japan: Electrical Goods and the Making of the Japanese Consumer* (Berkeley: University of California Press, 1999), 69.

39. See Partner, *Assembled in Japan*, 194–95.

40. Personal interview with Professor Wu Rung-shun, Taipei National University of the Arts, December 22, 2015. Professor Wu, a disciple of Hsu Tsang-Houei and one of the most important and prolific field recordists and ethnomusicological scholars in Taiwan, has been responsible for preserving, collating, and documenting Hsu Tsang-Houei's archival collections.

41. It seems that at least one of the Revox tape recorders used in the movement may have been procured through the offices of Shih Wei-liang's German colleague and collaborator Alois Osterwalder, with whom he had founded the Arbeit Gemeinschaft China-Europa, now known as the Ostasien—Institut, in pursuance of his goals.

42. Personal interview with Wu Rung-shun, December 22, 2015. Much of the technical information about the recording process was also confirmed in conversation with Fred Chiu, January 16, 2016.

43. Personal interview with Wu Rung-shun, December 22, 2015.

44. The tapes have been made available to the public in a box set on Chen Da containing two CDs of audio material and a book. See Xu Lisha and Lin Liangzhe, *Hengchun bandao juexiang—youchang shiren Chen Da* [Swan song of the Hengchun peninsula: the wandering troubadour, Chen Da] (Ilan: National Center for Traditional Arts, 2006).

45. The venture, likely funded by the KMT's China Youth Corps 救國團, was associated with Hsu and Shih's Center for the Study of National Music, established in 1967, and produced a series of studies of various European composers, including Bartok and Debussy, many penned by the two musicologists themselves. The

Center also maintained a music library called the China Youth Library 中國青年圖書館, located at Shih's home at Siwei Road in Taipei. The press later folded, apparently as a result of Shih's lack of managerial acumen.

46. For an informative and stimulating account of the neighborhood and its social and industrial history from a sonic standpoint, see Li Zhiming, *Dansheng dao: chengshi de shengyin yu jiyi* [One track street: Urban soundscapes and memory] (Taipei: Lianjing, 2013), 25–35.

47. See Sun Qingshan, "Zhanhou Taiwan dushi zhi chengzhang yu tixi" [The expansion and structure of urban areas in postwar Taiwan], in Cai Yongmei and Zhang Yingmei, eds., *Taiwan de dushi shehui* [Taiwan's urban society] (Taipei: Juliu tushu, 1997), 76–77.

48. Sun, "Zhanhou Taiwan dushi zhi chengzhang yu tixi," 83.

49. See Zheng Qiushuang, *Hong Jianquan de shiye zhiye: dajia de guoji pai* [Hong Jianquan's industrial calling: Everybody's National brand] (Zhonghe: Xusheng, 2004), 44–50.

50. See Shih, *Minzu yueshou Chen Da yu ta de ge*, no page numbers provided.

51. Shih, *Minzu yueshou Chen Da yu ta de ge*.

52. Shih, *Minzu yueshou Chen Da yu ta de ge*.

53. Shih, *Minzu yueshou Chen Da yu ta de ge*.

54. For an interesting blog entry on the "drifter" theme in Taiwanese popular music, see Emery, "Taibei, Taibei, ligan you tingdao?—Liuxing yinyue shi li de Taibei liulang gushi" [Taipei, Taipei, can you hear us? Migrating to Taipei in popular music history], http://gushi.tw/archives/26186. Accessed August 2, 2016.

55. The song's lyrics were written by the prominent songwriter Yu Junlin 葉俊麟.

56. See Li, *Dansheng dao*, 26–28.

57. See Peng Zhaomei, "Fazhan dianzi gongye yingxun de fangxiang" [The direction the development of the electronics industry should follow], *Jingji ribao* [Economic Daily News], December 28, 1970.

58. See Li Zhongtian, "Fuyu de nongcun" [A prosperous countryside], *Jingji ribao* [Economic Daily News], September 13, 1967. For a revealing autobiographical essay on the transformative effect of the presence of a record player and pirate records of American rock and roll and soul music in a rural home in Kaohsiung county in these years, see Chung Yung-feng 鍾永豐, "Wo de houzhimin tongnian" [My postcolonial childhood], in Chung Yung-feng, *Wo deng jiu lai chang shange* [Let's sing our mountain songs] (Shanghai: Shanghai wenyi chubanshe, 2015).

59. For an account of the early years of television broadcasting in Taiwan, see Yu-fen Ko, "Dianshi yu xiandai shenghuo: dianshi pujihua guocheng zhong de guo yu jia" [Television and modern life: Nation-state and home in the popularization process of TV, 1962–1964], *Taiwan shehui yanjiu jikan* [Taiwan: A Radical Quarterly in Social Sciences] 73 (March 2009). Taiwan TV's range was initially limited to the northern half of the island but expanded rapidly. See "Taiwan Dianshi gongsi de

guangbo shoushi quyu" [Regional reception of TTV broadcasts], *Dianshi zhoukan* [TV Weekly] 8 (December 3, 1962), 3.

60. For the "TV decade," see Tom Davenport's diary, September 1969. Fred Chiu's report on the movement is prefaced by a lengthy and passionate screed against the rural dissemination of popular music. See "Xian jieduan minge gongzuo de zong baogao" in Qiu, *Jimu tianye*, 7–12.

61. For scheduled pop music programming on Taiwan TV, see "Benzhou jiemu" [This week's programs], *Dianzhi zhoukan* [TV Weekly] 1 (October 10, 1962). The station soon inaugurated the perennial variety program "All Stars Affair" (Qunxing hui 群星會). The Telstars appeared on Taiwan TV as early as 1962 and had a weekly program on China TV by 1968, as well as serving as a backing band for recording artists such as Teresa Teng and Yao Surong. See Wang Susu, "Dianxing yuedui" [Telstar band], *Zhongguo dianshi zhoukan* [China TV Weekly] 12 (January 11, 1969).

62. Specifically, Chen Da asserted that the tunes "Caomin nong jigong" 草螟弄雞公 and "Hengchun minyao" 恆春民謠 were of indigenous origin, a claim Shih finds a challenge to our "traditional beliefs." See Shih, *Minzu yueshou Chen Da he tade ge*, no pagination.

63. See Xu and Lin, *Hengchun bandao juexiang*, 20–24.

64. The clearest example of this hybridity on *Musician of Our Nation* comes on track 7, in which Chen Da melds melodies from "Taidong Beinan bashe fandiao" [Barbarian song of the Beinan tribal settlement], "Pingpu diao" [Song of the plains tribe], and a Hakka tea-harvesting tune to paint a verbal portrait of the geographical features of the Hengchun peninsula.

65. Shih, *Minzu yueshou Chen Da yu tade ge*, no pagination.

66. Wen-Shu Juan 阮文淑, "Chong shu yice chuanqi: lun Chen Da yu 'Sixiang qi' zai qiling niandai Taibei de qiguan hua licheng" [Retelling a legend: On the spectacle forming process of Chen Da and "Su Siang Ki" in '70s Taipei], master's thesis, Graduate Institute of Musicology, National Taiwan University, 2012.

67. See Xu and Lin, *Hengchun bandao juexiang*, 56–60.

68. Xu and Lin, *Hengchun bandao juexiang*, 61–63. Chen Da posed for a picture alongside then President Chiang Ching-kuo at the reception for the visiting oldsters. A clip of this appearance is available at https://www.youtube.com/watch?v=OieBZxYYxlE. Accessed August 8, 2016.

69. For an early profile of Chang Chao-Tang, see "Chang Chaotang de sheying shengya" [Chang Chao-Tang's photographic career], *Zhongguo dianshi zhoukan* [China TV Weekly] 11 (January 4, 1969). For a series of essays on his life, photography, and work as a music critic, television producer, and documentarian, see Lin Ping, ed., *Suiyue ding'ge: Zhang Zhaotang* [Frames within time: Chang Chao Tang] (Taipei: Taipei Fine Arts Museum, 2017). Chang's series of "rock dinners," held at the Youshi ("Young Lion") publishing house, introduced attendees to rock and "new folk" 新民歌 and included artists as diverse as Pink Floyd and Leonard Cohen, whose songs, according to Chang's introduction in the accompanying "Menu,"

were "like betelnut: their flavor emerges only after repeated chewing." See Xiang Zilong, Chen Yanjing, and Chang Chao-Tang, "Menu," unpublished pamphlet. For Chang's music journalism, see the series of articles he published beginning in 1973 in the pioneering music magazine *Music and Stereo* (音樂與音響).

70. See Chang Chao-Tang, "Dilun wenhua" [Dylan culture], in *Yinyue yu yinxiang* [Music and Stereo] 1 (1973): 46–47. See also Chang Chao-Tang, "Zhe yidai de minge" (Folk songs of this generation), *Yinyue yu yinxiang* [Music and Stereo] 3 (1973): 30–39.

71. Xiang, Chen, and Chang, "Menu."

72. See Xu and Lin, *Hengchun bandao juexing*, 70–78. The plaintive and accusatory tone with which Chen Da's stint at Scarecrow between December 1976 and January 1977 was advertised in *Rock Magazine* (*Gunshi zazhi*) was symptomatic of the divide between rural music and urban listeners. Above a black-and-white photo of Chen Da taken by Chang Chao-Tang, the copy reads: "Come listen to Chen Da sing songs. . . . Among Taipei's music halls and coffee houses, only Scarecrow dares to bring Chen Da here from afar, since his songs are neither commercial nor popular, but instead remind people of the muddy earth, of longing for our rural home, of places far away. If you have listened to the Beatles, the Rolling Stones, and Bob Dylan, and never heard of Chen Da, that can only mean that your mind is not yet open, and your life is too narrow . . . in a word, that your rock and roll spirit is fake." See Tau Hsiao-ch'ing and Yang Chia, "Shei zai xi canting chang ge" [Who sang at Western restaurants?] in Tau and Yang, eds., *Minge 40*, 39.

73. The most comprehensive history remains Chang Chaowei's book-length study, *Shei zai nabian chang ziji de ge: Taiwan xiandai minge yundong shi*.

74. The Foundation, led by Hong Jianquan's daughter-in-law Jian Jinghui 簡靜惠, was also responsible for opening an innovative "Audio-Visual Library" 視聽圖書館 in Taipei in 1975, publishing some of the liveliest print journals of the era, including *Shuping shumu* (Book review and bibliography), and providing the seed funding for what remains the island's most celebrated and globally renowned modern dance troupe, Lin Hwai-min's Cloud Gate. See Zheng, *Hong Jianquan de shiye zhiye*, 140–51. Wen Shu Juan analyzes the significance of Chen Da's participation in the production at length. See her "Chong shu yice chuanqi: lun Chen Da yu 'Sixiang qi' zai qiling niandai Taibei de qiguan hua licheng," 71–105.

75. For a thorough account of the production and Chen Da's role in the production, see Xu and Lin, *Hengchun bandao juexing*, 84–95.

76. For an account of the incident that attempts to disentangle facts on the basis of eyewitness accounts from the myths that have grown up around it, see Ma Shih-fang, "Yijiuqiliu nian na zhi kele ping" [That Coke bottle from 1976], in *Zuori shu* [My back pages] (Taipei: Xin jingdian wenhua, 2010), 62–71.

77. See Hsu Tsang-Houei, "Women xuyao ziji de yinyue: da Shi Weiliang xiansheng de gongkai xin" [We need our own music: A reply to Mr. Shih Wei-liang's open letter], *Lianhe bao* [United Daily News], July 10 and 12, 1962.

78. For an account of Li's performance and the dialogue with Tau, see Chang Chaowei, *Shei zai nabian chang ziji de ge: Taiwan xiandai minge yundong shi,* 121–23.

79. Wen Shu Juan, "Chong shu yice chuanqi: lun Chen Da yu 'Sixiang qi' zai qiling niandai Taibei de qiguan hua licheng," 43–44. The writer and singer Jiang Xun was also among those who wrote about the evening. See T. C. Yang, *Yaoyuan de xiangchou* [Distant homesickness] (Beijing: Xinxing chubanshe, 2007), 81.

80. Wen Shu Juan, "Chong shu yice chuanqi: lun Chen Da yu 'Sixiang qi' zai qiling niandai Taibei de qiguan hua licheng," 44.

81. See Yang Zujun (T. C.Yang), *Yang Zujun,* Synco Records VS-011, 1979.

82. For a helpful account of these years, see Yang Chia, "1970 niandai de liuxing yinyue: huashuo dangnian qingchun de xin" [Popular music of the 1970s: Speaking of our youthful hearts] and Tau Hsiao-ch'ing, "Wode 'remen yinyue' jiemu yu dangnian huohong de xiyang yinyue" [My "Hot music" program and the red hot Western music of those years]. Both pieces are collected in Tau and Yang, eds., *Minge 40*. Tau points out in particular the popularity of songbooks such as Yang Guangrong's 楊光榮 *Minyao jita ji* (Folk guitar collection) as a vector for spreading Western pop song forms. Tau and Yang, eds., *Minge 40*, 20. Tau herself compiled a series of four songbooks under the rubric "Zhe yi dai de ge" (Songs of this generation), all of which were published by Crown Publishing between 1979 and 1980. See Tau Hsiao-ch'ing, "Cong Xiyang gequ dao chang ziji de ge" in Tau and Yang, eds., *Minge 40*, 33.

83. See *Minyao feng,* Haishan Records LS-7057, 1978.

84. See, for instance, Pao Meisheng, Shin Lee VS-009, 1978.

85. See Li Tai-hsiang, *Xiangtu minyao* [Native soil folk], Shin Lee Records VM-01, 1978, and *Xiangtu minyao,* vol. 2, Shin Lee Records VM-03, 1979.

86. See Chen Da, *Chen Da yu Hengchun diao shuochang,* First Records FM-5008, 1979. Chen Da insisted that it was a real story and titled it "The Harbor Incident" 港口事件, while Hsu Tsang-Houei and his collaborator in the production of the record, Qiu Liangkun, retitled it "Ah Yuan yu Ah Fa fuzi de beican gushi" (The miserable story of Ah Yuan, the father, and Ah Fa the son).

87. See Taida jita she, ed., *Minyao jita zhi yue* [The key to folk guitar] (Taipei: Tiantong chubanshe, 1982).

88. Hsu, "Minge caiji riji," 138.

89. Hsu Chao-ch'in, *Wuxianpu shang de Xu Shi* [Xu Shi Notated] (New Taipei City: Huafeng wenhua, 2015), 70.

90. Interestingly, several of these compositions are actually included in Huang Chunming's *Suite of the Native Soil* section devoted to postwar balladry, indicating their inclusion in the popular canon.

91. The song appears on "Melodies of Taiwan," King Records KLK-60, 1962.

92. A contemporary performance by the Cuban Boys is available at https://www.youtube.com/watch?v=RZkdHwEA3oM. Accessed August 9, 2016.

93. For a blogpost on Liu Fuzhu's version, released on Wulong Records, see http://roxytom.bluecircus.net/archives/008201.html. Accessed August 9, 2016.

94. See Wen, "Chong shu yice chuanqi: lun Chen Da yu 'Sixiang qi' zai qiling niandai Taibei de qiguan hua licheng," 20.

95. Chen recorded a tribute to Chen Da entitled "Red Eye Chen Da" 紅目達仔 on his acclaimed 1990 release on Crystal Records, "An Afternoon of Taiwanese Opera" 下午的一齣戲. For a videotaped performance of this cover, see https://www.youtube.com/watch?v=G-Mr-Sa-5y0. Accessed August 9, 2016.

96. See Wen Shia, *Wen Shia chang (chang) you renjian wuyu*, 42. I first learned of this incident in conversation with Wen Shia. Personal interview, Taipei, December 30, 2014.

## 6. Teresa Teng and the Network Trace

1. For a comprehensive study of "sloganeering stations" in Kinmen and the surrounding islands, see Lin Mei-hua, "Qingting zhandi de shengyin: Jinmen de zhandi guangbo" [Listening to the sounds of a battlefield: Broadcasting in wartime Kinmen, 1949–1992], master's thesis, National Kinmen Institute of Technology, 2009. For an account of broadcasting activities on the mainland side of the straits, see *Xiamen guangbo dianshi shilüe, 1935–2007* [Historical sketch of broadcasting and television in Xiamen, 1935–2007] (Xiamen: Xiamen daxue chubanshe, 2009).

2. See Kyle Devine, "A Mysterious Music in the Air: Cultural Origins of the Loudspeaker," *Popular Music History* 8, no. 1 (2013): 5.

3. The opening salvo in this campaign against Teng's music and the resurgence of prerevolutionary pop was a now notorious guidebook by the editors of the official journal *People's Music*, titled *How to Distinguish Yellow Songs*. See Renmin yinyue bianji bu, eds., *Zenyang jianbie huangse gequ* [How to distinguish yellow songs] (Beijing: Renmin yinyue chubanshe, 1982).

4. Another popular variation on the phrase, according to Lin Mei-hua, was "I only love Little Deng, not Big Deng" 只愛小鄧，不愛老鄧. See Lin, "Qinting zhandi de shengyin," 85.

5. See Emily I. Dolan, *The Orchestral Revolution: Haydn and the Technologies of Timbre* (Cambridge: Cambridge University Press, 2013), 78.

6. Dolan, *The Orchestral Revolution*, 78.

7. Dolan, *The Orchestral Revolution*, 89.

8. See Michael Denning, *Noise Uprising: The Audiopolitics of a World Musical Revolution* (London: Verso, 2015), 174.

9. Albin J. Zak offers an ear-opening study of the art of studio recording as a compositional process in *The Aesthetics of Rock: Cutting Tracks, Making Records* (Berkeley: University of California Press, 2001). For a useful introductory guide to specific recording practices, from tracking to signal processing to mixing, see Jay Hodgson, *Understanding Records: A Field Guide to Recording Practice* (New York: Continuum, 2010). Profiles of some of the most important innovators in

studio recording are provided in Virgil Moorefield, *The Producer as Composer: Shaping the Sounds of Popular Music* (Cambridge, Mass.: MIT Press, 2009). *The Cambridge Companion to Recorded Music* provides a rich historical and conceptual overview of recording practices from the acoustic to the digital age. See Nicholas Cook, Eric Clarke, Daniel Leech-Wilkinson, and John Rink, eds., *The Cambridge Companion to Recorded Music* (Cambridge: Cambridge University Press, 2010). Interestingly, many of these effects are geared precisely toward the "retro-technological" evocation of a historical "real" by way of digital algorithms that emulate the sound of, say, a spring reverb unit.

10. For profiles of several of the most prominent innovators in modern studio practice, see Moorefield, *The Producer as Composer*.

11. Lin, "Qingting zhandi de shengyin," 25.

12. The theoretical and strategic basis of broadcasting as a form of psychological warfare had already reached the Republic of China during the Second World War. A handbook titled "Broadcast War," published in the wartime capital of Chongqing, for instance, provides a comprehensive look at the history and practice of radio-borne information warfare, with particular attention to practices in the United States, Europe, the Soviet Union, and Japan, and prescriptions for the conduct of such operations in the Chinese front. See Peng Leshan, *Guangbo zhan* [Broadcast war] (Chongqing: Zhongguo bianji chubanshe, 1943). For coverage of the mission and the changing "psychological warfare" strategies used by state broadcasters in Taiwan with respect to the mainland, see Wu Daoyi, *Zhongguang sishi nian* [BCC 1928–1968] (Taipei: Zhongguo guangbo gongsi, 1968), 319–24.

13. For an account of these events, as well as a fascinating ground-level portrait of life in Quemoy during these years, see Michael Szonyi, *Cold War Island: Quemoy on the Front Line* (Cambridge: Cambridge University Press, 2008), 64–78.

14. Lin, "Qingting zhandi de shengyin," 74.

15. This propensity of broadcasters on both sides to break the silence between barrages and make use of calm, nocturnal conditions conducive to sound traveling is testified to by Chen Feifei, a broadcaster who worked for nearly thirty years at the Xiangshan station on the mainland side. See Lin, "Qingting zhandi de shengyin," 75.

16. See Szonyi, *Cold War Island*, 95–98; Lin, "Qingting zhandi de shengyin," 73–79.

17. Lin, "Qingting zhandi de shengyin," 80.

18. This is the testimony of a former broadcaster named Deng Rongrong, as interviewed by Lin Mei-hua, "Qingting zhandi de shengyin," 81.

19. Lin, "Qingting zhandi de shengyin," 85, 133.

20. Lin, "Qingting zhandi de shengyin," 139.

21. "On the Front Lines with You" is accessible on Taiwan TV's YouTube channel: https://www.youtube.com/watch?v=sHIrz8ZhYr4. Accessed December 10, 2017. An account of Teng's career as a military entertainer is included in Jiang Jie, *Juexiang: Yongyuan de Deng Lijun* [Swan song: The eternal Teresa Teng] (Taipei: Shibao wenhua, 2013), 272–311.

22. See https://www.youtube.com/watch?v=npMzzKFmMcI. Accessed December 10, 2017.

23. The full slogan reads, "Open up the battlefield of the soul / call out the resonance of our heart's desires" 開闢精神戰場，喚起心聲共鳴.

24. Visitors to Quemoy's broadcasting stations at Beishan and Mashan these days—many of whom are mainland tourists taking advantage of the new mobility enabled by unencumbered ferry travel across the straits—are regaled by an unending tape loop of this same performance, interspersed with recordings of Teresa Teng's greatest hits.

25. For an account of Teng's background and her family life, see Jiang, *Juexiang*, 18–60.

26. The show was in competition with the long-running "Meeting of the Stars" 群星會 variety show on Taiwan TV (TTV), which began to present audiences with a popular music revue format beginning in 1962. For early promotional material on the show, see "Qunxing shanshuo" [The stars sparkle], in *Dianshi zhoukan* [TV Weekly] 5 (November 1962).

27. For Teng's introduction into the orbit of China TV, see Jiang, *Juexiang*, 70–71. Interestingly, the long-playing Yeu Jow release of Jingjing from 1968 includes an unattributed Mandarin cover of Sagara Naomi's "A World Just for the Two of Us," titled "The World Is So Beautiful" 世界多美麗.

28. See "Taiwan diqi muqian you duoshao dianshi ji?" [How many TV sets are there in the Taiwan region?], *Zhongguo dianshi zhoukan* [China TV Weekly] 9 (December 1969).

29. K'o Yu-fen has published a pair of indispensable articles charting the early history of television in Taiwan. For a study of the early years of TTV, see "Dianshi yu xiandai shenghuo: dianshi pujihua guocheng zhong de 'guo' yu 'jia,' 1962–1964 [Television and modern life: "Home" and "nation" in the installation process of TV sets, 1962–1964], *Taiwan shehuixue yanjiu jikan* [Taiwan: a radical quarterly in social sciences] 72 (March 2009). For a sense of the push and pull of the ideological and industrial imperatives, as well as the lingering Japanese colonial imprint that shaped the adoption of TV in Taiwan, see "Dianshi de zhengzhi yu lunshu: yijiuliuling niandai Taiwan dianshi shezhi guocheng" [The politics and discourse of television: The formation process of television in 1960s Taiwan], in *Taiwan shehuixue yanjiu jikan* [Taiwan: A Radical Quarterly in Social Sciences] 69 (March 2008).

30. See, for example, Wang Susu, "Deng Lijun: shiqi sui de yingge hongxing" [Teresa Teng: seventeen-year-old star of song and screen], *Zhongguo dianshi zhoukan* [China TV Weekly] 7 (1969).

31. See "Deng Lijun yin chi Yinni huzhao zai Ri beikou" [Deng Lijun detained in Japan for holding Indonesian passport], *Lianhe bao*, February 19, 1979. A critique of her actions, as well as the diplomatic loss of face by which it had been precipitated, was printed on the same day. See "Why Should a Proper Chinese Sneak Around like a Thief" [Tangtang zhengzheng Zhongguo ren, guiguisuisui gan shenme?], *Lianhe bao*, February 19, 1979.

32. See Raymond Williams, *Television: Technology and Cultural Form* (London and New York: Routledge, 1990), 24.

33. Szonyi, *Cold War Island*, 10.

34. Szonyi, *Cold War Island*, 33.

35. For an account of Quemoy's local broadcasting systems, see Lin, "Qingting zhandi de shengyin," 132.

36. Ma Duosi, "Touting Deng Lijun de rizi" [The days of listening in secret to Teresa Teng], *Beijing jishi* [Beijing Document] 6 (2013).

37. See Ah Cheng, "Ting di tai" [Listening to enemy radio], in Bei Dao and Li Tuo, eds., *Qishi niandai* [The 1970s] (Beijing: Sanlian, 2009), 150. For an English translation of the entire essay, see Ah Cheng, "On Listening to Enemy Radio," trans. Yurou Zhong, published by the Modern Chinese Literature and Culture Resource Center, http://u.osu.edu/mclc/online-series/zhongyurou/. Accessed January 13, 2017.

38. For another such memoir, this time set in a small county seat in Guangdong, see Ye Kai, "Danka luyinji li de Deng Lijun" [Listening to Teresa Teng on a cassette player], *Meiwen* [Belles-lettres] 3 (2011).

39. Two notable examples are Jia Zhangke's *Platform* (*Zhantai*, 2000) and Feng Xiaogang's *Youth* (*Fanghua*, 2017), both of which attempt to register the historical whiplash of the immediate postsocialist "new era" by following the vicissitudes of performing arts troupes (*wengongtuan* 文工團) as they try and fail to make the transition to a market economy. In *Platform*, a provincial troupe's falling away from a settled socialist life world into the restless mobility and economic insecurity of the entrepreneurial 1980s is precipitated by its main characters secretly listening to Teresa Teng through the earpiece of a transistor radio. In a pivotal scene in *Youth*, the much-admired "living Lei Feng" of a military troupe is initiated into a new world of romantic feeling when a female colleague surreptitiously plays a Teng cassette for him. Listening under a pink mosquito net—to provide the properly suggestive atmosphere as well as to conceal their transgression—our revolutionary naïf, previously the very model of selfless collectivist kindness, is suddenly imbued with heretofore unheard-of private desires and declares his passion for the female lead, a transgression for which he is harshly rebuffed. The consequences for him and for the troupe as a whole are disastrous. He is punished by demotion and sent to the front of the Sino-Vietnamese conflict of 1979, where he loses an arm. The troupe itself is disbanded, having been rendered irrelevant by the powerful solvent of a liberalizing commodity culture.

40. See Cai Xiang, "Qishi niandai: modai huiyi" [The 1970s: Memories of the end of an era], in Bei Dao and Li Tuo, eds., *Qishi niandai*, 342.

41. Cai Xiang, "Qishi niandai: modai huiyi," 342.

42. Perhaps the most important example of such sentiment is provided by the huge popularity in the 1960s and 1970s of the Chinese translation of a Russian ballad, "Moscow Nights" (Mousike jiaowai de wanshang) by Vasily Solovyof-Sedoi. Why is it that Teng's "Story of a Small Town" is remembered to have triggered tears and a newfound sense of interiority, while the lyricism of "Moscow

Nights," beloved by a generation of listeners, is not remembered with quite the same epochal intensity? Translated by one of the leading interpreters of foreign songs in post-1949 China, Xue Fan, "Moscow Nights" was one of the only unabashedly romantic pieces included in an influential songbook, *Songs of the World* (*Shijie gequ*), released by the Shanghai wenyi chubanshe in 1959. The song was circulated largely by way of written scores rather than recordings and was often sung to the accompaniment of an accordion or a balalaika during private gatherings during the Mao years. My sense, and the argument this chapter advances, is that the impact of "Moscow Nights" was quite different from that of Teresa Teng precisely because of its status as a text within the ambit of the Socialist circuit, one moreover usually performed by peers, and assimilated to local linguistic norms. Teng's music, in contrast, was received through the exoteric ether of enemy radio, or on cassette tapes. "Moscow Nights," while undeniably romantic, was thus not coupled with the same indelibility to the particularities of Teng's otherworldly Mandarin intonation, nor was it associated with the electronically mediated timbral intimacies afforded by the radio receiver or cassette player. For an account of "Moscow Nights" and its history in China, see Xue Fan, *Gequ fanyi tansuo yu shijian* [Exploration and practice in the translation of song] (Wuhan: Hubei jiaoyu chubanshe, 2002), 7–28.

43. See Zhang Hong, "Wenhua zousi shidai de Deng Lijun" [Teresa Teng in the era of smuggled cultural goods], http://zhanghongreview.blog.163.com/blog/static/1245951822013722931024. Accessed March 15, 2017.

44. The song is included in the collection "Wei Mao zhuxi yulu puqu" [Quotations from Chairman Mao set to music], China Records S-103, 1966.

45. Wang Min'an, *Lun jiayong dianqi* [On household electrical appliances] (Zhengzhou: Henan daxue chubanshe, 2015), 65–66.

46. Wang, *Lun jiayong dianqi*, 60–61.

47. For an account of the early years of television and collective listening in the 1970s, see Nicole Huang, "Sun-Facing Courtyards: Urban Communal Culture in Mid-1970s Shanghai," *East Asian History* 25/26 (June/December 2003): 161–82. For radio adaptations of films and voice artists, see "Listening to Films: Politics of the Auditory in 1970s China," *Journal of Chinese Cinemas* 7, no. 3 (2013): 187–206.

48. See Wu Yongyi, "Yi zhong jingshen de fushiji: renshi woguo sanshi, sishi niandai huangse yinyue de renshi" [An agent of spiritual corrosion: Recognizing the yellow music of the 1930s and 1940s], in Renmin yinyue bianji bu, eds., *Zenyang jianbie huangse gequ* [How to distinguish yellow songs] (Beijing: Renmin yinyue chubanshe, 1982), 1.

49. Wu Yongyi, "Yi zhong jingshen de fushiji: renshi woguo sanshi, sishi niandai huangse yinyue de renshi," 3–7.

50. Zhou Yinchang, "Zenyang kandai Gangtai 'liuxing gequ'" [How to view "popular songs" from Hong Kong and Taiwan], in Renmin yinyue bianji bu, eds., *Zenyang jianbie huangse gequ*, 9–27.

51. Zhou Yinchang, "Zenyang kandai Gangtai 'liuxing gequ,'" 11–12.
52. Zhou Yinchang, "Zenyang kandai Gangtai 'liuxing gequ,'" 22–23.
53. Zhou Yinchang, "Zenyang kandai Gangtai 'liuxing gequ,'" 23–24.
54. Zhou Yinchang, "Zenyang kandai Gangtai 'liuxing gequ,'" 24.
55. Zhou Yinchang, "Zenyang kandai Gangtai 'liuxing gequ,'" 24–27.
56. Zhou Yinchang, "Zenyang kandai Gangtai 'liuxing gequ,'" 24.
57. For the origins of crooning and its relation to the microphone, see Anne McCracken, *Real Men Don't Sing: Crooning in American Culture* (Durham, N.C.: Duke University Press, 2015).
58. The musical press of the time provides a good sense of the way in which stereo was normalized as a standard listening practice in Taiwan, presenting "how-to" explanations alongside copious advertisements for stereo components. See, for one instance, Yi De, "Shenme jiaozuo 'litisheng'" [What is "stereophonic sound"?], *Yinyue feng* [Music Trend] 66 (January 1, 1977): 53–56.
59. For a history of the "sweet spot" in the mythology and mechanics of home audio, see Tony Grajeda, "The 'Sweet Spot': The Technology of Stereo and the Field of Auditorship," in Paul Théberge, Kyle Devine, and Tom Everett, eds., *Living Stereo: Histories and Cultures of Multichannel Stereo* (New York and London: Bloomsbury, 2015).
60. Zhang, "Wenhua zousi shidai de Deng Lijun."
61. For a detailed and lavishly illustrated account of the history of the boom box and the cultures of listening and musical creativity with which it was associated in the West, see Lyle Owerko, *The Boombox Project: The Machines, the Music, and the Urban Underground* (New York: Abrams Image, 2010).
62. Xu Xingfa, Mou Tianxiong, and Lin Rongting, "Guochan heshi luyinji chanxiao yuce" [Production estimates for domestically produced radio–cassette recorders], *Shanghai jinrong yanjiu* [Shanghai Financial Research] 7 (1981): 28–29.
63. See Zhou Dafeng, "Yin shili dao, xunxun shanyou: tan Gang'ao liuxing yongsu gequ de canru" [Riding the wave to help turn the tide: On the influx of vulgar pop Hong Kong and Macao], in Renmin yinyue bianji bu, eds., *Zenyang jianbie huangse gequ* [How to distinguish yellow songs] (Beijing: Renmin yinyue chubanshe, 1982), 38.
64. See, for instance, Dianjian, "Zenyang tiaoxuan heshi luyinji" [How to select cassette recorders], *Jiadian yingyong jishu* [Home Appliance Technologies] 3/4 (1985): 52–54. For a comprehensive list of imported models and their features, see Lan Gao, "Changjian jinkou heshi luyinji xingneng jianjie" [A summary of the features of commonly imported cassette recorders], *Jiadian yingyong jishu* [Home Appliance Technologies] 1 (1984): 36–48. For a book-length pamphlet, see Ma Degong, *Zenyang yonghao heshi cidai luyinji* [How to make use of your cassette recorder] (Zhengzhou: Henan kexue jishu chubanshe, 1981).
65. Cai Xiang, "Qishi niandai: modai huiyi," 341.
66. See Zhang Shuzhen, "Zhongguo luyin zhipin chuban shiye bashi nian, 1908–1987" [Eighty years of the Chinese record publishing industry], *Zhongguo yinyue xue* [Chinese Music Studies] 1 (1994): 92.

67. For the global impact of cassettes, see Peter Manuel, *Cassette Culture: Popular Music and Technology in North India* (Chicago: University of Chicago Press, 1993), 28–36. For a compelling study of the technology's uses in the context of Muslim devotion in Egypt, see Charles Hirschkind, *The Ethical Soundscape: Cassette Sermons and Islamic Counterpublics* (New York: Columbia University Press, 2006).

68. See Zhang Hong, "Shengyin zousi shidai: Deng Lijun de shengyin 'fense' geming" [The era of sonic smuggling: Teresa Teng's "pink" revolution in sound], *Xiamen hangkong* [Xiamen Airlines] 2009: 6.

69. Hirschkind, *The Ethical Soundscape*, 4.

INDEX

Abing, 141
A-Da, 168
Adorno, Theodor, 226n3
aesthetics, 6, 54, 105, 143, 173; cultural, 207n33; folk, 16; musical, 18, 187; transistors and, 7, 71
Afonso, José, 11
Ah Cheng, 185, 189
Ah-Mei, 97, 98, 101, 104, 108, 231n59
*Air Hostess* (film), 33, 38, 50, 94
"Airmail Letter from Hawai'i," 87
"Airport" (Teng), 181
Aiwa, 192
Akai, 146
Allende, Salvador, 11
"All You Need Is Love" (Beatles), 4, 5
"Along the Sungari River," 195
*Analects*, 58
*Analfabeto, El* (film), advertisement for, 84 (fig.)
"Anping Reminiscence," 164
*Anthology of American Folk Music* (Smith), 131
*Anthology of Chinese Folk Music*, 131
April Revolution (1960), 8
Arbeit Gemeinschaft China-Europa, 242n41
"Ariel's Song," 213n86

Armed Forces Network, 92, 115, 121, 129
*Around the World in Eighty Days* (film), 82
Asahi, 146
Asaoka, Yukiji, 33
Asian Film Festival, 52
Asia Records, 45, 85, 86, 87, 92, 121, 166, 218n41, 227n13
"At Home in Taipei," 93
Australian National Radio, 184, 185
Auto-tune, 174
"Autumn Song, The" (Yao), 34

Bach, J. S., 4
Baez, Joan, 12, 136, 157, 161
ballads, 156, 157; folk, 16; *pingtan*, 24; pop, 7; Taiwanese, 138, 227n16
Bardot, Brigitte, 111
Bar-Kays, 104
Bartok, Bela, 138, 139, 140, 242n45
Battle of Shanghai (1932), 25
Bayi people, 194
BBC. *See* British Broadcasting Corporation
Beatles, 2, 4, 19, 34, 51, 75, 81, 110, 125, 147, 150, 155, 206n32, 232n2,

256  INDEX

245n72; eastern sounds and, 205n20
*Because of Her* (film), 31, 35, 38, 51; stills from, 32 (fig.), 39 (fig.)
Beethoven, Ludwig van, 143
Beijing Radio Equipment Factory, 68, 69
Beijing Railway Station, 3
Beishan Broadcasting Station, 169 (fig.)
Beka, 24
Belafonte, Harry, 42
Bell Labs, 5, 67, 116, 146
Bell Sound, 127
Benjamin, Walter, 100
*benshi,* role of, 97
Bernards, Brian, 216n21
*Billboard,* 122, 215n16, 219n51, 235n30, 235n32
Black Cat Records, 125, 127, 217n36
"Black Is Black" (Los Bravos), 111
Bloch, Ernst, 80, 226n3
"Blowin' in the Wind" (Dylan), 158
Blue Cheer, 81, 102
"Blue Hawai'i," 92
blues, 137; African American, 16, 136; Mississippi Delta, 37
Bo, Ivy Ling, 46
"Bottoms Up by the Harbor Side," 90
Bourdaghs, Michael, 228n27
Bowie, David, 203n1
Braun, Ernest, 5
Bravos, Los, 111
"Bridge over Troubled Water" (Conniff), 111
British Broadcasting Corporation (BBC), 3, 184
broadcasts, 24, 69, 175, 183, 248n15; enemy, 184; radio, 59, 172
"Broadcast War" (handbook), 247n12
Bûn Hā Hawai'ian Band, 87, 225n1
Byrds, 30, 213n1

*cabaretera* films, 42
Cai Wenhua, 86, 227n13, 227n15
Cai Xiang, 186, 192
calypso, 12, 41, 42, 43, 217n35
campus folk, 15, 124, 130, 135, 136, 161, 162, 238n7; impossibility of, 155–59
Cantinflas (Fortino Alfonso Moreno Reyes), 82–83, 92, 226n5, 226n6
"Caomin nong jigong," 243n62
capitalism, 47, 75, 194
"Capitol of the World" series, 33, 37, 215n14
Capitol Records, 33, 37, 43, 215n13, 215n14, 215n16, 228n27
Carnation Revolution (1974), 11
Carter, Jimmy, 130
Caruso, Enrico, 24
Cash, Johnny, 111
cassette players, 116, 192, 193, 250n42
Castro, Fidel, 44
Cathay, 45, 214n3, 217n34
Cathay Organization, 31, 39, 52
CBC (Canada), 3, 129
CCP. *See* Chinese Communist Party
censorship, 15, 94, 125, 227n11
Center for Research in Chinese National Music, 138
Center for the Study of National Music, 242n45
Central Bureau of Investigation, 146
Central Motion Picture Corporation (CMPC), 47, 93, 94, 109, 111, 113, 229n32
Central News Agency, 232n2
Central People's Broadcasting Station, 3, 184
Central People's Radio, 185
cha-cha, 35, 42, 86, 166, 199
Chailley, Jacques, 139
Chan, Anita, 68

Chang, Grace (Ge Lan), 12, 22, 29, 47, 178, 213n2, 217n34; films of, 38, 40–41, 42, 51, 94, 178; Hong Kong cinema and, 33; mambo and, 30, 35, 44; musical cinema and, 45; music of, 31, 37, 43, 50; photo of, 32, 34, 39
Chang Chao-Tang, 156, 157, 244n69, 244n72
Chang Chao-wei, 159, 245n73
Chang Tieh-chih, 238n9
Channes, Claude, 76, 78
Chao, Y. R., 31, 35, 41, 51
Chaplin, Charlie, 14, 82, 97, 102, 231n59
Chen Chen, 110
Chen Da, 85, 136, 158, 160 (fig.), 162, 166, 167; acoustic environment and, 150; analogy about, 156; balladry of, 156, 157; Coca-Cola incident and, 159; country blues and, 137; death of, 168; described, 143–44; folk balladry of, 16; folk revivalism and, 156; Hsu Shih and, 138, 147, 149–50, 152–53, 163; Hsu Tsang-Houei and, 130, 138, 142, 144, 241n35; life of, 16, 149–50; LP format and, 147–55; migration of, 135; music of, 16, 131, 138, 150, 159, 163, 240n24, 241n34; recordings of, 142–46, 148, 149, 152–53, 242n44; Scarecrow and, 244n72; story-telling sessions by, 162–63
*Chen Da and Hengchun Tune Minstrelsy* (Chen), 162
Chen Feifei, 248n15
Cheng Ling, 110, 111, 113–14
Chen Ming-chang, 168
*Chen Village* (Chan, Madsen, and Unger), 68
Chen Xiuxi, 159
Chen Yingzhen, 142

"Cherry Pink and Apple Blossom White" (Prado), 42
Chiang Ching-kuo, 110, 244n68
Chiang Kai-Shek, 13, 44, 117, 170, 176, 194, 227n9
Chiao, Roy, 38
*Children of the Storm* (film), 25
Chi Lu-Shyia, 87, 227n16
China Broadcasting Company, 121
China Publications Center, 59, 75
*China Reconstructs* (magazine), 75
China Records, 28, 59, 72, 213n82, 220n19
China Television, 93, 151, 156, 178, 243n61, 248n27
*China TV Weekly*, 179 (fig.), 218n40
China Youth Corps (KMT), 139, 242n45
China Youth Library, 242n45
"China Youth National Salvation Corps," 139
Chinese Communist Party (CCP), 9, 13, 20, 21–22, 59, 73, 117, 170, 172
Chinese language, 60, 146, 207n42, 233n4; nonstandard/regional forms of, 207n40; standard, 144; vernacular, 41
Chinese Nationalist Party (KMT), 13, 14, 25, 33, 40, 41, 43, 45, 47, 83, 87, 90, 93, 134, 139, 159, 170, 177, 178, 195; censorship by, 15, 125; dominance, 110; Mandarin films and, 124; rule by, 129
Chinese Revolution, 1, 2, 15; transistor technology and, 6–7
Ching Chuan Kang (CCK) Air Base, 118
*Chinoise, La* (Godard), 19, 75; still from, 77 (fig.)
Chion, Michel, 237n2
Chiu, Fred, 141, 144, 240n19, 243n60; photo of, 147

Chiung Yao, 109
Chunghwa Market, 121, 133, 148; photo of, 149
Chung Ing-ssu, 111, 113
Chyi Yu, 161
cinema: acoustic sound in, 237n2; Chinese-language, 111; dialect, 93–94; Hokkien, 45, 218n43; Hong Kong, 33; musical, 12–13, 45; nonstandard, 95; Taiwanese, 13, 80; *Taiyu*, 47
circuits, 35, 37, 115–17; closed, 8; commercial, 12; communications, 175–76; disparate, 159, 161–67; electronic, 116; film exhibition, 52; folk, 137, 148, 153; ground and, 6–19; labor, 155; local, 116, 117; Mandarin, 93, 94; media, 30, 53; migratory, 162; musical, 35, 116; oscillator, 28; pop, 12, 115, 116; semiconductor, 14; transistor, 71; transnational, 130; urban, 138, 151
civil aviation, 23, 30, 39, 51, 90
Clark, Gene, 213n1
Clark, Paul, 220n8
Clayton, Buck, 24
*Clockwork Orange, A* (Kubrick), 113
Clooney, Rosemary, 42
Cloud Gate, 157, 245n74
CMPC. *See* Central Motion Picture Corporation
Coca-Cola, 111, 158, 159, 192
Coderre, Laurence, 69
Cohen, Leonard, 244n69
Cold War, 1, 4, 12, 14, 17, 26, 29, 53, 58, 81, 82, 83, 114, 115, 130, 137, 158, 170, 172, 177, 181, 183, 194; East Asia and, 110, 117; Taiwan and, 7, 15, 109, 146
*Collection of Modern Chinese Folksongs, A* (album), 157
"Collective Listening," 61 (fig.)
collectors, 116, 120–25

colonial rule, Japanese, 83, 101, 123, 148, 153
Coltrane, John, 10, 213n1
Columbia Records, 120, 213n1
Columbia Record Store, photo of, 120
*Company of Birds, The* (Loke), 219n56
"Concert for Democracy in China," 194
Connery, Christopher Leigh, 205n14
Conniff, Ray, 111
consumer electronics, 5, 13, 80, 116, 137, 172
copyright laws, 15, 95, 237n52
copyright violations, 114, 122, 235n28, 236n49
counterculture, 4, 12, 136, 137, 142, 158
"Country Boy" (Huang), 151
Cream, 111
Cuban Boys, 246n92
Cultural Renaissance, 83, 141, 227n9
Cultural Revolution, 3, 25, 28, 54, 56, 58, 68, 70, 72, 73, 75, 83, 184, 187, 188; cultural products of, 18
Cumings, Bruce, 15, 233n12
Curtis, Scott, 104

Daguangli, 149, 156
"Dangwai" movement, 159
Davenport, Tom, 142, 149, 150, 151, 152, 240n24
Davis, Miles, 10
"Death of a Mummy, The" (Lennon), 125
Debussy, Claude, 138, 139, 140, 242n45
decolonization, 1, 4, 8, 9, 14, 24, 25, 81, 85, 110, 136
Delfino, Ollie, 42, 217n34
Deng Xiaoping, 172
Denning, Michael, 10, 22, 23, 173–74
Denver, John, 161

Derrida, Jacques, 71, 71–72, 74
Devine, Kyle, 170
Dexter, Dave, Jr., 33–34, 215n14
*Dinah Shore Show, The*, 34, 35, 45; still from, 34 (fig.)
"Disraeli Gears" (Cream), 111
Dolan, Emily, 173
Donkey Radio, 66 (fig.)
Donovan, 11, 157
"Don't Think of It" (Yan Zhexi), 211n74
Dostoyevsky, Fyodor, 76
*Drifter with a Sword* (film), 96
"Drifting Girl" (Wen), 88 (fig.)
*Drifting into Taipei* (Huang), 151; cover of, 152 (fig.)
Du Fu, 26
Dylan, Bob, 11, 12, 124, 142, 147, 155, 156, 157, 161, 213n1, 245n72; Newport and, 136, 158, 206n25

*Early Train from Taipei, The* (film), 48
"East Is Red, The," 19, 21, 25, 26–27, 209n56, 209n58, 212n77, 302n2; "All You Need Is Love" and, 4, 5; ascension of, 211n73; birth/dissemination of, 209n59; broadcasting, 1, 22; Great Proletarian Cultural Revolution and, 3; impact of, 2; precursors to, 27; recording of, 213n82
"East Is Red 1, The" (satellite), 1, 3, 6–7, 28
"East Is Red 101" (record player), 69
"Eight Miles High" (Byrds), 213n1
Eisenhower, Dwight D., 117
Electrical and Musical Industries (EMI), 24, 31, 33, 35, 40, 46, 219n51, 236n35; Pathé and, 23, 39, 180
electrification, rural, 17, 68, 223n30, 224n40
"Elegy for Sun Yat-sen, Father of Our Country" (Li Jinhui), 158

EMI. *See* Electrical and Musical Industries
*enka*, 30, 46, 48, 87, 90
*Escaped Lunatic, The* (film), 100
ethnicity, 23, 35, 144, 148
*Everything Was Forever, Until It Was No More* (Yurchak), 74

Fairport Convention, 11
Fan Dunxing, 64, 67
Fan Jiyun, 138
Feld, Steven, 215n15
Festival de Música Popular Brasileira, 11
Field, Andrew, 210n69
Fifth Dimension, 118
Filipino Air Force Band, 44
film industry, 24, 33, 82, 214n8, 230n39
filmmaking, 80, 94–95; Japanese, 83, 230n39; Mandarin, 94, 124
"First Love by the Harbor Side," 90
First Records, 15, 131, 148; case study of, 125, 127–30
"Five Works" (Mao), 56
folk music, 12, 15, 20, 28, 37, 54, 86, 134, 143, 145, 158, 165, 178; Chinese, 25, 35, 85, 144, 200; derivations, 140; fate of, 16; Hengchun, 163; Hungarian, 139; indigenous, 131; modern, 157; popular music and, 137, 220n5; Taiwanese, 117, 162, 168
folk revivalism, 10, 11, 16, 124, 131, 136, 138, 143, 156, 158; *minyo*, 12; Taiwanese, 137, 168
folk-rock, 10, 11, 136
Folk Song Collection Movement, 138, 140, 141, 144, 152, 238n7, 240n18, 240n26, 241n33
folk song movement, 136, 159, 166, 238n7; modern, 140; Taiwanese, 135, 238n9

Folkways Records, 131
"Folk Wind" series, 161
"Formosa" (song), 159
"Formosa Mambo," 44
Formosa Plastics, 129
Four Sisters, 80, 81, 93, 96, 98, 103, 104, 105, 108
foxtrots, 24, 86
Free China, 7, 40, 45, 81, 125, 158, 192, 200
*French Connection, The* (film), 111, 113
Fu, Poshek, 39

Gaisberg, Fred, 34, 215n14
*Games People Play, The* (Berne), 142
Gaud, William, 18
General Instrument, 14
"Getting to Know You," 33
"G.I. Blues," 92
Gil, Gilberto, 11
GIO. *See* Government Information Office
Godard, Jean-Luc, 19, 75, 76, 78
Goethe, Johann Wolfgang, 76
*Goodbye, Taipei* (Wen), 14, 80, 81, 92–98, 99 (fig.), 100–102, 103 (fig.); copyright laws and, 95; opening of, 95; release prints of, 96; stills from, 107 (fig.)
Gosse, Phillip, 114, 115
Government Information Office (GIO), 90, 127
"Grândola Vila Morena" (Afonso), 11
"Grandpa and Grandma Travel to Taipei" (charity program), 156
"Grassroots Folk" concert, 159
Great China Records, 24, 26
Great Hall of the People, 2, 28
Great Leap Forward, 63, 67, 69
Green Revolution, 9, 13, 17–18, 23, 81, 136
"Greensleeves," 4

*Guitar in Hand* (Kobayashi), 91 (fig.)
guitars: acoustic, 137; electric, 206n32; Fender, 228n20; Hawaiian steel, 86, 87; manufacture of, 206n32; pedal steel, 26
Gunning, Tom, 95, 231n55
Guoji Shudian, 221n18
Guthrie, Woody, 11, 159

Haishan Records, 128, 161
Hakka language, 16, 41, 83, 85, 124, 138, 207n40, 227n7
Hamilton, Mary Beth, 143
Han Hyung-mo, 42
Hansen, Miriam Bratu, 41, 216n28
*Hanyu Pinyin*, romanization of, 28, 225n1
Happy End, 11
"Happy Sailor, The," 90
Harrison, George, 205n20
Hattori Ry ichi, 33, 38, 214n8
"Hawaiian Nights" (Koji), 88 (fig.)
"Hawaiian Nights" (Wen), 86, 87
*Hawaiian Nights* (Wen), cover of, 89 (fig.)
"Hawai'ian Nocturne," 87
He Lüting, 27, 28, 211n76, 212n79, 212n80, 221n13
Hengchun, 131, 135, 138, 143, 145, 149, 153, 154, 155, 156, 162, 163, 165, 167
"Hengchun minyao" 243n62
He Qifang, 21, 22
Hershey, Burnet, 24
"Hey Jude" (Beatles), 81, 103
"Highest Directives" (Mao), 75
*High Plains Drifter* (film), 96
Hinton, Carma, 203n3
hippies, 110, 111, 136
Hirschkind, Charles, 193
Hogtail, 143
Hokkien language, 16, 41, 45, 46, 94, 158, 207n40, 218n42

Hoklo language, 83, 85, 87, 124, 138, 148, 207n40, 226n1, 227n7
Hollywood, 12, 35, 37, 41, 51, 76, 80, 90, 92, 95, 97, 113, 216n24
Holy Hawk Records, 123
*Home Sweet Home* (Pai), 93
Hong Guo-juin, 46
Hong Jianquan, 148
Hong Jianquan Educational Culture Foundation, 157, 237n56, 245n74
Hong Kong, 7, 22, 30, 37, 41, 46, 51, 94, 121, 133; musical imports from, 189; Taiwan and, 12
Hong Kong Airways, 39
"Hong Kong Mambo" (Puente), 41
*Hong Kong's Grace Chang* (album), cover art for, 36 (fig.)
Hong Yifeng, 44, 46, 47, 48 (fig.), 85, 86, 121, 124, 219n49; feedback loop and, 80; mambo and, 13; musical cinema and, 45; voice of, 48
hook, 55, 73–74
*Hot Meat Rolls* (film), 49; still from, 50 (fig.)
"How Could I Not Miss Her" (Chao), 31
*How to Distinguish Yellow Songs,* 189, 247n3
*How to Recognize Yellow Music,* 192
"How to View 'Popular Songs' from Hong Kong and Taiwan," 189
Hsiang Tzu-Long, 157
Hsieh Teng-hui, 44, 166
Hsimenting, 28, 101, 133, 148, 199
Hsu Pi-kui, 164
Hsu Ping-ting, 164, 166, 168
Hsu Pi-yun, 164
Hsu Shih, 163–64, 165, 166; cover for, 165 (fig.); folk revival and, 168; photo of, 166, 167
Hsu Tsang-Houei, 16, 28, 85, 135, 137, 139, 140, 141, 145, 146, 157, 161, 163, 164, 165, 166, 168; acoustic map of, 133; anticolonialism and, 158; Center for the Study of National Music and, 242n45; Chen Da and, 130, 138, 142, 144, 241n35; collections of, 242n40; folk music and, 136, 162; modernist aesthetic of, 143; noise pollution and, 134; notation and, 241n34; report by, 142, 143; speech by, 131
Hu, Brian, 38
Huang, Nicole, 188–89, 220n7
Huang Chungming, 142, 158, 162, 246n90; cover for, 160 (fig.)
Huang Guolong, 85
Huang Xitian, 151, 152 (fig.)
Huang Ziping, 27, 74, 75
Hu Defu, 157
Huimei Records, 148
Hurt, Mississippi John, 16, 136

Ibuka Masaru, 146
"I Look Up as I Walk" (Sakamoto), 35
"I Love Calypso" (Chang), 42
Incredible String Band, 205n20
infrastructure, 18, 53, 54; media, 17, 170, 186; military, 115; musical, 26, 172, 184, 186, 192
*International Screen* (MP&GI), 33, 42
Ishihara Yujiro, 90, 93, 228n20
*Island Nation Love* (Teng), 191
*Island Nation Love, Volume 2* (Teng), 189–90
"I Want to Fly up to the Blue Sky" (Chang), 29, 38
*I Want to Sing* (film), 178

Jameson, Fredric, 8, 9, 10, 20, 226n3
Japanese Imperial Army, 25, 195
jazz, 24, 25, 26, 48, 55
Jet Set, 213n1
Jia County People's Government, 21
Jiang Qing, 54, 55, 72, 75
Jiang Wenye, 139

"Jing Jing," 178, 180
*John Lennon and the Plastic Ono Band* (album), 125; cover of, 128 (fig.)
Jolivet, André, 139

Ka'ai, Ernest, 24
Kai Tak Airport, 31, 51
Kang Ding, 82–83, 94, 97, 104–5, 108; album by, 79; films of, 92
*Kang Ding Adrift in Taipei*, 92
"Kang Ding's Chinese New Year Celebration," 84 (fig.)
*Kang Ding's Tale of Heartbreak* (Kang), 79, 82
Kaohsiung, 14, 15, 118, 119, 123, 161, 243n58
Kaser, David, 122
*kayōkyoku* pop, 81
Keaton, Buster, 14
Keystone Cops, 14, 80
*Key to Folk Guitar, The* (National Taiwan University), 162
King, Carole, 161
*King and I, The* (film), 34
"King" label, 164
"King of Cats," 92
Kingston Trio, 11
KMT. *See* Chinese Nationalist Party
Kobayashi Akira, 90, 91 (fig.), 93, 228n20
K'o Yu-fen, 178, 249n29
Kraus, Richard, 221n13
Kubrick, Stanley, 113
Kuncheng Li, 90
Kuningtou, 169, 170
Kurosawa Takatomo, 141, 240n19

landscapes: media, 54, 58–59, 69, 76, 80; musical, 210n62; social, 67
language, 41; Cantonese, 12, 41; Hoklo, 83, 85, 124, 138; Japanese colonial rule and, 226n7; local, 144,
227n7, 233n4; musical, 140, 163; nonstandard, 85; Taiwanese, 46, 79, 81. *See also* Chinese language; Hakka language; Hokkien language; Hoklo language; Mandarin Chinese
Larkin, Brian, 18, 19
*Last Train from Kaohsiung, The* (film), 48
Latour, Bruno, 144
Laurel and Hardy, 97
Leadbelly, 136
"Learning from the Beatles" (Poirier), 204n8
*Legacy* (album), 157
Leico, 127
Lei Feng, 250n39
Lennon, John, 5, 75, 125; recording of, 126 (fig.), 128 (fig.)
Lewis, Furry, 16, 136
Liang Maochun, 58, 72, 219n1
Liao Jinfeng, 93, 226n2
Liaoning People's Radio Station, 66 (fig.)
*Liberation Daily*, 21
Li Jiefu, 58, 73, 221n13, 221n14
Li Jinhui, 158
Li Jinqi, 21, 209n59
Lin Biao, 57, 58, 75, 221n13; death of, 53; Little Red Book and, 56
*Lingering Lost Love* (film), 47, 48, 83; still from, 48 (fig.); title sequence of, 49 (fig.)
Lin Hwai-min, 157, 245n74
Lin Keping, 38, 50
Li Shuangze, 15, 137, 158–59, 161, 166–67; death of, 159; performance by, 158; popular songs and, 163
"Listening to Songs in the Streets of Taipei" (Hsu), 134
Li Tai-hsiang, 161, 168
*Literature Quarterly*, 142
Little Red Book, 19, 54, 56–59, 75, 76

Little Theater, 142
Liu, Alan P., 222n20
Liu Fuzhu, 166, 246n93
Liu Zhiming, 121, 151
Li Youyuan, 21
Li Zengzheng, 21, 210n60
Loke Wan Tho, 31, 39, 40, 219n56; death of, 52
Lomax, Alan, 136, 142, 143
Lomax, John, 136
Longshan Temple, 133, 199
"Lost Girl, The" (Wen), 101
loudspeakers, 18, 65–66, 68–69, 70, 75, 96, 134, 169, 170–71, 187; balanced armature, 65; high-frequency, 73; horn reflex, 19, 72, 225n50, 225n52; increase in, 63; iron cone, 65; network of, 60; photo of, 169; transistorized, 70 (fig.)
*Love in a Cabin* (Pai), 109, 114, 124; culture and, 117; pirate records and, 123; redux, 130–31; space of emancipation in, 110; still from, 112 (fig.)
"Love Longing on the Passage to Hawai'i," 87
*Love Story of Uncivilized Girls* (film), 194
Lu Feiyi, 95
Lumumba, Patrice, 9
Lu Xun, 139, 141
Lu Xun Academy of Art, 20
lyrics, 101, 225n59; Chinese, 85; Taiwanese, 90, 228n25

Ma, Jean, 213n2, 217n35
MAAG. *See* Military Assistance Advisory Group
Macdonald, Stuart, 5
*Madame Freedom* (melodrama), 42
Madsen, Richard, 68
Malaysian Airways, 39
mambo, 7, 12, 13, 30, 33, 35, 40, 41, 42, 44, 199, 216n32

*Mambo* (film), 42
"Mambo Girl" (Chang), 12
*Mambo Girl* (film), Chang and, 35, 42, 44, 217n34
"Mambo in Stereo," 218n41
"Mambo Italiano" (Clooney), 42
"Mambo No. 8," 41
Mandarin Chinese, 14, 28, 32, 41, 45, 79, 80, 94, 95, 138, 146, 158, 178, 180; hegemony of, 12, 83, 124
"Man in Black, A" (Cash), 111
Mao Zedong, 9, 68, 188, 220n6; cult of personality and, 2–3, 53; "East Is Red" and, 1, 4; Lin and, 53; as media-effect, 71–76, 78; praise for, 220n5; quotations of, 55–56; quotation songs and, 21, 72, 73; Red Guard and, 70
Mao Zedong Thought, 54, 56, 57
"March of the Volunteers, The" (national anthem), 3, 25
"Marseillaise, La," 4, 25
Martin, George, 174
Mashan, 176, 248n24
Ma Shih-fang, 110, 235n31, 238n7, 238n9
Matsu, 118
Matsushita Electric Industrial Company, 13, 148, 183, 237n56
May 4th movement, 32, 41, 138, 141
McGrath, Jason, 225n55
McGuinn, Roger, 29, 30, 213n1
McLuhan, Marshall, 5, 204n7, 204n9, 205n12; electronic interdependence and, 63; global village and, 4, 63; media theory and, 205n12; technological triumphalism and, 7
media: consumption, 183; digital storage, 130; dispensation, 188; global, 3; interactivity, 56; mass, 9, 25, 30, 55, 56, 58, 59, 68, 109; modern, 130; portable, 70; regimes,

55; socialist, 19, 56; topology, 54, 137; transistorized, 70, 178; visual/aural, 59; wired, 18
media effect: Mao as, 71–76, 78
"Melancholic, The" (Chouren), 90
*Melodies of Taiwan* (Hsu), 164, 165 (fig.), 166
Messiaen, Olivier, 139
"Mexico" (Ventures), 103
microphones, 23, 69, 86, 227n15
migration, 17, 30, 37, 101, 136
"Migration Song, The," 21, 27, 210n60
Military Assistance Advisory Group (MAAG), 117, 118, 119
Miller, Glenn, 4
Mingfeng Records, 129, 148
Misora Hibari, 90
Mitchell, Joni, 124, 156
Miyashita Tsuneo, 87
modernism: black musical, 215n15; folk, 138–42; vernacular, 41, 216n28
modernization, 13, 18, 51, 60, 65, 80, 137, 143, 144, 166, 172
Moore's Law, 5
*Morning Sun* (film), 203n3, 209n56
Morrison, Van, 156
"Moscow Nights," 250–51n42
Motion Picture and General Investment (MP&GI), 31, 33, 38, 40, 42, 47, 48, 51, 214n3, 214n8
"Movement for a Chinese Cultural Renaissance" (KMT), 83, 141, 142
*Mr. Tambourine Man* (album), 29, 213n1
"Mr. Tambourine Man" (Dylan), 213n1
"Muchacha" (Hattori), 38
Mushanokōji Saneatsu, 141
music: Afro-Caribbean, 30; Anglo-American, 117, 199; beat, 152; Cantonese, 45, 215n17; Chinese, 17, 22, 150, 278, 207n42, 241n34; communication and, 156; globalization of, 115; Hawai'ian, 211n70; hit, 15, 50, 121, 124, 130, 138; Hokkien, 45; hot, 50; Japanese, 85, 90; Javanese, 140; light, 86, 103; mass, 10, 27–28; media technology and, 7; mixed-blood, 46, 87, 90, 92, 138, 151, 219n49, 228n17; national, 150; protest, 8, 205n19; quality, 128; revolutionary, 69; swing, 54; Taiwanese, 15–16, 102, 121, 131, 135, 199, 238n9; vernacular, 10; world, 31, 34, 35; yellow, 55, 172, 189, 199, 210n61
musicals: Chinese-language, 29; Mandarin, 138, 178; Taiwanese-language, 30; *Taiyu*, 45
*Music and Stereo*, 156, 244n69
*Musician of Our Nation: Chen Da and His Songs* (Chen), 16, 147–48, 155, 157, 163, 244n64
"Muss I Denn," 92
"My Home Is on the Other Side of the Mountain," 194, 195
"My Mummy's Dead" (John Lennon and the Plastic Ono Band), 125; recording of, 126 (fig.)

Nanyang circuit, 39, 216n21
National, 148, 183
National Academy of Music, 139
National Educational Television (NET), 3
*National Geographic*, 142
Nationalists, 25, 43, 83, 117, 118, 140, 170, 195
National Museum of Taiwan Literature, 227n7
National Taiwan Normal University, 111, 118, 134, 139, 161, 162, 198

Native Soil literary movement, 158
NBC, 35
Nettl, Bruno, 19–20, 209n52
networks: acoustic, 56, 150, 175; "Black Atlantic," 36; broadcast, 56, 59, 60, 63, 65, 193; electrical, 56; fixed, 70; global, 233n12; literary, 208n43; maritime, 23; media, 7, 12, 53, 55, 172, 187; musical, 6, 22; wired, 60
Newport Folk Festival, 11, 136, 158, 206n25
New Village movement, 141
NHK, 3
Nie Er, 25
"Night Mist" (Teng), 190
Nikkatsu Studios, 92
Ninth Party Congress, 54, 55, 220n5
"No American war provocation whatsoever can intimidate the Chinese people!," 171 (fig.)
Nobuyasu, Okabayashi, 11
North China Radio Equipment Factory, 68
*nueva cancion*, 11, 136, 206n28

*On Folk Song* (Shih), 140
Ongg, Judy, 152
"On Some Motifs in Baudelaire" (Benjamin), 100
"On the Front Lines with You" (TTV), 176
opera: Cantonese, 37; *huangmeidiao*, 37, 46, 121; *koa-a-hi*, 28, 95, 104, 133, 199, 200; Peking, 33; *po-te-hi* (budaixi) puppet, 232n65; "yellow plum," 37
*Orchestral Revolution: Haydn and the Technologies of Timbre, The* (Dolan), 173
"Orient Pirate Playground" (*Billboard*), 122
Ostasien-Institut, 242n41

Osterwalder, Alois, 242n41
*Our Dream Car* (film), 33
"Our Hope Is Placed on You," 187
"Our World," 4

"Pacific Festival," 33
Pai Ching-jui, 93, 109, 111, 124
Pan American World Airways, 118
Panasonic, 13, 237n56
Panda brand, 69, 224n40
Pao Mei-sheng, 161
Paris World Exposition (1889), 140
Pathé Records, 22, 24, 27, 31, 33, 211n74; EMI and, 23, 39, 180; expulsion of, 26; house band, 25
Peace Hotel jazz band, 44
peasantry, 17, 18, 65, 142
Pentangle, 11
Peony brand, 69, 223n38
*People's Daily*, 1, 55, 58, 59, 68
People's Liberation Army (PLA), 53, 56, 170
*People's Music* (journal), 189, 247n3
People's Republic of China, 7, 17, 26, 53, 130, 141, 142, 181; relations with, 157
Percy Faith Singers, The, 111
Perez Firmat, Gustavo, 41
Perez Prado, 41, 42, 44, 218n41
"Periodizing the 1960s" (Jameson), 8
Pesnyary, 11
Peter, Paul, and Mary, 11
Phoenix Sisters, 108
"Pingpu diao," 244n64
Pink Floyd, 244n69
Pinky and Killers, 104
"Pipeline" (Ventures), 104
piracy, 117, 125, 127; history of, 114–15; music, 15, 17, 119, 120, 237n52; Taiwanese, 17, 122, 129–30, 235n33
pirate records, 117, 119, 120, 121, 131, 158, 162; Anglophone, 123;

ethics of, 235n28; Korean, 233n10; Taiwanese, 114, 115, 118, 123, 235n28; trade, 122–23
Plastic Ono Band, 125; recording of, 126 (fig.)
*Platform*, 250n39
Poe, Edgar Allan, 100
Pojuschie Gitary, 11
Polydor Records, 181, 189
popular music, 15, 30, 54, 55, 75, 85, 86, 90, 102, 114, 133, 149, 168, 175, 176; Anglo-American, 121, 137; Chinese, 20, 22, 162, 172, 210n62, 214n8; commercial, 164; consumption of, 115, 233n11; cosmopolitan, 22; East Asian, 116; folk music and, 137; history of, 10, 33; import of, 7; Japanese, 87, 108, 180, 199, 206n30, 226n4; Mandarin, 15, 37, 39, 44, 50, 121, 130, 155, 161, 162, 172; quotation songs and, 73–74; social divisions and, 124; syntax of, 165; Taiwanese, 13, 44, 80, 116, 120, 124, 168, 235n27, 243n54; urban, 155
popular songs, 4, 155, 189, 199; Anglo-American, 81; Cantonese, 216n24; form of, 137, 163; Japanese, 82, 85, 104, 197, 198; Mandarin, 152, 178, 200; mass-mediated, 55; performance of, 85; proliferation of, 226n4; structure of, 163; *Taiyu*, 14, 151, 153, 164, 166; Western, 178, 246n82
*Possessed, The* (Dostoyevsky), 76
Presley, Elvis, 92
privatization, 172; mobile, 177–78, 180–81, 183–84
propaganda, 55, 228n23; Communist, 146; Maoist, 6; political, 60, 222n21
psychedelia, 10, 14
psychological warfare, 170, 175, 247n12

Puente, Tito, 41
Puyuma melodies, 154

Qideng Sheng, 142
Qing rule, 143, 154
Qiu Wangshe, 108, 231n59
"Queen" label, 164
Quemoy, 118, 169, 170, 174, 176, 177, 183–84, 194, 195
Quemoy crisis (1958), 118
"Que rico el mambo," 41
*Quotations of Chairman Mao, The*, 19, 54, 56, 57, 58, 71, 72, 74, 76
quotation songs, 19, 54, 55–56, 58–59, 76; phenomenon of, 72; popular music and, 73–74; youth culture and, 75

radio, 1, 5; commercial, 163; enemy, 184, 185; popularization of, 183; portable, 68, 184; programming, 67; reception, 60; rural, 59–60, 63, 65; shortwave, 184. *See also* transistor radios
*Radio in the Fields* (Wu), 63 (fig.)
radio listening stations, 60
Radio Peking, 59, 76, 142
Radio Shanghai, 59
"Rainy Harbor Love Song," 90
"Rainy Night Flower," 158
RCA, 42, 86
record industry, 211n72; Cantonese, 218n44; Chinese, 24; Taiwanese, 51, 85, 115, 122, 123, 235n27
*Record of Music, The*, 140, 197
Red Army, 20, 25
Red China, 12, 39, 83; Taiwan and, 110
Red Guard, 3, 8, 55, 69, 70, 71, 72, 110, 185
"Red Records," 27, 212n77
reggae, 10, 136, 206n23

# INDEX     267

Republic of China (ROC), 110, 117, 118, 170, 176, 184; diplomatic relations of, 15; hippies and, 110
"Revolution" (Lennon), 75
Revox, 146, 242n41
Rhee, Syngman, 8
"Riding a White Horse," 21, 210n60
RingRing Records, 148
Ritek, 129
RKO, 41
ROC. *See* Republic of China
rock and roll, 11, 12, 32, 42, 206n24, 210n62
*Rock Magazine*, 244n72
Rodgers, Jimmie, 219n50
Rodgers and Hammerstein, 34, 90
Rolling Stones, 19, 245n72
Royal Hawaiian Troubadours, 24
rumba, 23, 24, 25, 44, 199
Rural Electrification and Its Discontents, 67 (fig.)
rural roots, 13, 60,147

Sagara Naomi, 108
*Sailor, The* (Wen), 91 (fig.)
"Sailor's Love Song, The," 90
Sakamoto, Kyu, 35, 36, 92, 215n14, 228n27
Salazar, António, 11
Samsung, 183
Sanyo, 146, 191, 192
satellites, 1–2, 3, 6–7, 28
Scarecrow Restaurant, 157, 244n72
Schaefer, R. Murray, 134
Schaeffer, Pierre, 134
Schmalzer, Sigrid, 17
Sea Dragon Officer's Club, 119
"Season of Love, The," 104, 105 (fig.)
Seeger, Pete, 159
*Selected Shaanbei Folk Songs* (He), 21, 22
"Sesame Oil," 21

"Sgt. Pepper's Lonely Hearts Club Band" (Beatles), 125
Shakespeare, William, 213n86
"Shandong Mambo" (Wang), 43
Shanghai, 3, 22, 25, 26, 27, 44, 172, 192; colonial culture of, 189; film industry in, 33; jazz in, 24; music in, 33, 35; night clubs of, 211n70; population of, 23
Shanghai Broadcast Ensemble, 27
Shanghai Broadcast Orchestra, 211n76
Shanghai Conservatory of Music, 27
Shanghai Radio Equipment Factory, 68
Shanghai Record Manufacturing Company, 27, 212n77
Shao Yiqiang, 123, 235n28
Shaw Brothers, 31, 46, 50–51, 52, 94, 214n8
"She Loves You" (Beatles), 4
Shenyang Conservatory, 58
Shih, Evelyn, 95
Shih Wei-liang, 16, 17, 135, 137, 141, 145, 155, 157, 166, 168; anticolonialism and, 158; Bartok and, 140; Center for the Study of National Music and, 242n45; Chen and, 138, 147, 149–50, 151, 152–53, 163; folk music and, 136; KMT and, 139
Shinjuku Popular Music Festival, 180–81
Shin Lee Records, 161
Shirakaba group, 141
Shisan Mei, 38
Shore, Dinah, 33; photo of, 34
Shulinkou Air Station, 117, 234n18
"Signature Event Context" (Derrida), 71
Silver Convention, 118–19
Simon and Garfunkel, 110
Sinatra, Frank, 29
Singer, Ben, 100
Sino-American Joint Commission on Rural Reconstruction (JCRR), 13

Sino-American Mutual Defense Treaty, 117
sinophone, 207n42, 208n42, 214n8
"Sishuang zhi," 166
"Sixiang qi" (Remember when), 16, 138, 145, 155, 158, 163, 165, 168
*60 Minutes*, 156
Sledge, Percy, 81
sloganeering stations, 170, 246n1
Smith, Harry, 131
Snow, Valaida, 24
"Society for the Study of Chinese Folk Music" (Lu Xun Academy of Art), 20
song and dance epic, 2
songbooks, 21, 22, 59, 162, 245n82
Song Jwu, 127
"Song of Longing by the Harbor Side," 90
"Song of the Soil, The" (forum), 142
songs: anti-Communist/anti-Soviet, 200; art, 32; dance, 152, 166, 178, 200; Hengchun, 165; modern, 22, 25, 26, 35, 172; mountain, 20, 200; resistance, 198; revolutionary, 187, 211n76; screen, 24; tea-picking, 200, 244n64; village, 194
Songshan Airport, 49, 93
Sony Corporation, 68, 116, 146, 183, 192
soul music, 10, 14, 81
"Soulfinger" (Bar-Kays), 104, 232n65
"Sound of Silence, The" (Simon and Garfunkel), 110
soundscapes, 7, 81, 103, 134, 185, 193; local, 81; rural, 69; socialist, 187; urban, 7
*South Pacific* (Rodgers and Hammerstein), 90
"Space Oddity" (Bowie), 203n1
Spector, Phil, 174, 204n11
"Spring the Year Round," 155
Stalin, Joseph, 74

*Star* (magazine), cover of, 89 (fig.)
"Star a Day, A": Teng and, 178
Statistical Information Analysis Division (SIAD), 234n19
Steen, Andreas, 211n76
stereo systems, 116, 129, 174, 193, 238n2
Sterne, Jonathan, 241n30
Stevens, Cat, 124
Stone Shih, C. S., 44, 217n37
*Story of a Small Town* (film), 185, 250n42
"Streetlamp at Midnight," 164
"Student Sound, The," 123–24
*Suite of Our Native Soil: A Selection of Taiwan's Folk Songs* (Huang), 159, 162, 246n90; cover of, 160 (fig.)
"Sukiyaki" (Sakamoto), 35, 36, 228n27
"Summertime Blues" (Blue Cheer), 81, 102
Sun Tribe, 93
Sun Yat-sen, 58
"Symphonie Folksongs of Taiwan," 164
Szonyi, Michael, 183

*Ta Kung Pao*, 40
Taichung, 52, 118, 119, 123
Tailong (Taro), 97, 98, 104; identity of, 99 (fig.)
Tainan, 85, 118, 119, 164, 168, 218n41, 234n24
Taipei, 14, 44, 49, 51, 79, 83, 85, 97, 101, 103, 110, 118, 123, 125, 133, 138, 142, 147, 151, 155; furloughs in, 234n20; industrial districts of, 13; music in, 19, 197, 198–99, 200; population of, 148; urbanites in, 137
Taipei Air Station, 101, 118, 234n18, 234n24

# INDEX 269

Taipei Bridge, 102, 135, 148, 200
*Taipei Nights* (film), 95
Taitō Sugar Company, 153–54
Taitung, 154, 162
Taiwan, 98, 115, 123, 147; Chinese rule and, 81; Hong Kong and, 12; musical imports from, 189; music of, 7, 50; positioning of, 92; Red China and, 110; songs of, 200; soundscapes of, 81; urbanization of, 47
Taiwan Cuban Boys, 44, 166
Taiwan Defense Command, 117, 118, 234n18
"Taiwanese Native Folk Song Concert," 164
"Taiwan Melody" (Yao), 40, 47
Taiwan Music Institute, 241n33
Taiwan Peanuts, 164; photo of, 166
Taiwan Relations Act, 130
Taiwan Straits, 170, 175
Taiwan TV (TTV), 44, 152, 176
*Taiyu pian*, 46, 81, 82, 92, 93, 94, 95, 96, 97, 100, 103, 124
Takarazuka Dance Revue, 232n69
"Talks at the Yan'an Forum on Art and Literature," 20
Tang, Alan, 111
tape recorders, 10, 191, 192; photo of, 147
Tatung, 13
Tau Hsiao-ch'ing, 158, 239n9, 245n82
Tau Moe, 24
Taylor, James, 124, 161
Taylor, Jeremy, 218n43
Tcherepnin, Alexander, 27
Technicolor, 92, 93, 94
technology, 54, 67, 69, 100, 116, 183, 193, 238, 252n67; media, 7; mediating, 173; noise reduction, 192; recording, 86–87, 241n30; sound, 170–71; tape recording, 242n38; transistor, 5, 6, 13, 30, 146, 204n10

television, 30, 116, 148, 152, 178, 183; age of, 218n46; Taiwanese, 243n58
Telstar, 1–2, 243n61
"Telstar" (Tornados), 205n11
Tel-Star Band, 152
*Tempest, The* (Shakespeare), 213n86
Teng, Teresa, 22, 43, 152, 166, 173, 250; advertising campaigns and, 181; album cover for, 180 (fig.); mobile privatization and, 177–78, 180–81, 183–84; music of, 17, 172, 174–75, 185, 186, 189–90, 191–92, 194, 195; performance of, 186–87, 191; photo of, 179; popularity of, 180–81; voice of, 176, 177, 185, 190, 191–92, 194
"Terra" (Veloso), 203n1
"Thanks, Mr. Manager," 178
Tiananmen Square, 58, 68, 194
Tian Han, 25
timbre, 10, 73, 173–74, 187, 189, 190
Tin Pan Alley, 24, 25, 35
"Today's Themes for Young Lovers" (Percy Faith Singers), 111
Toho Film Studios, 46, 87
Tokyo Communications Manufacturing, 146
Tokyo University, 8
Toshiba, 116
tourism, 37, 39, 51, 90, 91
"Transistorized Loudspeaker Schematic," 70 (fig.)
transistor radios, 6, 7, 10, 13, 19, 68, 69, 81, 116, 121, 148
transistors, 53, 67, 68, 69, 183; open borders and, 7
Treaty of Mutual Cooperation and Security (ANPO), 8
Trinh Công So'n, 11
*Tropicália*, 8, 136
Tsuruta Kōji, 87, 89 (fig.); recording of, 88 (fig.)

TTV. *See* Taiwan TV
Tunghung Ho, 123, 124
Tuo Xian, 108, 231n59
"26 Bars in Taipei," 119 (fig.)

Underground Record Club (URC), 11
*Understanding Media* (McLuhan), 205n12
*Underwater!* (film), 41
Unger, Jonathan, 68
Union Record, 127
*United Daily News*, 140, 232n2
United States Agency for International Development (USAID), 13, 18
Unit 93 Military Entertainment Band, 177
Universidad Nacional Autonóma de México (UNAM), 8
urbanization, 47, 81, 148
U.S. Information Service, 215n12
U.S. Navy Hospital, 118

Veloso, Caetano, 11, 203n1
Ventures, 103, 104, 206n32, 232n65
Victor, 24, 27, 42
Victrolas, 24
Vietnam War, 15, 78, 81, 115, 119, 120; protesting, 8, 10, 11
"Village Girl Who Sells Watermelon" (Teng), 189
"Visiting Family," 21
Voice of America, 184
Volland, Nicolai, 208n43
Vysotsky, Vladimir, 11

walls of sound, 169, 170, 187, 194
Wang Fei, 43, 44, 217n36
Wang Guangji, 141
Wang Min'an, 187, 188
"Washington Square" (Village Stompers), 232n65
Wen Feng, 93
Wenhua Fashion Store, 87

Wen Shia, 45, 82, 85, 91 (fig.), 95, 98, 101, 103, 108, 121, 124, 151, 155, 168, 219n47, 226n1; Cai and, 227n13; cinematic past of, 97, 102; filming and, 232n61, 232n65; Four Sisters and, 80, 81, 93, 96, 105; lyrics of, 87, 90, 228n25; music of, 14, 15, 87, 90, 92, 104; pictures of, 228n19; recordings of, 86, 88 (fig.); sixth sense and, 230n41; steeplechase and, 97
"Wen Shia's Drifter Chronicles," 92, 101
"Wen Shia's Sailor," 90
"Wen Shia's Whirlwind," 102
Wen-Shu Juan, 156, 245n74
Wen Xiang, 93, 230n41
"We're Separated by Myriad Mountains," 25
"When a Man Loves a Woman" (Sledge), 81
White, Douglas A., 142
*White Album* (Beatles), 205n20
Whiteman, Paul, 24
Wiazemski, Anne, 76
Wien Records, 217n36
*Wilhelm Meister* (Goethe), 76
Williams, Raymond, 183
*Wired Broadcasting*, 60, 72
"Wired Broadcasting Is Developing Rapidly in the Countryside," 62 (fig.)
"Wired Village Networks," 64 (fig.)
*Wireless Magazine*, 61 (fig.), 71
"Wooden Heart" (Chou), 92, 228n25
"Working Class Hero" (John Lennon and the Plastic Ono Band), 125; recording of, 126 (fig.)
"World Just for the Two of Us, A" (Sagara), 108, 107 (fig.); cover for, 106 (fig.)
"World Sixties, The" (Connery), 205n14

Wu Baizhen, 53
"Wukong Tune," Chen and, 155
Wulong Records, 79, 148, 246n93
Wu Rung-shun, 241n35, 242n40
Wu Sanlian, 129
Wu Yongyi, 189

*Xiachao* (journal), 159
Xiamen, 45, 170, 192; speaker array at, 175
Xiamen University, broadcasts from, 176
Xiangshan station, 174, 248n15
Xiao Wang, 93, 97–98, 101, 102, 105, 108; pop music and, 104
Xiayu, 45
Xu Guolong, 217n36, 219n54, 241n35

Yamaha "Passola," advertisement for, 181, 182 (fig.)
Yan'an, 20, 27, 209n59, 221n13
Yang, Evan, 33
Yang, T. C., 157, 159
Yang Lihua, 95
Yang Sanlang, 164
Yangtze River, 200
Yang Xian, 157
Yang Yinliu, 141
Yan Heming, 27, 212n77
Yao Lee, 25, 26
Yao Min, 25, 33, 40
Ye Jintai, 129, 130, 131
Ye Junlin, 46
Yeu Jow Records, 178, 248n27
Yi Wen, 33
Yongxin, 94
"Young China," 159
*Youth,* 250n39
*yueqin,* 16, 85, 130, 131, 145, 150, 154, 155, 162, 163
Yu Guangzhong, 142, 157
Yurchak, Alexei, 74

*Zhang Di Seeks A-Zu* (film), 95
Zhang Hanhui, 195
Zhang Hong, 186, 189, 191, 193, 195
Zhang Songru, 21
Zhang Xigui, 82
Zhonghe, 148
Zhou Enlai, 27, 170
Zhou Lanping, 194
Zhou Xuan, 25
Zhou Yinchang, 190, 191
Zhou Zuoren, 141

**ANDREW F. JONES** is professor and Louis B. Agassiz Chair of Chinese at the University of California, Berkeley. He is author of *Like a Knife: Ideology and Genre in Contemporary Chinese Popular Music*; *Yellow Music: Media Culture and Colonial Modernity in the Chinese Jazz Age*; and *Developmental Fairy Tales: Evolutionary Thinking and Modern Chinese Culture*.